The Primacy of the Subjective

The Primacy of the Subjective

Foundations for a Unified Theory of Mind and Language

Nicholas Georgalis

A Bradford Book
The MIT Press
Cambridge, Massachusetts
London, England

MIT Press books may be purchased at special quantity discounts for business or sales promotional use. For information, please email special_sales@mitpress.mit.edu or write to Special Sales Department, The MIT Press, 55 Hayward Street, Cambridge, MA 02142.

Set in Stone Sans and Stone Serif by The MIT Press. Printed and bound in the United States of America.

Library of Congress Cataloging-in-Publication Data

Georgalis, Nicholas, 1944–
The primacy of the subjective : foundations for a unified theory of mind and language / Nicholas Georgalis.
    p. cm.
"A Bradford book."
Includes bibliographical references (p.) and index.
ISBN 0-262-07265-3 (alk. paper)
1. Philosophy of mind. 2. Subject (Philosophy) 3. Intentionality (Philosophy)
4. Languages and languages—Philosophy. I. Title.
BD418.3.G46   2005
128'.2—dc22   2005047473

10 9 8 7 6 5 4 3 2 1

Contents

Preface

It is not an exaggeration to say that virtually every substantive point made in this book relies on the concept of *minimal content*. 'Minimal content' is a technical term. It represents the subject of an agent's intentional state *as the agent conceives it*. Minimal content is a subjective, first-person, narrow concept. It does not presuppose any phenomenal features (chapter 1). Nevertheless, when we examine phenomenality we find that a variant concept of minimal content is similarly fundamental for an adequate analysis of the phenomenal. I call this narrow concept *phenomenal minimal content*. This concept individuates the phenomenal aspect of the perception *as the agent perceives it* (chapter 3). Minimal content and phenomenal minimal content have the same logic. Though both require consciousness, only the latter involves phenomenal features. Minimal content is the foundation for my theory of mind and language.

Any being that has states with minimal content is able to have non-inferential knowledge of it; she has a very narrowly circumscribed privileged access to her minimal content (chapters 1 and 2). Such special access results from the fact that minimal content is not simply a function of how things are; it is a function of how the thinker conceives things—minimal content is *constituted* by the agent. It is a first-person, individualist, or internalist notion. It is a substantive sense of narrow content, one distinct from any other in the literature. Since minimal content itself is not some sort of ontological being but a concept introduced to make sense of, analyze, and relate issues in the study of mind and language, it is not heavily burdened with problematic metaphysical baggage. It does not, for example, turn on troublesome concepts such as "the nature of the mental" or "the essence of mind."

The concept of minimal content is also fundamental for certain concepts that I deploy in the treatment of the topics of meaning and reference. In chapter 8 I introduce *intended reference*, a first-person concept derived from minimal content. The application of this concept is undertaken in the context of Quine's theses of the Indeterminacy of Translation and Inscrutability of Reference, though general results about meaning and reference are obtained. I mention here, though without argument, that I think the concept of intended reference has obvious and unifying applications to a number of other specific issues in the philosophy of language, often recasting them in a new light. I hope a reading of chapter 8 will make this clear. Some examples of such applications are to issues concerning rule following, Donnellan's referential/attributive distinction, and Kripke's puzzle about belief, among others. Thus, if my arguments are correct, minimal content plays a pivotal, unifying, and foundational role in both the philosophy of mind and the philosophy of language.

It is important to realize that I do not contend that minimal content is itself sufficient content for the tasks at hand. A second sense of content is also required for an adequate theory of mind: *objective content*. It is a wide, strictly third-person concept that indicates the subject an objective observer of the agent would ascribe as the subject of the agent's intentional or phenomenal state (chapter 1). When we turn from mind to language, the narrow concept of intended referent must also be supplemented with the wide concept of *objective referent*. The role of this concept relative to language is similar to that of objective content relative to mind (chapter 8). Still, the new narrow concepts introduced and issues associated with them occupy the bulk of my discussion.

The central theses of this book are as follows:

- A new *non*-phenomenal narrow concept of minimal content is required to understand mind and language.

- A strictly third-person methodology in the philosophical study of the mind and language is untenable; it must be supplemented with a first-person, subjective methodology. The augmented methodology is, nevertheless, objective.

- Consciousness—without phenomenality—is as strongly implicated in intentionality as in phenomenal states.

Beyond what I have already said about the first thesis, I argue that an agent constitutes minimal content, and that this act results in a unique intentional state: the *Fundamental Intentional State* (chapter 1). All other intentional states presuppose this special intentional state; its logic differs from all others.

In regard to the second thesis, I demonstrate that any *strictly* third-person methodology in the philosophical study of mind or language fails to identify minimal content and, in consequence, I argue (especially in chapters 2, 5, 7, and 8, though the point is made in various ways throughout), suffers from a number of fundamental and debilitating limitations that can be corrected only by the incorporation of a first-person methodology. I argue further that a methodology augmented in this way yields objective results, despite its incorporation of a first-person methodology. Therefore, an objective understanding of the subjective is possible with this expanded methodology (chapters 1, 3, and 5).

There is a further point regarding the second thesis, one that is also related to the third. Though some others emphasize the importance of first-person methodologies, they typically restrict its application to phenomenal states. This has resulted in a misleading partitioning of the problems of phenomenality (qualia) and the problems of intentionality into two distinct categories. The acceptance of this taxonomy is abetted by the all-too-common belief that phenomenal states have subjective aspects and involve consciousness but intentional states do not. On my view, the latter part of this is an illusion. Arguments for this are presented in chapters 1–3.

There are others who also reject the partitioning just indicated. These philosophers have expanded the application of the first-person perspective to intentional states by arguing that these too have certain phenomenal features—"phenomenal intentionality." I argue in chapter 3 that this is the wrong way to implicate consciousness in intentionality. My theory is importantly different from this approach, as well. Whereas on my theory consciousness is as crucial to intentionality as it is to phenomenality, my theory implicates consciousness in intentionality independent of phenomenal features (chapters 1 and 3).

One important reason that has led philosophers to adopt either of the approaches described and rejected in the previous two paragraphs is the almost universal tendency, even among widely divergent theorists of mind, to conflate consciousness and subjectivity with phenomenal experience. Of course it is true that phenomenal experience is subjective, and certainly it is often conscious, but my point is that intentionality implies subjectivity and consciousness without phenomenal aspects.

The tendency just described has contributed to the failure to recognize a different "explanatory gap problem" than the usual one. Of the two broad problem areas in the philosophy of mind—intentionality and phenomenality (qualia)—it is the latter that is typically viewed as posing the "hard problem" for consciousness. The very idea of the "hard problem" of consciousness is miscast, however, when it is restricted to problems concerning phenomenal states (qualia). I argue that the hard question, properly framed, is broader in scope. In short, there is an explanatory gap problem for both phenomenal and intentional states. My theory provides a framework that goes some significant distance in closing both gaps in a similar way (chapters 3–5, especially 4).

The failure to adequately recognize that there is a hard problem for intentionality is related to a certain common view regarding representation. It is widely believed by philosophers and cognitive scientists of almost every persuasion that there are unconscious representations. In chapter 5 I argue for an account of representation which has the radical consequence that representation itself requires consciousness: There are no unconscious representations. If I am right about this, to the extent that any explanation of intentionality must utilize the concept of representation, this provides a basis for another argument to the conclusion that intentionality requires non-phenomenal consciousness.

Other problems that are widely viewed as applying exclusively to phenomenality are also extended to intentionality. Specifically, corresponding to the problems of inverted and absent qualia is the problem of inverted and absent (non-phenomenal) minimal content. Whereas strictly third-person methodologies simply conjecture that these are phenomenal possibilities (a conjecture that some dispute), on my theory they are verifiably possible outcomes with regard to inverted and absent minimal content; moreover, such outcomes are on occasion not only verifiable but actual (chapter 1). Nevertheless, with my augmented methodology, there are grounds for holding that we can make objective claims regarding both another's minimal contents and another's qualia (chapter 3).

Various scientific identities (e.g., heat = kinetic energy of molecules) are often touted as models for some sort of reduction of the mental to the physical. Although I hold (in chapters 3 and 4 especially, but also in chapter 5) that the *having* of certain brain states is what constitutes a conscious state, the traditional identities are inadequate models to explain the relations between the mental and the physical (as are those models that depend on some sort of supervenience). I examine the traditional identity claims in both science and the philosophy of mind in detail, and I evaluate them in a novel way that reveals the inadequacies I have alleged. My analysis is based on an independently argued for systematic ambiguity in sensory terms. These results also imply a different way of evaluating disputes between "objectivists" and "subjectivists" regarding color and other sensory modalities. Yet another outcome of this line of reasoning reconciles Wilfred Sellars's manifest and scientific images and also reconciles Arthur Eddington's "two tables" (chapter 6)

In addition to the above, I argue for a number of negative results. A widely accepted externalist attempt to explain privileged access fails. Higher-order theories of intentionality are false. The motivation for and the plausibility of such theories is an artifact of applying a strictly third-person methodology. Functionalism is false. It can accommodate neither minimal content nor a limited privileged access to minimal content. Putnam's Twin-Earth thought experiment does not establish that thought content is wide. (All these negative results are argued for in chapter 2.) Burge's arthritis thought experiment is challenged in a new way, one that does not rely on a "reinterpretation strategy." That experiment does not, after all, support anti-individualism (chapter 7). I show that Quine's reading of his own thesis of indeterminacy of translation is vacuous, and, given his reading, that his explicit attempts to rescue reference from nonsense fail. (Minimal content via the concept of intended reference provides the basis for a non-vacuous reading of the Indeterminacy of Translation, while also rescuing reference from nonsense; minimal content thereby provides a basis for determinate meaning and reference, as already indicated above.) I show Quine's realism to be incoherent with the rest of his view. In chapter 9 I argue that ontological issues, in their traditional guise, should be abandoned.

Early in this preface I said that the concept of minimal content does not depend on "the nature of the mental." This point is important and relates to the conclusion just stated. Throughout the book I eschew ontological questions. I do so because I think such questions are groundless, even meaningless (chapter 9). I also think they distract us from making progress on substantive issues. (I illustrate the latter throughout the book, but chapter 6 may provide the clearest illustration.) Though I am concerned with the phenomena that come under the headings 'mental' and 'physical', and with how these phenomena are related to one another, I do not view this as some ontological venture. I view my task as showing how the concept of minimal content provides the means to unify a number of important statements regarding mind, body, and language—statements that most philosophers, regardless of their "ontological positions," would accept—and to resolve a number of problems that acceptance of those statements generate. I would like my theory, particularly the concept of minimal content, to be judged by how successfully and extensively it does this: To what extent does the deployment of minimal content advance our understanding of the phenomena we call 'mental' and 'physical' and of the relations between them? What light does minimal content shed on problems in the philosophy of language? The injection of ontological considerations in the discussion of such questions only serves to obfuscate the associated issues with irrelevancies. I believe that advances in the understanding of such issues can and should be made without recourse to ontology.

I have made many substantive and unorthodox claims regarding what I purport to establish in what follows. Skepticism regarding my success is understandable, indeed called for. The courage to make so many ambitious claims has been fortified by many years of labor directed at nursing the arguments in support of them. The task of determining whether I have succeeded now falls to you, my not too gentle (I trust) reader. I invite and welcome your efforts.

Acknowledgments

I have grappled with confusions regarding intentionality for many years. During this period, my reading of others on intentionality led me to believe I was not alone in this. This changed when I discovered John Searle's book *Intentionality*. It was instrumental to dispelling the confusions and enabling me to develop the theory presented here. So, my greatest philosophical debt is to him. But my debt to John extends into another dimension. In small but important ways, he has offered occasional friendly encouragement and support of my endeavors for a good many years now. This proved particularly important to the continuation of my project, as I have labored in relative obscurity to develop and argue for these many unorthodox views.

Uriah Kriegel scrutinized a version of parts of chapter 5. His perceptive comments resulted in substantial improvements. I am most grateful to him. William Lycan offered critical comments and some praise of some of my earlier work on these topics. While I did not always agree with his criticisms, they helped me improve my arguments. The attention he afforded me over the years also helped sustain me in my endeavors. I am grateful to him. I'd also like to express my thanks to Ümit Yalçin and John Bickle for vigorous, informative, and enjoyable discussions. Others to whom I am grateful are cited in notes.

East Carolina University afforded me one semester without teaching, which contributed to the book's progress.

Tom Stone, Senior Editor for Acquisitions at The MIT Press, was amazingly helpful, reassuring, and responsive to my many queries. The same should be said of Paul Bethge, who had the task of copy-editing my manuscript. I am most grateful to both of them. Though my contacts with others at The MIT Press were more limited, without exception they performed at the highest level of professionalism and efficiency, while being wonderfully cordial.

Finally, I am grateful to my parents, who nurtured those traits in me that enabled this undertaking and, importantly, its completion. I regret that they did not live to see this book.

Credits

Chapters 1 and 2 incorporate material from my papers "Asymmetry of Access to Intentional States" (*Erkenntnis* 40, 1994: 185–211) and "Awareness, Understanding and Functionalism" (*Erkenntnis* 44, 1996: 225–256). Here 'objective content' replaces 'subject component', the locution I used in those papers. Chapter 2 also incorporates material from "No Access for the Externalist" (*Mind* 99, 1990: 101–108).

Chapter 3 includes small parts of the 1994 and 1996 *Erkenntnis* articles mentioned above.

Chapter 4 includes much of my essay "Minds, Brains, and Chaos," published in *The Caldron of Consciousness*, edited by R. Ellis and N. Newton (John Benjamins, 2000). The section that argues that there are no unconscious representations is included in chapter 5.

The ninth section of chapter 5 ("Clarification of the Scope of the Arguments: Teleological Views Do Not Escape") was added in response to a referee's comments on my 2006 article "Representation and the First-Person Perspective." A number of other substantive improvements in that article, incorporated in the present chapter 5, were made in response to the referee's objections and questions. A version of the aforementioned section was presented at the 2005 meeting of the Southern Society for Philosophy and Psychology in Durham. Justin Fischer was the commentator. I am grateful to him for pointing out an infelicitous characterization of Millikan's view.

Chapter 7 includes material from my papers "Rethinking Burge's Thought Experiment" (*Synthese* 118, 1999: 145–164) and "Burge's Thought Experiment: Still in Need of a Defense (*Erkenntnis* 58, 2003: 267–273), but here informed by the concept of minimal content.

The Primacy of the Subjective

1   The Fundamental Intentional State

Two crucial aspects of the human mind are phenomenal experience and intentionality. Under the influence of behaviorism, functionalism, and early identity theories of the twentieth century, accounts of these two aspects have been advanced that are independent of each other; certainly the two have received separate treatments by these theories.[1] Moreover, insofar as consciousness has been considered at all, it has typically been associated with phenomenal experience. The separation of the two and the alignment of consciousness with just phenomenal experience are fundamental errors resulting in distorted accounts of both aspects, especially of intentionality. I argue that the major source of these errors is the reliance on a strictly third-person methodology.

Both phenomenal experience and intentionality are conscious phenomena, and a proper and unified understanding of them requires a first-person methodology. Although others also emphasize the importance of first-person methodologies, they typically apply it only to phenomenal states. Recently this has changed. A few now exploit the first-person perspective in an attempt to expose phenomenal or phenomenological features of intentional states.[2] To the extent that the latter efforts are designed to bring intentionality back under the umbrella of consciousness I am sympathetic to them; nevertheless, I am dubious of the means used to achieve this end.[3]

My theory differs from all such efforts. I deploy a first-person methodology to uncover a unique kind of non-phenomenal narrow content, which I call *minimal content*. This novel content plays a fundamental and crucial role in my analysis of intentionality. It makes clear that consciousness is as strongly implicated in intentional states as it is in phenomenal ones. Indeed, I will argue below that minimal content gives rise to what I shall call *the fundamental intentional state*. This intentional state has a unique logical structure, distinct from all other intentional states, but all others are rooted in it. Minimal content plays a similar foundational role in phenomenal states too, as I will explain in chapters 3 and 6. Minimal content, therefore, is a fundamental and unifying concept for a theory of the mind. I will argue in chapter 8 that it is fundamental in the philosophy of language too.

Some Preliminaries

Any theory of intentionality must confront at least two striking and apparently contradictory features:

(I)   There is an asymmetry between oneself and others with regard to access to the contents of thoughts.[4]

(II)   An individual may neither know nor be in a better position than someone else to ascertain what his own thought is about.

The resolution of this apparent conflict turns on the recognition that a correct analysis of intentional states involves not only two kinds of content but also two kinds of methodology. I will argue that the sense of 'content' that preserves the first feature requires a first-person analysis, for it is invisible from the third-person perspective. The sense of 'content' that saves the second feature requires a third-person analysis. Both are required. An exclusive use of either type of analysis must fall short of an adequate theory of intentionality.

Advocates of a strictly third-person analysis of content abound, but in order to be successful they must either provide for the first feature or show that it is a mere appearance. Including the first-person perspective in the study of the philosophy of mind runs counter to the views held by a formidable array of contemporary philosophers. For example, consider Daniel Dennett's unequivocal rejection of the first-person perspective: "I declare my starting point to be the objective, materialistic, third-person world of the physical sciences." (1987, p. 5) Dennett himself characterizes this starting point as "the orthodox choice today in the English-speaking philosophical world" (ibid.). And later in the same work he says: "I propose to see just what the mind looks like from the third-person, materialistic perspective of contemporary science. I bet we can see more and better if we start here, now, than if we try some other tack." (ibid., p. 7) In between these quoted passages, Dennett disparagingly cites a notable exception to the orthodoxy: Thomas Nagel's insistence on the importance of the first-person perspective, or the subjective, for a proper understanding of a number of things about humans and the world. I think Nagel is right. However, in this chapter my employment of the first-person perspective will not consider the qualitative or phenomenal aspects of mental states often associated with Nagel's work. (I will turn to them in chapter 3, and to sensory phenomena in chapter 6.) Instead, I will argue that the first-person perspective plays an indispensable role in uncovering a non-qualitative kind of content, one that plays a crucial role in studies of intentionality. Keeping faith with the orthodoxy, rather than enabling us to "see more and better," runs a significant risk of derailing the whole endeavor, since the content I identify is invisible to the orthodox methodology. There is no need to choose between the exclusive use of one or the other methodology in studies of the mind. Excluding either one is a mistake.

In what follows, I ask my readers to realize that at times they must adopt the perspectives of the individual thinkers I consider, and to think of the situation described as though they themselves were in the situation. Where I am not explicit, I let the context of my discussion serve as clues as to whether the first-person or the third-person perspective is the appropriate perspective to adopt. This is necessary because if I am right about minimal content, it is invisible from the third-person perspective; thus, my interlocutor must at least temporarily assume the first-person perspective if she is to fairly criticize what I say. My arguments for awareness of minimal content cannot even be comprehended unless one assumes that perspective on the cases I develop. This is a harmless request, since temporary adoption of the first-person perspective should not in itself beg any questions against opposing views.

Some possible misunderstandings of what follows may be avoided if I unequivocally state at the outset that I am not concerned with the ontology of mental states, whether they are intentional or phenomenal mental states. My interest lies with the *analysis of statements* concerning such states. The analysis is constrained by various simple statements that we find difficult to reject upon considering our experiences, notably the apparently conflicting statements ((I) and (II) above) regarding features of intentional states. Of course, there is also the pivotal constraint that the analysis provides an account of the fact that intentional states are "about" something or some state of affairs, that they are "directed." Giving an account of this "aboutness" that can be reconciled with (I) and (II) is my central task. Much if not all of what else we can correctly say about intentionality will follow from this analysis. The analysis is neutral regarding ontological commitments. Others, if they wish, may attempt to draw ontological conclusions from my analysis, but they are not my conclusions, nor are they forced by what I say. I will return to why ontological claims should be avoided from time to time in this and subsequent chapters, and in chapter 9 I will offer a more systematic discussion concerning my general conclusion regarding the idleness or vacuity of ontological claims.

Privileged Access and Minimal Content

The asymmetrical access we have to our own thoughts is sometimes referred to as *privileged access*. Many different conceptions of the latter have been advanced, but two general reasons why privileged access is held in disrepute by some are that exaggerated claims have been made on its behalf, and it has kept company with dualism. However, privileged access is not necessarily connected to dualism, and certain alleged features (such as complete transparency and incorrigibility) may be dropped while still preserving an important point to the special access we have to some of the content of some of our states. The special access at issue amounts to no more than one's ability to non-inferentially know the content, in some sense, of at least some of one's thoughts. It is in some such limited guise that privileged access remains a compelling doctrine.[5] Although the asymmetrical access amounts to no more than this, we shall see the consequences are great and have not been adequately recognized.[6]

Let no one worry that if this privileged access is allowed all the work necessary for understanding intentionality is (mysteriously) done. Frankly, the access that the first-person perspective provides does not explain anything; still, it is what exposes the content to which we have special access and which is invisible to a strictly third-person methodology. Privileged access and this content are central features that must be explained or shown to be mere appearance. They cannot be ignored.

As an illustration of the kind of access in question, consider an example introduced by John Heil (1988). Suppose you ask me to form an image of my grandmother. On informing you that I have done so, you inquire how

I know it is an image of her and not of someone else. For such an inquiry to make sense, it must be possible that I could be mistaken when I think the image I formed is an image of my grandmother. But insofar as I formed it expressly to be of my grandmother, such a possibility must be ruled out: *It is constitutive of the forming of the image that it is of her.*

There is room for error on the agent's part of a sort, one that is harmless to the point here. For example, the woman whom I have come to think of as my grandmother may really be an impostor. In that case, however, I would not be making a mistake about whom my image is of; rather, it is a mistake about my blood relationship to her. Another kind of case that may be put aside is one where some image randomly comes to my mind. Here, although the image is mine, I would be in no privileged position to ascertain of whom it is; indeed, it would appear to be no more *of anything* than are the "stars" I experience on receiving a blow to the head. If one were to maintain that the image was of someone in particular, the criteria for deciding would be at best unclear. In any case, I certainly would not be in any privileged position to know this in such a case.

Thus, although I can be wrong about images of mine in some ways, I cannot err in identifying whom my image is of when I deliberately form it to be of some particular individual. I cannot err in the latter simply because the possibility of error in these circumstances does not make any sense, not because I have some special mental powers or because I am cognizant of a special kind of entity. That an image is of the particular individual in question is a *constitutive* element of the very act of forming the image. It could not be *that act* if it were not *of that individual*. Given this, plus the fact that the content at issue is only part of the content of a thought, such "infallibility" is not to be confused with the Cartesian kind.

Someone who holds a "resemblance" criterion for what an image is an image of might think there is a possibility of error here. Suppose the image I formed bears a rather poor resemblance to my grandmother. The image itself may even be an excellent resemblance of someone other than my grandmother; nevertheless, the degree of visual faithfulness to my grandmother is irrelevant. It is, after all, the image I deliberately formed to be of her. The criterion determining who or what it is an image of cannot be based on what it is the most (visually) similar to. It is not as if I conjured up an image and then began to wonder who it depicts; the image was conjured precisely to be an image of my grandmother.

Resemblance could be relevant in a very different kind of case: Were I to find a photograph of someone, I might well wonder who is depicted in the photo and use resemblance as one criterion for deciding. In this case resemblance would be appropriate because of the different circumstances and causal relations involved in producing the photo. The relevant circumstances and causal relations are radically different in the case of a deliberately formed image, however; since here resemblance is irrelevant as a factor in the determination of the individual represented by the image. The formed image is a direct result of my act to produce not simply an image but an image of a certain individual. That being a constitutive element of the act, I cannot perform the act without the result being of that particular individual; otherwise, it would be a different act.

The same point could be made in regard to a sketch, which has the advantage of being publicly observable. If you ask me to sketch my grandmother, the result may indeed look more like your neighbor than my grandmother, and we may even agree on this. But a poorly drawn sketch of my grandmother is still a sketch of her. That is why it is said to be *poorly* drawn; it is not said to be a (well-drawn) sketch of whomever it most closely resembles. In parallel to the imagery, and in contrast to the photo case, there is neither a possibility of error on my part as to whom my deliberately drawn sketch is of nor any need for me to make any inferences to determine this. There is a possibility of error in your judging whom my sketch is of, and your judgment will be based on inference and may rely on resemblance, but my judgment does neither. That difference is just a manifestation of the asymmetry of access.

I examine another example[7] to illustrate further both the kind of privileged access that is at issue and the kind of content to which we have this special access. Suppose I make a diagram while lecturing on the battle of Borodino. I make Xs to mark the locations of Napoleon's troops and Os to mark the locations of Kutuzov's. Though there are countless errors I may make in my lecture and in the accuracy of my diagram, it makes no sense to ask me how I know that the Xs represent Napoleon's troops rather than Kutuzov's. Since the diagram is mine, the Xs cannot fail to represent what I intend them to represent. Suppose that, upon looking at my diagram, I have the thought that Napoleon had too heavy a concentration of troops in the northeast. On having this thought, I non-inferentially know that an X represents (a certain number of) Napoleon's troops. I know this straight out, without recourse to a thought about this thought. It would make no sense for me to look for evidence of this, to puzzle whether an X really represented (a certain number of) Kutuzov's troops. It does make sense that you might be puzzled about such a matter; you may have to infer on the basis of evidence, which could be as simple as the fact that I told you, what my Xs represent. Although I may be wrong in thinking there were too many troops in the northeast (as a matter of military strategy), I cannot be wrong in thinking that one of my Xs represents (a certain number of) Napoleon's troops.

Now consider a new twist on the case just presented. I may wonder what Kutuzov would have done had he been in Napoleon's position, my speculations being based on my knowledge of his psychology. But now the Xs represent (a certain number of) Kutuzov's troops. When I consider this situation from my first-person perspective, it is evident that here too I know this content of my thought straight out. My having this non-inferential knowledge clearly does not require a second-order thought, as is commonly supposed. This is in marked contrast to another's acquiring knowledge of the shift in my thought content. Someone else would have to consider a second-order thought in order to ascertain what my thought is about, and would also have to make inferences from evidence. (Further support of these contentions is offered in chapter 2.)

Not only do the cases just presented illustrate a relevant asymmetry of access, a kind of privileged access; they also help to identify a restricted kind of content: What each of us has non-inferential knowledge of in these examples is basically the "subject of one's thought." Just what is meant by this locution is unclear at this stage, however. It is a central contention of mine that this locution requires two distinct decompositions. I will call one *minimal content* and the other *objective content*.

Minimal content represents the subject[8] of the intentional state as the agent conceives it.

Objective content indicates the subject an objective observer of the agent would ascribe as the subject of the agent's intentional state.

I will argue that both minimal content and objective content are required in the analysis of what a thought is about, and that each signals what the thought is about in a different way. Neglect of either is neglect of a critical element required for a complete analysis of intentionality. As the examples suggest (and I will develop the point further below), the thinker plays a *constitutive* role in determining the minimal contents of her thoughts.

The privileged access in the above examples was to the minimal content, the subject of the agent's thought *as she conceived it*. It is this that was non-inferentially known in each of the above examples.[9] It is worth pointing out here, while the cases are "fresh," that one's special access to what is represented in such cases is known *straight out* by the thinker. One may non-inferentially know the subject of one's thought in the sense of minimal content and do so without having to have a further thought about the initial thought. I take it that the above cases demonstrate this—but they do this only if they are considered from the first-person perspective.

Intentional States and Minimal Content

A peculiar feature of an intentional state is that it is directed at an object, the intentional object. The explanation of this directedness and what the intentional object consists in is difficult; different authors provide considerably different accounts. These differences have serious consequences. My theory builds upon John Searle's theory of intentionality, so I will explain the basics of his theory first.[10]

For Searle, the intentional object just is the actual object or state of affairs to which the intentional state is directed. For example, if someone loves Sally and also believes that it is currently sleeting outside, then the intentional objects for these two states are the flesh-and-blood woman Sally and the coming down of freezing rain, respectively. But these states also have representative contents, which represent, respectively, the woman and the relevant state of affairs. (Searle sometimes calls the representative content *intentional content*.) On the other hand, there are intentional states that have no intentional object, though they must still have a representative content. For example, Ponce de Leon, in searching for the fountain of youth, was in an intentional state that had a representative content (consisting in part of a representation of what he was seeking), but his intentional state did not have an intentional object. Thus, on Searle's view, every intentional state has a representative (intentional) content, and it is by virtue of this content that the intentional state is directed at an intentional object, but not all intentional states have intentional objects.

It is of paramount importance to keep the intentional object and the representative content distinct. In particular, in those cases that Searle would describe as failing to have an intentional object, one must resist the temptation of identifying the representational content with the intentional object. The temptation to do so is abetted by the consideration that the thought must be about something—it is not about nothing. Since there is no relevant actual object or state of affairs for it to be about, the reasoning continues, it must be about the representative content.[11] The idea behind such views is that, if one is to avoid talking or thinking about "nothing," there always must be an intentional object of some sort.[12]

Sometimes the representative content is propositional in form, as when one believes that a certain state of affairs obtains; sometimes it is not, as when one desires a certain object. In either case, however, an object is "signaled" by the representative content. I endorse everything in Searle's view of intentionality that I have presented to this point, but central to my theory is a specific addition. It is my contention that in the *analysis* of any intentional state there are *two* distinct but correct ways of characterizing the object signaled: minimal content and objective content.

Both minimal content and objective content are restricted to the subject of a thought; neither includes what may be thought of the subject, what may be attributed to it. Just as minimal content and objective content must be kept distinct from one another, neither is to be identified with the intentional object. The latter is an actual object or state of affairs, whereas minimal content and objective content are concepts employed in the analysis of intentional states. They correspond to first-person and third-person descriptions, respectively, of what is the subject of the agent's intentional states.

Minimal content and objective content must not be identified for several reasons: (1) They play different roles in the analysis of intentional states. (2) They may signal different objects. (3) The agent's access to these two contents is importantly different. Because of this difference in access, I spoke above, and i will continue to speak, of minimal content's *representing* and of objective content's *indicating* what the thought is about. Though these terms mark a difference, I do not claim to explain the difference here. When a generic term is required, I will speak, as I did above, of *signaling* what the thought is about.

The situation may be depicted as follows: The schema for an intentional state is $\Psi(R)$, where Ψ is some psychological mode (e.g. believing or desiring) and R is the representative (or intentional) content and is distinct from the intentional object, as defined by Searle.[13] If I am right, any such schema also requires a twofold decomposition:

(i) $\Psi(\Phi(m))$

and

(ii) $\Psi(\Phi(o))$,

where m is the minimal content, o is the objective content, and Φ is what is attributed to "the subject of one's thought."[14]

That one of these contents is subjective and the other objective follows directly from the thinker's different relations to them. This is crucial in explaining why (I) and (II) in the first section of this chapter are both true despite the appearance of conflict. The relevant contents in (I) and (II) are different, corresponding to minimal content and objective content, respectively.[15] Since the contents are different, any apparent conflict between (I) and (II) disappears.

Those who exclude a first-person methodology in the analysis of intentional states cannot countenance minimal content. Hence, the employment of a strictly third-person methodology encourages, if it does not imply, the extremely counterintuitive rejection of (I) for the sake of (II). Since the orthodox methodologies in contemporary analytic philosophy of mind employ a strictly third-person methodology, it is not surprising that minimal content has gone unnoticed and that (I) and (II) have appeared to be in conflict.

In maintaining the importance of a subjective first-person perspective in the analysis of intentionality, I am not denying the possibility of an objective account of it. Indeed, my introduction of the notion of minimal content and my analysis of any intentional state into two characterizations, $\Psi(\Phi(m))$ and $\Psi(\Phi(o))$, are steps in this direction. (Further steps are advanced in chapter 3.)

Illustrative Applications of the Concepts

To further clarify these different concepts of content and to illustrate the fruitfulness of deploying both, consider the following example. A mid-eighteenth-century chemist might have thought that phlogiston was abundant in charcoal. The objective content of such a thought could not indicate phlogiston, since there is no such thing; nevertheless, the minimal content of the chemist's thought, the subject of her thought as she conceived it, did represent phlogiston. While the chemist had a special access to her minimal content, she certainly had no special access to the objective content or what it indicates. This absence of special access to the objective content and what it indicates is not simply because, as is the case in the present example, that there is no such thing. Even when the indicated object exists and is co-extensive with what the chemist's minimal content represents, there is still no privileged access to *it*, the existing intentional object. This last point is simply the familiar one that whatever privileged access there is, there is none that we have to actual objects in the world.[16]

Though the objective content and one's minimal content may signal different objects, they need not. Suppose I am correct in thinking that a certain woman is my grandmother, but I have many false beliefs about her, and there are a number of important things true of her of which I am ignorant. Suppose I entertain the thought that my grandmother was a gracious woman. The correctness of that judgment is a function of what she actually did or would do in certain circumstances. My judgment will be a function of what I believe, rightly or wrongly, about her. I may harbor so many false beliefs pertaining to my grandmother that another, someone who has a more accurate view of her, would say of me, in a colloquial vein, "He does not know her at all." Despite my lamentable epistemological status, any of my intentional states concerning my grandmother will have a minimal content that represents her (the right woman), and I can know this non-inferentially. Thus, both the minimal content and the objective content can signal the same object, in spite of all the misinformation I may have regarding the intentional object.

My grandmother is relatively easily to individuate, even if I labor under a vast amount of misinformation about her. Lest it be thought that that is why the minimal content and the objective content can signal the same subject, consider this: Suppose I entertain the thought that quarks are difficult to experimentally detect. Suppose also that the physicists who theorize about such things are right in thinking that there are quarks. Although I have barely the foggiest idea of what quarks are, it is still plausible that my minimal content and the objective content of my thought signal the same object. For, at the very least, had the physicists not developed their theory of quarks, I would not have my (foggy) thought about quarks. Because I have so little knowledge of quarks, the subject of my thought, as I conceive it, is intended to be whatever the physicists are talking about. I do not add to it in any way that could make what is signaled deviate from the objective content from what those in the know take it to be. (Here, perhaps, a germ of truth in direct theories of reference is operative.)

The above is not to say that to be meaningful my thoughts require that the objects signaled by them exist (as with Russell's logically proper names), as the phlogiston example should make clear. Quite the contrary, it is the claim that minimal content represents something to me—whether what is represented exists or not, whether or not my representation of it is accurate or not, whether I have or do not have correct collateral information pertaining to it—and that it does so on pain of nonsense. Constitutive of my entertaining some particular thought is that its minimal content be what I conceive it to be. *It would not be the thought that it is if it did not have the subject that I conceive it to have.* For, at the very least, I must have *some conception* of what I am "thinking about"; without this, the very meaningfulness of the claim that *my thought*—as opposed to some sentence I might utter—is about anything is brought into question. It is for reasons such as these (more support will come later) that the thinker plays a constitutive role in determining her minimal content. It is also why I call this kind of content minimal.

When my minimal content does match the objective content, but I labor under a number of false beliefs regarding it, I clearly have limited understanding of the object represented, and my ability to explicate my thoughts pertaining to it is thereby limited. I explain below the contrast between *being aware of* and *understanding* what is represented by one's minimal content. For now, I simply point out that to have a thought about something (e.g. quarks) I need have no great understanding of them; indeed, they need not even exist. When my understanding is slight, I will, no doubt, be unable to explain my thought adequately. Still, to have such a thought at all, I must be able to somehow represent quarks in thought and, therefore, to individuate them to some degree.

Partial Recapitulation

The analysis of a single intentional state requires both a minimal content and an objective content, because what the thinker takes her thought to be about may not in fact exist, or may be seriously misconceived by her, or may be entirely different from what it is about objectively. The occurrence of any or all of these mishaps in no way vitiates the thinker's awareness of the subject of her thought as she conceives it, though they may mislead another thinker who is not adopting her point of view. Ideally, what is signaled by minimal content and objective content is one and the same, but this cannot be guaranteed. To allow for the possibility of either a match or a divergence in what is signaled by these two contents, a correct analysis of an intentional state requires both kinds of content; but one has privileged access to only one of them: one's own minimal contents.

Further Development of Some of the Fundamental Ideas Presented

I now introduce a series of cases in order to clarify a number of central ideas:

1.   minimal content

2.   what it is for an individual to be aware of minimal content

3.   the character of an individual's privileged access to her minimal contents

4.   the difference between being aware and understanding one's own minimal contents.

The words 'awareness' and 'understanding' are widely used but vague. It is certainly questionable whether they have univocal uses in their wide applications. In this section I will contrast the two terms and show when each is preferred. (I do not claim that the contrast I have developed is or should be universally used, but it does mark, I think, an important difference.) *Awareness*, when taken as non-inferential knowledge, is preferred in discussions pertaining to the individuation of the subject of a thought, construed as minimal content. *Understanding*, on the other hand, comes to bear when the explication of a thought or the determination of its subject, construed as the objective content, is at issue. I will clarify this by reminding you of some familiar truths about formal theories.

Consider a formal theory that has as one of its models the natural numbers. It is well known that such a formal theory has other models—for example, a model that has sets, and not numbers, in its domain. So the theorems may be viewed as truths about numbers or as truths about sets. Now consider two individuals, A and B. Individual A learned the theory as axioms about natural numbers, and only them; she doesn't even know that the theory has other models. Individual B learned the same formal theory as axioms exclusively about sets.

What seems quite uncontroversial is that each of these individuals can increase her respective understanding of the theory as she explores ever further the consequences of the axioms. The increase in understanding may be measured by the extent to which A and B can prove theorems and explain their proofs. Suppose, somewhat artificially, that A and B are identical in their symbol-manipulating abilities—that A can go on in fascinating detail with truths about numbers, and B can go on in equally fascinating detail about sets. The point, of course, is that their capacities to respond differentially and appropriately to the symbols are, by hypothesis, identical. There is absolutely nothing that would differentiate their responses vis à vis the manipulation and concatenation of the symbols of the theory. Yet A and B take themselves to be proving truths about different things; their respective minimal contents are different and represent different objects.

We, too, may acknowledge that what A and B take their respective contents to be are quite distinct, for the one it is numbers, for the other it is sets, and we may do so without our making any ontological commitment to the nature of either numbers or sets.[17] Indeed, we may acknowledge that A and B conceive themselves to be thinking about different objects even while *we* hold that they are ultimately not different (the numbers just are certain sets), or that neither numbers nor sets are actual objects at all (say, along nominalistic lines). In short whether our ontological commitments coincide with A's or B's or neither, it will have no bearing on our discussion of what *their* minimal contents are. Thus, while we acknowledge what are clearly the respective minimal contents of our theorists' thoughts, it might well be that the objective content of one or the other's thought indicates something other than what is represented by her minimal content.

The above is intended to bring out, in a preliminary way, the importance of keeping the discussion of issues surrounding symbolic manipulation, understanding, and ontology separate from the discussion of issues surrounding minimal content. This follows from the fact that A and B are identical with respect to their symbol manipulation and understanding, yet they have different minimal contents, and that all of this is consistent with several different ontologies. Furthermore, though A's minimal contents represent numbers, as A becomes more sophisticated she may conclude that there are no numbers but only, say, sets. A's minimal content could on occasion still represent numbers, though she does not believe that there are any numbers, just as we may entertain thoughts of mermaids without believing that any mermaids exist.[18] Thus, symbol manipulation, understanding, minimal content, and ontology are independent in at least the ways indicated here. For the next few pages I will focus on how awareness of minimal content is largely independent of both understanding and symbol manipulation. I will also touch on the relation between the latter two. I will not address any ontological questions as such.

Recall that understanding involves the ability to determine a thought's objective content and to be able to explicate the thought in such a way that there can be inter-subjective agreement among qualified experts. It is undoubtedly the case that a significant factor in the measure of one's degree of understanding is the extent to which there are appropriate and differential responses to a relevant set of symbols. Such differential responses probably are extremely relevant to accounts of understanding. At the very least, they would be essential as a *measure* of one kind of understanding. However, whatever bearing differential symbol-manipulating capacities have, or do not have, vis à vis the question of understanding, they do not have much to do with the concept of minimal content or with the fact that an individual is sometimes aware of her minimal content.

When I hold that one's minimal content is *independent* of symbol manipulation, I am not holding that one can have and be aware of minimal content *without* being able to engage in some relevant symbol manipulation. The claim of independence results from my argument that the symbol manipulation, no matter how sophisticated, may remain constant while the minimal content (i.e. sets or numbers) varies. Qua minimal contents, A's and B's understandings differ, despite their identical symbol-manipulating abilities. A's minimal content represents numbers and B's represents sets, and this is so regardless of what the true ontology includes (numbers but no sets, sets but no numbers, both, or neither). This is not to say that either A or B would have any understanding if she were unable to perform some relevant symbol manipulations, only that symbol manipulation is not sufficient to determine understanding since, at least in this case, it is not sufficient to determine either the thinker's minimal content or the objective content of her thought.

Furthermore, as the consideration below of the theorist C will show, one may be aware of the same minimal content as A, even though one's symbol-manipulating ability is considerably inferior to A's. Although such inferior symbol-manipulating ability may well be a sign of a poorer understanding of numbers, it in no way diminishes the fact that the agent's thoughts are about numbers. Just how much symbol manipulation is required for awareness of minimal content is not clear. What is clear is that *different* minimal contents are consistent with identical high symbol-manipulation abilities (e.g. the theorists A and B) and that the *same* minimal content is consistent with radically different levels of symbol-manipulation abilities (e.g. the theorists A and C). Thus, rapid and smooth symbol manipulation is not necessary for one to be aware of one's minimal content, and very little is sometimes enough. (Compare my discussion of Van Gulick in the next chapter.) To this extent, and in this sense, awareness of minimal content is independent of symbol manipulation. Let me explain further.

Consider a third individual, C, who, like A, learned the formal theory strictly as a theory about numbers, but is not nearly as adept at proving theorems as is A. On the basis of the disparity in their symbol-manipulating skills, we would say that A has a better understanding of the theory of natural numbers than does C. Yet C, though bumbling in her symbolic manipulations, still knows without inference the minimal content that those symbols or her corresponding thoughts have for her. Her difficulty consists in providing proofs of particular truths about numbers. In spite of this, whether it is a statement (thought) that she can prove easily or one that she cannot prove at all, she is equally aware that it is a statement (thought) about numbers (whatever their ultimate ontological status). What is important here about minimal content is that C is directly aware of the same content in both cases and that in either case it is correct to say that C has the same minimal content as does A, in spite of A's greater facility at theorem proving. (The latter is indicative that A's understanding of number is greater than C's.) In contrast, B's minimal content differs from both A's and C's, despite the fact that B's symbol-manipulation ability is identical to A's.

The results drawn from our consideration of the three theorists depended on our projecting ourselves into their respective circumstances—that is, adopting their first-person perspective. When we do so, it is evident that, while each can be aware of the minimal content of her thoughts as she manipulates symbols, the appropriate differential responses themselves have very little, if anything, to do with either what that minimal content is or the agent's awareness of it. What they conceive the objects to be is the same or different independent of those responses—independent in the sense explained above.

C's limitations in her theorem proving may well indicate limitations in her understanding of number (or, perhaps more accurate, limitations in her understanding of number theory), though this limitation affects neither what her minimal content represents nor her awareness of it.[19] Any proper account of understanding, undoubtedly, will be one that admits of degrees of understanding. Indeed, the varying degrees of understanding may well be reflected, if not partly constituted by, the varying degrees of successful symbol manipulation. In important contrast, *awareness of minimal content does not admit of degrees.* Either our theorist is aware that she is proving (or attempting to prove) theorems about numbers or she isn't. The relative ease with which she is able to construct such proofs appears irrelevant to her awareness of her minimal content. She may prove, say, "2 is a prime number" or "There is no greatest even number" with ease, but despite her best efforts she may be unable to prove, say, "Every number has a prime factorization." In *any* of these cases, however, C is *equally* aware that her minimal content represents number, be it a specific one, as in the first sentence, or number in general, as in the latter two.

To repeat, it is not the theorist's symbol-manipulating ability that determines which minimal content she has, nor does it determine her awareness of it. Clearly, then, no matter what the full account of understanding is, it is importantly different from one's awareness of what the minimal content of one's thought represents. Our understanding admits of degrees; our awareness of minimal content does not. Though we may well have more or less understanding of, say, numbers (as evidenced by how adequately and thoroughly we can explain or prove that numbers have certain properties), it is nonsense to say that one's awareness of numbers has increased or decreased (or is more or less than someone else's awareness of numbers). C, our weak number theorist, knows that her thoughts are about numbers. Period. It does not matter whether it is a thought that she can easily prove or explain, or not. Nor does it matter that *generally* she is not very good at explaining the properties of numbers, or at proving theorems about them. These abilities bear on the strength of her understanding and give rise to talk of degrees of understanding. Such abilities and the resulting degrees are not transferable to awareness of minimal content.

I have exploited the familiar idea of multiple models for a single formal theory in my discussion of the theorists A–C. Additional light may be cast on the idea of one's being aware of one's minimal content by considering a converse relation: cases where the same object is characterized by different formal theories. Rota et al. (1989) argue that such situations are quite common in the practice of mathematics. Among other examples, they discuss the real number line and groups as cases where the practicing mathematician has a pre-axiomatic grasp, an understanding of these objects that is free from any particular axiomatization.[20] This grasping of the object is critical, Rota et al. claim, to identifying different axiomatizations as being axiomatizations of the same object.[21]

Rota et al. recognize that a student learning a theory will sometimes be unavoidably dependent on some particular axiomatization of that theory. This dependency is especially strong in a case such as group theory, much less so in other cases, e.g., the real number line. But, in any case, it is a dependency that is overcome once a student becomes familiar with the theory. Becoming familiar with the theory is becoming aware of, say, groups. In my terms, it is becoming aware of a minimal content that represents groups in a way that transcends the particular axiomatization by which the student was introduced to groups. Rota et al. argue that "to the mathematician, an axiom system is a new window through which the object, be it a group, a topological space or the real line, can be viewed from a new and different angle that will reveal heretofore unsuspected possibilities" (1989, p. 382). In holding this, Rota et al. are neither arguing nor claiming that these "grasped" objects have some special ontological status: In particular, they insist that they are not arguing for Platonism, and that they are just "acknowledging the actual practice of mathematics" (ibid.). Nor are they arguing that the mathematician is exercising any special faculty, mental or otherwise, when grasping these objects. They take a neutral stand with respect to both the ontological status of these objects and the character of the faculty by which one is aware of them. Their analysis is developed from the first-person perspective of a practicing mathematician, not from a third-person perspective. Thus, their approach is methodologically similar to my own, and it is appropriate to characterize the mathematician's grasping of the objects of his own thoughts as another characterization of one's being aware of the minimal content of one's thought.

One of the distinct advantages of the concept of minimal content is precisely that it permits us to avoid the troublesome issues surrounding the concept of understanding while still allowing an advance in the analysis of intentionality. The scope of the word 'understanding' is clearly broader, if not also vaguer, than is one's non-inferential knowledge, awareness, of one's own minimal content.

Understanding, Explicating, and Individuating

Near the end of his 1988 paper "Individualism and Self-Knowledge," Tyler Burge draws a distinction related to the one I have drawn between awareness and understanding. He distinguishes thinking a thought and explicating it. It is correct to do so. I can think the thought that mercury is one of the elements (Burge's example) without being able to give a proper explication of that thought. When I am unable to explicate my thought, presumably it is because I do not adequately understand it. I may know very little about the periodic table and how mercury fits into it, its atomic structure, etc. But Burge mistakenly conflates *explicating* with *individuating*: "One clearly does not have first-person authority about whether one of one's thoughts is to be explicated or individuated in such and such a way." (1988, p. 662) I agree that one does not have first-person authority over the *explication* of one's thought, say, that mercury is an element, but *to have the thought at all* one must be able to somehow *individuate* mercury as what is represented by the minimal content of that thought, no matter how ignorant one might be or how many misconceptions one might have of mercury. Explicating is strongly related to understanding, but individuating a subject of a thought, in the sense of being aware of one's minimal content, is quite independent of both explicating and understanding.

There are two problems here. The first is the problem, just mentioned, of conflating individuating and explicating. The second turns on the dual analysis of the reference of the subject of a thought. Take the latter first. Earlier I indicated a schematization of a thought as $\Psi(R)$ and stated that it must be decomposed into two schemes: $\Psi(\Phi(m))$ and $\Psi(\Phi(o))$ (where Ψ is some psychological mode, Φ is some attribute, m is the minimal content, and o is the objective content of the thought). Now, insofar as the quotation from Burge pertains to a thought in the sense of $\Psi(\Phi(o))$, I have no disagreement with him. There is no first-person authority over one's thought in this sense of thought. But things are quite different when the thought is construed as $\Psi(\Phi(m))$. Here the conflation of individuating and explicating comes to bear.

To have a thought at all, in the sense of entertaining it, one must be able to individuate the thought, even when one is unable to explicate it. An inability to explicate one's thought manifests one's lack of understanding, but still the thinker would have first-person authority with regard to how the thought and its minimal content are individuated. Individuating a thought or a minimal content is different from explicating either of them, as I now will explain.

To individuate a thought $\Psi(\Phi(m))$, one must be able to differentiate it from other thoughts—either because the minimal content is different or something different is attributed to the same minimal content. Obviously, one must have already individuated the minimal content to do either. And one must be able, when the occasion arises, to re-identify it as the same thought as one had before. To explicate a thought, on the other hand, one must explain how that thought relates to other thoughts. One must state a good number of properties the represented object is to have and, where appropriate, show that it possesses those properties. In the case of numbers, this amounts to providing proofs of and commentaries on theorems. Again, our not-very-competent theorist C is unable to do this to any great extent, and so C cannot explicate many of her number thoughts. Her shortcomings, however, do not interfere with her ability to individuate her thoughts and their minimal contents. But her inability to explicate her thoughts does provide reason for our saying that she does not understand them, or, at least, that she does not understand them well.

One can be aware of one's thought $\Psi(\Phi(m))$ and its minimal content m without being able to do much explicating; nevertheless, one cannot even begin to explicate a thought unless one has already individuated it. This is true no matter how inadequate one's explications may be. Understanding entails the ability to explicate a thought, and doing this presupposes that one has individuated the thought. But individuating one's thought requires individuating its minimal content, regardless of whether the minimal content matches the objective content of the thought. Therefore, understanding presupposes minimal content.

In saying this I am *not* holding that either the identities of concepts or the meanings of terms are ultimately determined by the individual. Thus, when Burge elsewhere maintains that "the meanings of many terms . . . and the identity of many concepts . . . are what they are even though what the individual knows about the meaning or concept may be insufficient to determine it uniquely" (1992, p. 46), there is—in one sense—no disagreement with what I say. Individual ignorance is varied and extensive. Such ignorance pertains to the objective content and what may be correctly attributed to it, and, thus, to how much one's understanding of one's minimal content may diverge from a correct understanding of the thought's objective content. Still, in another sense, I do disagree with Burge: There is first-person authority over what one's thought is about in the sense of minimal content, the subject of the thought as conceived by the thinker, regardless of the extent of the thinker's misconceptions pertaining to the thought's objective content.[22] The greater one's misconceptions, the less one is able to correctly explicate one's own thought, the less one understands it. One neither has first-person privilege over the objective content nor over what counts as understanding, but this is different from individuating or knowing the minimal content of one's thought. Here, one does have first-person privilege.

If I read Burge's comments as pertaining to the objective content, I am in complete agreement with him. Specifically, there is no privileged access to the objective content of one's own thought. But I have argued that any analysis of intentional states must countenance minimal content in *addition* to the objective content, and the situation is quite otherwise with respect to minimal content, as I have tried to show.

It is precisely because minimal content and objective content play distinct roles in the analysis that we are able to avoid talk of understanding and still have something significant and new to say about intentionality or representation. Once we distinguish awareness of minimal content from knowledge of the objective content or understanding the thought objectively, we can go further than we have in showing that the capacity for responding differentially to symbols is not sufficient for determining awareness of minimal content. To see this we can collapse our two individuals A and B into one, dropping the restriction that the individual doesn't know about alternative models. Call our new theorist D. The syntactic strings that D manipulates are identical whether the theorem she is proving is "about" numbers or sets. Yet on some occasions D's minimal contents represent numbers and on others they represent sets; she may alter what the symbols represent to her at will. (This is similar to the "new twist" on the Kutuzov example discussed earlier.) Surely it is wrong to say that D's differential symbol manipulations account for, or in any way determine, the different contents that she can be aware of, for these are identical though the minimal contents are different. Nor, for the same reason, does the converse relation hold. Thus, appropriate differential responses to symbols, on the one hand, and awareness of one's minimal content, on the other, are once again seen to be utterly independent in the sense described above.

The Fundamental Intentional State

I am now in position to make a rather singular and remarkable claim:

The subjective constitution by an agent of her minimal content makes it a different and unique intentional state—one that is presupposed by all other intentional states.

This subjective constitution is what characterizes the fundamental intentional state. Here is how it differs from all other, "normal," intentional states. Generally, intentional states involve an agent S having a certain psychological attitude Ψ (believing, desiring, and so forth) toward a representational content R. Schematically, $S(\Psi(R))$, where R may represent a thing or a state of affairs. Call states having this structure *normal intentional states*. It is fundamental on my theory that R requires *both* an objective (o or $\Phi(o)$) and a subjective (m or the $\Phi(m)$) characterization. Now, the minimal content, m, being *about* something, is itself "directed," but, crucially, not in the way that representational content as objectively characterized is directed. On the objective reading of R, R is not constituted by the agent. In contrast, on the subjective reading of R, as m or $\Phi(m)$, it or a component of it is subjectively constituted. Thus, while one's having a minimal content is itself an intentional state, it is a unique one. Its logical structure differs from that of normal intentional states. The having of minimal content *cannot* be characterized as a *psychological attitude directed at something else*, as normal intentional states are.

Unlike all other contents, the agent constitutes minimal content. Minimal content does not merely represent; it has the uniquely singular property of *representing in virtue of the agent's constituting the content*. The minimal content of the act and the act itself—the constituting—are *not logically separable*. Thus, if one were to attempt to construe the constituting act as a psychological attitude, it would be distinctively different from the usual psychological attitudes, since all of those are logically separable from their contents. Therefore, the *aboutness* relation involved with minimal content is unique.[23] This is a wonderful consequence, since if it had the same logical structure as that of normal intentional states there would be a danger of infinite regress.[24]

Minimal content is at once different from and presupposed by all normal intentional states. It is *the fundamental intentional state*. I call it fundamental because there can be no normal intentional states without it. I call it intentional not because it has the same logical structure as normal intentional states (it does not) but because it has the central feature of such states ("aboutness," though, as I have emphasized, it is about things in way peculiar to it)—unlike normal intentional states, it involves a constituting relation that is logically inseparable from the content it constitutes.[25] This difference goes to the very heart of the ambiguity in the locution 'what a thought is about', an ambiguity that is accommodated by the introduction of the distinction between minimal content and objective content. If I am right about minimal content, however, the fundamental intentional state is not similarly ambiguous. It follows that the subjective side of the ambiguity is logically prior to its objective side.

The New Problems of Absent and Inverted (Non-Phenomenal) Content

The concept of minimal content has other interesting consequences. I argued in my discussion of the theorists A–D that, no matter how correct and elaborate the symbol manipulations are, *such manipulations are not sufficient to individuate one minimal content from another; still, the content is easily and directly individuated and differentiated by the agent, she is aware of what it is, and all this is achieved from her first-person perspective.* Theorists A, C, and D differentiate numbers (or particular numbers) and are able to distinguish them from sets (or particular sets). This ability and their awareness of minimal content do not require that they make an inference, though an observer of them must make inferences regarding their contents.

I have also argued that a difference in minimal content for an individual does not require a difference in symbolic manipulation. (Compare theorist

D.) Thus, the symbol manipulation is neither necessary nor sufficient for determining different minimal contents. Since the symbol manipulation is not sufficient to determine either A's or B's minimal content, there is here a sort of indeterminacy of minimal content from the third-person perspective, though each theorist has a definite minimal content that is different from the other's and is directly accessible to the theorist who has it.[26] As a result of this, we have an analogue to the problem of the inverted spectrum. Given the behavior of A and B as observed from a third-person perspective, we can attribute thoughts about numbers or sets to either A or B, but we cannot determine on that basis which minimal content the thinker has— an inverted minimal content problem.

We can now go further. Such manipulations, which are accessible from a third-person perspective, are not sufficient to say that the symbols have *any* content for the processor. Programs for proving theorems can and have been developed. Some are able to prove more difficult theorems than others, and to do it more efficiently.[27] Still, we have no reason to think that the symbols have any content for the program or for the machine running the program.[28] We could even build into the program the "disposition" to display 'number', or '2', when asked appropriate questions. The incorporation of this little programming task yields no basis for holding that the computer running the program has special access to its minimal content, not even that it has minimal content. None of this would provide reason to hold that the symbols it manipulates have content *for it*.[29]

Indeed, the same result that applied to a computer running a program could be achieved with a person. Let E be yet another theorist who learns the same formal theory as did A and B, but learns no semantics for it beyond that for the logical constants. E may still become quite adept at manipulating the symbols in accordance with the *formal* rules and *uninterpreted* axioms of the theory, as adept as A and B. But with E we go beyond this indeterminacy of minimal content relative to the third-person perspective. Here we have *absent content*. All the relevant symbol manipulations may be realized in E's activities, but E has *no* minimal content relative to these symbols or their manipulations.

The expression 'absent content' is obviously chosen because my point parallels one that Ned Block (1978) raised against functionalism. The general idea Block argued for, in opposition to functionalism, was that, though all the functional roles that a functionalist might require could be in place in some system, it would still be plausible in some such cases to deny that the system has any qualia. My arguments establish that all the relevant functional roles could be in place, yet a *non-phenomenal* narrow content—minimal content—would not be thereby determined or is in fact absent. Theorists A and B exemplify the minimal-content analogue to the inverted spectrum. Theorist E is the minimal-content analogue to the absent-qualia problem and is also a special case of the intentionality analogue to the "zombie case." However, my support for absent and inverted minimal content is stronger than the support offered by others for the inverted spectrum, absent qualia, and zombie problems. My arguments, unlike the others, *do not depend on mere conjectures of possibilities—they are verifiable from the first-person perspective.*

Constituting and Grasping Minimal Content: Fregean, Cartesian, and Searlean Comparisons

We have seen that from the first-person perspective that there is a kind of direct "grasping" of content that does not admit of degrees and is distinct from understanding the content. This grasping of minimal content, our non-inferential awareness of it, is largely a function of the fact that we subjectively constitute it. I make no claim as to just how we are able to constitute minimal content, but the various cases presented (forming an image, the battle diagram, with and without the "twist," the various theorists recently considered) make evident that we do constitute minimal content. Because of the subjective character of such constituting, this is evident only if one considers these cases from the first-person perspective. The crucial subjective features thus revealed are opaque from a strictly third-person perspective. Saying this, however, no more makes the act of constituting minimal content "spooky" or mysterious than is any other empirical phenomena *that* we know occurs without yet knowing *how* it occurs. ·

Frege

The minimal content of a thought is the subject of a thought as conceived by the thinker. Some may be tempted to assimilate minimal content to a Fregean sense, understood as a "mode of presentation," for it is natural to take the expression 'as conceived by' as though it were under a certain mode of presentation, or the subject of the thought under a certain "guise."

Such temptations must be resisted, for such a construal would be seriously misleading. My view of minimal content departs significantly from Frege's concept of sense. First a minor difference: By definition, both minimal content and objective content can only signal an object, whereas Fregean senses may also signal states of affairs. A much more critical difference is that I hold that a *single thought* is properly analyzed as having *both* a minimal content and an objective content; for Frege a thought has only one sense. Finally, and most important, minimal contents, depending as they do on how the *individual* conceives things, are *subjective* in a way in which Frege insisted senses are not.[30]

The last point is of great importance when making a comparative evaluation of Frege's claim that we grasp senses and my claim that we grasp minimal contents. The idea of grasping plays a central role in both of our views. But since minimal contents are unabashedly subjective and are in part constituted by the thinker, the idea that we grasp our own minimal contents seems clearly right. In contrast, just how a thinker is to grasp an objective Fregean sense, a sense that the thinker does not even in part constitute, does appear a bit mysterious; it is not addressed by Frege. The concept of minimal content clearly differs from and has a clear advantage over the concept of Fregean sense, at least in this respect. From the first-person perspective, it is *constitutive* of my entertaining some particular thought that it has the minimal content that it has. It simply would be a different thought if it did not have the subject that I conceive it to have. The grasping of minimal content by the thinker is unproblematic because the act of thinking that particular thought is a subjective act constitutive of its minimal content.

Descartes

Does our awareness of our minimal content amount to a privileged access of the Cartesian sort? The latter is typically portrayed so that the contents of one's mind are completely and infallibly transparent to oneself. I am not convinced that this is a fair portrayal of Descartes, but I will not attempt here a scholarly defense of a different reading of him.[31] The common interpretation of Descartes' view, whether it is his view or not, has been widely and rightly criticized. Certainly, the objective content is not completely and infallibly transparent to the agent. I do not challenge this. So long as 'content' is construed as the objective content there is no privileged access to it, none whatsoever. But this is no reason for *all* privileged access to *any kind* of content of one's thoughts to fall into disrepute. Minimal content is a distinct content from either the objective content or the representative content.[32] The privileged access that I endorse applies only on certain occasions and is severely restricted to minimal content, m. Moreover, any infallibility with regard to what the minimal content represents which results from this privileged access turns on the *senselessness* of an attribution of error, not upon our having some special ability or faculty. Thus, a limited, non-Cartesian form of privileged access is preserved.

Searle

My view is most sympathetic to Searle's; indeed, it builds upon it and so shares a number of its features. Importantly, the capacity for awareness of minimal content, being a necessary condition for an agent's having intentional states, is a commitment to intrinsic intentionality. Searle emphasizes intrinsic intentionality, as distinct from derivative or metaphorical intentionality, though he does not identify minimal content as a critical component of it.

Searle's idea of intrinsic intentionality is famously (or infamously) presented in his Chinese Room thought experiment.[33] One might wonder whether I have presented a remodeled Chinese Room. In Searle's thought experiment, the central concept is that of *understanding*; whether the room system has subjective phenomenal states is not at issue (pace Van Gulick—see chapter 3). Though Searle does not speak explicitly of content in that work, clearly it is involved; the question "Does the system understand?" may fairly be put as the question whether the strings of marks have any content for the agent (or system) manipulating them. Though I fundamentally agree with Searle regarding his views of intrinsic intentionality and the Chinese Room, casting the associated issues in terms of awareness of minimal content has several advantages over talk of understanding and natural languages.

First, rather than trying to contrast the Chinese Room with a genuine speaker of Chinese who "understands" (with all the attendant murkiness of this notion), the contrast is instead drawn in relatively simple and clear terms: straight out, one is aware that one's minimal content is, say, sets or numbers. So we take several steps back from understanding to awareness of minimal content. Crucially, and unlike understanding, minimal content does not come in degrees. As a result, we do not have to rely on, or attempt to resolve, conflicting intuitions as to whether or not a system such as the

Chinese Room understands. In the cases I considered, each individual clearly is aware of their respective minimal contents—despite radically different levels of understanding—whether those contents are the same (e.g. theorists A and C compared) or different (e.g. theorists A and B compared).

Another advantage is that a move against the Chinese Room commonly made by functionalists and others is defused. They often wish to bring in causal interaction of the system with its environment. Since such interactions are relevant in our own case for language understanding, they argue that such causal interaction must also be extended to the room system, prior to its getting any serious attention. I think this move is fundamentally mistaken (see chapters 2 and 3); still, the importance of such interaction may initially seem plausible when it is a question of language understanding in general. In part, it may seem plausible because of the pervasiveness of terms referring to things that occur in our environment. Whatever the reasons, it is clear that such causal interaction with the environment (other than the trivial ones for input and output) is not even initially plausible when we speak of abstract contents such as numbers or sets.

Explaining the Appearance

Given that it is at least initially plausible that we sometimes have some limited privileged access to the content of our intentional states, a special restriction is placed on any proposed account of intentionality: It must either include an account of this feature or explain why it appears to be the case but is not.

The force of this restriction might be made clearer by an analogy. George Berkeley argued that material substance did not exist (or rather that the notion itself was incoherent). But ordinary thinking and ordinary experience seem to present material things as uncontroversial data. In sections 34–81 of *A Treatise Concerning Principles of Human Knowledge*, Berkeley particularly addresses himself to objections based on this type of consideration—objections that his view denies various obvious truths, or that it obliterates various obvious distinctions, such as that between a real thing and a chimera.[34] In point of fact, while rejecting material substances, he took great care to show exactly why one cannot, say, simply walk through real walls, whereas one can "walk" through imagined walls, even though on his view both are collections of ideas. (Whether he was ultimately successful is entirely immaterial to the little moral I wish to draw from my discussion of him.) In doing so, Berkeley offered an explanation of how certain obvious data that seemed to refute his view were not only consistent with but explained by his account.

That Berkeley did explain why such obvious data are in accord with his theory is precisely why Samuel Johnson's famous "refutation" of Berkeley,[35] though cute in its vivid and immediate appeal to what seems to be a conflicting datum, can never be taken seriously. Had Berkeley failed to provide these explanations, Johnson would have had a formidable point. Unlike Berkeley, many present-day philosophers prefer to reduce, eliminate, or give an objective externalist account of the mental rather than rejecting the material; nevertheless, if they are to avoid a Johnsonian refutation (in reverse), they, too, must explain certain appearances, though their task is quite different from that which Berkeley confronted.

It is the kind of privileged access to one's (minimal) contents brought out by the various examples discussed earlier that constitutes the sort of data that produce such severe obstacles for strictly third-person methodologies. The obstacles thus raised are raised as data. Such data do not require some elaborate theoretical analysis (internalist or otherwise) to shore them up so that they can play this role. Not only do we have mental states; we also sometimes directly know (some of the) content of those states, its minimal content. When I speak here of 'being aware of the content' or 'knowing what the content is', I repeat that I do *not* refer to its *ontological* status, but only to how it is described in virtue of the subject's non-inferential knowledge of it. Whatever its ultimate ontological status, it is data of the utmost importance.

Heil (1988, p. 247) cites with approval Davidson's claim that we are victims of a certain misleading picture of the mind—to wit, ". . . the content of one's mental states are taken to be based on inward glimpses of those states or on the grasping of particular entities." Davidson recommends abandoning such a picture, and Heil claims that once we do so we "remove at least one of the reasons for supposing that externalism undermines privileged access" (ibid.). I applaud this abandonment. However, this picture is not the only obstacle for externalism or for strictly objective accounts. Abandoning it does not clear the way for such accounts of privileged access.

When I argue (in the next chapter) that these accounts cannot provide for any privileged access to contents, I do not rely on any analysis of this privileged access that presupposes such "inward glimpses of those states or on the grasping of particular entities." I am not committed to this model of introspection or to the grasping of *entities*. The metaphor used to characterize or single out the datum is inconsequential relative to the datum itself. I do not think that content is an entity, nor do I think we have "inward glimpses" of it, nor do my arguments depend on any such assumptions. *Still, we are sometimes aware of content.* We are not, however, aware of it in the sense of having special or detailed knowledge of its nature or ontological status. To hold the latter would be to invoke the thoroughly discredited view that our privileged access to our own mental states gives us infallible and incorrigible knowledge of the *very nature* of those states. I certainly do not hold that view.

Nor should my recent comments be construed as my harboring some view such as that there exist "pure data," that there is a "given," or that common-sense beliefs are somehow epistemically privileged. I hold no such views. Such views are, to my mind, also thoroughly discredited. Though there are no "pure data," it is far from evident that the indicated datum—that sometimes we have privileged access to (at least part of) our own content, our minimal contents—is such that it is essentially dependent on this particular (wrong-headed) picture of the mind. Rejecting the picture does not, ipso facto, eliminate the datum in question; puzzles remain regarding an account of this datum.

As I see it, any account that employs an exclusive third-person methodology must fail in accommodating privileged access to (minimal) content or even recognizing the latter. If that is correct, the only option for someone employing a strictly third-person methodology is to dissolve the datum by explaining it away as mere appearance—that is, by showing that privileged access to our own contents is just an illusion. If a theory fails in the latter and lacks the resources to account for the appearance, then the theory must be rejected.

If I am right, minimal content and awareness of it are fundamental to a theory of mind. Recognition of this provides a better foundation for the analysis of mind than can any theory based on a strictly third-person methodology. Since reliance on the latter methodology has dominated the philosophical study of the mind, and since minimal content is evident only from the first-person perspective, it is not surprising that minimal content has gone largely unnoticed.

2 Minimal Content and Some Failures of Third-Person Methodologies

In this chapter I attempt to strengthen the case for the acceptance of the first-person concept of minimal content by way of exposing some fundamental inadequacies that are characteristic of various orthodox theories that employ a strictly third-person methodology, inadequacies that are overcome through the employment of minimal content. By so doing, the pervasiveness and indispensability of the concept of minimal content to the philosophical study of the mind is further demonstrated.

Externalism and Higher-Order Thoughts

Externalism (or anti-individualism) embraces the orthodox methodology. It is the view that the content of a subject's mental state is determined by some state of affairs outside of that mental state, in virtue of occurrences in the physical or social environment of the subject. Given that it is so determined, a question arises as to whether we could ever have privileged access to the content of any of our thoughts, since we certainly do not have privileged access to external states of affairs. A number of externalists believe that their theory can accommodate privileged access to content and typically invoke a higher-order thought (or perception) to do so. I argue that such invocation is neither necessary nor sufficient for privileged access. The basic reason for this turns on the fact that the fundamental intentional state has the unique logical structure that it does.

Higher-Order States Are Not Necessary

To see this, recall theorist D, who knew her formal theory had different models with different domains (numbers and sets). D can switch her minimal content from number to set at will and know, without inference, which her thought was about on any given occasion. She knows her minimal content straight out, and it makes no sense to question whether she is right about this. In stark contrast, our ascertaining D's minimal content is necessarily based on inferences from her behavior, and it does make sense from this perspective to question whether we have made the right inference. It is easy to see, therefore, that if we were to restrict ourselves to an exclusively third-person methodology in the analysis of such cases, we would endorse the view that D *herself* must have a second-order thought to be aware of what her thought is about, since we in assessing her content must do so. However, the examination of D's case in the previous chapter shows that D need not do this—that from D's first-person perspective this is not required. Therefore, the claim that a higher-order characterization is necessary is seen to be an artifact of employing an exclusive third-person methodology.

The various versions of the view that a second-order thought is required for this kind of knowledge are known as Higher-Order Theories of Consciousness.[1] Insofar as these theories *require* a higher-order state in their analysis of consciousness, they must be rejected if I am right that D's awareness (hence, consciousness) of her own minimal content is first-order. The earlier examples—theorists A–C, the grandmother image, the battle diagram with and without the "twist"—serve as additional counterexamples to the widely held claim that a second-order state is required for such knowledge. But, again, these counterexamples can be recognized as such only if one adopts the first-person perspective, for the considerations to which I appeal on their behalf are invisible from a third-person perspective. *That this is so is a direct manifestation of the important asymmetry of the first- person and third-person perspectives.* Thus, the cases provide reason to reject theories of consciousness that rely on exclusive use of a third-person methodology.

Higher-Order States Are Not Sufficient

There is the separate important question whether within an externalist's framework such moves can successfully account for any privileged access there is to one's own states. I address this question through a refutation of one such attempt. My objections, however, are of a sufficiently general nature that they pose problems for any externalist account of privileged access that relies upon higher-order thoughts (perceptions).

John Heil (1988) offers such an account; it is widely cited as providing an externalist account of privileged access. Heil acknowledges that there is a skeptical problem with self-awareness for the externalist—a skeptical problem that goes even deeper than traditional skepticism, for it questions "the presumption that we think what we think we think" (245).[2] Nevertheless, he holds that, despite various skeptical reasons to think the contrary, we can "accept a relational or externalist explication of intentional content and retain the conviction that access to one's own states of mind is epistemically privileged" (243). He accepts the asymmetry (238), but he holds that "if we can be externalists about content, then we can be externalists about an agent's awareness of content."[3] I argue for the denial of the consequent of this conditional. Thus, if the asymmetry between first and third person access is not mere illusion, an externalist account of mental content is untenable.

Heil thinks the skeptic's problem arises from a "fundamental mischaracterization of externalism" (245). By way of a solution, he proposes the following:

We are supposing that externalism is correct, hence that the content of M' [a second-order introspective state that "encompasses," his word, a first-order state M] is determined by some state of affairs, A', that is at least partly distinct from M'.

Heil then asks:

What, now, is to prevent A' from determining the intentional content for M' that *includes* the content of M? What, for instance, keeps our simplified theory from allowing that a causal relation of a certain sort endows my introspective thought with a content encompassing the content of the thought on which I am introspecting? (245)

Heil's implied answer, of course, is "Nothing." He elaborates in the following terms. Externalist theories do not require that the thinker having mental states know or believe that certain conditions obtain, only that they obtain. So, Heil asserts, "the same must be true for second-order states of mind. When I introspect, the content of my introspection will be determined by its being caused in an appropriate way, not by my discovering that it was caused in that way." (246) In addition, the content of the second-order thought "encompasses" the content of the first-order thought. Heil concludes his section on externalism and skepticism by holding that "the content of *both* thoughts [first- and second-order] is generated externally" (247).

There are two separate issues here: whether the content of a thought is determined ("generated") by external conditions and whether externalism has the resources to account for the asymmetrical access, privileged access, to the content of one's thought. Let us suppose, with Heil (p. 247), that the first- and second-order thoughts and their contents are determined by external conditions. One may also suppose that the content of the second-order thought "encompasses" the content of the first-order thought (p. 245). Granting all this, the question remains: How does that provide for privileged access to the content of one's thought? How does that allow us to, as quoted above, "retain the conviction that access to one's own states of mind is epistemically privileged"?

Heil's talk of a further external condition determining a content that encompasses the content of a first-order thought is part of his attempt to show how, the skeptic notwithstanding, externalism can account for privileged access. But content determination is one thing and privileged access to content is another. One problem is that it is not evident how the appeal to external conditions' determining content, or of a content's "encompassing" another content can do the job of providing an account of privileged access.

The crux of Heil's externalist account of privileged access does not merely rely upon the assumption that the contents are externally determined and the encompassing feature, however. Also critical is the additional claim that, although external conditions must obtain, the subject need not know or believe that they obtain:

. . . externalist theories of the sort under discussion require only that certain conditions *obtain* in order for a given state to have a particular intentional content. They do not, or anyhow need not, require in addition that one know or believe these states to obtain. When I introspect, the content of my introspection will be determined by its being caused in an appropriate way, not by my discovering that it was caused in that way. (246)

Now, Heil recognized that the mere occurrence of such thought-determining and content-determining causal relations of the first-order thought were not sufficient to provide for the thinker's privileged access to her content in the first instance; hence the move to a second-order thought, one that included, encompassed, the content of the first-order thought. This second-order thought is determined by another causal relation, different from that required for the first-order thought, which also need only obtain, but of which the subject need not be aware.

It is a mystery how such inclusion of content and an appeal to yet another (unspecified) causal relation can be any more revealing of the thinker's awareness of content, her privileged access, than it was of her first-order thought. If there was a puzzle at the level of the first-order thought regarding the thinker's privileged access, it is not resolved by moving to a second-order for which the same type of conditions are in play. The mere inclusion of some content within another more inclusive content cannot account for the awareness of the initial content; yet that seems to be the only relevant difference. In both the first-order thought and the second-order thought, causal relations to external states of affairs determine the content and the subject is not required to be aware of these. If one is not aware of content in the first instance, or if the causal relation determining content in the first instance does not explain the subject's awareness of content, why should content within content make a difference relative to awareness of the first content? If there are no different factors, what could account for the privileged access?

It is held that if the content of the first-order thought is externally determined then so too is the content of the second-order thought that "encompasses" the content of the first-order thought; moreover, in neither case need one know the external conditions that determine these contents. All that, of course, is a standard externalist line on *content*, but the issue at hand is not just that—it is a thinker's *privileged access* to her content. As already observed, content is one thing and privileged access is another. Clearly, simply providing a theory of how the content is determined, no matter how successful the theory is in that respect, does not, in itself, address the question of the thinker's privileged access to content.

Indeterminacy in Determining the Content, and More on Second-Order Thoughts

Putting privileged access aside until the end of this section, I will examine another problem for the externalist. It concerns the use of expressions such as "the content is determined [generated or caused] by external conditions." There is widespread indeterminacy and outright vagueness in contemporary philosophical use of such expressions. After examining this locution, I will then be able to show why, with or without reliance on second-order thoughts, the externalist cannot accommodate privileged access.

Many external causal conditions are necessary in order that I be aware of a given content on any given occasion. That there is a proper amount of oxygen in the atmosphere is an external condition that clearly must obtain if I am to be aware of any content. It is equally obvious that I need not be aware of the oxygen in the atmosphere in order that I may be aware of the thought content of my occurrent state. Many such necessary external conditions must obtain—for example, the proper functioning of my heart and the temperature of the ambient air. Clearly it is not required that the thinker know or believe that such conditions obtain. It is also clear that such conditions, though necessary, clearly do not *determine* the content in any way relevant to the present discussion.

What does it take for an external condition to determine the content of a mental state? Perhaps a clue will be found above: Those conditions were *irrelevant* to determining the content since they would be required for us to have *any* content. They would play no role in determining the specific content. They would be merely "background conditions" for humans' having content. Consider the obvious claim that for a condition to determine content it must, in some way, be specific to the particular content at issue. In the example of the battle diagram discussed in chapter 1, there certainly are some causal external conditions specific to my perception of Xs. For example, for each token of the symbol type X, there must be certain patterns of ink on paper and proper lighting interacting with the ink and with my perceptual apparatus, etc. Call these conditions C_1. It is that very pattern of ink obtaining and my causally interacting with it in the right way that determines my perception of each token of an X. So it is that C_1 determines my perception of Xs. But the *content* of which I am aware is not the individual tokens of Xs, nor is the content the type X. *It is what I conceive the type X to represent*, namely (a certain number of) Napoleon's troops. C_1 does not determine that.

Different conditions, though not substantially different ones, might have obtained; for example, my diagram may have been drawn with chalk on a blackboard rather than with ink on paper. Call the analogous but different set of conditions C_2. Again, C_2 may well determine my perception of chalk tokens of the symbol type X, but not what that type represents. Of course, too, I could have imagined the whole diagram (assuming it is not overly complicated) and, as a result of doing so, had the same thought and be aware of the *same content* as I was under either C_1 or C_2, but this time substantially different external conditions (call them C_3) obtain. (Here, even if the conditions are not external to my body, they are surely external to the particular thought or state.) My imagined Xs may well have radically different conditions determining them than those that determined the visually perceived tokens,[4] yet, whatever those conditions are, they, like the conditions C_1 and C_2, are conditions that determine the tokens, not what is represented by them.

Each of the three different sets of conditions, C_1, C_2, and C_3, is specific to the occasion of a mental state's having a particular content. In each case, however, only a token of a symbol type is determined, but neither the token nor the type is what one has asymmetrical access to. (In a sense, then, what is determined by these specific external conditions is twice removed from the content of which I am aware.) The difference between determining the token (or the type) and determining what in particular is represented is important to a proper understanding of representation.[5] Is there some other external condition, one common to the three sets, that determines the content? Perhaps.[6] I, for one, am at a loss as to how to specify it, within externalist constraints, so as to avoid the result just brought out.

Thus, in each case I hold that the external conditions considered only determine the token used to represent content; they do not determine the content. Various tokens of a symbol type are determined by external conditions, but neither the tokens nor the type is the content of the thought. To clinch this conclusion, consider the new twist on the battle diagram (or theorist D), introduced in chapter 1. Given the battle configuration at a given time and the different psychologies and abilities of Napoleon and Kutuzov, I might wonder what Kutuzov would have done if he were in Napoleon's position—that is, if the Xs (tokens), positioned as they are, represented Kutuzov's troops rather than Napoleon's. *I may change the content without changing the external conditions.* Clearly, this content is independent of the external conditions.

One thing I have tried to bring out here is that, although talk of external conditions determining content has a "solid ring" to it, what it actually amounts to is quite elusive. The externalist trades on the obvious fact that a number of external conditions are necessary for one to be aware of content. Vaguely alluding to these external conditions fails to show that they determine the *content*, however. Many are just what I called 'background conditions' for content. Other conditions, though in some sense specific to the content, do not determine it, but only tokens that represent the particular content, and the latter, as we have just seen, can vary independent of the former. But since the relevant sense (if there is one) must be specified, I lay down a challenge to those who hold that the content is determined by some external condition. The challenge is to show how one could possibly specify an external condition in a manner that would not be subject to the arguments above—arguments which establish that said specified condition merely determines tokens of a symbol, rather than what in particular the symbol represents, the particular content.

There is the further important consequence from the case involving the "twist" on the battle diagram (or theorist D), already explained. It pertains specifically to privileged access rather than content. Should I shift my content from Xs representing Napoleon's troops to Xs representing Kutuzov's, I do not need to *infer* (as you might) that these very same tokens now represent Kutuzov's troops—*I know this straight out, and I have no need to move to a second-order thought.* Thus, not only is the content independent (in the sense just explained) of external conditions, but one's special access to it does not require a second-order thought.

The externalist has problems. The problem recently canvassed concerns the vagueness and inadequacy of the word 'determining' in the locution 'determining the content'. This resulted in a failure to specify a particular content. Second, there is the earlier objection concerning eternalism's failure to account for privileged access to content, despite the appeal to second-order thoughts. This problem is significantly compounded by the observation that one can have privileged access to one's content without recourse to second-order thoughts. Therefore, even if an analysis based on second-order thoughts were successful for some cases, such higher-order thoughts would not be necessary for privileged access. The externalist would still owe us an account of privileged access to the content of first-order thoughts.

There is yet another problem. Just what is content? There is a tendency on the part of externalists, which stems from their basic thesis, to identify the determiner of content with content itself. Some of Heil's statements exemplify this. Consider the following: "Thus, even if I happened to be right about what *caused M*, hence about *M's intentional content*, my access to that content would hardly be direct or privileged." (Heil 1988, p. 245) A bit later Heil says "I might err in identifying the *cause of M*, hence err in my assessment of *M's content*" (ibid., emphases added). In the context of a defense of privileged access to content, this is strange, to say the least. As Heil recognizes, there certainly can be no privileged access to the causes; so, if an error in identifying the cause of a mental state M implies (note the 'hence' in the passage just quoted) an error in my assessment of M's content, there can be no privileged access to content or intentional content. End of story.

Of course, the repeated claim that the thinker need not know the determiner of content, only that it obtains, coupled with the move to a second-order thought, is supposed to free the externalist from this unwanted consequence. But does it? As I showed earlier, content determination is one thing and privileged access to content is another. Although these moves could conceivably rescue the externalist's position regarding the former, they erect an insurmountable barrier to an externalist account of privileged access.

I think some of the confusion on content—just what it is and what is our relation to it—stems from an incomplete or confused view of intentionality. Heil says that "intentional states, by and large, exhibit two components, a particular content and an attitude or disposition of some sort toward that content" (1988, p. 241). I am not sure why Heil inserted the qualification "by and large," but there appears to be a glaring omission in this characterization of intentional states that is not rectified by the qualification. What of the intentional object? Arguably one could say that this omission is acceptable since Heil is speaking of intentional *states* rather than intentionality. Generally I would agree with this, but it is of no help to Heil. I think that Heil here is referring to the intentional object, not to the intentional content proper, when he uses 'intentional content' in the passage quoted above.[7] Apparently, Heil fails to distinguish them, at least here. His comments (quoted above) regarding the relations between causes and either contents or intentional contents suggest that his use of 'intentional content' in that context is closer to Searle's use of 'intentional object'. That does not mean that Heil is wrong. Labels are not important; however, since intentional object and intentional content play quite different roles in intentionality, Heil must either show that one of these roles is unnecessary or provide for it in his discussion. He does neither. Certainly, one must not conflate them.

Perhaps the tendency to conflate intentional content and intentional object stems from an effort to be in accord with the externalist's desire, advanced by Putnam, to locate meaning (content) outside the head. (The Twin-Earth case is discussed below.) Perhaps externalists and others tend to avoid distinguishing the two in order to get away from some earlier (misguided) traditional usage, where the intentional object is, itself, mental, a Meinongian object. The latter can be and is avoided, however, while still keeping intentional contents in the head, as Searle does. (See Searle 1983 and my extension of Searle's theory in chapter 1 above.) If intentional content is in the head, then there is a prima facie better chance of giving a satisfactory account of privileged access to at least some of it, as I have tried to do, than there is if it is not in the head. Additionally, putting content in the head does not (at least need not) put meaning there; the two are not identical on my theory. (See chapter 8 below.)

Let me make it clear that according to my theory externalism might be acceptable as a *partial* theory of the content of an agent's mental state. The part the externalist may have gotten right is the objective content, o, or even $\Phi(o)$. But the externalist has no place for the internalist concept of minimal content, the m of $\Phi(m)$. Since externalism only countenances objective content and there never is privileged access to this, externalists' efforts to account for privileged access are doomed to failure. In my criticism of Heil's account, however, I did not rely on this general and fundamental inadequacy of externalist theories. As I have tried to make clear, the failure of Heil's appeal to second-order thoughts to explain privilege access has its own explanation, separate from an appeal to minimal content. Ultimately, though, the explanation of Heil's failure is secondary to the root cause: Privileged access is access to *minimal content*, a content that is inconsistent with their theory; moreover, one's awareness of it is, or can be, first-order. If I am right about this fundamental cause of externalism's failure to account for privileged access, then no amount of tinkering with second-order thoughts or with the principles of externalism will rectify the deficiency.

A Failure of Functionalism

Functionalism is another philosophical theory of the mental that typically restricts itself to the orthodoxy of a strictly third-person methodology. It too lacks the resources to account for our privileged access to content. Robert Van Gulick is a particularly clear example of a functionalist philosopher who, while sensitive to the problem of providing a place for first-person awareness of what our thoughts are about, makes what are to me two typical errors. The first ultimately results from his reliance on the orthodox methodology. The second is to think of consciousness generally, and that involved in privileged access in particular, as somehow strongly associated with phenomenal experience. Both errors are widespread in philosophy. I will treat of the first error as it is manifested in Van Gulick's functionalism in this section, and as it is manifested in functionalism generally in the next section. I will examine the second error in the next chapter.

Van Gulick subsumes knowing what one's thought is about to understanding. Central to his account of understanding is the concept of *semantic transparency*[8]:

> [Semantic transparency] concerns the extent to which a system can be said to understand the content of the internal symbols or representation on which it operates. The more the system understands the content of its representations (as manifested in its behavior with respect to those symbols) the more those symbols can be said to be semantically transparent to the system. The behavior manifesting the relevant understanding will consist in part of behaviors connecting the symbols with the external world through input and output relations, but will also include behaviors relating internal symbols to each other in ways that are sensitive to their content. (1989, p. 223)

Thus, the greater that one's understanding of the content of the internal symbols is, the greater their semantic transparency, and semantic transparency is manifested by the rapid manipulation of the internal symbols: it "consists in large part of the fact that I can instantaneously connect those representations to other semantically related representations" (224). In addition, these symbols are connected to the external world through input and output relations, and the internal manipulations are, as in Van Gulick's words quoted above, "sensitive to their content."

Clearly, input/output relations are required on any account. Just how the internal relations are sensitive to the content of symbols is of course a crucial issue when the topic is privileged access to content. I presume Van Gulick intends semantic transparency to provide for that sensitivity to content since it pertains to the fluency of the internal relations to the symbols, which "concerns the extent to which a system can be said to understand the content of the internal symbols or representation on which it operates" (quoted above). Since Van Gulick says nothing further about "sensitivity to content," I assume that he thinks that his account of semantic transparency takes care of that.

Presumably, then, more rapid manipulations produce greater transparency and understanding. (This much fits with my discussion in the previous chapter of *degrees of understanding* or *measures* thereof.) Although these quotations occur in the context of a discussion of phenomenal representations, the subsequent discussion will make it clear that Van Gulick intends the concept of semantic transparency to apply to understanding in general.[9]

Van Gulick attempts to give an account of first-person awareness of what our thoughts are about:

On the whole, when we have a conscious experience, we know what we are conscious of. . . . We know what they [internal representations] represent *in virtue of our capacity to instantaneously and effortlessly connect those representations with other semantically related representations*. (1989, p. 224, emphasis added)

Finally, he states:

It is *the awareness of these transitions among representations* in the seemingly continuous flow of experience *that provides the subjective experience of understanding, our conscious feeling that we know what we are thinking about*. (ibid., emphases added)

To see why this does not succeed in accounting for the fact that we know what we are thinking about recall theorists A and B considered in chapter 1. They engage in the same symbol manipulations, and so, on Van Gulick's account, they have the same understanding, the same "awareness of these transitions among representations." However, this cannot be what accounts for their understanding or their "conscious feeling that [they] know what [they] are thinking about," since they are thinking about *different things* while the transitions are the same and occur with equal rapidity. Furthermore, our not-very-competent number theorist C's transitions between symbols are hesitant or halting; her transitions certainly are not as rapid as A's. Yet C knows, as clearly as does A, that her thoughts are about number.

Thus, semantic transparency, *insofar as it involves the smooth and rapid transitions* between representations, is neither necessary (consider A and C, who are very unequal in their transitions but both think about numbers) nor sufficient (consider A and B, who are equally smooth and rapid in their transitions but think about different things: numbers versus sets) for "our conscious feeling that we know what we are thinking about." Nor is semantic transparency sufficient for a symbol manipulator to be "sensitive to the content" (Van Gulick 1989, p. 223) of the symbols manipulated, contrary to Van Gulick's claim. For again, the semantic transparency of A's and B's symbols are identical, but *the contents are distinct*. A and B are each "sensitive to the content," since each is aware of their respective minimal content, each knows what she is thinking about, but they are not sensitive to this in virtue of semantic transparency. Case E supports the claim that semantic transparency is irrelevant to a thinker's awareness of content, since E's symbol manipulations do not differ from A's and B's, but E's symbols have *no content for* E. (E is the absent-content case.) Van Gulick's attempt to provide for privileged access fails.

I argued in chapter 1 that the concept of understanding is much broader and less definite than the concept of minimal content, and that for that reason alone consideration of it should be postponed until simpler and more fundamental matters have been handled. In addition, consideration of understanding naturally brings symbol manipulation to center stage, since understanding surely involves inferential relations between thoughts. Such inferential relations and symbol manipulations are accessible to a strictly third-person methodology and are definitely associated with the concept of understanding. Therefore, the exclusive use of this sort of methodology encourages these misleading directions. But, as I argued earlier, symbol manipulation is crucial neither to minimal content nor to our awareness of it, and understanding presupposes awareness of (one's) minimal content.

A General Argument against Functionalism

A major and prominent strictly third-person analysis of intentionality is provided by functionalism. If a functionalist is to give an account of our special access to our own minimal contents, it must be achieved under the constraint that the differential responses to symbols or various relations internal to the thinker may be specifically due to the content. The cases of theorists A–E developed in chapter 1 and my discussion of Van Gulick count against that claim. The same differential responses are consistent with some of the symbols' having different minimal contents for the symbol manipulator (e.g., theorists A and B) and different differential responses are consistent with the same minimal contents (e.g., theorists A and C). Thus, such responses are not sensitive to the particular content. The above results are the same whether these differential responses are overt or occur "in the head." Since the syntactical relations that are the basis for these differential responses model the sort of relations one finds in conceptual (functional or computational) role semantics, the narrow content of conceptual role semantics is too coarse to determine a particular content.[10]

Not even the much weaker claim that the differential responses are specifically due to some equivalence class of contents, equivalence with respect to certain functional roles, is justified. For the fact that a digital computer running the appropriate program may also make these same correct differential responses as, say, theorist A, while the symbols clearly have no content for it, counts against even this weaker claim, as does the case of theorist E in chapter 1. In none of these cases is the response due specifically to the content of the symbols; nor need different contents result in different responses, in spite of the fact that in some of the cases the same functional roles are instantiated.

Not only is the narrow content of conceptual role semantics too coarse, it is also too fine. There are different formal theories for the same content; these theories are the basis for different syntactical or functional roles. Think of different formalizations for set theory (say, NBG and ZF), or the different formalizations of group theory mentioned by Rota et al. (see chapter 1 above). Since the different theories just mentioned involve different functional roles, if one were to individuate the content in virtue of the operative functional roles one would be committed to different contents for theories that are widely believed by mathematicians, philosophers, and others to have the same contents. The minimal content for someone operating with NBG or ZF is sets, despite the different functional relations instantiated in these two theories. The narrow content of functionalism does not capture this content; functionalism is too fine grained. But, as we have seen, functionalism is also too coarse grained, since it is unable to distinguish, for example, D's minimal contents, which included sets and numbers.

Now consider an objection a functionalist might raise to what I have argued here. The functionalist might respond that the various theorists considered have different verbal dispositions depending on whether their contents are numbers, sets, or something else. Since these different verbal dispositions are realized in the different theorists, the theorists differ in functional organization. Thus, though the differences in content for the theorists are not revealed in the symbol manipulations within their respective theories, if we take a sufficiently broad view of their functional organization—a view that includes their different verbal dispositions in their background languages and their respective formal theories as a proper part—their differences in content will be reflected in differences in functional organization. The latter difference will eventually show up as some difference in symbolic manipulation, even if it does not do so within the theories themselves, contrary to what I argued above.[11]

A preliminary response to the objection: The plausibility of holding that our different theorists had different minimal contents, which they could know without recourse to second-order thoughts, in no way turned on their actually having a disposition to utter one term rather than another. One might even imagine the cases considered to be restricted with a further proviso, viz., that our theorists have no such dispositions. It may in fact be impossible to so restrict our theorists; however, it is not obviously impossible, and adding that restriction would in no way hinder the formulation of the cases as already presented. It does help to bring out the plausibility of holding that our theorists' having different minimal contents does not depend on their having such dispositions. After all, it is easy enough to imagine the cases, to imagine that they are aware of various minimal contents, without presupposing anything about such dispositions that they may or may not also have. This initial response is less than conclusive, so I will now meet the objection head-on.

The more rigorous response to the functionalist's objection is two-pronged. I show that the objection is deflated for two independent reasons:

(i)   It depends on a criterion of functional equivalence that no one has yet provided.[12]

(ii)   Even if such a criterion were provided, the functionalist would have to show, not just assert, that any functional relation offered as the basis for some mental property (in this case minimal content or awareness of it) can in fact account for the property. This has not been done.

As to (i), suppose, plausibly enough, that different verbal dispositions imply different functional organization, and consider two number theorists, each of whom has the same disposition to utter the word 'number' when appropriately stimulated. Still, each will undoubtedly have many other dispositions in which they differ. Thus, though these two theorists share what has been alleged to be the relevant disposition, they are not functionally equivalent. That gets to the point that undermines the objection:

(*)   Given any two individuals, there will always be *some* functional difference between them; no two individuals are functionally equivalent *in all respects*.

As a result of (*), what is needed is a non-ad-hoc way of determining the relevant type of functional equivalence (hence, also non-equivalence) for any given case. Without a criterion for relevant functional equivalence, we surely cannot permit the mere specification of *some* functional difference, whatever its initial plausibility, as a sufficient reason to hold that an alleged counterexample to functionalism fails because the individuals involved are not functionally equivalent. If we were to allow the latter, the existence of a counterexample would be a priori impossible (since there is always *some* functional difference between any two individuals). Therefore, the non-ad-hoc specification of just what is to count as functional equivalence is of the utmost importance. This is a serious lacuna in functionalists' accounts.

So, even if we suppose different theorists, say, A and B, do have different verbal dispositions, the question remains: *Is this sufficient to say that they are not functionally equivalent vis à vis either their respective minimal contents or their awareness of those contents?* As already indicated, an answer to this question is stymied by the lack of an adequate criterion of functional equivalence. Without such a criterion, the claim that different verbal dispositions are sufficient for saying the theorists are not functionally equivalent is unsupported. On the other hand, even if we had an adequate general criterion for functional equivalence, this would not be enough. Since (*) is the case, (ii) comes into play: Whenever a particular functional difference is offered as a basis for functional non-equivalence, *that particular* functional feature must be shown to be sufficient for the specific mentalistic property at issue. For the case at hand, the functionalist would have the responsibility of demonstrating that verbal dispositions are sufficient for determining minimal content or one's awareness of one's own minimal content. Only then would the fact that there are two individuals with different verbal dispositions warrant the inference that they have different minimal contents. If the functionalist fails to provide such an account, whether in terms of verbal dispositions or some other specific functional feature, the functionalist has failed to give an account of minimal content or one's awareness of it. Since neither (i) nor (ii) has been overcome, the functionalist has failed in this respect.

Let me elaborate on the immediate issues. Talk of verbal dispositions here is just a distraction unless it is supplemented with an account of how verbal dispositions determine minimal content or one's awareness of it. *If* functionalism is true, *there is a relevant functional difference between theorists A and*

B, and it accounts for both their different minimal contents and their respective awareness' of it. For a functionalist, a difference in verbal dispositions between A and B is, perhaps, a likely first place to look for the relevant difference. (We shall see below, however, that verbal dispositions are not plausible after all.) Moreover, if it should turn out that the difference in verbal disposition fails to be the locus of the *relevant* functional difference, and, *if functionalism is true*, then there must be some *other* functional difference to be found between A and B. But *whether functionalism is true is centrally in contention*, so it is exceedingly important for the functionalist to show that whatever particular functional difference she proposes is, indeed, responsible for the difference in minimal content or the awareness of it. Failing to do so is to fail to enter into the battle. Simply suggesting a plausible candidate, having already assumed the truth of functionalism, not only begs the question but also fails to complete the job. I am pessimistic that this is a job the functionalist *can* complete.

Even if functionalism is true, the difference in verbal dispositions of two theorists is a suspect basis for holding that they have different minimal contents. To see this, consider a German-speaking number theorist. When she and our English-speaking number theorist are similarly prompted, they will respond with different words. They have different dispositions, even though it is correct to say that they have the same minimal content. Of course, the prompting will be via different symbols, German or English, but this in itself is no reason to think that the difference in responses to the different typescripts has any special bearing on what the German-speaking theorists' or the English-speaking theorists' minimal contents represent.[13] To make this even clearer, suppose that our German-speaking theorist becomes fluent in English and now works equally well with number theory formulated in either language. Now, when she utilizes the theory formulated in English, her differential responses to different symbols mirror exactly those of the monolingual English-speaking theorist, and they differ from her own responses when she is working in the German formulation; still, her minimal contents are the same regardless of which formulation she is utilizing. So, once again, we see that what is represented by the minimal content is independent of appropriate differential responses to different stimuli (typescripts).[14] (Compare the discussion above of externalism and the difficulty of specifying the external condition that determines the content of a thought.)

This brings us to another problem confronting the functionalist regarding the issues before us. The response considered on behalf of the functionalist has been that the difference in, say, A's and B's minimal content is, in fact, dependent on their different verbal dispositions and, hence, on their different functional organization. I have argued that the appeal to verbal dispositions fails, but I now wish to indicate a further source of trouble for the functionalist. How is this peculiarly first-person aspect—that we have minimal contents and can be aware of what they represent—to be explained in terms of a third-person account deploying functional relations? One possibility is that the difference in dispositions causes a difference in minimal content and awareness of it; another is that the minimal content or the awareness of it is identical or logically reducible to the actualizing of a certain verbal disposition. These alternatives exhaust the helpful possibilities for my objector.[15]

When I entertain the thought that 2 is a prime number, neither the minimal content nor the awareness of it seems to be of a dispositional type. Yet the possibilities for the "depends" relation just listed require a causal relation, an identity relation, or a logical relation between the minimal content (or the awareness of it) and a disposition. Thus, all of these require relating two items that are prima facie of distinctly different types. If functionalism is true, then, undoubtedly, one of these relations holds. But, as before, if the functionalist is to gain the advantage here, she cannot do so simply by assuming that functionalism is true. She must explain the appearance that, although minimal content and dispositions are of apparently distinct types, they are nevertheless related in one of the ways indicated. One could close this gap by showing that they are identical, or by producing the relevant reduction, be it logical or causal. Of course, that is asking a lot. On the other hand, a sketch of how they will be related is not too much to require.[16] Such a sketch, need I say it again, must not presuppose that functionalism is true. But not even this much has been done.

The above assumes that the functionalist is concerned to give an account of how a thinker is sometimes and in some way privileged regarding what her thought is about (as, for example, Van Gulick is). There is another alternative to the problems posed by these first-person aspects articulated here. The functionalist may deny that there is minimal content and may also deny that there is any sort of privileged access to the content (of whatever sort) of a thought on the part of the thinker. For such a position to be taken seriously, however, it would be incumbent on the functionalist to explain the *appearance* that the thinker sometimes is in such a privileged position.[17]

In rejecting functionalism, am I just relying on the intuition that we are aware of our minimal content and claiming that the functionalist can't account for this intuition? No. First, my argument does not simply rest on an intuition, one that others may or may not share. As I developed the cases for the various theorists (A–D) and the other examples treated earlier, they were attempts to demonstrate that each theorist is, in fact, aware of the minimal content of her respective thought. The cases were developed for the purpose of strengthening the support for this conclusion. This was done from the first-person perspective; how it would be for the individual theorists. If I have failed, then there must be specific shortcomings in my development of the cases treated or the conclusions drawn from them; these must be pointed out. As I initially warned, my case for the theorists' being aware of their thoughts' minimal contents cannot be even assessed from a strictly third-person perspective. So my interlocutor must, at least temporarily, adopt the first-person perspective. For example, the functionalist must show that first-person-perspective awareness of number, as demonstrated in the cases I develop, is accountable from a strictly third-person perspective, or that it occurs is an utter illusion, a mere appearance. I have argued that the functionalist cannot succeed here. I may be wrong, but my argument does not simply rest on an appeal to an intuition.

Minimal Content and Twin Earth

I have discussed above how certain third-person accounts, including externalism or anti-individualism and functionalism, fail to account for privileged access. Third-person accounts of intentional states and their contents commonly maintain these two claims:

(A)   A causal interaction of a system with its environment is necessary to determine or individuate at least some contents.[18]

(B)   Two systems might be identical molecule for molecule but differ in the content of their intentional states because of their respective environments.

I argue that if one holds both (A) and (B), there is no possibility that a system has special access to its minimal contents. Thus, anyone holding both (A) and (B) is forced to deny the asymmetry of access discussed; hence, any such person must also explain the contrary appearance as a mere illusion. Here is why: Suppose both (A) and (B) are true. Whatever differences in content there are for the two individuals so placed, the differences depend on their being in different social environments (Burge-type arguments; see chapter 7) or in different physical environments (Putnam-type arguments; see below), since, ex hypothesi, the agents' internal states are identical. Given our third-person perspective of them and our knowledge of the environments, *we* may have reason to attribute different contents to their respective states, but *the individuals* would have no reason to do so from their first-person perspectives. We have reason because we have knowledge that the environments are different. Because we have that knowledge, there will be differences in *our* internal states, depending on which environment we are considering.

Any such differences of content must be opaque to the thinkers themselves. Otherwise, a thinker could be in two relevantly different environments while in identical internal states and, nevertheless, somehow detect the difference. Short of magic, differences in the environment cannot be differences for the thinker causally interacting with the environment unless there is also a corresponding difference in her internal states. Hence, the "wide content" that results from the causal interaction is precluded from being content for that thinker—it cannot be content that the agent is aware of.

Though I came to this argument independently, Jerry Fodor had already presented a similar pattern of reasoning, but had reached a different conclusion. Fodor argued that, for purposes of causal explanation in psychology, mental states must be individuated narrowly[19]:

... you *can't* affect the causal powers of a person's mental states without affecting his physiology. That's not a conceptual claim or a metaphysical claim. . . . The mechanisms by which environmental variables affect organic behaviors run via their effects on the organism's nervous system. Or so, at least, all the physiologists I know assure me. (1988, pp. 39–40)

Both Fodor and I are appealing to the general point that individuals cannot have different properties—be it causal powers of their thoughts or their asymmetrical awareness of certain contents of their own thoughts—without some differences' being registered in their bodily states. I have argued that if there are no differences in the states of the organisms' nervous systems, it is simply mystifying how the subjects of their thoughts, *as they conceive them*, could possibly be different. So, if, as the various third-person accounts would have it, the contents are different for two such systems, *they are not differences as conceived or detected by the system itself.* As such, the contents that such approaches identify have no bearing on what an individual is aware of, no bearing on whatever privileged access (to her minimal content) the individual has. Since the preceding argument is quite general and may even appear to beg important questions, let us apply the concepts I have introduced to a Twin-Earth context and draw some lessons other than the usual ones.

Hilary Putnam's Twin-Earth argument purports to show a crucial role the physical environment plays in determining the content of an individual's thought. I attempt here to deflate that argument, while at the same time clarifying minimal content. Tyler Burge's famous thought experiment claims a similar role for the social environment of the individual. In chapter 7, I argue that Burge's thought experiment does not establish anti-individualism and that it leaves internalism or individualism unscathed, but here I concentrate on Putnam-type views.

A common assumption in discussions of Twin-Earth cases is that what is in the head of my Twin and me is the same. A troubling question related to this common assumption is "Do my Twin and I know about the underlying stuff that prompts our respective water thoughts?" If the answer is affirmative, then it is not clear that what is in our respective heads could be the same. For when I have water thoughts, they are connected (computationally/inferentially or somehow) with H_2O thoughts (among others), while my Twin's water thoughts are similarly connected to XYZ thoughts. Given that our respective water thoughts are connected to different thoughts in our respective heads, whatever type of an account one gives of how thoughts are realized in a head, it is clear that what is in our heads must be different, contrary to the standard assumption required to get Twin-Earth cases off the ground. Thus, the thought experiment is incoherent if the answer to the question above is affirmative.

What if the answer to the above question is negative? In that case we still have grounds for saying what is in my Twin's head and what is in my head are identical. Note, however, that in this case, if one says what is usual in Twin-Earth-type cases (viz., that because of the differences in our respective environments, my Twin and I have different contents to our thoughts, and our word 'water' means different things), then *these are differences of which my Twin and I are entirely unaware.* Of course, one or both of us could become informed as to the underlying stuff that tends to prompt water thoughts or 'water' utterances. In such an event, we would immediately be back to the previous case, which undermines the thought experiment.

So the thought experiment is deflated: Either the conditions of the experiment are incoherent or the differences in content are not differences available to the thinkers. The experiment does not show that different extensions imply different contents; *not so long as the content of the thought in question is content available to the thinker having the thought, and the extension at issue is the actual extension.* Still, there is a clear sense in which what the thinker's thought is "about" is available to him whether or not he has got the actual extension right. The content that is available to both my Twin and me is clearly not wide content, it is not conceptual role content, nor is it narrow content in Fodor's sense. Fodor's narrow content is not semantically evaluable, it cannot be articulated, and the agent who has the narrow content isn't aware of it as such. In contrast, my minimal content has all these properties, and having these properties squares with the data in ways that not having them does not.

There is no strangeness at all in saying that a thinker does not know what is "really" prompting her thoughts or utterances. But it makes no sense to say that she does not know what it is that she *thinks* is prompting her thoughts or utterances; at least, it makes no sense in such simple cases as when she is considering a glass of clear, colorless, tasteless, odorless liquid. There is also no strangeness in describing what the thinker *thinks* her thought is about, in a subjective first-person sense, as being *part* of the content of *her* thought, all the while granting that in another sense (an objective third-person sense) her thought is about something entirely different. The very possibility of making such mistakes requires the possibility that what is signaled by the thought be something other than what prompts or causes it. The subjectively conceived content is often, in some way, peculiarly available to the thinker in a way that the objective cause or prompt never is. These are exactly the two contents introduced earlier: minimal content and objective content. To make sense of the situation just described requires both.

Let us explore these last considerations in more detail. Often when I have water thoughts my minimal content represents H_2O. Presumably I am correct in this, H_2O being the actual chemical composition of water on Earth. Thus, the objective content of these thoughts of mine also indicates H_2O.

Suppose that I am now, unbeknownst to myself, transported to Twin Earth to take the place of Twin Me. The minimal content of any of my water thoughts still represents H_2O, and I still believe that the actual extension, the objective content, is H_2O. I have no reason (at least not yet) to think otherwise. On the other hand, my companions on Twin Earth have good reason to think otherwise, and do so. The minimal content of their water thoughts represents, as it has, XYZ. Further, the objective contents of their thoughts indicate XYZ. Since they know that the water stuff on their planet is XYZ, their minimal content represents that which their objective content indicates, the actual object in their environment. Importantly, they take my expressions of my water thoughts to be about XYZ while I, in my ignorance, take my and their utterances of 'water' to be about H_2O. Nevertheless, since the actual stuff prompting my thoughts on this occasion is XYZ, it is appropriate from a third-person perspective of one in the know to hold that my thought is about XYZ, even though from my perspective it is about H_2O. (Recall the two seemingly contradictory features of intentional states noted at the beginning of chapter 1.)

Two different analyses of 'about' are at issue here. The notion of minimal content is meant to convey one of them—the subject of a thought as conceived by the thinker. It is only part of the content of a thought and it is, in part, subjectively determined. It depends on the thinker's first-person perspective. There is another analysis of 'about'. This analysis depends on an objective third-person perspective on what the subject of a thought is, and it is this sense that the objective content is meant to capture. Thus, in the case just considered, it is correct for the Twin Earthians to say of me that XYZ is the subject of my thought when, while on Twin Earth, I say "There is a glass of water on the desk," despite my thinking, also correctly, that H_2O is the subject of *my* thought.

Well, what is my thought about? Most discussions of Twin Earth assume that this question has a univocal answer, emphasize third-person aspects, and ignore or overlook the first-person perspective. Hence, the consideration that my Twin and I could have type identical internal states while the extensions of our thoughts are different has led many to the conclusion that thought or sense does not determine extension; additionally, it is of course true that there is no privileged access to the extension of a thought in this sense. I agree with this twofold conclusion when the term 'extension' is understood to denote the objectively determined objects. A thought is the vehicle for the objective content, which does indicate the objectively determinable extension. *But it is not only that.* It is also the vehicle for one's minimal content, and the latter need not signal the same object(s) as the objective content. According to my theory, it is a fundamental error to suppose that there is a univocal answer to the question as to what an individual's thought is about.

Third-person accounts presented in various externalist or anti-individualist positions maintain that the contents of the thoughts of two molecular twins are different because they are in different environments. I agree with this so long as the contents of which they speak are the objective contents of the twins' respective thoughts. It is clear that neither twin can have any privileged access to this kind of content. It is equally clear, however, that both twins do have privileged access to their respective minimal content, to the subject of their respective thoughts as they each conceive it.[20] Thus, by failing to provide a place for the first-person notion of minimal content, such accounts introduce a serious distortion in our understanding of intentionality. In particular, the way we sometimes do have privileged access to our contents is disregarded, while third-person factors, such as causal relations between a thinker and her environment, are overplayed. This leads to needlessly paradoxical results.

In the situation just described, from a third-person point of view my thought is about XYZ, but I do not know this, and, as yet, I have never even heard of XYZ; thus, though my thought in this case is quite simple, in a sense I do not know what I am thinking about. Still, it is absurd to say that the content of *my* thought is XYZ *and leave it at that.* From the first-person perspective I certainly do know what my thought is about: It is about H_2O, not XYZ. To know this, I need not be right as to what is actually prompting the thought or what I think about it,[21] and the object represented in my thought need not even exist. My point is not to deny the relevance of the third-person perspective, but to display the importance of including minimal content as another component in the analysis of intentional states—a component that derives from the first-person perspective.

Let us now revert to the original situation: I am on Earth, and Twin Me is on Twin Earth. My minimal content represents H_2O (which matches the actual stuff around me), while my twin's minimal content represents XYZ (which matches the stuff around him). Clearly, though, what is in our respective worlds does not determine what our minimal contents represent.

Whatever determines it, it cannot be that I am causally interacting with H_2O that determines my content. For when I go to Twin Earth my internal state can be identical while I am causally interacting with XYZ, and my minimal content still represents H_2O. Thus, when I think there is a glass of water before me, that particular belief is false, at least insofar as it entails that H_2O is before me at the moment. From my perspective, the minimal content is the same, there is no change in my belief from what it would have been had I been in qualitatively similar circumstances on Earth. Many externalists are wont to say that under these circumstances my belief has changed.[22] But it is hard to see what grounds there are for holding this other than trying to save an externalist theory. If such simple beliefs of mine can thus change without my knowledge, then the sense in which they are *my* beliefs seems to consist of hardly more than that I have mouthed certain words, the meanings of which I do not know. For the externalist, this extreme result exacerbates the difficulty of accounting for first-person authority.

One may object that, although it is true that when I am on Twin Earth I am causally interacting with XYZ and my minimal content still represents H_2O, this has little force against the position I am attacking.[23] It is my causal history that determines the content of my water thought, not merely my current causal relations. Let us see why this consideration does not undermine my objection.

Suppose that at some time in the future, as a result of some radical scientific revolution, the idea of molecules is abandoned, except perhaps for the convenience of ordinary discourse or even for ease in the discussion of some laboratory manipulations (just as we now use Newton's equations rather than the more complicated relativistic ones when velocities are small enough). In this imagined future time, one speaks not of molecules but of various states of strings. Even if we recognize this outcome as a possibility, *right now* my causal history is no different than it would be were things to develop so as to leave the molecules intact. Thus, even though right now I may well be causally interacting with states of strings rather than H_2O molecules, this causal interaction is not sufficient to force me to conceive my thoughts on such matters as being of states of strings. The main point is that, even though I have been causally interacting with the ultimate or "real" underlying structure of the stuff water (as even Thales was in ancient times), whatever it is, and have been doing so for some time, those causal relations cannot force my minimal content to represent it. After all, it is not as though our "ideas are copies of the underlying structure," to permute a bit on a classical empiricist theme.

An analogous point can be made by reference to an actual historical episode. When chemists thought phlogiston was released from a substance when it was burned, they did so in part because of their causal relations with their environment. Their causal interactions with their environment were such that they thought phlogiston existed. That they were wrong, that the underlying stuff with which they were causally interacting was not phlogiston, in no way undermines the claim that their minimal content was a representation of a stuff they called 'phlogiston'.[24] Further, that they came to that particular representation was in large part a result of their causal history—of their conducting various experiments, observing the results, and interpreting them in light of their evolving phlogiston theory.

Above I described a permutation on the classical empiricist's claim that ideas are copies of impressions. If the latter were true, the content of ideas would be determined by the environment in the strongest possible way. Though this idea has rightfully fallen into disrepute, I think it still, in a subterranean way, maintains a grip on the thoughts of a number of philosophers. Some sophisticated, though weaker, variant of it is, I believe, one root of various third-person analyses of content. The weaker versions, however, are not adequate to determine the content to the required specificity.[25] To see this, consider a dominant species of third-person-type analysis of content that goes under the name 'anti-individualism'. A leading advocate of this view characterizes it as follows:

Anti-individualism is the view that not all of an individual's mental states and events can be type-individuated independently of the nature of the entities in the individual's environment. There is, on this view, a deep individuative relation between the individual's being in mental states of certain kinds and the nature of the individual's physical or social environments. (Burge 1992, pp. 46–47)

Just what the alleged "deep individuative relation" alluded to by the anti-individualist is has yet to be characterized. The resulting vagueness of the claim may be instructively compared to the vagueness of the externalist's claim that external conditions "determine the content" of a thought, discussed in an earlier section. Nevertheless, if there are such individuative relations, they may well be required for the objective content. With regard to this kind of content, I have not disputed the anti-individualist's claim, and I will not do so here. To say this is to allow that such individuative relations may determine the subject of a thinker's thought in an objective sense, i.e., from the third-person perspective of someone who knows that these relations between the thinker and his environment obtain. The subject of a thinker's thought in this sense, however, may be unknown to the thinker, and it may well diverge from what the thinker conceives his thought to be about. In contrast, what the thinker *conceives* that *very same thought* to be about is completely determined (indeed constituted) by the thinker; but it is clearly *not* completely determined by the presumed objective individuative relations.

The points just made are exemplified in some of the situations discussed earlier in this section, those where minimal content and objective content diverged in what is signaled: When I am on Twin Earth the minimal content of my water thoughts is still H_2O even though what is in the environment, what the objective content of my thought indicates, is XYZ. The phlogiston chemist individuated phlogiston as the minimal content of some of his thoughts, even though there was no such thing as phlogiston in his environment. Finally, there was the case involving the hypothetical evolution of science that replaced talk of molecules with states of strings. In each of these cases, certain contents are individuated on the part of the thinker. The thinker is non-inferentially aware of them, but they are different from the objective content of the thought.

Concluding Thoughts

To the extent that appealing to causal relations between the thinker and her environment allows contents to vary with the environment without changes in the internal state of the thinker (as is the case in Twin-Earth-type examples), such contents are independent of how the thinker conceives things. In addition, the thinker cannot detect a difference in contents under these conditions, for there is no change in the thinker's internal state. Any such contents, therefore, are contents that *we* can ascribe to the thinker's states, but they cannot be contents for the thinker. We can ascribe contents to the thinker's states because we have knowledge of the environments' being different. Because we have that knowledge, there will be differences in *our* internal states depending on which environment we are considering.

In a very broad and trivial sense, it is undoubtedly true that there are many varied causal relations between an individual and his social and physical environments that contribute to the individual's being in a certain intentional state. Moreover, one's past causal interactions with the environment certainly are determining factors of one's current thoughts. I do not deny these platitudinous remarks on the causal relations between what exists in the environment and what our intentional states are. Furthermore, such casual interactions and the histories that result are certainly instrumental in our having any thoughts at all. But the fact remains that, though the external objects of such relations may well co-vary with the objective contents of our thoughts, they need not, and sometimes do not, co-vary with our minimal contents.

It is also undoubtedly true that such causal relations are essential to our learning the thoughts we learn. Learning, however, is not perfect. The imperfections are broadly of two kinds. First, our teachers often are themselves ignorant of or misinformed about aspects of that which they instruct. Second, even when our teachers have it right, we may err in the uptake. These imperfections contribute to the necessity of our analyzing the expression 'the subject of a thought' into two kinds of content: minimal and objective. Exclusive attention to features accessible from the third-person perspective, such as the objects in the environment upon which there is inter-subjective agreement and the causal relations between these objects and some agent, has resulted in gross neglect of minimal content's existence and of its independent role in the analysis of intentional states. In consequence, there has been a corresponding distortion in accounts of intentionality and consciousness.

Minimal content is a first-person, individualist, or internalist concept. It provides a determinate and substantive sense of narrow content unlike any other in the literature. I have argued that minimal content cannot be accommodated by exclusively third-person methodologies. It is not itself some sort of object, and nothing is presupposed as to whether what it represents actually exists[26]; therefore, it is not heavily burdened with problematic metaphysical baggage. It is a large step away from the much more complex and perplexing notion of understanding. It does not turn on any troublesome concepts, such as meaning, proposition, or the nature of the mental.[27] It is a crucial and essential step away from the objective content of a thought. Still, it is a notion of content that saves and makes more precise what our privileged access to content consists in, and in conjunction with objective content it provides a resource to resolve many problems in the philosophy of mind—for example, those raised by Twin Earth. Therefore, not only does my type of analysis save the appearances and enhance our understanding of the structure of intentionality; it also provides the means to preserve what is true in both first-person and third-person accounts.

That a thinker is at some times and in some way in a privileged position regarding what his thought is "about" is a kind of "datum." I have tried to give an account of this datum via the fundamental concept of minimal content. Others may wish to offer a different account of this datum, one not involving minimal content. I have argued, however, that advocates of a strictly third-person methodology lack the resources to do this. Still others may wish to deny the datum itself. But any analysis of intentionality must either account for this datum in some way or show it to be a mere illusion. Failing to do either would leave them justly open (in a way that Berkeley was not) to a simple sort of refutation, one that employs a Johnsonian methodology.[28]

3 Consciousness and Subjectivity

No adequate theory of the mind can be silent on consciousness and subjectivity. However, the meanings of the terms 'consciousness' and 'subjectivity' and their range of application are neither clear nor univocal, and various authors use them rather differently. Such disparities are inevitable. Ultimately, it is a theory of mind that determines the meanings and applications of these terms, and there are a number of theories of mind in circulation.

The pivotal concept in my theory of mind is that of *minimal content*. It is a subjective first-person concept that is invisible from a strictly third-person perspective. An agent can have privileged awareness of her minimal content, and when she does so she is conscious of it. I have argued that an analysis of intentional states requires this concept; but not it alone—the third-person concept of objective content is also required for an analysis of intentional states. My discussion to this point is, among other things, an attempt to show that both contents are required, to explain minimal content and what being aware of it consists in, and that exclusive third-person methodologies lack the resources to provide for minimal content.

In this chapter, I explain how the concepts of subjectivity and consciousness function in my theory. In the process, I illustrate and oppose an almost universal tendency, even among widely divergent theorists of mind, to conflate consciousness or subjectivity, on the one hand, with phenomenal experience, on the other. Of course it is true that phenomenal experience is subjective and (if not always, often) conscious. My point is that subjectivity and consciousness do not occur only in phenomenal experience; they are as strongly implicated in intentionality. Importantly, when consciousness is implicated in intentionality, it is not in a phenomenal guise. As I tried to show in chapter 1, separating consciousness from intentionality is a serious mistake. Call this Mistake 1. Attempting to show that consciousness is related to intentionality by arguing that there is phenomenal aspect to intentionality is a different but related mistake, one that is also serious. Call this Mistake 2. Each mistake introduces radical (though different) distortions in the direction of studies in the philosophy of mind.

Diagnosis of Mistakes 1 and 2

Since about the middle of the twentieth century, issues concerning the mind have been divided into two broad categories: phenomenal experience (qualia) and intentionality.[1] Under the influence of behaviorism, functionalism, and early identity theories of the twentieth century, accounts of these two aspects have been advanced that are independent of each other; certainly the two have received separate treatments by these theories. Most philosophers who considered consciousness at all restricted it to phenomenal or qualitative experience.[2]

In the 1950s and the early 1960s, it was mistakenly believed by many that behaviorism could give an adequate account of intentional states. This was the avowed position of U. T. Place (1956). The problem of consciousness that remained was that of showing how sensations (phenomenal states) are brain states. The failures of behavioristic accounts of intentionality soon became evident; however, confidence on the part of many regarding the possibility of a strictly objective analysis of intentionality apart from consciousness was quickly renewed by various functionalist accounts of intentionality. To this day, more than a few philosophers persist in this belief.[3] Still, there never was much optimism regarding the success of either a behaviorist or a functionalist account of qualia or of phenomenal experience—this "residue of consciousness," as Place referred to it. For the early identity theorists, if there were recalcitrant problems of consciousness they concerned its phenomenal or qualitative manifestations.[4]

Thomas Nagel contributed to the tendency to think of consciousness in terms of the phenomenal. In his classic 1980 paper he was clearly concerned with phenomenal sensory experiences, be they of humans, bats, or Martians. He introduced the locution "what it is like" (hereafter abbreviated WIL) to characterize these subjective conscious experiences. Thus, with the now ubiquitous WIL, Nagel abetted the tight link between the phenomenal and consciousness that had already been forged. Frank

Jackson's classic 1986 paper "What Mary Didn't Know" continued this trend.

The earlier division between intentionality and phenomenal experience may well have influenced Nagel's and Jackson's focus on phenomenal aspects of conscious states in their much-discussed papers, but there can be little doubt that their papers are largely responsible for the subsequent pre-occupation with these states when the topic is consciousness. Burge makes the connection between the phenomenal and consciousness explicit. He claims that the connection is one of implication: " . . . access consciousness—indeed, *any sort of consciousness*—in an individual presupposes the existence of *phenomenal* consciousness in that individual" (1997, p. 426, emphasis added).

So the concepts of consciousness, phenomenal, and "what it is like" have formed a rather tight circle in contemporary philosophy of mind. Consciousness was separated from intentionality and was associated with the phenomenal via the WIL operator. Given this history, once philosophers began to suspect that consciousness was implicated in intentionality, it was natural for them to try and fix on some phenomenal (conscious) aspect of intentionality to secure their suspicion. Thus, I suggest, Mistake 1 gave rise to Mistake 2. There was a swing from phenomenal consciousness to intentionality with the hope of locating some role for consciousness in intentionality.

It is of some further interest to observe that given the divide between intentionality and phenomenality, others have attempted to swing in the opposite direction. The latter is exemplified by *representationism* or *intentionalism* regarding qualia.[5] These philosophers try to apply an eviscerated sense of intentionality, one bereft of consciousness (at least in my sense of that term), to an analysis of phenomenality. If an analysis of intentionality could be given without consciousness, and if an analysis of phenomenality could be given in terms of intentionality, then the role for that "residue of consciousness" that Place worried about could be resolved if not eliminated. One might call this Mistake 3: Phenomenality is analyzable in terms of intentionality, without consciousness implicated. I will not examine Mistake 3 here, since, insofar as it treats intentionality as independent of consciousness, it is, if I am right, a non-starter.[6]

My arguments in chapters 1 and 2 support my contention that Mistake 1 is, indeed, a mistake. Before giving a general argument against Mistake 2,

I illustrate and criticize (in the next two sections) some attempts that tend to merge consciousness issues with those of phenomenality.

Problems of the Conscious Aspects of Intentional States Are Not Dependent on Problems of Phenomenal States

There is a somewhat weaker position than one that denies that consciousness is implicated in intentionality. It holds that whatever problems intentional states and special access to some mental states have regarding consciousness and subjectivity are due to these being somehow connected to phenomenal states. Martin Davies and Glyn Humphreys, in the fine introduction to their 1993 collection of essays, are guilty of this move, and they exemplify the tendency to skew consciousness toward the phenomenal. They, however, see it neither as a skewing nor as a problem. They state:

It is the notion (a) of phenomenal consciousness that is the focus of attention for those philosophers who stress the theoretical elusiveness of consciousness. To the extent that the other two notions carry an air of mystery about them, it is largely inherited from phenomenal consciousness. (1993, p. 14)

The other two notions referred to in this passage are

(b)   the notion of a state with conceptualized semantic content (that is, the notion of a state with the kind of intentionality characteristic of propositional attitudes like belief) (13)

and

(c)   the notion of a state which is such that, provided only that the subject possesses the concept of that state, she is in a position to judge that she is in that state. (13–14)

Borrowing from Ned Block (1997), Davies and Humphreys call (c) 'access consciousness' and characterize it as "the idea, roughly, of availability of content for verbal report—[an idea that] applies most directly to thoughts"; whereas 'phenomenal consciousness' is "the 'something it is like' notion to which Nagel calls attention—[and] applies most directly to sensations and other experiences" (13–14).

In marked contrast to this, on my theory, awareness of minimal content is a kind of "access consciousness" to the subject of the intentional content of a propositional attitude (construed as minimal content, not the objective content) and, thus, involves at least something like both (b) and (c): On my theory, it is not necessarily connected to (a), phenomenal consciousness.

My treatment of minimal content is in opposition to the claim that the deep problems associated with (b) and (c) ("the air of mystery about them") is inherited from (a). Thus, I deny Davies' and Humphreys' claim that the elusiveness "trickles down from phenomenal consciousness to access consciousness, via the notion of intentionality" (1993, p. 14). Intentionality and "access consciousness" have their own deep problems *quite apart from phenomenal consciousness*. Furthermore, while phenomenal consciousness also has its own very deep problems, many of them are a result of intentionality and access consciousness, not the other way around.

If I am right about consciousness and intentionality, then the problems of intentionality do not "trickle down from" those of phenomenal consciousness, and the alternatives of phenomenal or access consciousness that Block offers are not exhaustive.[7] Indeed, it turns out that the analysis of phenomenality requires a structurally similar analysis to that of intentionality (see chapter 6); an analysis of either requires both minimal content and objective content. The common conscious element of intentionality and phenomenality is minimal content consciousness—not phenomenality.

Another Illustration of the Collapse of Consciousness to Phenomenal Consciousness

I now turn to an example of how the misconception of consciousness in terms of phenomenal consciousness leads to distortions and mistakes in the study of mind. My criticism of Robert Van Gulick in chapter 2 focused on the inadequacies of his notion of semantic transparency to provide either an account of understanding or our first-person awareness of what our thoughts are about, but the idea of phenomenal consciousness also corrupts his view. Consider Van Gulick's reformulation of Searle's Chinese Room Argument:

1.   The difference between those symbol manipulating systems that have genuine intentionality and those that have only "as if" intentionality is that the former actually understand the symbols on which they operate, i.e., the symbols in the former case are semantically transparent to the system.

2.   The sorts of representations associated with conscious phenomenal experience involve a high degree of semantic transparency;

3.   Therefore, a capacity for conscious phenomenal experience is a necessary condition for having states with genuine intentionality. (1989, p. 224)

Van Gulick states that he is "inclined to agree with both of the argument's premises; however the conclusion obviously does not follow" (ibid.). Van Gulick thinks that for the conclusion to follow "one would need a premise asserting that conscious *phenomenal* experience is a necessary condition for semantic transparency" (ibid., emphasis added).

Van Gulick's reformulation of Searle's argument is unsatisfactory. First, to my knowledge, Searle no where in his discussion or presentation of the Chinese Room speaks of "conscious *phenomenal* experience," though he does speak of "conscious experiences" and "understanding." In fact, Searle is rather unique in recent philosophy in that he discusses consciousness apart from phenomenal experience (though he does not neglect the latter). What the Chinese Room lacks, according to Searle, is an understanding of the content of the syntactic strings manipulated. Neither Searle's argument nor his discussion turns on that content's being phenomenal. Nagel's famous discussion certainly focuses on phenomenal features; Searle's does not. So Van Gulick's reformulation is importantly inaccurate. Secondly, I already argued (chapter 2) that Van Gulick's casting of genuine intentionality in terms of his concept of semantic transparency is a further mistake. Not only does Searle not rely on it; semantic transparency is neither necessary nor sufficient for genuine intentionality (as I have also argued), phenomenal states aside.

The distortion that is of particular interest here occurs when Van Gulick suggests the following:

. . . if semantic transparency is required for genuine mentality (as premise 1 asserts) and the *only* semantically transparent representations with which we are familiar are those met in phenomenal experience, then it is easy to see why *phenomenal* experience might *seem* to be a necessary condition for genuine mentality. But unless we can show that phenomenal experience is in fact the only way to achieve a high degree of semantic transparency (and I do not see a way to do so) such intuitions must be regarded as unfounded. (1989, p. 225, emphases on 'phenomenal' and 'only' added)

There is much that is wrong with this passage.[8] But the important error for present purposes is the suggestion, despite its conditional nature, that conscious experience *in us* invariably involves phenomenal experiences. (Such a misconception on Van Gulick's part would explain why he thinks his reformulation of Searle's argument in terms of phenomenal consciousness is acceptable, though in fact it is not.) Much of Van Gulick's discussion supports the view that he does hold this. For example, he introduces two "why" questions: "*Why* do phenomenal representations involve a high degree of semantic transparency? And *why* do we humans use representations with phenomenal qualities to construct our self-model?" (ibid.) Van Gulick's answers to these questions are interesting, but for present purposes here it is enough to point out that he closes that discussion as follows: "I hope these three partial answers shed a little light on *why our human model of self requires conscious phenomenal experience. . . .*" (1989, p. 228, emphasis added) This, coupled with the fact that, for him, having a self model is required for the task of knowing what we are thinking about, leaves little doubt that he believes (falsely, according to me) that conscious experience in us does require, or at least invariably involves as a contingent matter, phenomenal experience.

Of course, Van Gulick is also concerned to leave open the possibility that phenomenal experience is only contingently tied to consciousness—it may not be necessary for understanding or semantic transparency. (He makes much of this early on in his essay.) I support him on this. But not only is it possible—*it is actual.* My discussion of theorists A–D in chapter 1 clearly indicated that their understanding could involve a great deal of what Van Gulick calls "semantic transparency" without having any phenomenal experiences.[9] So it is not even contingently true that all our conscious experience involves phenomenal experience. Those cases, however, also show that semantic transparency is not sufficient for understanding what one is thinking about. Thus, Van Gulick's question whether "phenomenal experience is in fact the only way to achieve a high degree of semantic transparency" is a double red herring. Neither phenomenal experience (just argued) nor semantic transparency (chapter 2) is at the heart of the issue. Consciousness must be seen to have non-phenomenal manifestations. The non-phenomenal aspects of consciousness are crucial to a study of intentionality.

Analysis of Mistake 2: The Fiction of Phenomenal Intentionality

Insofar as the history of the subject over the last few decades (sketched above) confined the study of consciousness to phenomenal states, once philosophers began to suspect that consciousness is also involved in intentionality, it was natural to look for some *phenomenal* aspect of intentional states, as a number of philosophers have, calling it "phenomenal intentionality."[10] (Thus, we see how Mistake 1 has contributed to Mistake 2.) To my mind this is a deep error.

Those who argue for phenomenal intentionality typically attempt to support their thesis by appealing to the claim that *there is something that it is like* to be in an intentional state. The *something that it is like* experience, of course, goes back to Thomas Nagel's classic paper, where he offered it as a necessary and sufficient condition for conscious mental states:

> . . . an organism has conscious mental states if and only if there is something that it is like to be that organism—something it is like for the organism. (quoted on p. 160 of Block 1980)

Nagel's idea here is typically discussed in connection with phenomenal qualities, and Nagel himself focused on the qualitative or phenomenal aspects of conscious states. Insofar as his account of consciousness is restricted to phenomenal consciousness, it is incomplete.[11] Later I will show how Nagel's central idea about consciousness can and should be interpreted to remove this incompleteness. First, I argue that efforts deploying the "what it is like" phenomenon (in the restricted sense defined below) to secure the conscious aspects of intentionality are deeply flawed.

Many would agree that states produced via sense organs, phenomenal states, do have a WIL aspect to the individual having them. Many who argue for phenomenal intentionality press this WIL aspect into service in their attempts to show that consciousness is, if not necessarily, then, at the least, importantly involved in intentional states. They hold that there is a WIL experience that applies to the having of an intentional state. These arguments, invoking as they do the "what it's like" for the agent in a given intentional state, thereby implicate a first-person methodology. It is right to import a first-person methodology into the usual third-person ones in the study of intentionality. The trouble is not with the augmented methodology. The trouble is in conceiving of that first-person methodology in terms of phenomenality. This in turn obfuscates the connection between consciousness and intentionality and, worse, undermines the arguments for the connection.

Advocates of phenomenal intentionality extend the use of 'phenomenal' in a vague way, and the WIL phenomenon is mistakenly thought to secure the extended use of 'phenomenal'. That vagueness, when coupled with a crucial asymmetry between the original and extended range of application of 'phenomenal' (spelled out below), undermines the arguments for "phenomenal intentionality."

Let us grant that at least in some broad sense there is something that it is like to think, say, that it is raining, or to wish that it would stop raining. There are at least two important questions regarding this WIL for intentional states: "Is it essential to the intentional states?" and "Can it do the same work for intentional states as it does for conscious *sensory* experiences?" I have already answered the first question in the negative; here I address the second question.

We may distinguish a restricted and an unrestricted use of the locution 'what it is like':

1.   *Restricted*—the original, Nagelian sense—what it is like to have an experience produced by the sense organs (ours and those of bats, Martians, etc., assuming they are conscious). That is, some transduction of external stimuli via some organ producing a WIL experience for the conscious perceiver: what it is like to have a sensory experience.

2.   *Unrestricted*—extended sense—what it is like to have an experience as above but *also* as in what it is like to have some particular propositional *attitude* (belief , desire, etc.) and/or what it is like to entertain a *particular content* p of an attitude.[12]

What the advocates of phenomenal intentionality require to support their claim of phenomenal intentionality is the unrestricted sense of WIL, or at least one of the alternatives of 2; the restricted sensory sense does not suffice for their purposes. Is this manner of extension of the restricted Nagelian sense of WIL warranted?

First, notice a general point. The deployment of the WIL phenomenon—be it in connection with the phenomenal or the intentional—imports a first-person methodology in an essential way. I have no objection to this. Still, the introduction of a first-person methodology introduces certain difficulties regarding the inter-subjective resolution of disagreements regarding first-person reports of individuals that third-person methodologies avoid. Such disagreements are not inevitable whenever a first-person methodology is deployed. Importantly, they do not (typically) arise when there is an appeal to what it is like regarding sensory experiences, the restricted sense. Matters are quite otherwise when advocates of phenomenal intentionality apply this methodology to secure their position. This I will now show.

When I am stimulated by various diverse items, such as certain apples, ripe tomatoes, stop signs, and fire trucks, my different experiences have a *type-identifiable uniform feature* that I call 'experiencing red': what it is like to experience red is the having of one of those or similar (in this respect) experiences. Importantly, there is a certain aspect *uniformly* picked out in these diverse sensory experiences by appeal to the WIL to have them that warrants the claim that there is something that it like to experience red. Similar remarks apply to the other sensory modalities.

The uniformity described is crucial to the claim that there is something that it is like to experience red, smooth, sweet, or any other sensory experience. In the sensory modalities, there is not only the *intra*-personal but also an *inter*-subjective uniformity regarding what it is like. When others type-identify their sensory experiences, they do so in a way that maps "smoothly" to the way I do it; our sensory quality spaces are isomorphic. Now one might think that the possibility of inverted spectra counts against my claim of *inter*-subjective uniformity. On the contrary, this possibility supports my contention. For even if others had an inverted spectrum relative to mine, there would still be *uniformity within their type-identified WIL experiences*, even if the sensory appearances they experienced were systematically different from my own. The very coherence of the inverted spectrum problem presupposes that others would type-identify the same class of stimuli as I do. Those experiences type-identified by WIL for the inverted individual would present a uniform appearance to her, even if the appearances presented to her were to differ qualitatively from what I experience when prompted by a stimulus from the same class. Failing such uniformity, there would be verifiable differences between us and inverted spectrum problems would be undermined from the onset. So the uniformity of a type-identifiable sensory aspect via the WIL phenomenon holds equally in the subjective and inter-subjective cases.

The occurrence of a uniform feature in each of the classes of experiences individuated by an appeal to WIL is necessary if the WIL phenomenon is to succeed in type-identifying some feature, say red. *The question we must confront here is whether the WIL phenomenon similarly type-identifies a uniform feature when it is applied to occurrent intentional states, as it does when applied to sensory experiences.* Note that in asking the question in this way I am *not* challenging whether it is true to say that there is something that it is like to instantiate some particular occurrent intentional state. I am granting that for the sake of argument. Rather, the issue is whether such supposed WIL experiences pick out *uniformly identifiable features* on different occasions. If

I am right that this is necessary to secure phenomenal intentionality via the WIL phenomenon, the failure to type-identify a uniform feature in the case of intentional states would prove the irrelevance of appeals to WIL *in this way* to any analysis of intentional states, even while granting that there is in *some* sense something that it is like to be in some particular occurrent intentional state. Therefore, any support for a necessary role of consciousness in intentional states would have to rely upon something *other than this sort* of appeal to WIL to have them.[13]

I have argued that showing that occurrent intentional states involve consciousness by an appeal to WIL to have them can *only* have value in establishing the existence of phenomenal intentionality, if by so doing such WIL experiences pick out a uniformly type-identifiable feature on different occasions. Establishing the latter is potentially tricky, however, as it necessarily involves reliance upon the first-person reports of various individuals, and these may conflict. It is important to notice, again, that the use of the first-person perspective does not always lead to such problems. We have seen that such reliance does not pose an obstacle when sensory experiences are at issue, since there is little or no disagreement among individuals in these cases. The reason for the agreement regarding sensory experiences is that in such cases an appeal to WIL does type-identify a uniform phenomenal aspect across a wide range of experiences; moreover, we saw that the very formulation of inverted spectrum problems presuppose that this is so. Things are quite otherwise when the WIL phenomenon is turned toward occurrent intentional states; here there is disagreement both as to its occurrence and regarding the relevance of it to our understanding or analysis of intentional states. As before and for the sake of argument, I am willing to grant that there is a WIL experience in the having of occurrent intentional states. The crucial issue here is whether such WIL experiences type-identify some uniform aspect when applied to occurrent intentional states.

Given the essentially first-person nature of appeals based upon WIL, if there are disagreements on this, how are they to be resolved and what do such disagreements show? I do not see how such disputes can be resolved. In such matters, there appears to be no way of trumping another's (sincere) report of WIL for her. One might be able to persuade others to *think* about their experiences differently, or even *train* them to experience them differently, be they phenomenal or intentional, but that would *alter* their WIL experiences and would not change the initial WIL phenomenon. If there is anything to the claim of phenomenal intentionality, it must apply to the initial experiences as well as the supposed altered ones. Notice that such disagreements do not exist when it is sensory experience at issue and, in this case, no persuasion or special training is required to get others to see the point. It is clear methodologically that when the first-person perspective is in play, one can expect reliable results only when there is agreement among individuals' first-person reports, agreement that is lacking in the type of case before us, which I now demonstrate.

When I turn my attention to my occurrent intentional states, I fail to find a uniform feature type-identified by "what they are like" to me. That is a sincere report from my first-person perspective. What it is like to entertain the *beliefs that* P, Q, R, . . . on different occasions, though all instances of believings do not seem to me to share some uniformly identifiable phenomenal or qualitative feature, at least not when I attend to my own "inner life." To the extent that there is some vague phenomenal WIL for me on these different occasions, there is no uniformity; furthermore, the WIL that I do find seems largely influenced by a plethora of varying background conditions, most of which are irrelevant to the specific believing attitude. I find a similar lack of uniformity when I consider classes of other occurrent attitudinal states. Things are no better (for me) when I attend to the contents themselves. What it is like to have some occurrent belief *P* seems to share no easily characterized WIL phenomenal feature that is common to the different occasions that I entertain *P* and that is somehow specific to that particular content. Moreover, whatever WIL aspects I do find seem affected by the specific background conditions in place on those different occasions, not the content *P*,[14] as we saw is the case for the attitudes themselves. The situation is no different (from my first-person perspective) when I consider the intentional state itself (attitude plus content).

Now this is not to deny that such states *can be* type-identified as *believings*, *desirings*, or some other attitude. We do that. Nor is it to deny that such states can be type-identified via their *contents*, *P*, *Q*, or whatever. We do that, too. Such type identities *can be* and *are* found in these different states. Just how we do these things is at issue, however. The proponent of phenomenal intentionality is making a specific claim regarding how this is secured. To support that thesis, she cannot simply rely upon the fact *that* we do type-identify them, not without begging the question. For the fact that we do this does not by itself support the claim that there is a uniform *phenomenal*

WIL feature of these states, let alone that it is in virtue of such features that
we succeed. What is at issue is whether the attitudes or contents *themselves*
have a special type-identifiable uniform phenomenal WIL aspect, as the
sensory experiences clearly do, not whether they can be type-identified in
some way or other.

One may object to my claim that there is no type-identifiable uniform
feature to intentional states that is secured by the WIL experience as follows: Fearing *P* is an intentional state. Certainly, there is a WIL experience
of fear, which type-identifies a uniform phenomenal aspect. The same may
be said for the other emotions. So there is, after all, phenomenal intentionality, at least for these kinds of intentional states.[15] I think not, though I
accept everything but the last sentence. I agree that there is something that
it is like when one is happy, afraid, angry, sad, etc. There may well be a type-
identifiable WIL experience of happiness along a continuum range,
"shades" of happiness, much like there is, say, a type-identifiable WIL to
sense red across a continuum of shades of red. It seems that what I just said
for happiness applies as well to all other types of emotions mentioned.
Emotions have, it seems to me, phenomenal aspects and a very rich phenomenology; indeed, that is what makes them such compelling forces in
our private lives.

My having said that, however, does not commit me to phenomenal
intentionality. Emotion is one thing; intentionality is another. These are
distinct even when the attitude of an intentional state is an emotion. The
central feature of intentionality is its directedness to something other than
itself. *The analysis of intentionality must give an account of this directedness.* If
one can correctly speak of the phenomenology (or phenomenal aspects) *of
intentionality*, the phenomenology or the phenomenal aspect must be *of the
directedness itself*; otherwise, one is talking of a mere contingent accou-
trement of an intentional state, not of something that is essential to it.

Long ago, John Searle pointed out that the term 'mental state' is broader
in its extension than 'intentional state' precisely because one could be in an
undirected generalized mental state of, say, being anxious, where the anxiety is not directed at any particular object or state of affairs. Such an emotion, a generalized state of anxiety, would indeed have a phenomenology
and the WIL to be in that state, a non-intentional one, may be similar to
the WIL experience when one is anxious *that R*, an intentional state.
Whatever phenomenology there is to the former, no doubt, it is of the same

type that is realized when one finds some phenomenology of the latter intentional state. However, since that phenomenology can be present *without* an intentional state, it clearly is not sufficient for intentionality. Nor is it necessary, since one could recognize that one is anxious that R without manifesting any of the WIL aspects of anxiety on that particular occasion.

More generally, since there are intentional states without any relevant or type-identifiable phenomenal aspect or phenomenology, as argued above, whatever phenomenal aspects my be associated with them on this or that occasion, they are not necessary for intentional states. Therefore, talk of "phenomenal intentionality" or the "phenomenology of intentionality" adds nothing to an analysis of intentionality itself, to an analysis of the directedness of such states.

The prospect of showing that there is some phenomenal aspect or phenomenology that is relevant to the analysis of intentional states whose psychological attitude is an emotion—such states as fearing that P, happy that Q, angry that R, sad that S—would appear to be quite slim. Matters are even worse when we move to the paradigm intentional state: believing that P, or even, understanding that P. For while the indicated emotional states themselves *do* have a type-identifiable WIL aspect, I just argued that this is neither necessary nor sufficient for an analysis of their correlative intentional states, the phenomenology or phenomenal aspect of the former are at best just accoutrements to the latter. Matters are worse in this regard for any alleged phenomenology of intentional states such as believing or understanding, occurrent or otherwise, since these do not even have any type-identifiable WIL aspect, as the emotions do, or so I have argued.

Earlier I raised the questions as to how disagreements concerning WIL of intentional states could be resolved and what they show. One might respond to the occurrence of such disagreements regarding subjective experiences by claiming that they simply reflect individual differences among different subjects and are not important regarding the claim that there is a WIL to intentional states. Aside from the fact that such a response would give up the general point regarding intentional states, it is unacceptable unless it were coupled with a refutation of my earlier argument that the unrestricted sense of WIL must type-identify a *uniform* feature, as the restricted sense does. To my knowledge, no advocate of "phenomenal intentionality" has even attempted to do this, let alone recognize the need to do so. In any case, the kinds of proposals scouted earlier in response to disagreements, if successful, would merely serve to deflect rather than resolve the disagreements.

This brings us to my other more important question: What do such disagreements show? It certainly reveals a dramatic contrast with the remarkable ease with which there is intra-subjective ability to type-identify a uniform WIL aspect *when the WIL is used in the restricted sensory sense*. This contrast between the sensory and the intentional is equally stark at the inter-subjective level. Therefore, there is a critical asymmetry regarding WIL reports pertaining to sensory experiences, phenomenal experiences in the restricted sense, and those pertaining to occurrent intentional states, "phenomenal experiences" in the extended sense.

Advocates of phenomenal intentionality have appealed to the not implausible fact that there are occasions when "how it seems" to one to be in this as opposed to that intentional state is different. They then expropriate the already imprecise expression 'what it is like' to make their point. This elastic expansion of 'what it is like' to include the intentional must be resisted. Whatever vagueness the locution has when applied within the sensory domain is overridden by its ability to type-identify a uniform feature within that domain of experiences; moreover this is done in such a way that there is no inter-subjective disagreement regarding such uniformity. It is this that makes the WIL of sensory experience informative and significant.

Talk of the phenomenal is closely associated with talk of WIL: phenomenal qualities are those for which there is something that it is like to have them. Both concepts are significant and important in their applications to the sensory domain, for the reasons given. It is the legitimacy of the *particular manner* of extension of these concepts to the intentional that is at issue. The asymmetry between sensory experiences and intentionality in this regard was argued for above; this asymmetry implies that what makes these concepts informative and significant in the sensory domain is not operative—in the same way—when they are applied to intentionality. Advocates of applying these concepts to intentionality must provide an analysis of them that is specific to this domain. Simply trading on the success of their deployment in the sensory domain is not sufficient to secure their relevance regarding intentionality. Uncritically extending the application of the locution 'what it is like' or 'phenomenal' to intentional states in the ways discussed, rather than expanding our understanding of the intentional, obfuscates both the concepts *phenomenal* and *what it is like*. In consequence, it also makes claims regarding the connection of consciousness and intentionality hopelessly vague.

A Different and Legitimate Application of WIL to Intentionality

While I reject phenomenal intentionality,[16] I clearly do not reject the essential role consciousness plays in intentionality. Nor do I deny that there is some relevant sense of "what it is like" that plays a role in securing the connection between consciousness and intentionality. In chapter 1, I deployed the first-person perspective to uncover a *non*-phenomenal narrow content, minimal content. In essence, this was a tacit appeal to WIL of a certain and different kind than is found in sensory experience. This deployment shared with the WIL (restricted sense) of phenomenal states a certain advantageous feature: the relatively straightforward and unproblematic type-identification of something. One typically has no problem intra-subjectively identifying one's minimal content from one occasion to another. Moreover, to the extent that another can identify someone else's minimal content, she can have good objective reasons for thinking it is either the same or different on different occasions. Thus, my earlier implicit deployment of the WIL operator to intentionality is different from and not subject to the criticisms that I have raised of its use by advocates of "phenomenal intentionality."

We can now further see that the idea of minimal content is itself operative in phenomenality. In the case of intentionality, minimal content is the *subject* of the thinker's thought *as the thinker conceives it*. When we examine phenomenality, it is the *phenomenal aspect* of the perception *as perceived* by the perceiver. Call this *phenomenal minimal content*. Phenomenal minimal content and minimal content share an important feature: neither can be recognized except from the first-person perspective. Moreover, in chapter 6, we will see that phenomenal minimal content, like minimal content, has a corresponding objective content, but that the relation between these two kinds of content is importantly different in the case of phenomenality than it is in intentionality.

With these two now different but legitimate applications of WIL in hand, I suggest an unorthodox reading of Nagel's requirement for a conscious state (quoted above). I bend his requirement to emphasize that consciousness is involved in both intentional and phenomenal states, while recognizing that the WIL of each is relevantly different, my suggestion is that we understand the phrase "something that it is like *to be* that organism" as pertaining to phenomenal consciousness, and that we understand the alternative clause (also present in Nagel's original formulation) "something it is like *for* the organism" as applying to minimal content consciousness or, more generally, to non-phenomenal consciousness.[17]

I agree with Nagel that there is an especially tight relation between subjectivity and an agent's having a "point of view," but this tight relation extends to the agent's non-phenomenal and asymmetrical awareness of minimal content that she sometimes has from her privileged first-person perspective.[18] Reading Nagel's requirement in the way suggested is not essential to my point that non-phenomenal consciousness poses some of the same problems as phenomenal consciousness does for a strictly third-person methodology, but it is a way of removing the indicated incompleteness in his criterion for consciousness, while respecting his ground-breaking paper. (I do not know whether Nagel would endorse this reading.)

Phenomenology

Part of the above may be viewed as terminological recommendations, but I hope to have convinced you that it is not merely terminological, since the particular wider applications of the locutions 'phenomenal' and 'what it is like' that I have criticized have serious negative consequences. That said, I would also like to briefly comment on some recent uses of the words 'phenomenology' and 'phenomenological', particularly by proponents of phenomenal intentionality and make an alternative suggestion regarding their use. (Again, though this is in part terminological, I think it is much more that that.)

There appears to be a growing tendency to use the words 'phenomenological' and 'phenomenal' interchangeably. Typically, these terms are not explicitly defined, though one is often explained by an appeal to the other, and both are sometimes explicated by an appeal to "what it is like" to be in this or that mental state.[19] These tendencies must be resisted. To my mind, the uncritical deployment of these locutions not only engenders confusion regarding them; it also seriously it impedes progress in our understanding of the relationship between consciousness and intentionality. I have already tried to show that while it is understandable that philosophers would try to ground the consciousness of intentionality in certain phenomenal aspects—given various historical factors—doing so is seriously flawed.[20]

Once freed of the encumbrance of phenomenality, consciousness is better understood and the role it and the first-person perspective plays in intentionality becomes manifest.

What bearing do these matters have on discussions of the phenomenology of intentional states? I think it provides an understanding of 'phenomenological' that is distinct from that of 'phenomenal' and, yet, does justice to what I take is the legitimate point that drives those who argue for phenomenal intentionality, namely, that there is a subjective, first-person aspect implicated in intentionality. It is just not phenomenal in character. What I suggest, therefore, is that a method is *phenomenological* only if it requires an appeal to a first-person methodology.

The advocates of phenomenal intentionality and I agree that that there is an unavoidable first-person aspect to intentionality, so that intentionality implies consciousness. The advocates of phenomenal intentionality are also rightly taken by the apparent fact that "there is something that it is like" to be in some particular intentional state. Their problem, according to me, was to think of the WIL on the model of the restricted sense of WIL and to try to extend this model to intentional states without further ado. But because of the asymmetry between intentional and sensory states regarding the deliverance of a uniform phenomenal feature via the WIL operator, demonstrated above, such an extension fails. Once this is corrected and the first-person aspect of intentional states is recognized, which involves a new and different kind of WIL, it follows that—while there is no "phenomenal intentionality"—there is a phenomenology of intentionality.

Common Treatment of Problems of Intentionality and Phenomenality

I certainly am not denying that phenomenal states are both subjective and (at least frequently) conscious. But if I am right in what I have argued to this point, the coupling of conscious and subjective states exclusively with phenomenal states is misleading as to the nature of subjectivity and consciousness, as well as their relations to intentionality. Non-phenomenal consciousness is an essential component of intentional states, and no strictly third-person methodology can accommodate it. (See chapters 1, 2, and 7.) Awareness of minimal content is a subjective conscious experience, but it need not involve any phenomenal features, at least none essentially tied to it. Mistake 2 is a mistake.

The subjectivity of awareness of minimal content derives from its tie to the first-person perspective. As Nagel puts it, "every subjective phenomenon is essentially connected with a single point of view" (quoted on p. 160 of Block 1980). Minimal content, as opposed to the objective content, is the subject of a thought *as conceived by the thinker*; so, it satisfies Nagel's criterion for subjectivity, as it is tied to the thinker's point of view. The discussion of the number and set theorists in chapter 1 displayed cases of minimal content without phenomenal or qualitative features. Apart from that technical treatment, it is rather obvious that when I think that 2 is a prime number, or even wonder whether Aristotle was a good teacher, these experiences do not necessarily involve any phenomenal experiences[21] (though they may as a contingent matter of fact). Importantly, they are tied to my point of view, since the minimal contents of these thoughts are so tied. Therefore, *not all subjective experiences are phenomenal.*[22]

Both intentional and phenomenal states are subjective and involve consciousness. Generally, issues concerning intentionality pertain essentially to *aboutness*. Frequently, though not always, so do issues concerning phenomenal states. Troubles commence, however, when questions of subjectivity or consciousness are cast in terms of phenomenal consciousness, as my extended recent discussion was meant to show. But other problems arise too. For example, when perceptual elements are introduced and questions peculiar to them are brought into play, questions naturally arise as to what are the relevant causal relations between our states and items in our environment. However, my belief that two is a prime number is just as assuredly about a number as my perception that asparagus is on the dish is about a certain kind of physical object, as I conceive numbers and asparagus. In both cases, the element of "aboutness" is resolutely involved (notwithstanding, whether or not there are numbers or physical objects), as is subjectivity. But clearly, there are no causal relations between one's minimal content and, say, numbers or sets. So questions pertaining to such causal relations are not common to all intentional states. Because they are not common to all intentional states, emphasis on them skews the analysis.

On the other hand, problems of aboutness and subjectivity are just as central with non-perceptual intentional states as they are with perceptual ones. Thus, a more satisfying resolution is to be expected if we concentrate on the common aspects, rather than what is peculiar to phenomenal states. The framing of the problem with a focus on phenomenal states diminishes the possibility of a common treatment of both intentionality and phenomenality.[23] Of course, there are also substantial differences between the two, but these differences must not be allowed to obscure and distort a deeper understanding of their common root in consciousness and subjectivity.

An Objective Study of Subjectivity Is Possible, Though a Strictly Third-Person Methodology Is Inadequate

Though I think it is important to keep phenomenal and intentional states distinct, they are both subjective, at least in part. As a result, I think that they share an important additional feature: the recognition of the existence of either can only be achieved by a being or system that is capable of having a first-person perspective. Data restricted to what is obtainable using a *strictly* third-person methodology contains nothing that would in and of itself give any clue that subjective states were instantiated. If an investigator herself did not have subjective states, she would fail to recognize that they were realized in another. Moreover, there are no purely objective grounds that would lead the investigator to even think to look for subjective states in another, the suspicion that another has them *would not even occur to her*. This is to say that any investigation of the subjective utilizing a strictly third-person methodology must fail.

To see this, consider a variant of Frank Jackson's case of Mary. Think of Sally, who like Mary is confined from birth to an exclusively black and white room. But assume that Sally, unlike Mary, does *not* know every physical fact; in particular, assume she knows nothing of the neurophysiology of color perception and does not even know that others have color perceptions. Let Sally have great scientific acumen such that within the confines of her room she develops extensive objective theories about the world; she even develops an extensive brain theory that explains and predicts much of the behavior of those outside the room. My contention is that in spite of all her scientific ability, Sally, left to her own resources, would not produce the neurophysiology of color perception; she would not even hit upon the idea that those outside the room have color perceptions.

Suppose Sally examines the brains of others who are outside of the room and who, unknown to her, are perceiving colors. Given the plethora of brain states that would be simultaneously present, it is highly improbable that Sally would—on her own—individuate the relevant type of brain states for color perception. To do this, one minimally one would have to correlate certain brain states with color perceptions but of the latter, Sally knows nothing.

One might attempt to overcome this obstacle by supposing that someone outside the room gives Sally some instruction. Sally might be told, for example, that when someone on the outside looks at (certain) apple trees, they have "color perceptions" that they call 'red' (apples) and 'green' (leaves), and so forth. (Scare quotes are used because Sally would not be able to get the content of this locution.) Now Sally can extend her investigations to correlate individuals' reports using color terms with corresponding brain states. We may suppose that she gets very good at this, obtaining highly reliable correlations of types of brain states with types of color terms reported.[24] Although this is an advance of sorts, it brings her no closer to a correlation of *color perceptions* and brain states. Correlations of brain states and the vocalizations of color terms is another matter, different areas of the brain are activated by language use and visual perception. Perhaps, Sally would have greater success in discovering relevant correlations were she instructed by someone outside of the room to examine the visual cortex of those outside the room. Even so, there is an intrinsically odd feature in these attempts. Sally is attempting to establish correlations between brain states and, well, what? From Sally's perspective the items of one side of the desired correlation are invisible to her.

As bad as this is, there is an even more fundamental matter that undermines any such attempts to counter my claim that there is nothing in data that is restricted entirely to what is available from a third-person methodology that would lead one to even suspect the existence of subjective states. For what drives these cases is the presupposition that there is someone else who *does* have the subjective states that Sally lacks and is coaching her in light of their awareness. So long as this is a necessary requirement for success in such circumstances, they cannot undermine my claim—they support it.

Sally, while in the room, lacks subjective states of a type that those outside of the room have non-inferential, subjective access to. Lacking these and left to her own devices and limitations, there is no reason to think that Sally would individuate the relevant brain states. Of course, the brain states that do realize the subjective states of others are in principle know*able* to Mary; I am not denying that. She may even fortuitously come to know those very brain states that are operative in these circumstances. What she still would not know is that they enable *color perceptions*, certain particular kinds of subjective states, in the people whose brains are in those states.

We must be careful in saying even this much though. We often glibly talk of "states" of this or that as if something determinate was being said, as when I just said that the brain states that enable the color perceptions of others may be knowable to Sally. Quite the opposite is the case. Brain states are not like discrete physical objects that we can discover—even unfamiliar ones—among other physical objects. A brain state is represented by a certain ordered *n*-tuple of values of relevant brain variables. Such states are determinable only if the relevant variables are specified; these are not readily available to ordinary observation. Nor do they emerge simply by applying more sophisticated observational techniques via the use of instruments. One must have a viable theory of the brain: The theory of brain employed is what would determine the relevant brain variables, and it would provide the understanding of the type of instrumentation required to obtain relevant readings.[25]

Determining these relevant variables, hence the relevant brain states, is exceedingly difficult because of the complexity and plethora of possibilities that exist. While these variables would have determinate features, they are not determinate in the sense that an untrained eye or uninformed person could "pick them out of the crowd," so to speak, as one can do with ordinary though unfamiliar physical objects. Any investigation that would successfully isolate them would be strongly dependent upon extensive background knowledge, theoretical and observational. These usual complexities in scientific investigations on the way to discovery of relevant state variables grow exponentially for the case at hand. Any brain theory for, say, color perception, must provide for the fact that certain types of brain states enable color perceptions. Supposing that the investigator not only lacked color perceptions, but also lacked knowledge of them—as subjective states—would, at the very least, make the identification of the relevant variables practically impossible. For the color perceptions that would be part of the requisite background knowledge would be absent.

I think these claims are partly supported, in a backhanded sort of way, by the fact that without exception, whenever one argues that certain objective features of some non-human being or system are sufficient for it to perceive or understand, there are always others ready to argue that the identified objective feature is not sufficient. Any strictly objective data appealed to in these disputes clearly does not force the conclusion. I take it that this is *some* further evidence, though it *hardly* proves the case, that if we ourselves did not have such states, we would never suspect other beings or systems to have them. Certainly the chief, I would say the only reason we are brought to look for such states in any non-human being or system is that we find those states in ourselves and rightly think we are not unique.

Crucially, we find these states in ourselves only because we enjoy a first-person perspective regarding them. It is just that perspective which allows for the identification of those states apart from any objective variables. This is important precisely because of our massive ignorance regarding the objective basis for our subjective states. We simply would not find them if we lacked a first-person perspective. Undoubtedly, there are objective facts that enable our subjective states. Because the latter are readily identified from our first-person perspective, we can proceed to investigate their objective basis in us. We can attempt to discover the brain theory that would specify the relevant variables. Once we know what objectively accounts for subjective states in us, we will know what to look for, in a third-person sort of way, in other systems.[26]

I will not discuss Fred Dretske's provocative paper "How Do You Know You Are Not a Zombie?" in any detail, but I cannot let the opportunity pass without a pertinent observation. In this essay Dretske argues that there is "no identifiable way" that we know we are not zombies. As one would expect from him, his argumentation to this conclusion relies upon a strictly third-person methodology: The "ways," just alluded to, that he considers and finds wanting are so confined. Dretske and I are in agreement on this. Consciousness is invisible to a strictly third-person methodology. The unexpected result is that Dretske proves my point regarding the invisibility of subjectivity or consciousness to this methodology. But while he thinks that an exclusively third-person methodology is the only proper one, I have tried to show that this mistaken. If I am right that we clearly do know from our first-person perspective that we are not zombies, Dretske's argument is a reductio of the claim that we should restrict ourselves to a third-person methodology.

If I am right in the above, this is yet further reason than I have already given for denying that a methodology employing a strictly third-person perspective is adequate for the investigation of intentionality, subjectivity, or consciousness.[27] For if I am right, it is at best an illusion that the first-person perspective is not implicated in such endeavors: Advocates of a strictly third-person methodology must be implicitly employing data or information garnered from their first-person perspective in order that they may have some clue as to what to investigate from a third-person perspective, to even know what is being "talked about" when subjective states are at issue. Better to forthrightly acknowledge the implicit assumptions, refine them, and expand our conception of the objective.

I have not, nor will I deny that others in considering an agent's states may obtain *knowledge* of that agent's subjective states; indeed, I argue that we can have objective knowledge of another's subjective states, including others' minimal contents. I speak here of 'knowledge' rather than 'access' to reflect a difference: from the third-person perspective one can never have "access" to another's subjective states *in the same way* as the agent has to her own states, for this special access determines at least an aspect of what is thus detected. Since the subjectivity itself determines an aspect of these states for the individual having them, they are known differently by another or not at all.

This unequal "accessibility," however, neither implies that we cannot have objective accounts of these phenomena, nor that we cannot have objective knowledge of another's subjective states.[28] It does suggest that only those who share that point of view, those who have subjective states, are even going to think to try to give any account, objective or subjective, of such phenomena, or even look for them in other systems. Without a similar first-person perspective of those states, they simply would not even be noticed. Here is another way in which the study of the mental irreducibly involves a first-person methodology. In chapter 1, I argued that minimal content and awareness of it is invisible from a strictly third-person perspective; we now see some reason to hold that subjectivity in general is opaque to an exclusively third-person methodology.

Inadequacy of Third-Person Accounts of Subjective Knowledge: New Facts

The results of the previous section raise the question as to whether what is peculiarly known from one's subjective point of view is a distinct fact from any fact that a strictly third-person account can establish. In this section I will argue that there are good reasons to affirm that it is, and certain arguments to the opposite conclusion fail.

To begin to clarify this, think of human beings as complicated multipurpose detecting devices. (I ask the reader to indulge me some obvious comments by way of setting the context.) Various objective stimulations to our surfaces cause certain changes in our internal states. At the very least, changes in our brain states are caused. Some of these internal states thus caused are means for our detecting objective environmental features. If one screens the distal causes and does not intervene in some equivalent neuronal way, the internal states caused by them are no more. This much is no different for any simple detecting device, say, a voltmeter, than it is for us; nevertheless, there is an important difference that is pertinent here. We who have these states, we whose brains are in such states, experience them differently than someone observing us or our brains. In short, frequently when we detect external features, there is the "what it is like" aspect. No such claim can be made for simple detecting devices.

Certainly a crucial element in an agent's phenomenal subjective state is the particular perspectival view she enjoys. This is the kernel of truth in the view of those—for example, William Lycan (1996, 2001) and Gilbert Harman (1990)—who would analyze subjectivity, in part, as consisting in the subject's unique perspective. In a work published in 2003, Lycan calls it the *perspectival view*. Consider what Lycan says about "intrinsically perspectival views" and the "intrinsically perspectival representations" they deliver.[29] He discusses these in the context of a "quasi-perceptual" perspective, which he explains as follows:

Sense organs and other detectors, monitors etc. are intrinsically perspectival and deliver only intrinsically perspectival representations, in that (a) they show the objects they detect only from particular points of view, (b) they key on different properties of the objects, (c) they give you different packets of information about the same objects, and (d) they offer their representational contents under different modes of presentation. (2003, p. 392)

As Lycan speaks here not only of sense organs but also of "other detectors, monitors etc.," it would appear that he holds that ordinary detecting devices also have a perspectival view. With a caveat regarding (d), I can agree with him on this. In chapter 5 I will explain some difficulties with attributing representational contents to non-humans, but for the purposes of this chapter I can let that slide for now and allow that Lycan's (a)–(d) apply to human and non-human detecting devices alike, to this extent they both have a "perspective."

Despite these similarities, there are even more significant differences between human and non-human detectors. The most crucial difference has already been mentioned; we have the capacity to "experience" or to be "conscious" of some of those states, whatever that means, while ordinary instruments clearly do not. The other differences are all related to this fundamental fact; one of them is that the same individual may experience a single type of input stimulus differently on different occasions, and different individuals may experience the same stimulus type differently on the same occasion.[30] None of this is true for simple, properly functioning detecting devices. Another difference is that ordinary instruments are neither aware of their states nor do they "read" them—we read their states. We do not typically "read" our own objective states to determine our subjective, "perspectival," states, as we read objective states of non-human detectors to determine their "perspectival" states—we have experiences. This, of course, is to say that there is something that it is like to be a "detecting device" like us; whereas, there is no reason to say the same for, say, a voltmeter, certainly not in a univocal sense of WIL.

What explains the difference? An obvious though crude answer is that we, unlike, say, the voltmeter, are conscious. This is precisely why some of our internal states are considered to be subjective. A state is subjective or has a subjective aspect if and only if the agent who is in the state is conscious of it (or at least could be). What we know is that while both voltmeters' and our internal states yield a perspective that is dependent upon our respective constitutions, our constitution is such that not only can we be in or have such states, they have or can have a conscious aspect to them. It is as clear *that* we have the relevant constitution for this consciousness, as it is that we do not yet know *what* it is about our objective constitution that enables it. We are also confident that simple instruments lack the requisite constitution, even thought they have an "intrinsically perspectival view."

I have been neutral as to what relations may exist between brain states and subjective states. In the next chapter I will advance a hypothesis, with some empirical support, as to just what it is about our constitution that enables these remarkable states. Of course, Lycan too does not claim that simple instruments, even while having an intrinsically perspectival view, have subjective states. He recognizes that we are sometimes conscious of our inner states, in ways that simple instruments never are or can be. In short, he would not reject the crude and uninformative answer regarding the difference between humans and simple detecting devices that I suggested above, but his explication of consciousness differs markedly from mine. I will briefly consider Lycan's account below, but first I consider a rebuttal of his to Frank Jackson's famous thought experiment involving a color-deprived neuroscientist named Mary.

My sole purpose in examining this case is to reject Lycan's contention that Mary does not learn a new fact. I ask my reader to concentrate on just the question whether Mary learns a new fact. I ask this because I have found that the resistance to the claim that there is a new fact is largely based upon the belief (fear) that if this is admitted dualism follows. I think there is a new fact in this case and that on my view we can admit this without any ensuing commitments to dualism.

Lycan deploys his view of intrinsically perspectival representations to show the falsity of what he advances as a crucial (suppressed) premise in Jackson's famous argument:

For any facts: if F1 = F2, then anyone who knows F1 knows F2. (2003, p. 385)[31]

Against this assumption, Lycan maintains that "facts can be differently represented from differing perspectives, and that is why . . . [the cited premise] is false" (388); what appears to be a new fact is just the same old fact differently represented. To his credit, Lycan holds that there is more to it than just that. Indeed, he is willing to concede that Nagel and Jackson have proved something, viz., there is *information* that is not public, objective, and scientific that Mary gains upon leaving the room.

What is this distinction between fact and information? Lycan first introduces the idea of information under the heading of fine-grained "facts" (the scare quotes are Lycan's) via an appeal to Roderick Chisholm's 1976 book *Person and Object*. Chisholm argued that water splashing is a different fact from that of H_2O moving. The previous section prepared the way for my own support in favor of some such fine-grained view of facts—no scare quotes. I will further advance it in chapter 6. Here I will show that Lycan's fact/information distinction cannot do the work he intends for it. Here is what Lycan says:

I do not think anyone could credibly insist that one of these two ways of counting "facts"—the chunky or the Chisholmian [fine-grained]—is *correct* to the exclusion of the other. I make the following terminological proposal. Let us continue to use the term "fact" in the more usual chunky way, with which we began, and let us call Chisholm facts "pieces of information." (387)

Four pages later, Lycan says:

The introspective representations' contents are going to be non-physical pieces of information.

And that, says the perspectivalist, is why Mary can know all the scientific stuff about experiences of red and not know [what it is like] to experience red. It is because, never having had a first-order experience of red herself, she cannot represent that experience from the introspective perspective.

What Mary (in the room) lacks is a quasi-sensory perspective. With this I agree, but Lycan also holds that this perspective only yields *information*, not *fact*, so that when Mary leaves the room and acquires this perspective, she does not learn a new fact, only new information. With this I disagree.[32]

What is this allegedly same fact, before and after release? There are two candidates depending on whether we consider the perceiver's brain or an external object. In the latter case, it is simply that some external physical object has a certain physical property, say, a certain spectral reflectance. In the former case, the candidate for the same fact would be that a brain is in a certain state. As this case is more complex, I elaborate some of the issues. Mary, while in the room and examining (via some instruments, let us suppose) the relevant brain state of someone gazing at green grass will know their brain state under some, say, neuronal description. When she's released and looks at, say, grass, she herself has color perceptions. On investigating her own brain in this circumstance, utilizing her previous objective methods, she finds that her brain is in the same type of state which others were in when they were looking at grass. The second candidate for being the same fact is, then, this brain state, and Mary now knows she can identify it either subjectively or objectively. She has acquired a new perspective on this brain state. I agree that either way she identifies this brain state, it is the same fact. I also agree that the other candidate for being the same fact, a certain spectral reflectance, can now be known differently by Mary, depending on whether she uses her previous objective methods or her new subjective way.

But is there some other, new, fact that Mary learns? Let us see. Suppose (what is undoubtedly impossible) that Mary does an exhaustive analysis of her own brain states prior to her release and notices that many outside the room frequently have a certain kind of brain state (when they are having color perceptions) that she never has had. She may well wonder what it would be like to have such a state, that is, if *her* brain were in *that state*.[33] Once she leaves the room and is stimulated in a new way so that she now has color perceptions, and she undertakes her post-release objective investigation of her own brain, she knows what it is like because *her* brain is now in the corresponding state, and she is now having a subjective experience of a type that is new to her. Of course, that her brain is in that state is also new for her. Is Mary's being in this new state nothing more than the latter? If all that were new was simply that her brain is in a state it had not been in before, then this would be no reason to herald a new fact. There is more to it than that. The point that too many philosophers make too little of is that there is something involved in the *actual having* of certain brain states that is *quite distinct* from and additional to those brain states themselves.

To see this, contrast the fact that brain states themselves may be known by any number of different objective methods. These different methods yield the same objective knowledge of them; regardless of which of these methods is used, exactly the same objective fact is determined. This is not true for subjective states. When Mary (pre-release) objectively detected brain states of others which enabled their subjective states, she did not detect *their* subjective states, she did not detect any subjective states at all. But the subjective states of those individuals were additional features of their brain states. How else could those subjective states have come about, if not in virtue of those brain states? Barring dualism or magic, these brain states, which pre-release Mary was able to detect, *then* had an additional feature, which pre-release Mary was *unable to detect*.

What does this last point show? Consider this simple, general argument: Given any fact and any feature of that fact, *it would not be that fact if it lacked that feature*. When pre-release Mary determines that others have certain brain states, brain states that enables *them* to have subjective experiences, Mary is not cognizant of the latter feature. Mary failed to identify a feature of the brain states of others that those brain states *had*. So whatever fact it is that Mary identified, it had to be a *different* fact than the one she is able to identify post-release. Mary learns a new fact on acquiring this new perspective.

Having a subjective experience undoubtedly involves one's brain being in a certain state, but that it is a subjective state cannot be identified by objective means *alone*. The *having* of some brain state is a different phenomenon than that of the brain state itself. The means of detection is critical to an aspect of *what* is detected. *The first-person means of detection is (partly) constitutive of subjective states and, hence, of what is known.* The occurrence of a certain brain state is one fact—its occurrence *in someone* and the resulting subjective state is another. We may conclude that subjective experience is not simply identical to a brain state; it is identical to the *having* of that brain state. The specification of that brain state is one fact—the having of it another. This difference is not simply that it is a different instantiation of some brain state type, say, that it is instanced in this space-time region rather than that, for that would leave out the critical feature—the having of it.

I now turn to another kind of attempt to refute Jackson's argument as it, like Lycan's, presupposes that Mary does not learn a new fact. Lewis and Nemirow defend the claim that no new fact is learned by Mary by claiming that the difference is due to Mary's acquisition of a new ability. As with Lycan's attempt to support the "same fact claim," there is also something seriously wrong with Lewis' and Nemirow's appeal to a new ability to defend this claim.

To have some ability is to have a particular *potential* to do or realize something of a certain sort, given certain conditions. When the required conditions are in place and there are no overriding factors, the ability is activated and the appropriate result is realized. Absent the conditions for activation of the ability, the ability is not activated and the result is not realized. This account of having and exercising some ability (as far as it goes) seems to me to be completely uncontroversial. A simple consequence of it is that if one is deprived of the conditions that would activate an ability one should not expect the result that would have occurred had the exercise of that ability been activated. (I cannot ride a bike if no bike is available, notwithstanding my ability to ride one.) In such circumstances, however, the absence of the result in no way indicates the absence of the ability.

Applying this to the Mary case, we see that there is no reason to hold that there is some ability that pre-release Mary lacked and then gained.

That she now perceives colors for the first time does not imply that she earlier lacked the ability to do so. Clearly a required condition for the activation of that ability was absent while she was confined to the room, namely, being presented with colored objects. We have seen that under such conditions, we should expect the absence of the result (Mary's perceiving colors) even if Mary in fact had the ability all along. So the claim that Mary acquires a new ability is no more supported than its denial. Therefore, the explanation of the occurrence of the new phenomenon upon Mary's release as being a result of her acquiring a new ability and not to her learning a new fact is without support.

There is also something quite odd in the characterization of what happens to Mary upon release as the *acquisition of a new ability*, for the following reason: The acquisition of some ability requires practice in the activity that instantiates the ability (think of the ability to play the violin or ride a bike). Mary, however, requires no "practice" in seeing colors on leaving the room; she straight-away experiences them. So if it were correct to characterize the phenomenon in question as the acquisition of some ability, it would be a sui generis ability, one whose acquisition was different from all other abilities.[34] This is further reason to reject the idea that Mary acquires a new ability.

The attempts of Lycan, Lewis, and Nemirow to account for the new phenomenon which occurs when Mary is released from the room without acknowledging a new fact have failed, or so I have argued. These failures coupled with my positive argument clear the way to treat the new phenomenon as a genuine fact. In chapter 6, I will attempt to further advance this claim but in a way that implies neither substance nor property dualism.

Consciousness and the Explanatory Gap

The earlier discussion of what Lycan called *intrinsically perspectival views* and the *intrinsically perspectival representations* appeared to apply to simple instruments and to humans. But while we may well attribute perspectival views and representations in Lycan's sense to simple detecting devices, it is obvious that this provides no grounds for holding that there is something it is like to be, say, a voltmeter. This by itself, however, does not count against the perspectivalist view, since this view of subjectivity does not consist *just* in having such a perspective. The *Inner Sense Theory* that Lycan advances requires two further features for subjectivity or consciousness: (1) that the perspective comes about through some sort of self-scanning mechanism of the device's inner states and (2) that the representations of these inner states are of a "proprietary kind."

Now, it is easy to imagine, and indeed to construct, an augmented voltmeter (s-voltmeter)—one that has an additional mechanism that scans some of its inner states. The augmented voltmeter would satisfy feature (1) just mentioned. But there is nothing in this that allows us to see how adding this new mechanism could result in the augmented device's having subjective states. There is a particular reason why it is difficult to see how this could come about, and this brings us to a fundamental issue. It is unclear, to say the least, how something so radically new and different—subjectivity—can arise out of "more of the same" when "the more" is comprised of the same elements that initially lacked it, as the added scanning mechanism would be. *How could it possibly be that such additions would enable subjective states?* (I will refer to this as the "how question" or "how possibly"). The question is so perplexing because the features of the mechanism, original or augmented, are so radically different from what they supposedly give rise to.[35] Adding consideration of feature (2) of the Inner Sense Theory does not help since it is subject to the same problem as feature (1).[36] Of course, the same perplexity is, at this point, as stubbornly present for my theory too, but I will advance a solution in the next chapter.

We have reached that well-known great chasm, the "explanatory gap," that separates philosophers into camps with what often seems to be fundamentally irreconcilable differences. It is the radical difference in character of the "information" (to use Lycan's term) regarding brain states obtained from the first-person and third-person perspectives that poses what appears to be such an impenetrable problem as to their relations. Denying that first-person "information" are facts, as Lycan does, does not resolve this issue. Nor can the relation between the radically different features be resolved by appeal to further third-person concepts (such as scanning mechanisms), no matter how ingenious.[37] Even if (contrary to what I have argued) Mary does not learn a new fact, the physicalist still has the problem of explaining the "how" question, as we all do. Let me repeat that in pressing these points, I am not opposing physicalism. When I hold that Mary learns a new fact, I am not committed to its being some non-physical fact. A main point of my view is that the radical difference in character of subjective and objective states poses a problem *within* any theory of the mind, including physicalism. It is *not just a point to argue against physicalism*, though certainly this has been done. Universal acceptance of physicalism would not diminish the importance and need of physicalism to resolve this issue. It is my contention that regardless of any other virtues a physicalist (or anti-physicalist) theory of consciousness or subjectivity may have, it suffers from a major lacuna if it fails to resolve or at least to provide a framework for a resolution of this radical difference; it must show how the subjective states and the non-subjective states could possibly be related.

Concluding Remarks

Nagel maintains that an objective physical theory must abandon a single point of view. In a sense I agree with this, but I do not think that this eliminates the possibility of giving an objective account of the subjective point of view.[38] However, if we rely on a narrow construal of 'objective', one that constrains it to what is obtainable by *strictly* third-person methodologies, there cannot be an objective account of the subjective. Since both phenomenal and intentional features are in part constituted by a first-person perspective, there are facts that are accessible only from a subjective point of view, and there is no way that a theory exclusively employing third-person concepts can adequately accommodate them. Therefore, an adequate account of mind must be supplemented with a first-person methodology.[39] My introduction of the concepts of minimal content and objective content reflects my efforts to provide an objective and adequate foundation for a theory of mind. The objectivity at issue is one that recognizes the primacy of the subjective in this domain.

My theory is at odds with various orthodox views in a number of respects. One that I would like to emphasize here is that of the two broad problem areas in the philosophy of mind, intentionality and phenomenality, it is the latter that is typically viewed as posing the "hard problem" for consciousness, and the absence of a solution is the explanatory gap problem.[40] However, the very idea of the hard problem of consciousness is miscast when it is restricted to problems concerning phenomenal states.

The properly framed hard question is broader in scope. Simply and generally put, there is a similar explanatory gap problem for both phenomenal and intentional states. Whether the attempts of others succeed in closing the phenomenal/physical gap or not, they have not addressed this new gap problem. On my theory, the closing of both gaps is done in a unified way, although the details differ. In the next chapter, I will provide a common framework for closing both gaps.

4 Physicalism, the Explanatory Gap, and Chaos

Physicalism comes in a variety of forms. Common to all such forms is the view that everything is physical and there is a physical explanation of every fact. Just what 'physical' means varies in these formulations; sometimes it is left undefined. I will recommend below one account that draws its inspiration from a well-known episode in the history of physics.

It is widely agreed that our phenomenal states pose a particularly "hard problem" for physicalism, however construed, since there seems to be an "explanatory gap" between, say, brain states and phenomenal experiences. Here I will discuss an important solved analogue to the explanatory gap problem. It provides us with a concrete understanding of just what it is we ought to seek when we seek to close the explanatory gap. This case also demonstrates that, contrary to some, an entailment relation is not necessary to close the gap.

My account of physicalism and how the explanatory gap should be closed preserves the gap as the serious problem it is, but shows that it poses no serious threat to physicalism properly understood. Still, I will show that physicalism must avoid certain evasive "ostrich" strategies, and that any appeal to fundamental mysteries also should be avoided. I have also generalized the problem: Not only is there a gap not only between brain states and phenomenal states, there is also a gap between brain states and non-phenomenal contentful mental states, such as beliefs and desires. (Chapters 1–3 support the latter.) I will propose a model that provides a framework that goes a considerable distance toward closing both of these gaps. The same model will shed light on another "hard problem": that of mental/physical causation.

Physicalism and the Explanatory Gap

What is the solved analogue to the explanatory gap problem, alluded to above? Consider an investigator at a relatively early stage of chemistry, perhaps a fictitious stage: Suppose that it is known that H_2O molecules constitute water, but suppose that little is known about intermolecular bonds. Molecules are (roughly) *discrete entities*, yet water presents itself as a *continuous and flowing stuff*, a liquid. When I use the word 'liquid' here, I do not mean it in its technical, physiochemical sense; rather, it should be understood as a straightforward observation term. It is what a speaker of English would understand, even if she were entirely ignorant of chemistry and physics. It is this sense that is relevant if the analogy is to work.[1] That is, the gap in the water case is between its discrete molecular constitution as described in physical chemistry and its ordinarily observed continuous flow in daily life. When they are so disparate in nature, how could the former give rise to the latter?

We can understand this once we know that H_2O molecules can form weak intermolecular bonds, such that the bonds between large clusters of them can easily break and reform with other large clusters, the clusters themselves changing over time, thereby "sliding" across one another.[2] Furthermore, it is a familiar fact that small discrete entities in near proximity to one another may give the appearance of continuity, especially when viewed from a distance. Thus is dispelled the "mystery" that might justifiably be raised concerning the gap between water's ordinarily observed continuity and ability to flow and its discrete molecular constitution.[3] Saying this indicates how for this case it could possibly be that "more of the same" can indeed enable or give rise to something quite different.

While the actual theory of molecular bonding is quite complicated, the explanation just given does not turn on any arcane knowledge of that theory. Only some of the simplest general features of the theory, coupled with continuity considerations are needed to provide an adequate account of the liquidity of water. With that slim knowledge, what might have been mysterious is comprehensible to us.[4]

This account is not tantamount to simply saying that liquidity supervenes on a certain type of molecular bonding, though it may do so. Merely to talk of supervenience here (without appealing to, say, intermolecular bonds and continuity considerations) would be merely to name the mystery; it would not provide a plausible "mechanism" for the supervening property. While many different properties may "supervene" on various sets of base properties, mere statement of a supervenience relation between the sets of properties is nearly vacuous. One must also state *how* the base properties determine the supervenient ones. The importance of specifying the dependence relation becomes all the more evident once it is realized that these dependence relations will certainly vary from case to case. Thus, though weak intermolecular bonds may constitute the dependence relation in the molecule/liquid case, no one would expect that same dependence relation to be operative in the brain state/mental state case, even if one holds that mental states supervene on brain states.[5]

The gap problem between brain states and mental states appears impenetrable because no one has identified any plausible "mechanism" connecting brain states and mental states that enables us to understand how the one *could* give rise to, enable, or be identical to the other. The "how possibly" question was raised in chapter 3. This lacuna is exacerbated because the features of the former are so radically different from the latter. A solution to the gap problem requires the *specification* of some "mechanism" that would make it comprehensible to us that the one enables the other, something that could play a similar role to the intermolecular bonds in the molecule/liquid case. Merely saying that mental states "supervene" on brain states is, as already indicated, virtually vacuous and seems little more than an expression of faith in physicalism; it certainly advances no understanding.

Hypothesis: Some unknown entities, states, processes, or features, X, of the brain are to phenomenal or, more generally, to conscious mental states as intermolecular bonds are to liquidity. There may be no such X, but any physicalist research program one of whose goals is to solve the explanatory gap problem must seek such an X.

For definiteness, I will assume throughout that a solution lies in neuroscience. (I also believe it.) Whether current neurophysiological theories and approaches are sufficient to uncover such an X, if it exists, is an empirical question. With this caveat in mind, there seems to be three options:

1. Current neurophysiological resources are generally sufficient to uncover such an X, though certain relevant details or connections among them have yet to be determined.

2. The current resources are not adequate—a scientific revolution in neurophysiology, of the kind Kuhn has described in other fields, is required.

3. There is no such neurophysiological X.

The current intractableness of the problem of the explanatory gap, while not conclusively establishing that option 1 is a dead end, does make it implausible. The analogy provides the reason for saying this: the solution to the molecule/liquidity gap did not rely on any technical or detailed knowledge of the character of intermolecular bonds, *but only on some of their simple most general aspects*. But while we have a rather good understanding of the firing rates of neurons and some of the various chemical neurotransmitters, *this does not offer the slightest clue how any such features could give rise to phenomenal states*. If specialized knowledge is not required and we already have the essentials of what we need, the gap problem should have been solved already, or at least the outline of its solution should be at hand. But it is not, and we do not even have a plausible line on it. Some exploit this recalcitrant fact to the extent of claiming that it shows physicalism is false, that is, they endorse option 3, or some generalized version of it, maintaining that it is an unsolvable mystery, beyond our capabilities. We shall see that such a conclusion is premature. For although option 1 currently seems unlikely, that is not the only way physicalism could be saved and the explanatory gap problem solved. There is still option 2: that we need a new science.[6]

For the reasons cited above, I reject option 1. (Later, I will give a more conclusive reason why option 1 is not tenable.) I further hold that, given a plausible understanding of physicalism, we must reject option 3. To see this, consider first a simple-minded view of Physicalism, one no one would take seriously today. It holds that all things, events, states, or processes are explainable within a Newtonian framework. Clearly, physicalism thus understood is false. Today no one would be tempted by such a narrow physicalism; however, such a view would have been, indeed was, held by many in the late eighteenth century and in the first half of the nineteenth century.

The history of this case is well known. A relevant problem then was to account for electromagnetic phenomena in Newtonian terms. (I am not advancing this as a gap problem, though one might; I exploit it for its bearing on the concept of physicalism.) All such efforts failed. The Newtonian laws required supplementation with those of Maxwell. Maxwell's success exposed the incompleteness of Newtonian Mechanics and, therefore, a defeat of physicalism narrowly understood in Newtonian terms. Was this a refutation of physicalism? No one, I think, would say so, not even then. It did, however, expose a shortcoming of Newtonian mechanics, and it was a defeat for physicalism narrowly understood in Newtonian terms. The reaction was to enlarge the concept of physicalism. To my mind, this was a rational reaction. Newtonian mechanics enjoyed huge successes and held out tremendous promise in its early years, but subsequent sustained scientific investigation determined that more had been anticipated than could be fulfilled; furthermore, the Maxwellian enhancement, which solved the target problems, was good science by all relevant standards. Subsequent scientific developments, the special and general theories of relativity and quantum electrodynamics, expanded our conception of the nature of the physical even more.

What bearing does all this have on ruling out option 3? The point is that any attempt to limit the concept of physicalism to currently successful scientific theories is a mistake. Among other reasons, it unjustifiably assumes that our current science has "got it essentially right." Not only is such a belief contrary to the inherent tentative nature of science; it is inductively unsound, given the various dramatic changes and upheavals in scientific theories over the centuries that has resulted in our expanded view of the physical.

Physicalism understood as restricted to current science is most probably false. If one were to adopt this restricted view of physicalism, then, given the apparent hopelessness of closing the gap with the resources of current science, one would be pushed toward option 3. I have attempted to show that such a restriction is unjustified. If the exact character of physicalism is understood as characterized by our best science, not taken as an essentially finished product, but as ongoing and open-ended, then physicalism is very probably true. For thus understood, it is simply the stricture that we will not count any natural thing, process, state, or feature as explained until we have a scientific account of it, *whatever that is*. This makes physicalism a rather uncontroversial, indeed, trivial thesis, since all that is ruled out is non-scientific accounts, say, supernaturalism.

Given this conception of physicalism, endorsement of option 3, in its general interpretation, would be tantamount to giving up and declaring the explanatory gap to be an unsolv*able* mystery, as some have done. Such a stance bears a trace of arrogance in that it unjustifiably presupposes foreknowledge of what future science will bring (more accurately, what it will *not* bring). We *may* never have the requisite science to close the gap (though I think it is at hand, as I will explain); still, it is difficult to see why, at this stage of infancy of brain science, we should draw the pessimistic conclusion that closing the gap is forever beyond our reach.[7]

A conception of physicalism constrained to some particular stage of scientific development is, while more dramatic, also far more problematic. Certainly, the restriction to current science is quite dubious, as there is not even a single general and basic paradigm in neuroscience. Neuroscience has yet to produce its Newton or Einstein. What could decide in favor of such a narrow conception of Physicalism? Nothing short of its actual fulfillment; this is certainly not on the horizon.

Physicalism conceived as broadly as I have recommended, though so uncontroversial as to be trivial, has the virtue of shifting the attention to more productive discussions of the explanatory gap. Frequently physicalists and anti-physicalists alike view the explanatory gap as a threat to physicalism. The gap is only a threat if one adopts an unjustifiably narrow view of physicalism. Taking this narrower view, coupled with the (apparent) hopelessness of the current situation regarding the closure of the explanatory gap, results in a pernicious reaction by both sides. Physicalists tend to argue that the gap is not that big, that serious or even that it is an illusion, while anti-physicalists declare it is not solvable. If I am right, these defensive strategies on the part of physicalists (one might call them "ostrich strategies") are as misguided as the "mysterian" strategies of the anti-physicalist, for the narrow view of physicalism presupposed by both sides is unwarranted.[8] In short, we must shun "ostrich" or "mysterian" strategies, endorse the wider conception of physicalism, and get on with the work of identifying an enabling relation that makes the connection between mental and brain states comprehensible to us.

Some have rejected this line. For example, David Chalmers (1996, p. 118) has argued against the idea advanced here that we need a new science. (See also Churchland 1996.) Chalmers argues that all physical theories come down to two basic elements: structure and dynamics of physical processes. He says that "from structure and dynamics, we can only get more structure and dynamics" (1996, p. 118), and he concludes that new structure and function will not help in closing the explanatory gap, for it is just more of the same.

Chalmers supplements his general argument with two other requirements that he thinks advocates of a new science cannot fulfill. He says that it is difficult to evaluate the claim that it will take a new science in the abstract, holding that "one would at least like to see an example of how such a new physics [science] might *possibly* go" (1996, p. 118). Furthermore, he holds that "no set of facts about physical structure and dynamics can add up to a fact about phenomenology" (ibid.). A fair interpretation of his locution "add up" is that of entailment, as on the very same page he raises the rhetorical question "How could a theory that is recognizably a physical theory entail the existence of consciousness?" So the two further requirements are (A) a concrete proposal, or an indication of how the new science might go, and (B) that the new science entails consciousness.

As to requirement (A), I will present a specific proposal later. For now, I note that I have already indicated how a new science could possibly go. I did so by noting how science has gone with respect to a similar problem; namely, it uncovered an informative connection between the diverse elements of discrete molecules and continuous liquidity. But if one accepts requirement (B), one might protest that the analogy did not even accomplish that: It does not close its own gap, since the structure and dynamics of molecules does not *entail* liquidity.

I am inclined to agree that the entailment relation is lacking in the analogy, though it may well be that there are a number of plausible missing premises that would turn it into an entailment. Still, I am not inclined to mount such a defense, as I think the entailment requirement is too strong. Rather, I offer the analogy as evidence that the entailment relation is simply not necessary. We *do* see how understanding the loose intermolecular bonds render the gap between the disparate items solvable. Their relation becomes *understandable to us*, and *we see this without the benefit of an entailment relation*. If an entailment relation is not necessary to close this particular gap, why should we make it an a priori requirement in the brain/mental states gap? Where is the argument for the claim that the relation that closes the gap between diverse entities must be entailment?

To require that the relevant scientific theories entail that there are mental states is, to my mind, to set too high a standard. I, for one, would think that the explanatory gap between these disparate items would be closed, if one could give any account of their relations comparable to that given in the case of molecules and liquidity. If we could only just see how something so new and different could arise out of the brain states! Of course, none of this is to eschew entailment relations. All the better, if they can be produced. My point is simply that they are not necessary for closing the explanatory gap.[9]

Let us suppose, as seems true, that the molecule/liquid gap is closed without specification of an entailment relationship between the structure and dynamics of molecules and liquidity in its ordinary observational sense.

What seems to be operative in the closing of this gap is some "plausibility relation" between the disparate items. Given these disparate items and the weak intermolecular bonds, it is comprehensible to us that such structure and dynamics could give rise to the ordinarily observed liquidity.

Viewing the explanatory gap as a problem depends on a first-person perspective. Without first-person subjective states, there would be no gap (as one of the relata would not exist) and therefore no gap problem. As I argued in chapter 3, if an investigator (Sally) who lacked subjective states were to examine a being that had subjective states, she would find nothing in the *strictly* third-person data that would suggest to her the existence of subjective states, and she would not have a clue—left to her own devices—to look for them. The problem cannot even be appreciated if one is restricted to an exclusively third-person methodology.[10] That it is a first-person problem is precisely why the problem is one of making the connection between brain and subjective states a "comprehensible *to us*" problem and not an entailment problem.

There remains Chalmers' main general objection. According to him, what is essential to a physical theory is structure and dynamics, and a new physical theory will just give us more of the same; so, a new physical theory will not help in closing the explanatory gap. But Chalmers casts this argument at far too general a level. The *particular character* of the structure and dynamics is what makes a difference. Just as I earlier argued that talk of supervenience is empty without specification of the relevant determination relation, in this context, general talk of structure and dynamics is equally empty. In the molecule/liquid analogy, it is the *particular character* (weak intermolecular bonds) of the structure and dynamics of molecules that enables us to understand how liquidity can arise out of such qualitatively different items. So, too, we may expect that the *particular character* of the new dynamics is what will enable us to close the explanatory gap between brain states and mental states. Additionally, the analogy leads us to the hopeful expectation that detailed or highly sophisticated knowledge of the new dynamics may not be necessary to close the gap.

An Early Attempt to Explain Subjective Qualities: Galileo

I have stressed that a crucial element in closing the explanatory gap is to have an account that enables us to comprehend how certain kinds of qualities could possibly give rise to (or cause, or be identical with) others, even though the two kinds are, or appear to be, radically different from each other. This is a problem that I think Galileo faced and thought he resolved. Galileo's efforts in this regard are, I think, fascinating and not widely known. Since they illustrate an attempt to do what I have argued is required in closing the explanatory gap, I will give an abridged presentation.

Galileo did not talk of a mind as the seat of subjective experiences; instead, he held that the subjective experiences were the effects of objectives qualities on our *sensitive bodies*. Even at that, one can make the case that he was aware that "there was something it is like" to be a sensitive body. Indeed, it is precisely this difference between sensitive bodies and ordinary external objects (non-sensitive bodies) that grounds his distinction between subjective and objective qualities. He contrasts the effect of moving a hand over a living man and a marble statue. The motion and the contact can be identical, yet only the living (sensitive) body will experience a tickling, of which he says: "This latter affection is altogether our own, and it is not at all a property of the hand itself." (1623, p. 28) After he describes a similar case using a feather and the resulting titillation, he states:

. . . if the living, sensing body were removed, nothing would remain of the titillation but an empty name. (ibid.)

He continues with a generalization to other qualities, drawing this conclusion:

. . . I believe that many other qualities, such as taste, odor, color, and sound, often predicated of natural bodies, have a similar and no greater existence than this. (ibid., pp. 28–29)

Therefore, the having of subjective qualities results in the "what it is like states," given our "sensitive bodies." They are what Galileo calls "subjective qualities," and they have no existence apart from us.

Galileo attempts an explanation of how the objective qualities give rise to the subjective ones. The general idea is that our subjective experiences will vary depending on the shape, number, and velocity of the particles impinging on our sense organs. For example, standing near a fire on a cold day produces a warm, pleasant experience. As we approach the fire, the experienced heat intensifies and the pleasure may increase for a time but shifts to discomfort and eventually pain. The micro-explanation that Galileo offers of these macro-phenomena is that in the initial situation relatively few small particles are reaching our bodies and with little force; so they do not penetrate, or not very deeply. As we approach the fire, more and more sharp particles penetrate ever deeper and with greater force. So what began as a pleasant intrusion becomes an onslaught, until so many of these small sharp particles are impinging on the sensitive body at once and with such great force that they rend the flesh and hurt.

He applies the same ideas to the other senses.[11] I quote at length his account of smells and tastes because my summary does not do justice to his remarkable proposal:

Since certain material bodies are continually resolving themselves into tiny particles, some of the particles, because they are heavier than air, will descend; and some of them, because they are lighter than air, will ascend. From this, perhaps, two further senses are born, for certain of the particles penetrate two parts of our body which are effectively more sensitive than the skin, which is incapable of feeling the incursion of material which are too fine, subtle, or flexible. The descending particles are received by the upper surface of the tongue, and penetrating, they blend with its substance and moisture. Thus our tastes are caused, pleasant or harsh in accordance with variations in the contact of diversely shaped particles, and depending upon whether they are few or many, and whether they have high or low velocity. Other particles ascend, and entering the nostrils they penetrate the various nodes (*mammilule*) which are the instruments of smell; and these particles, in like manner through contact and motion, produce savoriness or unsavoriness—again depending upon whether the particles have this or that shape, high or low velocity, and whether they are many or few. (ibid., p. 29)

As far as such an analysis goes toward making "comprehensible to us" how the objective properties may give rise to the subjective ones, it ultimately fails. For the subjective aspects that are accounted for by the objective ones on such an analysis are those of intensity or pleasantness of, say, heat, smell, or taste, but not the heat, smells, or tastes themselves. Galileo's explanations essentially address the degree of intensity, strong or weak, and our psychological attitude, pleasant or unpleasant, in terms of the objective features of size, shape, velocity, and number. They strike me as good candidates for making comprehensible to us how *these* subjective features could arise from variations in objective features. Degrees aside, however, it is important that they do not begin to address how the objective (primary) qualities could produce other subjective (secondary) qualities so radically different in character. Even if it were a psychological fact that we associate, say, the impingement of smooth shapes with sweetness, while that of sharp shapes are associated with bitter tastes, and even if this "geometry of taste" were empirically supported, the residual and recalcitrant question would remain as to just why *these shapes* are associated with *these tastes*. How does it happen? Smoothness being so different from sweetness, how do smooth particles give rise to *sweet taste*? In this regard—explaining how something new can arise—the gap between the two kinds of properties remains as great as before.

Apart from these deficiencies in Galileo's analysis, it does illustrate an effort to make comprehensible to us how one kind of property could give rise to a radically different kind. In the process of doing that, Galileo exemplified another methodological virtue: Evidently he recognized the need to "explain the appearances."[12] For in denying that the subjective qualities are "indwelling properties of some external body," he recognized that this conflicted with the common-sense view; thus, he sought to explain how his view could be reconciled with the contrary appearances.[13] Having the benefit of some new science, I will in the next section offer a different and more successful way of addressing the "how possibly?" question.

Chaos and Subjective States

It is the fact that mental states are so radically different in character from brain states that gives rise to the conundrum of the explanatory gap. In short, we seem to get something entirely new and different out of the activity of neurons and neurotransmitters. A significant contributing factor to this mystifying situation is the implicit assumption that the relevant mathematics is linear. For within such models, it is true that "the whole is the sum of its parts." You do not get "more," and you certainly do not get anything "different" from the linear combination of the parts.[14] Mental states being so evidently different from brain states, showing how they could arise out of the latter seems to be an impossible, even logically impossible, undertaking, so long as inquiries are restricted to linear models. Until recently, non-linear models were eschewed in scientific investigations because of their complexity; moreover, linear models applied to the activity of neurons and neurotransmitters appear *logically inadequate* to close the gap, for the reasons given.[15] The situation, thus, seems desperate and is a compelling reason to reject option 1, listed earlier. In consequence, if one's sights are limited to linear models, option 2 appears as unlikely, and option 3, which leads to the mysterian conclusion, appears inescapable.

Prospects are brighter when *self-organized* systems governed by non-linear dynamics are considered.[16] These are open systems, some of whose properties are not completely explainable by properties of parts of the system. Consider a simple example. When oil is heated uniformly from below, the molecules become more energetic, the heat is randomly dissipated, but there is no macro-observational change in the properties of the liquid. However, a significant change occurs once a certain temperature is reached: the liquid abruptly assumes a lattice structure of hexagonal convection cells (Bénard cells). This new behavior is *not merely driven by input and initial conditions; the molecules collectively organize themselves*. This lack of external driving of the activity is what indicates that it is self-organized which, in turn, is characteristic of chaotic systems. Moreover, this collective behavior of large populations of elements of the system, known as *self-organization*, constrains the behavior of individual elements so that there is a kind of "top-down causality." All of this is contrary to the usual patterns of explanations. It turns out that such self-organized behavior is widespread; for example, it governs the dappling patterns of animals' coats, hurricanes, cellular slime molds, and even the formation of the visual cortex (Kelso 1997, pp. 6–15).

From such cases, we may extract a unique and peculiar attribute of non-linear interactions of elements that provides for at least the possibility of the closing the explanatory gap. It is the basis for the X of the previous section:

(*) The dynamics of self-organized systems, described by non-linear equations, yield properties of the system that are significantly different from any linear combination of microelements of the system.

Nonlinear dynamics is the only known candidate possessing this feature, and this is exactly the kind of feature that can resolve the basic conundrum the explanatory gap generates. For the central obstacle to closing the gap is the apparent impossibility of our understanding how we can get something more and so different out of interacting elements in the brain. The dynamics described by non-linear equations eliminate this obstacle.[17] Freed from the constraint of linear models and given (*), what appeared to be a recalcitrant mystery is transformed into a manageable, if still formidable, problem. The enormous (scientific) task to characterize the non-linear equations of brain state variables so that something more and different, mental states, can arise out of their interactions remains. Nevertheless, the apparently impenetrable "how possibly" question becomes manageable. Viewing the brain as a self-organized system governed by non-linear dynamics is the general core of a new paradigm, in the Kuhnian sense, of brain behavior that at least provides the framework for a solution, a solution that appears impossible against a background of linear models.

It is in such systems that new properties appear that are not just more of the same. The feature (*) is exactly what is *needed* to do the job. Noting this, however, falls far short of actually producing the relevant non-linear mathematics. Still, it is gratifying to realize the abstract point that there is this unusual and powerful feature of non-linear dynamics that provides a *framework or basis for our comprehension* of how brain states could give rise to mental states (even though they are so radically different from one another). This is rather like the situation with our earlier simple analogy. Knowledge of the general character of weak intermolecular bonds is sufficient for us to comprehend how liquidity can arise from a multitude of discrete entities, and no sophisticated knowledge of the theory of molecular bonds is required for this. It is no small point that, in a similar way, a most serious logical obstacle to closing the explanatory gap between the disparate items of mental and brain states is swept away. The helpfulness of this result is, of course, contingent upon brain dynamics being actually non-linear. We will see that there is some cause for optimism with regard to the existence of non-linear models of brain activity.

But there is more. In the discussion of the heated oil, we observed that the emergent property of the system, hexagonal convection cells, exerted a kind of top-down causality, properties of large collections of molecules constrain the behavior of individual molecules. This is a second powerful and unique feature of self-organized systems that provides the basis for removal of another major logical conundrum between brain and mind—mental causation. It appears that certain high-level mental states, such as beliefs and desires, activate certain microstates, the activation of motor neurons, which results in the agent moving to fulfill her desire. How to understand this mental/physical causation? A second unique feature of self-organized systems turns the trick:

(**) The dynamics of self-organized systems, described by non-linear equations, yield global properties of the system that causally constrain microelements of the system.

Assume, for the moment, that conscious thoughts and perceptions are just these sorts of emergent properties of self-organized brains governed by non-linear dynamics. (Two prominent neuroscientists, Earl MacCormac (1996) and Walter Freeman (1991, 1995) have so hypothesized, respectively.) The idea that conscious thoughts or perceptions actually bring about certain behaviors by means of certain sensory motor responses, is *demystified* on this assumption. For we have simple analogical illustrations (Bénard cells discussed above, other examples cited above and many, many more) of how such different states—different because the microstates lack the properties newly exhibited—can constrain microstates. So, self-organized systems have a feature that also goes to the heart of solving the general problem of "how possibly" there can be mental/physical causation.

Thus, a second apparently logically impossible realization of a relation between brain and mind becomes *comprehensible to us—given the new paradigm*. Again, as with (*), this only holds out the abstract possibility, one whose promise could only be fulfilled after completion of enormous scientific work, work demonstrating that brain behavior is governed by relevant non-linear equations that support such speculations. But, once again, it is a most gratifying abstract possibility, as it transforms a seemingly logically impossible situation into one that is within our grasp.

I suggest, then, that *the conundrums of the explanatory gap and mental causation may well be simply artifacts of methodologies based in linear microreduction models*.

Non-linear dynamics provides, however, even more gratification than mere abstract possibilities. Freeman successfully applied chaos theory to neurophysiological systems.[18] He did extensive work on the olfactory system of rabbits, which I will focus on, but similar results have been found in rats and cats, and in the visual system of monkeys (Freeman and Dijk 1987), cats (Eckhorn et al. 1988; Gray et al. 1989), and humans (Schippers 1990). Somewhat more tentatively, similar results were found in the somatosensory system of humans (Freeman and Mauer 1989). I must add that there is no way I can do justice to the extensive important scientific work already accomplished in this area. I will only touch on a few highlights of Freeman's varied experimental and mathematical support for his model and strongly encourage the reader to "follow his nose" in pursuing Freeman's extensive research.[19]

This approach is a candidate for a "new science" alluded to earlier. There is a significant split among brain researchers as to the importance of relatively local behavior of neurons (feature neurons or "grandmother cells"), on the one hand, or the global activity of large populations of neurons, on the other, for understanding perception and cognition. Freeman started in the former camp, but twelve years of experimentation using traditional methods on the olfactory system of the rabbit transformed him into a leading exponent of the importance of global activity and the application of chaos theory. His extensive attempts to find significant relations between odorants and relatively local neural populations failed.[20]

Here in brief are some of the details. The initial detection of an odor is by a spatial sheet of receptors in the nose. These receptors signal through the olfactory nerve another sheet of cells in the olfactory bulb. Although single neurons do fire in response to specific odors, the same cell fires in response to different odors and the same odor can excite many different cells. Freeman used electroencephalograms (EEGs) to record the activity. What he found was that the patterns of two successive sniffs of the same odor were as different from one another as were the patterns between two sniffs of different odors. The spatial patterns of the EEGs did not reliably correlate with the input stimuli. They changed not only when stimuli changed but when anything else changed. Change even occurred on reinforcement of an odor not previously reinforced. This change in reinforcement pattern for a particular odor had a ripple effect in that the spatial patterns for all the other odors also changed, indicating associative memory.

In brief, the receptors in the nose activate certain neurons in the olfactory bulb. The bulb then constructs a global spatial pattern that is dependent on past experience in that which neurons fire synchronously is a function of the specific past activations of neurons. It is the global pattern of cooperative activity of neurons that is transmitted to the olfactory cortex and other areas. Freeman allows that the sheets of receptors in the nose and at the initial input to the olfactory bulb are feature detectors that refine sensory input, but they do not constitute perception. Importantly, the raw sensory data recorded in these sheets is "washed out," not transmitted as such (though it can be "recovered" if the need arises before too long an interval). Stimuli destabilize neuronal populations, causing them to construct patterns that express the *significance* of the stimuli to the animal based on its experience; it does *not* express the stimulus per se.[21]

The EEGs for a particular odorant indicate an attractor. Although different sniffs of the same odorant produce differences in EEG as great as do different odors, the spatial patterns of EEG for a given odorant are similar, as remarked above. Each inhalation causes a burst of bulbar activity. Although each EEG tracing varies, a common waveform or carrier wave is embedded in the tracings, and the identity of the odorant is reliably identified in the bulbwide spatial pattern of the carrier wave amplitude. The aperiodic common carrier wave is everywhere in the bulb. It occurs not only during bursts but also between bursts, when there is no extractable stimulus. "The carrier wave is not imposed from outside the olfactory system by the receptors or by other parts of the brain. It emerges as a cooperative activity that is self-organized by the neural masses." (Freeman 1992, p. 468) As earlier noted, this lack of external driving of the activity is what indicates that it is self-organized; it is characteristic of chaotic systems.

The varying set of different receptor cells in the nose that cause the global activity in the olfactory bulb to exhibit this spatial pattern is its basin of attraction. Thus, one attractor can be entered from a variety of starting points. I emphasize that the particular array of receptor cells excited varies considerably from one sniff to another, even when of the same odorant, but each odorant has its own attractor and basin. Input to the basal chaotic attractor causes a burst to the appropriate chaotic attractor for the input. To Freeman, chaos is essential, as it is the only way to account for the observed rapid shifts from one brain state to another.[22]

According to Freeman, the general dynamics of perception is as follows. The brain seeks information by directing an individual to sense. Self-organizing activity in the limbic system directs the search by transmitting a search command to the motor systems and simultaneously sends what is called a reafference message to the sensory systems. The reafference message directs the sensory systems to prepare to respond to new information. The sensory systems strongly respond with a burst, every neuron in a given region participating in a collective activity. The resulting synchronous activity from these systems is then transmitted back to the limbic system, where they are combined and form what Freeman calls a 'gestalt'. In a fraction of a second, the process repeats. Freeman concludes: " . . . an act of perception is not the copying of an incoming stimulus. It is a step in a trajectory by which brains grow, reorganize themselves and reach into their environment to change it to their own advantage." (1991, p. 85)

Generalizing on some earlier work of others (Helmholtz, von Holst, Mittlestadt, Sperry), Freeman sees all goal-directed movement as initiated by the limbic system, with the entorhinal cortex playing a central role. All sensory systems converge in the entorhinal cortex, and the entorhinal cortex is involved in memory and emotion. It was already noted that the pattern of the burst activity associated with a sniff was a function of experience and did not correlate with the external stimulus itself. What all this suggests is that the experience that shapes the burst activity is not simply a recording of what has happened, but includes its emotional value or significance to the animal based upon its particular history.

This is of special note, since one would expect that the significance of the smell of a fox would be different for a rabbit and a dog; for the one, memories of chase and fear, for the other, food and expectation of a meal. According to Freeman, the bursts correlated with such smells are unique to the individual. It is a commonplace that one's emotions (based on one's past experiences) can affect one's perceptions and thoughts. Remarkably, the model of perception provided by Freeman would seem to provide some neurological basis for such a commonplace, as the reafferent messages transmitted to the sensory cortex from the entorhinal cortex apparently reflect the significance of the stimulus to the particular animal based on its peculiar experience.

Concluding Remarks

I argued above that a new paradigm of brain science is needed to close the explanatory gap. I argued that what was important in the new science is its *particular* structure and dynamics. I illustrated this in my recommendation of an analogy that provides a model of what we need to close the explanatory gap. We saw that the *particular* structure and dynamics must be such that they can make *comprehensible to us* how the interaction of certain elements and their properties can give rise to radically new and different properties.

The new science that appears to provide a basis for closing the explanatory gap between qualitatively different mental and brain states is that of chaos theory applied to brain activity. The new *particular* feature that this theory provides, and which is unique to it, is presented above as (*). We found yet another special feature of this theory, (**), which may well provide the basis to make comprehensible to us how there can be mental causation. Based on how the molecule/liquid analogy turned out, we expected and hoped that arcane knowledge of the new theory would not be required to make comprehensible to us how it can resolve the conundrums we face. Apparently, our hopes and expectations in this regard have been fulfilled. We may take further gratification in the fact that not only does chaos theory do all this at a rather abstract level, but also it already has been successfully applied to empirical questions of brain activity and perception.

I stand by arguments for what is needed to close the explanatory gap and why. I stand by arguments that chaos theory has a distinctive feature, (*), that can do what is required, as well as having a feature, (**), that can make plausible to us how there could be mental/physical causation. I know of no other theory that provides the requisite features. If the brain is not chaotic, and there are no other mathematical theories which have analogues to (*) and (**), then perhaps the mysterians are right. For, to my lights, without a theory that has such features, the conundrums of the explanatory gap and mental/physical causation appear unsolvable. Is brain dynamics chaotic? I do not know. While there appears to be some evidence that in some of its manifestations it is, it is probably too soon for an unqualified answer; moreover, the answer is best left to the brain scientists to determine.

There are, however, two general criticisms of a dynamical system approach to the brain that I now address. One alleges that this approach merely re-describes brain activity without explaining it. Without getting into the details of this criticism, it is easy to see that whatever merit such criticism might have is totally eclipsed by the possibility that such an approach provides the logical scaffolding for solving the problems of the explanatory gap and mental causation, as I have argued it does.

Others have criticized the application of chaos theory to brain activity because unlike, say, computational models, there is no clear or significant place for representations in chaotic dynamics, and it is a widely held assumption that representations (both conscious and unconscious) play a pervasive role in cognition. In the next chapter I will attempt to dispel this concern by arguing that there simply are no unconscious representations, though many take them for granted. (Undoubtedly, some will think that this "cure" is worse than the "disease.") My thesis is that *representations play a role only when conscious thoughts or perceptions are operative*. This is argued for independent of chaos theory, but my thesis is reinforced by it. Where genuine representations are operative, I hypothesize that they are manifested as bursts to attractor states. Such burst states constrain the firing of individual neurons in a top-down fashion; this is a manifestation of feature (**). Furthermore, we know that these bursts are self-organized and are not driven by external stimulation. By feature (*), we may expect that the resulting burst states are significantly different from their antecedent states ("unconscious representations"). This is exactly what we should expect if only conscious states are representational, and it undermines the second objection to the application of chaos theory to the brain.

Appendix

A general and brief explanation of some of the central concepts of chaos theory is here provided for the convenience of the reader. The relevant form of chaos is deterministic as opposed to entropic. Entropic chaos simply moves to increasing disorder, there are no emerging patterns of activity in the system. It is in accord with the ordinary understanding of 'chaos'. Where there is deterministic chaos, similar patterns appear and disappear periodically in the dynamical activity of a system, but they do so with a complexity that makes it difficult to detect and, therefore, appear to be entropic. The complexity is due to the iterative nature of the equations governing the behavior. In iterative equations, the outcome of each computation is the input for the next computation. A characteristic feature of chaotic systems is that very slight differences in the starting point or weak input can lead to huge differences in eventual outcome. This extreme sensitivity to initial conditions is referred to as the "butterfly effect." This results in the extraordinary feature that the outcomes are not predictable, even though the equations are often quite simple and deterministic.[23]

The last statement sounds contradictory. I think the idea that resolves this is that we are precluded from an *exact* measurement of the input, and since the minutest differences in input can make for radically different predicted outcomes, the outcome cannot "in principle" be predicted. This is in contrast to non-chaotic systems, where predicted results are not as sensitive to the exact input. In the latter systems, all that is required is "exactness" up to a certain degree of accuracy, since any accuracy beyond that will not make any difference in the predicted result.[24]

A central concept in chaos theory is that of a *strange attractor*. When a dynamical system settles into a certain pattern, that pattern is known as an attractor; there are several kinds of attractors. The simplest attractor is the *single-point attractor*. The point at which a pendulum subject to friction eventually stops typically illustrates it. When a pendulum is not subject to friction, it will continue in exactly the same pattern of motion forever. Such repeating patterns are known as *limit-cycle attractors*. There are a number of other kinds of attractors, which like the one just defined, continue to repeat the same pattern of motion. Earlier I stated that similar patterns are repeated in chaotic systems. The distinctive characteristic of these systems is that they *never* traverse the same path, unlike the ones just discussed, but the paths are similar and do trace recognizable patterns. Because of the uniqueness of each path, such patterns are known as *strange attractors*.

The set of initial values that terminate in an attractor is known as its *basin of attraction*. In chaotic systems, there are rapid *bursts* from one strange attractor to another and back to the basal state. These bursts are called *bifurcations*; they constitute significant phase transitions in the system. The transition from rest to walking, from walking to a trot or the shift from laminar flow to turbulence in fluid dynamics are all common illustrations of bifurcations.

5   Representation and the First-Person Perspective

A fundamental question that is rightfully receiving a great deal of attention in philosophy is how to give an account of the content of intentional states. It is impossible to ignore the concept of representation in any thorough attempt to provide an explanation of such content. Here are some of the questions regarding representation that I will examine in this chapter: How is it that contents of intentional states come to represent things to us? How can a physical token—be it a portion of a brain, a state of a nervous system, or some marks on paper—represent something else? What is required to determine which non-human creatures or devices have representational states? As has been my position in earlier chapters, I contend that answers to these and related questions must be informed by a first-person methodology.

Because representation also plays a central role in the study of both natural and artificial intelligence, the proper understanding of it is critical not only to philosophers but also to computer scientists, neurophysiologists, evolutionary biologists, and psychologists. There may well be no univocal notion of either representation or intelligence employed throughout (or within) these diverse investigations. Perhaps this is as it should be. If this is so, the different concepts must be made explicit to avoid equivocation. In any case, it is imperative that we isolate the concept of representation implicated in human cognition and behavior before we attempt to decide which non-human systems have *similar* representational states.[1] We must not utilize an equivocal concept of representation. Nor should we simply exploit a concept of representation, instances of which may be found in many species but which has not yet been demonstrated to be the operative concept of representation in the human performance of intelligent tasks.

Not many agree with this restrictive approach to representation. For example, long ago Daniel Dennett (1978, p. 91), after listing a wide variety

of things that he said represented (words, thoughts, thinkers, pictures, com-
puters, animals, sentences, mechanisms, states, functions, nerve impulses,
formal models), went on to say this: "It will not do to divide and conquer
here. . . . What is important is that there is something that binds them all
together, and we need a theory that can unify the variety." Later (1987, p.
5) Dennett explicitly rejected the idea that the first-person perspective is apt
for the development of such a theory: "I declare my starting point to be the
objective, materialistic, third-person world of the physical sciences."
Dennett correctly characterized this as "the orthodox choice today in the
English-speaking philosophical world." It is still the orthodoxy. Such a
wide-ranging theory as Dennett envisions[2] might be interesting in its own
right, but there is a definite risk that it would leave out what is distinctive
about *human* representational states. In view of the inadequacies of a
strictly third-person methodology for a study of mind that I detailed in
previous chapters, this risk is unacceptable.

The present chapter further advances the indispensable role of a first-
person methodology in the study of mind, for in it I demonstrate that minimal content is crucial in the analysis of representation in humans. I argue
that some of the items that Dennett and others (Patricia and Paul
Churchland, Fred Dretske, and Ruth Millikan, to name a few) would list
among the things that represent are more usefully classed as something
short of representation—something I will distinguish later as *information-
bearing states*. I give several arguments as to why the orthodox choice of
an exclusively third-person methodology must be abandoned to achieve an
adequate understanding of representation. Specifically, I show that an adequate theory of representation must do the following:

1. satisfy the *particularity requirement*
2. distinguish *representers* from *information bearers*
3. account for the *fundamental fact of representation*.

The emphasized concepts are explained and defended. I argue that the
orthodox methodology lacks the resources to do any of 1–3, but a new
theory of representation that I argue for that depends on the concept of
minimal content does satisfy these requirements. Thus, I am at odds with
many, if not most, contemporary philosophers and cognitive scientists,
both with regard to the theory I advance and with regard to the methodology adopted.

Others have emphasized the importance of the first-person perspective, but I use it to make several new points, notably the introduction of my central concept of *minimal content* and the resulting recognition of *the fundamental intentional state* (chapter 1). I now advance a methodological principle: *methodological chauvinism* that implements the first-person perspective. The expanded methodology enables a unique fact to be exposed: what I have called the *fundamental fact of representation*. If I am right about all this, no strictly third-person methodology can be adequate for the study of mind or representation and, importantly, consciousness is necessary for representation; indeed, I argue that there are no unconscious beliefs or representations.

The arguments presented in this chapter and in other chapters demonstrate the systematic failure of exclusively third-person approaches to a philosophical theory of mind. This is shown by examining some particular exclusively third-person approaches to representation and showing that they fail to accommodate the above requirements.[3] The failures of these arguments do not depend on details of the particular theories; they have to do with failure of those theories to accommodate the first-person perspective. Finally, I argue that the methodology I adopt is neither unscientific nor anthropomorphic, despite its employment of the first-person perspective. Ironically, it is the exclusive use of the third-person perspective that leads to anthropomorphism in the study of representation and of the mind.

Methodological Chauvinism

An organism or an artificial system may move in such a way that, when viewed from a third-person perspective, it would appear that it must have representational states. Nevertheless, as far as the entity itself is concerned, the idea of representation may be completely idle in giving an account of what has transpired. The subject in question may have so moved simply because of the way some part was causally connected to other parts of the subject.[4] If we assume that there are both genuine and merely apparent representational states, we are forced to ask how we may correctly distinguish them. These epistemological questions need have no bearing on the problem as to what is required for an entity to have a representational state; still, until we are able to say in virtue of what feature, or features, we do have representational states, we must respect this epistemological point by exercising restraint in the attribution of representational states to non-humans. Indeed my suggestion is that the point be raised to the status of a methodological principle.

Ideally a demarcation between genuine and apparent representational states would be determined through specification of the necessary and sufficient conditions for each. Unfortunately, it is not even known whether there is a single set of such conditions for representational states, much less what they are. Typically, some prominent feature of our representational states (e.g., certain causal, functional, or computational relations) is selected. When these features are found in various non-human entities and they exhibit certain relevant behaviors, they are alleged to have representational states on that basis. When different features are posited and different extensions of entities having representational states are thus determined, arguments ensue. Such debates typically involve each party accusing the other of begging the question. For example, Zenon Pylyshyn, in the context of discussing Searle's famous Chinese Room, offers by way of criticism the following:

> . . . we cannot take as sacred anyone's intuitions about such things or whether another creature has intentionality—especially when such intuitions rest (as Searle's do, by his own admission) on knowing what the creature (or machine) is *made of.* . . . Clearly, intuitions based on nothing but such anthropocentric chauvinism cannot form the foundations of a science of cognition. (1980, p. 443)

Such a charge is double-edged, however. It is no more legitimate to hold that a non-human being *has* intentional or representational states because it has Z, where the value of Z may be a certain computational structure (Pylyshyn's favored feature), or whatever, until it is established that we have intentional or representational states *because* of Z than it is to rely on intuitions about other non-humans' states based on what they are made of. Our merely having Z, even when Z is a plausible candidate for why we have intentional or representational states, is not sufficient reason to attribute those states to a non-human because it has Z. I will turn to where charges of anthropomorphism are properly directed in the last section of this chapter.

Despite widely differing intuitions as to what is central to a representational state, there are pertinent matters agreed upon by virtually all parties. It behooves us to exploit these points of agreement in the development of any theory of representation. They are as follows:

(1)   There is a fundamental and almost universal agreement that humans have representational states, whatever they consist in.

(2)   There is a fundamental and universal ignorance as to what exactly it is in virtue of that humans have them.

(3)   There are wildly divergent views as to what else has them.

We may capture these points of agreement in a principle that I call *methodological chauvinism*: The foundation for the development of any theory of representation should use a restricted database consisting of elements established from the first-person perspective to be representations or representational states.

The restriction imposed by this principle is justified because any theory of representation must account for the clear cases—our representational states. Furthermore, any instances initially excluded are not, thereby, forever consigned as non-representational. Any genuine cases of representational states among them are ones that will eventually be accounted for by a theory of representation developed from the restricted database. It is, if you will, a conservative principle of safety, one least likely to lead us astray, however great our initial ignorance of what constitutes a representation or representational state. The worst that would happen is that any genuine cases of representations that are initially excluded by the principle would be delayed in their inclusion among the representational.

In marked contrast, the current prevalent procedures violate methodological chauvinism and, as a result, lead to potential dead ends. To see this, suppose a kind of entity is initially included among those clearly having representational states (humans) because they (certain non-human kinds) have some features assumed to be sufficient for our having representational states. Suppose further that the features in question are not sufficient, and entities of that kind do not in fact have representational states of the sort that we do. This erroneous, yet possible, inclusion of such entities in the initial database will, at the very least, produce serious distortions in the developing theory. More probably, such inclusion will result in something other than a theory of representation, since it accommodates entities that (by hypothesis) do not have representational states. The prevalent and competing methodology allows, if it does not encourage, just such erroneous or distorting results. (Compare Dennett's remarks quoted above.)

One might object that the restricted data set endorsed by methodological chauvinism could just as well lead us astray. One might think that just this kind of distortion would have occurred had the early Newtonians adopted my principle and argued that the data for the laws of motions should be restricted to that of medium-size objects moving at moderate velocities; after all, the early Newtonians might have continued, "any theory of mechanics must explain at least the motions of these central objects." Of course, this procedure would have been confounded on learning that the very small, very large, and very fast do not behave in accordance with the Newtonian laws.[5] Well, surely there are no guarantees, still, applying the principle to representation is importantly disanalogous to mechanics and has an independent support for its application to representation.

First, a clarification, methodological chauvinism is not advanced as a methodological principle that should apply to all areas of investigation. As formulated above it is restricted to representation, and while it has more general application, to wit, to all those areas of investigation where there is a first-person perspective on the relevant domain, there is no reason to think that it should be relevant where that perspective is absent, e.g., mechanics. Thus, there is this crucial disanalogy between the cases of representation and mechanics vis à vis the methodological principle at issue. What distinguishes representation from most other areas, in particular mechanics, is the fact that we sometimes have a first-person perspective regarding our own representations.

There is also an important epistemic difference between the case of representation and that of mechanics. As I point out, there are serious and diverse disagreements regarding what other creatures or systems represent, or what enables it (as is illustrated by the Searle-Pylyshyn dispute, discussed above.) During the nineteenth century, there were no similar disagreements regarding the dynamics of the very large, the very small, or the very fast; there was unanimity in the belief that Newton's laws governed them all. Although they were wrong, Newton's successes and the lack of any reason (at the time) to think otherwise made it methodologically sound to proceed in this way. Regarding representation, we have nothing that comes close to being a generally accepted theory of it; moreover, we have severe disagreements on what counts as a genuine representation. Indeed, it just such radical divergences that speak to the advisability of the advocated principle: Not all these disputants can be right, so the more cautious approach endorsed by methodological chauvinism is fitting. Under such conditions, we should proceed from cases on which there is widespread agreement that they are genuine representations.

A further methodological point: If I am right about the indispensable role of the first-person perspective in the discussion of representation and the invisibility of minimal content from a third-person perspective, it has the important implication that *my interlocutor must at least temporarily adopt the first-person perspective in assessing my claims.* If I am right on these matters, my arguments in their support cannot even be comprehended unless this is done. This does not prejudge things in my favor; if I am wrong, such temporary adoption of the first-person perspective would prove innocuous, since it would be ultimately eliminable.

Representing Particular Things: The Particularity Requirement

What, then, accounts for the widespread agreement on the restricted database authorized by methodological chauvinism? The type of limited privileged access discussed in chapter 1 warrants the claim that, for some of our states, an individual is or can be aware that they are representational and that they represent not just something else but *something in particular* and *to that individual.*[6] Methodological chauvinism counsels that we base our investigation on such states. There are those who would doubt that either the conscious element or the first-person perspective implicit in all of this is necessary for being in a representational state. In this section I argue that consciousness is necessary to secure the particularity of a representation and that, whereas a strictly third-person methodology fails in this task, the incorporation of a first-person methodology via the concept of minimal content succeeds. Consequently, the capacity for consciousness is necessary for the capacity to secure the particularity of a representation and, hence, to represent.

Consider the fact that when an item represents something else—qua *that representation*—a *particular* object or state of affairs is represented. It would not be *that representation* if it did not have *that object.*[7] It is clear that a given physical item r, under the proper conditions, can represent something, say, t; yet it is equally clear that the same item r, under different conditions, can represent some other item, t', distinct from t. Few, if any, would maintain that any physical item—as such—*necessarily* represents some particular object or that it can represent *only* that object. (In speaking of a "physical item as such," I am speaking of a physical item examined from a strictly third-person perspective.) In short, no such physical item intrinsically represents some single particular thing. While this last point is obvious, one of its implications is not adequately appreciated: Since there is no necessary connection between a physical item serving as a representation and that which it represents, *if the representation is to do its job*, there must not only be a represented item, somehow *the uniqueness of what is represented must be secured.*

If a third-person methodologist were to demonstrate that there are physical structures that, as such, intrinsically represent, then much of what I have argued for would be refuted. Although much work has been devoted to how the content of representational state is determined, the question whether such accounts *uniquely* determine, hence, whether they provide for the particularity requirement, is typically ignored. David Armstrong is an exception; he not only recognized the need, he attempted to address this issue of particularity or uniqueness via the concept of intrinsic power to represent[8]:

Beliefs are to be thought of as maps which carry their interpretation of reality within themselves. Of their own nature, apart from any conventions of interpretation, they point to the existence of a certain state of affairs (though there may be no such state of affairs). They have an intrinsic power of representation. (1973, p. 4)

Armstrong tells us that this "intrinsic power of representation" consists in "the self-directedness of belief—and thought—states" (ibid., p. 54). After he distinguishes ideas from concepts and each of these into simple and complex, he puts the burden of self-directedness on simple concepts. Self-directedness is then explained by the claim that simple concepts have "certain sorts of selective capacity towards things that fall under the concept in question" (6).[9]

Armstrong was aware of the need to secure the uniqueness of representation. The fact is that Armstrong only tells us that these concepts *must be* self-directed—so that they may have an "intrinsic power of representation"—without telling how they possibly could be self-directed. At best his account of how these concepts can be self-directed takes refuge in some sort of ostension.[10] Surely this will not help; Wittgenstein and Quine have taught us that ostension is not adequate to secure unique reference. Furthermore, if this ostension is now to be some capacity of a simple concept or some inner state, a physicalist account of how this capacity could be realized is crucial to a physicalist and to Armstrong in particular, since he introduces it, in large part, to avoid Brentano's explanation of the directedness of, say, belief states in terms of an irreducible non-physical character of intentionality. (See Armstrong 1973, pp. 54, 68.) Armstrong fails to address this, and to my knowledge no one else has addressed it.

In claiming that the physicalist is unable to provide an account of the particularity requirement, intrinsic representation, I do not mean 'physicalist' in the sense developed in chapter 4; I am a physicalist in that sense. My remarks are directed to the typical physicalist who restricts herself to a strictly third-person methodology. The issue is not a difficulty in understanding what is meant by 'intrinsic representation' or whether such representations exist; rather, it is a question whether a strictly third-person methodology has the resources to provide for them. According to me, it does not: Any explanation of the directedness of intentional states requires inclusion of a first-person methodology.

The problems with a strictly third-person methodology securing a particular thing represented were already manifested in the discussion of theorists A–D (and other examples) in chapters 1 and 2. We saw that neither the symbols nor the inferential roles they shared with one another were sufficient for them to intrinsically represent, to fix a particular object as the subject of a thought. In contrast, the individual is able to constitute this by having and being directly aware of her minimal content. From the individual's point of view there is no problem knowing what in particular is represented. The symbols represented numbers or sets for each theorist, D having the ability to switch back and forth without any overt sign that she did so. In effect, each was operating with a particular mapping,[11] one that was known without inference by the agent through her asymmetrical awareness of her minimal content. Matters are completely different from a third-person perspective, where the available evidence is compatible with attributions of various objective contents. What has been said of symbols is with equal justification said of brain states.

Any explanation of the directedness of intentional states or that they have a unique referent requires inclusion of a first-person methodology.[12] The obstacles to satisfying the particularity requirement do not obtain on this expanded methodology. For example, the problems with ostension, mentioned above, result from attempts to determine the object of *another's* ostended object, *not one's own*. (See chapter 8.) An individual is able to determine one's own ostended object—as she conceives it—from her first-person perspective. From the individual's point of view, at least sometimes, there is no problem in knowing what in particular is represented in the sense of minimal content—as this is constituted by that very act of representation on the part of the agent. But it is the agent not, say, the concept itself (as Armstrong would have it), that secures the uniqueness of the representation (again, in the sense of its minimal content).

One might deny that it is the agent that determines which object is represented or which mapping is operative, hence, what is represented, and suggest instead that it is the physical item's (r's) *functional role* or the *purpose* to which it is put that determines the relevant mapping. One might argue further that this can be established apart from the agent as such, and that such matters as these are totally manageable from the third-person perspective. My response, argued for in chapter 2 (and more on this below), is that if r has one functional role, it has many, and if it has one purpose, it has many. Thus, individuation or specification of the roles or purposes is a process that does not in itself lead to a unique result, but every case of actual representation is a representation of *one*, not many different possible represented objects, events, or states of affairs.[13] Theorists using the same formal theory, manipulating the same symbols in the same way, could have as their minimal content numbers or sets, and it was argued that the functionalist cannot accommodate the limited privileged access the agent has to her particular content (chapter 2). So an appeal to purpose or functional role can neither determine the operative mapping nor what *in particular* is represented.

The Constituting of Minimal Content as It Relates to Representation

On my theory, it is through a direct act that the agent grasps what the subject of her thought is, her minimal content, and *it is constitutive of that thought that it be of that very object represented by her minimal content*. It is this that provides (though, clearly, not by this alone) for the uniqueness of what is represented by the physical item, be it symbol or brain state. When so engaged, theorist A could be explicitly or implicitly aware that she was proving theorems about numbers. Either way she was operating with a particular mapping that determined what objects she thought her statements were about. Similarly for theorist B, though for her the mapping was to sets, not numbers. A physical token of a type, say 3, represented some particular object, either a certain number or a certain set, depending on whether theorist A or theorist B was operating with that physical token. Theorist D could switch from one to the other at will.

Could a given item be mapped to a different object than the agent intends? Most assuredly, as the discussion in chapter 1 clearly demonstrates. Could the agent, therefore, be wrong in her determination of what is represented? No. Not only is error ruled out; as above in the discussion of minimal content, *it does not even make sense to talk of error here*. The agent's particular implementation, explicitly or implicitly, of a mapping is *partly constitutive of that particular act of representation*. I hasten to add that in holding that the agent cannot be wrong as to which mapping or object is intended, *I do not mean that she cannot be wrong in how she represents the world*. (Her minimal content may not match the relevant objective content.) What she cannot be mistaken about, at least in simple cases, is *which* object her minimal content represents. She certainly can be wrong as to whether the employed representation is an accurate representation of the relevant part of the world.

So the determination of a minimal content or a mapping is ultimately based on the actions of some agent. No matter whether the agent explicitly considers and selects the mapping or, as is typical, just tacitly operates with it. What is essential is that the agent was at one time aware of the mapping or what particular was represented by some item or symbol she employed, not that she be conscious of this whenever she uses the item. In saying this is achieved by the agent, I am not saying that this is always a private conscious act done in total isolation; nor need the agent *always* be a conscious of the mapping whenever she uses the representation; nor is it an act that is generally carried out independent of various conventions operative in the agent's community. The agent may select or operate with mappings in violation of her community's conventions, but typically she will not. When she explicitly does do so without putting her audience on proper notice, she will be undoubtedly and deservedly misunderstood. In these matters it is more typical that deviations from community norms are based upon the agent's ignorance, however.[14]

What does the implementation of a mapping by the agent consist in? The idea of privileged awareness of one's minimal content was explored and developed in chapters 1 and 2. Here I am developing a consequence of that. Since there are cases where what is represented by an item is in part *constituted* by the agent to whom this item is a representation, and the agent can have non-inferential knowledge of this, there is a kind of non-inferential "grasping" on the part of the thinker as to what she intends to represent and, thus, if only implicitly, of the relevant mapping too. The basis for this grasping and how it is an improvement over Frege's use of that expression was also discussed in chapter 1.What is of great importance is the fact that minimal contents are unabashedly subjective—*they are constituted by the individual thinker.* That *we constitute* our minimal contents makes the idea of "grasping" them readily intelligible. From the first-person perspective, it is constitutive of my entertaining some particular thought that it has the minimal content that it does, that it represents what it does. It simply would be a different thought or a different representation, if it did not have the subject that I take it to have—it is an intrinsic representation.[15]

It is the fact that the agent subjectively constitutes her minimal content that secures the *particularity of the representation.* Since this is so *and* that there is an asymmetry between the agent and an observer of her regarding this subjective constitution explains why a theory of representation restricted to a third-person methodology cannot satisfy the particularity requirement. Different particular items represented (say, numbers or sets) are equally warranted with this methodology.[16] The problem of multiply represented objects is an artifact of the reliance on a strictly third-person methodology. Abandoning this artificial restriction not only eliminates the non-uniqueness problem, a new point emerges: *The subjective constitution by an agent of her minimal content makes it a different and unique intentional state that is presupposed by all other intentional states.* This is the *fundamental intentional state,* introduced and argued for in chapter 1.

The Fundamental Fact of Representation

If, as I have argued, the constitution of minimal content is the fundamental intentional state, the particularity requirement must be satisfied, and third-person methodologies fail in the latter, then a plausible candidate (preliminary version) for a necessary condition on representation emerges:

For any item r to represent a particular item t, there must be an agent s *to whom* r represents t.

As just explained, the particularity problem is overcome when the agent s has the capacity to non-inferentially grasp her subjectively constituted particular minimal content. One's having this capacity is certainly sufficient to be a legitimate value of s and, thus, to be in a representational state in a robust sense. The proposed candidate for a necessary condition on representation also brings into prominence the third variable in the representation relation—r represents t *to s*—the "to whom" is essential. This raises two important questions: What kinds of entities are legitimate values of s? Must they be conscious to be a legitimate value of s? These questions are in effect questions as to what besides conscious humans can constitute minimal content.

Humans clearly do have the capacity to represent, though exactly what enables it is far from evident. *That* we can represent particular objects is evident from our conscious first-person perspective. Here we see the connection between the capacity to have this perspective and the third variable in the representation relation: the complete confidence that we are representers derives from our first-person recognition that on some occasions we are legitimate values of the third variable. I can be aware that some vehicle of representation r represents some particular t to me. When this capacity is present it is clearly sufficient to represent a particular object, and there is no reason to doubt that representational states in a robust sense are manifested. Furthermore, given the failure (to date) of a strictly third-person methodology to account for uniqueness in representation, unless conditions other than the limited consciousness I have argued for can be shown to be sufficient, then this capacity is also necessary.

Are there other sufficient conditions for uniqueness of representation exclusive of consciousness? Perhaps, but it is clear that where consciousness does not exist, or is not known to exist, controversy prevails as to whether various other features which do obtain are sufficient for the entity to represent, to be a value of the third variable; hence, there is controversy as to whether representational states are instantiated. (Compare what was said above of Pylyshyn's criticism of Searle.) This is precisely why the principle of methodological chauvinism is advanced. Given the history of discussions of representation, establishing that there are sufficient conditions exclusive of consciousness in a non-contentious way is at best a formidable task. Doing this in a way that also satisfies the particularity requirement appears to be impossible. If there is no set of conditions sufficient for representation that does not include consciousness, then consciousness is necessary for representation.

Thus, anyone who would deny that consciousness and the first-person perspective (in any form) are necessary for representation has a substantial additional burden. Any candidate for a representational state such a person proposes will either be a state of a human or not. If it is a state of a human, one must show that consciousness is not necessary to solve the particularity problem. If it is a state of a non-human, it is conscious or not. If it is conscious, one must address the same problem as in our case: One must show that the consciousness of that being is not necessary for its representational states. On the other hand, if the being is not conscious, one must show that some feature of that being is sufficient for representational states. Before one embarks on this task, however, a prior question must be answered (given methodological chauvinism): "*Does* the non-conscious being even have representational states?" One cannot rely on the claim that it is evident that the state is representational, for the cases are in dispute.[17] No one has established with the same degree of certainty, certainly not with widespread support, that there are other conditions that are themselves sufficient for representation, sufficient to secure the particularity of the representation, while avoiding an appeal to consciousness. Until this is done, the claim that the non-conscious being has representational states is not warranted.

Methodological chauvinism counsels the exclusion of any such other conditions until they have been independently established. This would be achieved if starting from our unquestionable representational states we were to determine that what makes them representational is independent of our consciousness. Then we could safely say of non-humans who had that feature that they had representational states, regardless of whether they were conscious or not. No such other conditions have been successfully advanced, though there have been extensive efforts. Add to this the difficulty (impossibility?) of satisfying the particularity requirement without consciousness, and we have, at the very least, strong inductive ground for holding that consciousness is a necessary condition for having representational states, as well as being sufficient. So, what was introduced as a candidate for a necessary condition on representation should be strengthened to include consciousness:

For any item r to represent a particular item t, there must be a *conscious* agent s *to whom* r represents t.

I call this the *fundamental fact of representation.*

The above certainly does not amount to a complete theory of representation. It is not intended to be one. I do wish to emphasize how consciousness via the first-person perspective informs us as to some salient and uncontroversial points that any theory of representation must accommodate. In particular, it highlights the importance of the third variable in the representation relation, that variable's relation to the first-person perspective, and a role that consciousness plays in satisfying the particularity requirement. The importance of the first-person perspective is often obscured by at least two facts. Frequently, perhaps typically, we use an item as representing something else (to ourselves, as well as others) without explicitly thinking that it is a representation or considering the operative mapping. Generally, these facts are tacitly understood—for example, when we sketch a map to provide someone with directions. The suppression of the third variable and the lack of any explicit appeal to consciousness in such cases is harmless, for there is no uncertainty that they are operative, and it is easy to make them explicit.

Another more insidious source of obstruction results from a systematic ambiguity in the expression "an item r represents t." Suppose that an entity, s, contains an item r which is adapted to some end, and that t is represented by r to some s' other than s, e.g., a human observer of s. In such situations there can be a quick slide to talk of representational states of s rather than s'. Clearly such situations do not warrant the claim that r (or, for that matter, anything else) represents t to s, even if it does to s'. Thus, potential values of the third variable may be conflated so as to misleadingly suggest that s has representational states, when possibly it is only the human observer of s, s', that has them.

Yet another consequence of the recognition of the importance of the third variable is that expressions such as "r represents t," "r is a representation," or "s is in a representational state" are incomplete in themselves. To even be meaningful, they must be implicit variants of "r represents t to s." (A fuller analysis of representation requires a fourth variable for context or circumstances: r represents t to s in circumstances u, but it is the crucially ignored third variable that is relevant here.) If the values of the missing variables are not obtainable from the context, one has not managed to assert anything at all.

Information Bearers Contrasted with Genuine Representers

Problems concerning the attributions of representational states just discussed result from ignoring the third variable in the representation relation and the neglect of the first-person perspective. These problems are exacerbated by a frequent implicit identification of *information bearers* with *representers*. It is a natural consequence of a faulty methodology; one that exclusively employs a third-person perspective, for this methodology lacks the resources to make the distinction, and the difference between the two is altogether invisible from that perspective. Failure to take pains to distinguish them has led to serious and deep distortions in the philosophy of mind. To see why, I first state what is meant by *information bearer*:

If a given property P of a system covaries with some other property P' and the covariance is not random, then the system bears information pertaining to P'.[18]

Given any information-bearing system and our third-person perspective on it, we can always take items in that system to represent other items, simply because we are representers. Under such conditions, we are the values of the third variable; this is certainly not an adequate basis for attributing representational states (in the same sense that we have them) to the information bearer itself. It is possible that the particular information bearer cannot be a value of the third variable, thus, has no representational system and no representational states.

Surely it should be granted that various information-bearing organisms are able to behave appropriately as a function of the information they bear. We also frequently bear information without it representing anything to ourselves, as is the case with many (most) of our physiological states, e.g., when the informational content produced by, say, over-drinking results in vomiting. No one doubts that we too are reliable information bearers. Given the kind of creatures we are, however, *that information can come to represent something to us*. But it is wrong to infer that other kinds of entities have the capacity to represent in this way simply because they are information bearers. It is misleading to speak of them as having representational states, if all we mean is that they are information bearers and certain informational items in them represent other things *to us*. On the other hand, even if a system is a representer, is a proper value of the third variable, we cannot maintain that it is simply because it is an information bearer. Nor can we maintain that certain informational states of a system are representational states simply because it is known that the system is *capable* of having genuine representational states. That a being has this capacity is not sufficient to say that some particular information-bearing state of it is representational—to it.

I now discuss some examples to clarify the distinction between representing and information bearing and the points just made. The first example shows that some of the problems I have indicated are not just operative when dealing with non-human systems. Because these problems also apply to us even though we are clear cases of representers, it is all the more crucial that we ascertain in virtue of what we are able to represent before willy-nilly attributing representational states to non-human systems or creatures—i.e., that we must apply the principle of methodological chauvinism.

The hot coffee that is now in my stomach most assuredly has caused me to have a certain brain state that bears certain information regarding the contents of my stomach. Suppose a neurophysiologist identifies that state and its informational content. She can also take my state, or its informational content, to represent *to her* (she is the value of the third variable) the following: Hot coffee in his (i.e., my) stomach. In such circumstances, the informational content embedded in my brain state *becomes* representational *to the neurophysiologist* through her actions. Still, it represents nothing *to me*, even though it bears information as to the contents of my stomach. (Similarly, her examination of my informational content will cause her brain state to have some distinct informational content but, *as such*, it represents nothing to her. Of course her informational content can become an object of attention,[19] and thereby represent something else to whoever has attended to it, just as mine has for the neurophysiologist.) No doubt the neurophysiologist is justified in making the general claim that anyone in that particular state, with its particular informational content, probably has hot coffee in his stomach. What she certainly is *not justified* in saying is that *that very informational content represents to the one having it*—the one in whom it resides—hot coffee in his own stomach.

A similar generalization to the one just given applies to non-human cases. For example, a snake's pit organ responds only if there is a warm object moving nearby, and information from that organ is sent to the optic tectum. In the tectum there is an integration of visual and infrared information

(Churchland and Churchland 1983, p. 16). It is very likely to be true that a snake is in proximity to a moving warm-blooded object, if it is in the indicated state that results from the integration of the visual and infrared information. That the snake has this informational content in no way warrants the claim that it represents *to the snake*: warm, moving object. Here is why. While there is no doubt that we are genuine representers, one may doubt that snakes are. Yet, since the informational content that resulted from my drinking hot coffee represents nothing *to me*, there certainly is no reason to think that the indicated snake's informational content, as such, represents anything *to it*.

Importantly, this result obtains even if in fact snakes are proper values of the third variable, even if they are genuine representers and not merely information bearers. We are similar to the snakes in this respect. Both snakes and humans often bear information that represents nothing to either us or to the snakes (which is not to deny that it may play an important causal role in the production of relevant behavior). Yet, there is an important difference between what is known and how in the cases of snakes and humans. From our first-person perspective we know that there are (other) items than these that can and do represent other things to us (even our own informational states can become representational to us, if we take appropriate actions). We can never—*in the same way*—know that this holds for snakes, or other non-human systems. So any temptation to make the inference that other types of organisms have representational systems on the basis that some item plays an informational role in their survival and it represents something to us must be resisted. (A similar argument would establish the same conclusion with 'causal' replacing 'informational'.) We know this because many such items occur in us and, yet, represent nothing to us.

Because the point is important, I consider schemata of two types of cases to elucidate the difference between mere information-bearing states and genuinely representational states manifested in humans.

Case 1:   Suppose a human subject, S, desires that a certain state of affairs, P, obtain. S, therefore, undertakes various behaviors, B, that S believes will contribute to the realization of P. (For example, having this book published is, at the time of writing, an unrealized goal. I represent that state of affairs to myself and undertake various activities to realize it.) An unrealized end cannot itself be the cause of the agent's behavior, insofar as it is non-existent in the causal order. Not many years ago, philosophers worried how some future end could cause some motion now. A solution to this problem is obtained by abandoning the idea that the behavior is caused by an unrealized end and holding that it is the current desire for the end, realized somehow in the agent, that plays the relevant causal role. But for such a proposal to succeed, it is necessary that the agent *represent* the desired end (the non-existent state of affairs P), and he must represent it *to himself*.

I fail to see how anything but a conscious being could "represent" a non-existent state of affairs. We cannot fall back on the concept of information bearing, as it would be most magical that a being could simply bear information regarding a desired non-existent state of affairs. Certainly no causal relation could exist between the agent's states and a non-existent state of affairs. Thus, in such situations, *what is represented must be manifest to S if S is to undertake various behaviors in order* to help produce P. The conclusion is inescapable: S must be conscious of what is represented.

Case 2: Consider again a human subject S, but suppose that various occurrent stimuli cause S to be in certain states or cause certain events of processes to occur in S, and that these in turn cause S to undergo various motions M. (I speak of motions rather than behaviors or actions in order to exclude any suggestion of mentality.) Once again, suppose that it happens that the motions M contribute in a significant way to the production of some state of affairs P. We may even suppose that P contributes to S's survival. If this is the whole of the relevant account (so far as S is concerned) of the production of P, then there is no reason to say that anything was represented *to* S. Under such circumstances, it also would be wrong to say that S has the particular desire that P be realized. S could not have had that desire, because P was a non-existent state of affairs and, though there were states of S that contributed to the eventual production of P, none of those states represented P, certainly not *to* S; they simply eventuated in P's actualization. Certainly, S is not conscious of a representation of P.

It is important to realize that the significant differences in cases 1 and 2 *can only be recognized from the first-person perspective;* they are *invisible* from the third-person perspective. But the differences here are not only grounds for distinguishing kinds of "representational" states; they are also grounds for distinguishing kinds of "purposive" activity, since having a representational state is a necessary condition for engaging in purposive activity. To repeat: One cannot act to bring about a non-existent state of affairs without having some existent representation of it, and *one cannot deliberately act* to bring about *that* non-existent state of affairs unless that *particular* state of affairs is represented (the particularity requirement is satisfied) and is represented *to the agent* (the agent is a legitimate value of the third variable in the representation relation). Thus, it would also be wrong to hold that, in situations like case 2, S undertook the motions M for the purpose of bringing about P, even if it appeared to be so from an objective third-person perspective. For this reason, the teleological component that is often added to various functionalist or naturalist accounts must be viewed with suspicion.[20] Given our first-person perspective, we know that *sometimes* we represent a non-existent state of affairs to ourselves, and that we undertake certain behaviors for the purpose of actualizing that represented (but non-existent) state of affairs. To have representational states and engage in purposive activity of the kind evidenced in case 1 requires the capacity for consciousness.

Representers, Information Bearers, and Methodological Chauvinism

We humans have representational systems and are proper values of the third variable; still, there are clearly occasions when we are not actual values. On those occasions, we fail to be in representational states (of the kind indicated in case 1) or to engage in the corresponding kind of purposeful activity; nevertheless, a strictly third-person perspective of these activities would suggest that there are representational states involved and that the motions are purposive even when neither is the case. Let no one think that the privacy of mental states is the issue here. Although there are certain epistemological problems pertaining to whether other humans, on a specific occasion, are proper values of the third variable, nothing I argue here gives any reason to doubt either that other humans have representational states or that they have as much (or as little) access to their own representational states as I have to my own. Nor do the questions I raise (such as whether certain motions of other types of entities are truly representational or purposeful) stem from some general skeptical position.[21] The point is simply that the difference between information bearing and representing is invisible from a strictly third-person perspective.

That we are unable to distinguish information bearing and representing from a strictly third-person perspective even when we know the subject is capable of representing, as is sometimes the case in humans, further exacerbates the difficulty of ascertaining when we may correctly attribute such states to non-human entities. For if we sometimes have difficulty discerning from a third-person perspective when representational states are operative in the activities of a human, whom we unquestionably know is capable of having representational states, then how can we possibly hope to discern representational states in non-human creatures or systems by relying on a strictly third-person perspective when we never have the privilege of the first-person perspective regarding the types of states those creatures or systems have and do not yet know in virtue of what it is that we have representational states? The grounds for maintaining that non-humans are *ever* proper values for the third variable in the representation relation are of necessity quite different from, and far more controversial than, the grounds for maintaining that we *sometimes* are. To know when to attribute such states to non-human creatures, we must first ascertain which of our *objective* features enable us to represent. If we were to identify such features, being objective, we could proceed to ascertain which non-human creatures have them and, therefore, are also representers and not merely information bearers. These are compelling reasons to adopt methodological chauvinism.

Given the above, we see once again that it is reasonable to withhold the status of representers from non-human information-bearing systems, at least until we dispel our ignorance as to what it is in virtue of that we do represent. Non-human candidates, such as snakes, *may* stand to all of their states the way we do to some of ours, viz., the ones that represent nothing to us, notwithstanding the fact that those states are information bearing and even may contribute to the creature's survival. Were that to be the case, they would not be genuine representers. I emphasize that I do not maintain that only humans have representational states. I do, however, maintain that we do not now know what objective feature enables this, and that until this is known we have no way of knowing what other creatures or systems represent.

It should be clear from earlier sections that consciousness is sufficient to satisfy the particularity requirement. It is our first-person perspective on some of our states that makes it unproblematic both that we are conscious and that we are capable of representing particular things. However, this perspective *does not reveal in virtue of what we are conscious and represent, only that we are and do.* Earlier I offered some reason to think that consciousness is not only sufficient but also necessary for robust representation. Should I turn out to be right about this, however, it would not by itself advance our understanding of which non-human beings represent, since we no more know what specific *objective* features enables consciousness than we do which enable representation. Our knowledge that we are conscious and represent derives from our first-person perspective on some of our own states. We obviously lack that way of knowing whether any other creature or system is conscious; moreover, the first-person perspective we enjoy regarding some of our own states does not itself reveal what objective feature enables it, and hence we are at a loss as to what to look for in other creatures or systems to determine whether they are conscious or represent. Until we know in virtue of what objective feature we are conscious or represent, we have no grounds for holding that various non-human creatures or systems are anything more than information bearing.[22] This is a main point of methodological chauvinism.

The third-person perspective in the study of representational states is of a piece with the attempt to obtain a theory for all manner of "representations" (as is manifested by Dennett's remarks quoted earlier). In response to my objections to this, an advocate of such an approach may protest that representation occurs in information-bearing states but that it is of a "simpler kind" than goes on in those cases that also involve a conscious element. That advocate might hold, for example, that paramecia do represent, it is just that their representations differ from ours in a number of ways.[23] Among the reasons this response is inadequate is that it encourages equivocation on the term 'representation'.

The fact is that all of nature's creatures are information bearers because we all are causally related to our environments. Certainly even thermostats and thermometers, which respond in a regular way to certain changes in their environments, are information bearers. Consider the simple case of a thermometer. While it is relatively easy to individuate the informational content in such systems, there is absolutely no temptation to hold that the states of such systems represent anything *to the system itself.* Of course, states of such systems may easily represent aspects of its environment *to us* (for example, the length of a column of alcohol in a glass tube represents a certain temperature of the ambient air to us), but it is sheer nonsense to say that that length represents anything *to the thermometer*. We are, but it is not, a possible value of the third variable. (Compare my discussion above as to the danger of conflating potential values for the third variable.) There certainly appear to be significant differences between how a thermometer "represents" and how we do it.[24]

No one questions whether humans, non-human animals, and even artifacts such as thermometers have in *some* common sense "representational states," say, that of informational states. But focusing on this common sense not only promotes obscurity, it misses an important point. The crucial question is this: Given the vast range of diverse information bearers, which among them are proper values of the third variable in the representation relation? For even if I am wrong in thinking that strictly informational states are not representational, there are tantalizing and difficult issues raised by the robust sense of representation that I advocate. For example, is it the "common" or the robust sense of representation that is operative in our performance of intelligent tasks? (Compare case 1 above.) What enables the robust sense? Which non-human entities, if any, are capable of possessing these more robust representational states. Studying the "common sense of representation" across beings does not touch these questions; indeed, it obscures them. But if we don't address them, we risk conflating representers and information bearers. If the difference is real, as I have argued it is, failing to distinguish them can only result in an impoverished, if not false, theory of mind, cognition, and representation.

Third-person views of representation violate methodological chauvinism; they thereby encourage the mistaken inference that a given entity has representational states because it bears information. These mistakes are abetted by the fact that third-person views ignore or inadequately treat the third variable in the representation relation. The failure to distinguish representation from information bearing is unacceptable.[25] To avoid confusion, it is better to withhold the application of the term 'representer' (and its variants) from entities not yet known to be legitimate values of the third variable in the representation relation, while allowing the application of the term 'information bearer'. If it were to be shown, contrary to my arguments, that the ability to be the value of the third variable does not, after all, involve anything distinctively different and important (viz., the capacity to have the first-person perspective) relative to the concept of representation from what is involved in the cases of information bearers, this discrimination would be unnecessary. In the meantime, at the very least, it must be acknowledged that there is at least an *appearance* that a system's capacity to be a possible value of the third variable and to be aware of its contents goes beyond its being simply an information bearer. This difference may be mere appearance, but until that is demonstrated it is an appearance that cannot be ignored. Should it turn out to be no more than a mere appearance, it still must be accounted for.[26]

The Churchlands: A Case Study

In this section I illustrate how one can unwittingly pursue the idea of information bearing and be deceived into thinking that one has thereby said something significant about representation.[27]

The Churchlands state the following:

> The brain is evidently a syntactic engine, for a neuron cannot know the distant causal ancestry or the distant causal destiny of its inputs and outputs. An activated neuron causes a creature to withdraw into its shell not because such activation represents the presence of a predator—though it may indeed represent this—but because that neuron is connected to the withdrawal muscles, and because its activation is of the kind that causes them to contract. (1983, p. 10)

I accept it as fact that the activated neurons' being connected appropriately is itself sufficient—apart from any representations as such—to produce certain movements conducive to the creature's survival. (Call such systems "hard-wired"; they are essentially of the type indicated in case 2 above and involve "representations," if at all, only as mere information bearers.) It is also evident that under such conditions the creature's movements will appear from a third-person perspective to be purposeful and to involve representational states. Precisely because of this appearance, doubt is raised as to when an entity's movements, which do contribute to its survival, are indicative of representational states in the robust sense that I advocate.

The quoted passage suggests that the Churchlands are sensitive to the distinction. I will show that they are not, and that what they do argue for is inconsistent with any such distinction. Moreover, their view does not have the resources to accommodate it. They typically take as a sufficient condition for the entity to have a representational system that it exhibits motion conducive to its survival, and so appears (from a third-person perspective) to be intelligent and purposeful.[28] This move on their part is clearly brought out in their discussion of a snake's striking at an object.

The Churchlands report that a snake's pit organ responds only if there is a warm object moving nearby, and information from that organ is sent to the optic tectum. In the tectum there is an integration of visual and infrared information, which we translate as "small warm-blooded moving object nearby." They further claim that this story provides "a useful conception *of the snake's representational attunement* to certain aspects of its environment" (1983, p. 16). An important feature of this "representational attunement" is *calibrational content*. The Churchlands define the latter as what is assigned to repeatable states of a given physical system that are causally produced by features of the environment and, thus, serve as more or less reliable indicators of those features.[29] Calibrational content is a species of informational content, as previously defined.

Reliable indicators to whom? We are, of course, invited to think that features of the environment are indicated to the snake, but even though the snake's movements in response to those "indicators" are appropriate to the conditions in which it finds itself and thus contribute to its continued survival, it does not follow that anything is indicated *to the snake*. Though a snake may have representational states in the robust sense, that is immaterial here. What is needed, but is not provided by the Churchlands, is some way of distinguishing cases that are representational in this sense from those that are not. Pointing to features that apply equally whether informational or representational states are operative is clearly inadequate.[30]

There is no question that calibrational content, as defined, is causally efficacious, but that content's relation to any relevant representation is left obscure. The Churchlands make comments that lead one to suspect that they believe an identity relation obtains between calibration content and representation, for they insist that the brain cells themselves do represent the world. For example, early in their 1983 paper they make the general claim that "densely crowded packets of excitable cells inevitably come to represent the world" (p. 5), and in the specific case of the snake "these cells represent small moving objects—their excited state contains calibrational contents to the effect that there are small moving warm objects nearby" (15).

There is a problem here. (i) Assume calibrational content is identical to a representation. What then is the point of holding (as the Churchlands apparently do in the passage quoted at the beginning of this section) that a creature's motions which appear to us to be both purposeful and to involve representational states may have come about simply as a result of how the activated neurons are connected to the muscles, *and not because of a representation.* Given the identity, the motions did come about because of a representation, even though one may describe the sequence of events without using that term. Such differences in description, however, are simply irrelevant to whether representation is operative; moreover, "representation" as calibrational content is not robust. Alternatively, (ii) assume calibrational content is not identical to representation. Then the problem just raised is avoided but a different one is generated for the Churchlands. Since they are centrally concerned with establishing how a system's representational system hooks up with the world, some further linkage between the representational system and the calibrational content is required. Putting aside for now the very real question as to just how such calibrational contents are to be individuated in the organism (I shall return to this below), there is still the problem of establishing a link between calibrational contents and the representational system, if their central concern is to be addressed. The value of the notion of calibrational content for this purpose is left unclear. Inasmuch as the calibrational content resides in the organism, certainly a causal connection between the *organism* and its environment is established, but this is hardly surprising to anyone except an extreme skeptic. The question the Churchlands pose does not concern *this* connection, but one between the system's representational system and the world. Moreover, even if calibrational content is linked to a representational system, the Churchlands are silent on what the representation is and on the presumed link between the calibrational content and the representational system. Thus, on the assumption that calibrational content is not identical to representation, the connection between the environment and the *representational system* is left vague and tenuous, at best.

This last point stands quite apart from any questions as to whether a genuine sense of representation is involved. Therefore, on the hypothesis of non-identity between calibrational content and representation (assumption (ii)), the notion of calibrational content does nothing to provide a connection between the representational system and the environment, and though the terms "representation," "representational state," and "representational system" are extensively used by the Churchlands, nothing is said as to what they are. The representational system, if it exists, remains mysterious and mysteriously embedded in the organism. In fact, the Churchlands have failed to demonstrate the representative character of that system.

The Churchlands, therefore, have the following dilemma: If a calibrational content is identical to a representation (assumption (i)), then a causal connection between a representational system and the environment is established, but then there is no basis for distinguishing motions that result from the organism's being hard-wired and motions involving representational states of the organism. Alternatively, if a calibrational content is not identical to a representation (assumption (ii)), then, although the *possibility* of drawing this distinction is still open, no connection between the representational system itself and the environment is established, contrary to their goal. Moreover, whether the creature has a representational system beyond calibrational content is not addressed; it is simply assumed.

Of assumptions (i) and (ii), I think the Churchlands endorse the first. I have already provided evidence that they typically go from talk of a creature's movements conducive to its survival to talk of its representational system. This strongly supports the view that they take calibrational content and representation as identical, despite the suggestion in the opening quotation of their endorsement of a distinction between being hard-wired to respond to environmental stimuli in ways conducive to one's survival and having a representational system.[31]

The identification of calibrational content with representation (assumption (i)) ignores the importance of the third variable and provides no room, or at least no consequential place, for how a system conceives things. The Churchlands themselves recognize that "in general, calibrational contents do nothing to reflect how the representing creature happens to conceive things" (1983, pp. 12–13) So if calibrational content and representation are identical on their view, they are, after all, committed to the conclusion that an entity's conceivings, if any, and its representings, in the sense just indicated, are independent. Thus, they leave no room for minimal content and no room for the difference between representing and information bearing.

These outcomes are unacceptable. Recall the problem mentioned above as to the individuation of calibrational content. No doubt the problem is easily resolved when dealing with a simple system (e.g., a thermometer), but it is hardly trivial to do so with more complex systems, say snakes or people. Interestingly, in such systems where it is relatively easy to individuate the

causally determined calibrational content, there is absolutely no temptation to hold that the states of the entities in question represent anything *to*
those entities. Of course, states of such systems may easily represent aspects
of its environment *to us*, e.g., the length of a column of alcohol in a glass
tube represents a certain temperature of the ambient air to us; but it is sheer
nonsense to say that that length represents anything *to the thermometer*. We
are, but it is not, a possible value of the third variable. (Compare my discussion above regarding the danger of conflating potential values for the
third variable.) There certainly appears to be a difference between how a
thermometer "represents" and how we do it.[32] Another reason why the
difference is crucial comes to the fore when one notices that in cases of
intermediate complexity (say, snakes, which may or may not be genuine
representers), the individuation of the calibrational content becomes far
from trivial, in contrast to the simple case of a thermometer, not to mention those unmistakable cases of representers, humans. *Such differences in
how things "represent" must be either explained or shown to be mere appearances.*
The Churchlands do neither. The appeal to calibrational content is not
successful, and there is no reason to think that vague references to varying
complexity of the systems will do any better.

Representers and Information Bearers: A Different Look

I now consider Fodor's response to a charge made by Dennett. It provides a
different angle on a relevant difference between information bearers and
representers.

   Long ago (1978), Dennett argued that attributing representations to
humans requires one to also attribute them—and in the same way—to
thermostats and paramecia. The temptation to slide from the former to the
latter is abetted by a fact already discussed, viz., information bearers often
move in ways that appear to involve representational states and appear
intelligent and purposeful from a third-person perspective. Fodor (1986)
responded that the slippery slope from humans to thermostats and paramecia is not as slippery as Dennett thinks. In that article Fodor attempted
to stop the slide by employing a distinction between nomic properties
(those that may enter into genuine laws, e.g., having mass) and non-nomic
properties (those that do not enter into genuine laws, e.g., being a crumpled
shirt). It is interesting that Fodor subsequently came to reject this distinc-

tion, for he came to think that it undermines an informational theory of content. I wholeheartedly agree that it does—indeed, I think it equally undermines causal theories of content—but I, unlike Fodor, think both these theories of content *should* be rejected as a basis for a theory of representation. So, though I now utilize Fodor's early distinction for my own ends, I do not take the current Fodor to endorse this employment.

In the case of non-nomic properties, the agent's behavior comes to be what it is in virtue of *the agent's representing to itself* an object as having the non-nomic property. It is a selective response to a non-nomic stimulus property. The resulting behavior is related in a law-like way to the subject's representing to itself the object as having the non-nomic property (given other psychological states); it is not, however, connected in a law-like way with any nomic property of the object.

Fodor's distinction allows that how an agent conceives things is relevant to how it represents them; thus, it also allows for a difference between information bearers and representers. How the agent conceives things is, of course, centrally important to my view, since this is constitutive of the agent's minimal content. In the case of a genuine representer, its behavior may, and frequently does, result from how it conceives an object, event, or state of affairs, and its conception may involve non-nomic properties. Another representer may conceive the same non-nomic property differently. Further, how a representer conceives a state of affairs to itself is important in that the state of affairs may be sought or avoided depending on this.

In contrast, an information bearer's motions can result only from its bearing information concerning nomic properties. Crucially, and unlike representers, all relevantly similar information bearers will bear that information in the same way. Alternatively put: *The only information* a strict information bearer may bear is that of nomic properties, and all (normal) information bearers of that type will bear the same information in similar circumstances. In contrast, *a representer may bear information of either kind of property, and may do it differently than other representers*. The importance of this is not diminished, even if how one conceives things amounts to no more than how it represents them, so long as the robust or genuine sense of representation is operative. For even at that, how it represents (conceives) things is different from bearing information.

The particular deployment of the distinction between nomic and non-nomic properties is not crucial. The crucial point is that anyone who is utilizing a sense of representation that allows for the difference between causally responding to input and responding (even causally) to a representation of some input must acknowledge a difference between an information bearer and a representer. Using the distinction between nomic and non-nomic properties is one way to state the difference. Stressing the importance of how one conceives things in discussions of representation makes vivid the role of the first-person perspective in driving a wedge between information bearers and representers. If nothing else, what I have argued in this chapter is that any strictly third-person account of representation must meet the challenge of providing a principled way of distinguishing representers from information bearers so that not every information bearer is a representer.[33]

Clarification of the Scope of the Arguments: Teleological Views Do Not Escape

My focus on the distinction between information and representation may misleadingly suggest to the reader a more restricted target of my arguments than their force merits. One might think that my targets are simply informational theories of representation, and that "teleological theories" would fall outside the range of my arguments. This would be a mistake. The arguments as they stand apply to any theory of representation that is restricted to a strictly third-person methodology.

This possible misunderstanding of the extent of applicability of my arguments is abetted by the fact that Fred Dretske and Ruth Millikan purport to distinguish informational from representational states. They even seem to share some of the concerns that I have been at pains to emphasize. For example, Dretske holds that a representation should have meaning in a system's cognitive economy and not merely be assigned meaning, say, by us. And Millikan holds that to be a representation an item "must be one that functions as a sign or representation *for the system itself*" (1989, p. 284). In this section I discuss these apparent similarities and show that they are only apparent. I also explain why their theories do not escape the arguments already presented. Ultimately, they fail in satisfying the particularity requirement and the fundamental fact of representation, the "to whom" requirement, because, despite their claims to the contrary, they fail to adequately distinguish representers from information bearers.

Millikan, in her challenge to causal/informational accounts of representation or mental content, argues that such accounts are unable to settle certain indeterminacies of informational states. (Of course, I agree with her on this.) She thinks that she overcomes this by stressing that it is how the system itself uses the representation: that representation *consumption* rather than *production* is the key. (Causal/informational theories emphasize the latter at the expense of the former.) By emphasizing the consumption side, she also thinks that she accommodates the idea that an item is a representation "for the system itself." These claims seem to recognize a distinction between information-bearing states and representation, seem to be in accord with my emphasis on the third variable in the representation relation (the "to whom"), and even seem ultimately to satisfy the particularity requirement. All this is mere appearance.

Millikan discusses Dretske's famous case in which there is a species of bacteria that possesses tiny magnets (magnetosomes) whose polarity is aligned in a way conducive to their survival: Given the hemisphere where the bacteria are located, the magnets pull the bacteria away from oxygen-rich water.[34] There is, however, an obvious informational indeterminacy in the bacteria's (magnetsomes') states, since they reliably covary both with the direction of magnetic north and the direction of less oxygen-rich water. So the question "Which is represented?" arises. Here we have a version of the problem of the particularity of the representation.

Millikan's biosemantics attempts to eliminate this indeterminacy: "What the magnetosome represents is only what its *consumers* require that it corresponds to in order to perform *their* tasks." (1989, p. 290) What the bacteria require for their survival is that the representation represents the direction of less oxygen-rich water, not that of the magnetic field. That is how the consumers, the bacteria, use the representation, and that is what is important on the biosemantic view, for it is this that it was selected for by the bacteria's evolutionary history. Thus, on Millikan's view, the magnetosomes' states uniquely represent the direction of less oxygen-rich water. This she rightly says does not make sense on the informational/causal view of representation.

This is an advance on informational/causal views of representation, but it is not sufficient to escape the arguments I have presented. First, notice that Millikan's discussion *presupposes* that the bacteria are representers. The considerations I have brought to bear on such cases bring such uncritical acceptance of "representations" into doubt. The presupposition that Millikan's criterion is sufficient for representation violates methodological chauvinism. Whereas I have argued that failure to abide by this methodological principle is mistaken, Millikan would clearly reject that principle. Thus, I cannot use the principle against Millikan's view without appearing to beg at least some questions; I do not so use it, but the conflict is worth pointing out.

The class of informational states may be partitioned in many ways. But simply partitioning the class does not by itself show that one of the resulting classes rightly includes the representational. Of course, Millikan has not offered an arbitrary demarcation; she identifies an additional feature that informational states must have to be representational, to wit, being selected for via an evolutionary history is not an initially implausible candidate to mark a genuine representation. Moreover, this is a powerful distinguishing feature. Once this class is identified, not only does the feature appear to distinguish representers from information bearers; in addition, both the particularity requirement and the fundamental fact of representation, which we may think of as the "to whom" requirement, appear to be satisfied. Still, I think Millikan's addition fails to rise above the level of informational to the level of the representational. Here is why.

It is indisputable that *we* can talk about the pull of the magnetosome *representing* the direction of less oxygen-rich water, as opposed to magnetic north. We do this because *we* can also identify the function of moving the bacteria away from oxygen-rich water as conducive to its survival. Thus viewing "representation" highlights an important aspect relative to this species of bacteria's survival. All of this, however, is just a case of *our* being the value of the third variable in the representation relation. Such facts, however, have no bearing on the question whether the state of the magnetosome represents *to the bacterium*, or whether *it* is a representer. (Compare the earlier discussion of the snake case and its relation to us.) That such states represent this to us in no way supports the claim that anything at all is represented to the bacterium. And the latter is so, notwithstanding the facts that bacteria causally respond to those states in a way conducive to their survival and that this feature was selected for by its evolutionary history.

In addition to what was just said against Millikan's view, there is a simple alternative explanation of the bacteria's behavior that makes it clear why no grounds have been offered to say that the bacteria (or the magnetosomes) are anything more than information bearers, despite the fact that their informational states have the additional feature she requires to distinguish them as "representational." The explanation I offer is, I submit, more plausible than Millikan's alternative. If I am right in this, no reason has yet been offered to think that the bacteria are representers, and certainly none to think that anything is represented to the bacteria themselves. This discussion will also reveal why Millikan's understanding of the statement "It must be one that functions as a sign or representation *for the system itself*" (1989, p. 284) differs importantly from mine, despite superficial similarities.

By my lights, given the structure of the bacteria, their inhering magnetosomes, and the environment in which they live, they are "wired" in ways that produce beneficial responses to stimuli from the environment. If the favorable feature of the environment (less oxygen-rich water) is not what is connected in a law-like way to the "proffered representation" (the state of the magnetosome), but something only contingently connected with it, as in the bacteria case, then so much the luckier are the creatures in question. Such is the power of evolution that traits only contingently connected to some environmental feature may be selected for. However, these are no grounds for holding that "the pull-in-a-direction-at-a-time *represents* the less oxygen-rich water" (290) *to the bacteria*, and certainly not to the magnetosome. The bacteria move in that direction simply because of the polarity of their magnets and the magnetic field in which they find themselves. That things are so arranged is precisely why they haven't died off (as they would have if the poles had been reversed). It does not follow that the states of the magnetosomes represent anything to the bacteria. Again, having such "content" does contribute to their survival, given their nature and the environments in which they occur; the contribution, however, is purely causal. As such, the contribution would still be made *whether or not* the state of the magnetosomes *represents* anything *to the bacteria*, and it would still be made even if no "representational" but only causal or informational content were involved.

I have just criticized Millikan's attempt to eliminate the indeterminacy in the information indicated above. In effect she tries to satisfy the particularity requirement by emphasizing the consumption side of representation rather than its production, and in the process her solution seems also to solve the "to whom" problem that I have raised in connection with the fundamental fact of representation. But Millikan's solution fails to satisfy the logically prior question as to whether a representation is even in play. Thus, there is no reason to think that she has satisfied the particularity requirement. She has relied upon the fact that the latter, and the other requirements mentioned, are satisfied *for us*. Clearly the latter is not sufficient to establish the satisfaction of these requirements *for the bacteria*. Adding that the content that we recognize contributes to the creature's survival is of no help unless one can show that the creature also had this conception or shared our value of survival. Is the bacterium "trying to survive," or is it just moving in accordance with its causal structure and its environment? Therefore, Millikan has not shown that these informational states are appropriately viewed as representations, even though they are distinguished from other informational contents by being selected for in the creature's evolution. Millikan's insistence that an item function as a representation for the system itself, the consumer, appears to involve the third variable in the representation relation as I have identified it, but it should now be clear that the similarity is only apparent.

The difference between Millikan and me may be brought into sharper focus by considering the concept of function. The following question is crucial to her case: Is the *function* of the state of the magnetosome—as opposed to its *causal role*—an objective feature? For Millikan's account to work, it must be. Millikan has done much serious work on the concept of function, proper and derived. I will not examine that work in detail here. What I will do is give an argument as to why functions are not objective. If they are not, then the appeal to them cannot help to circumvent my arguments against strictly third-person views of representation. The argument is borrowed from Searle, and I fully endorse it.

Searle reminds us that "one of Darwin's greatest achievements was to drive teleology out of an account of the origin of species" (1995, p. 16). My account above as to how the bacteria manage to flourish without anything being represented to them is in accord with this. It is not that the bacteria evolved so that the states of the magnetosomes are to represent this (less oxygen-rich water) rather than that (direction of the environmental magnetic field). It is not *for* the one purpose or function rather than the other. It simply happened that bacteria with magnetosomes that are aligned in a certain way in certain environments flourished and reproduced and so were selected for. Those in similar environments without this mechanism, or without some other mechanism that propelled them to less oxygen-rich water, simply died off and did not reproduce their kind. All this can and should be understood in accordance with Darwin's theory, quite apart from teleology or objective functions, and certainly quite apart from the idea that anything is represented to the bacteria, as I have argued.

Here is the argument of Searle's that I alluded to:

Either "function" is defined in terms of causes, in which case there is nothing intrinsically functional about functions, they are just causes like any others. Or functions are defined in terms of the furtherance of a set of values that *we* hold—life, survival, reproduction, health—in which case they are observer relative. (1995, p. 16, emphasis added)

This strikes me as exactly right. Millikan's talk of what the "*consumers* require . . . to perform *their* tasks" (1989, p. 290) is a projection of our values to the bacteria, as though their "task" was to flourish, as though *they* were *trying* to survive. It is futile to hold that the bacteria have any of these values—that they are trying to move in a certain direction *in order* that they might survive. It is quite peculiar—at best metaphorical, at worst anthropomorphic—to even think of their having "tasks." We take the state of the magnetosome to represent the direction of less oxygen-rich water, given our knowledge of the environment, its biological history, and our values of survival, reproduction, etc. We do so because *we* see that these states contribute to its survival, something we have the capacity to value. Whatever "functions" are involved in this characterization, they are not objective.

If functions are not objective, then the fact that the "function" of the magnetosome was selected for because of its contribution to the bacteria's survival gives us no reason to think that the magnetosome represents the direction of less oxygen-rich water *to the bacteria*. That it facilitates *our* understanding of the bacteria's evolutionary history is reason to hold that—from our perspective—it so represents, but it is no reason to hold the bacteria represent and, then, certainly not that it represents this in particular to it. To think otherwise is to exemplify what I warned against earlier: the conflation of values of the third variable in the representation relation between us and the creature or system we are investigating. In fact, the structure and behavior of these bacteria nicely exemplify the abstract schema of case 2, discussed in an earlier section, where something's behavior appears to involve representations from a strictly third-person perspective, when in fact no representations are involved in the creature's behavior.

It should be clear that my argument here does not depend on the (undoubtedly true) claim that the bacteria's "representations" fail to rise to the level of complexity of our representations. I have argued that we have no reason, as yet, to think that bacteria represent at all. This negative conclusion is reinforced by the explanation given above of their behavior that is in accord with evolution but that does *not* involve representations. Thus, when Millikan lists at least six fundamental ways in which simple organisms' representations differ from ours (1989, p. 294–297), this is not to my point. Of course, it is obvious and to be expected that simple creatures and devices—*if* they represent at all—will have representations which differ from ours in a number of significant ways. The identification of such features of our representations is useful. The important point, however, is that saying that these are ways our representations differ from those of simpler creatures *presupposes* an affirmative answer to the *logically prior* question as to *whether they represent at all*. If one holds that no reason has yet been given to say that they do, as I have argued here and throughout this chapter, then it is not reassuring to be told that their "representations" are simpler that ours.

I have argued that Millikan, despite appearances to the contrary, has not succeeded in distinguishing representation from information. In consequence, she has also failed adequately treat of the "to whom" problem associated with the fundamental fact of representation and to satisfy the particularity requirement. Moreover, the recognition that our representations are more complex than those of simpler creatures—assuming that they have representations—is no corrective to these shortcomings.

Dretske's view similarly appeals to the idea of function to explain representation and distinguish it from information. Like Millikan, Dretske has said much that is important about representation and information. My discussion of Millikan should make clear how I would deploy my arguments against Dretske's view, so I will give only a sketch of his view, highlighting the role objective functions play in it and the outstanding problem associated with them regarding the dialectic of our competing views. Dretske says:

The fundamental idea is that a system, S, represents a property, F, if and only if S has the function of indicating (providing information about) the F of a certain domain of objects. (1995, p. 2)

He divides representations between *conventional* and *natural*. Both are distinct from information in that an informational state may have multiple informational contents whereas a representation indicates a single property, depending on its indicator function. Its indicator function is determined by what the system was designed to do.

Some indicator functions have their informational functions derived from the intentions of its designers; these are the conventional representations. Thus, a pressure gauge, e.g., is designed to indicate pressure, though the same informational state carries information about temperature; still, since it was designed for the former and not the latter, it represents only pressure. In contrast, *natural representations* do not acquire their indicator functions from the intentions of a designer; they are, Dretske claims, naturally acquired. Clearly, if there are such functions then there are natural representations and we would have a genuine distinction between information and representation, contrary to what I have argued. For if there were such functions, they would be objective features of a state or system. Moreover, the particularity and the "to whom" requirements would appear to be readily satisfied. My thesis that no theory of representation that relies upon a strictly third-person methodology can succeed would be refuted, if there are objective indicator functions.

Are there such functions? Dretske thinks there are. Does he argue for this? No. In his characteristically straightforward style, he states:

I assume that there are naturally acquired functions and, thus, natural representations. I do not argue for this; I assume it. (1995, p. 7)

While Dretske recognizes that there are those few who deny the assumption (he cites Dennett 1987 and Searle 1992), he lists a host of others who endorse it. He also quotes Philip Kitcher's interpretation of Darwin in support of the assumption: "One of Darwin's important discoveries is that we can think of design without a designer." (1993, p. 380) The suggestion is that Darwin somehow showed us we can have designs, and hence indicator functions, that are not dependent on the intentions of a designer.

That the belief that there are naturally acquired objective functions is widely held is not in dispute. Whether the belief is true is in dispute. Does the quote from Kitcher support the assumption? No. In accordance with Searle's interpretation of this and the discussion above, we can allow that, yes, *we* can think of "design without a designer," but it does not follow from *our* so conceptualizing it that there *is* any such objective design, nor, importantly, does Darwinian theory require it. As Searle pointed out (quoted above), Darwin has shown that we can understand the origin of species without teleology—neither natural nor otherwise. Hence, while believers in naturally acquired objective functions may find comfort in Kitcher's interpretation of "Darwinian design," it offers no support for the assumption.

Attempts such as those of Dretske and Millikan to secure the distinction between representation and information rest upon an acknowledged unsupported assumption that there are objective functions. As I indicated above, I cannot simply appeal to methodological chauvinism to refute their views, but, by the same token, my view cannot be refuted by an appeal to this disputed assumption, no matter how widely held. Doing so on either part would simply beg the question. Were it the case that an appeal to such functions was necessary to explain the evolutionary development of biological systems, that would be a point in their favor, but my discussion of the magnetosome, which is in accordance with Darwinian theory, presents an alternative schema that is adequate for explanation of evolutionary development and which requires no appeal to function, objective or otherwise. This, of course, is not to deny that talk of such functions may provide heuristic assistance to us in explaining such developments. It is a mistake, however, or at the very least unnecessary, to project such functions onto nature's machinations, as I believe Searle's argument above shows.

Until advocates of teleological views provide counters to my earlier arguments or give independent support for the existence of objective functions in nature, they have failed to distinguish representers from information bearers. My arguments for the distinction between information bearers and representers are completely general. They are applicable against any theory of representation that rests upon a strictly third-person methodology.

There Are No Unconscious Representations

In this section I argue for what is perhaps my most controversial claim: that there are no unconscious representations.

Beliefs clearly involve representations. There is an innocent and straightforward sense of 'unconscious beliefs' such that no one, I take it, would deny that at any given moment each of us has a vast number of them. I have in mind quite ordinary beliefs that each of us has but is not currently entertaining. All non-occurrent beliefs that one has are unconscious in this sense. These include beliefs (expressible by sentences such as 'Gold is a metal' and 'Two is the only even prime number') that could be truly attributed to us even when we are not entertaining them. Just as clearly, any such belief is one that we could entertain and therefore, at times, be conscious of. Such beliefs easily pass from being unconscious to being conscious, and back. Being unconscious in this sense does not make them deeply hidden; they are not Freudian.

Thus understood, there clearly are unconscious beliefs, and each of them is, *in some sense*, is identical to its conscious manifestation. What identity there is between a conscious belief and an unconscious one is secured by the *sentence* expressing the belief, which is just to say that the *sentence* expressing the belief is the same whether the belief is conscious or unconscious. However, not everything we say of conscious beliefs is true of unconscious beliefs, because their realizations are different. One point at issue here is just what it is to *have* a belief; another is whether one *has* conscious and unconscious beliefs in the same way. I take it that when one "has" a belief, be it conscious or unconscious, it is realized in *some* way, be it neurobiological, computational, individuated somehow by its causal connections to the environment, or something else. We have every reason to expect that, no matter how a belief is realized, its conscious and unconscious realizations are different. (I will throughout assume the realizations are neurobiological.)

An objection that might be raised to my claim that conscious and unconscious realizations of the same belief are different might go as follows: Although the realizations are unlikely to be identical, there is a "common component" to both, one that constitutes or corresponds to the belief itself. They are not quite identical, however, because a conscious belief obviously requires something additional. For example, if one's unconscious belief state that p is realized by some brain state, then one's conscious belief that p is realized by that very same brain state plus others, or that brain state enters into different relations with other brain states when one is conscious of the belief, and these other states or relations do not obtain when the belief is unconscious.

The main thing wrong with this kind of move is that it is committed to a "storehouse" view of unconscious beliefs, as if each and every belief one has, including the unconscious beliefs, is somehow stored intact in one's head. But at any given moment one *has* indefinitely many (perhaps infinitely many[35]) unconscious beliefs, and according to this view distinct states for each one must somehow be realized. As is well known, this is at best highly implausible. Better to reject the idea of a common realization, even partial, and think, for starters, more along dispositional lines, in parallel with various dispositional physical properties. For example, that a glass *is fragile* is realized in its molecular structure. Importantly, the very same molecular realization of its fragility is *simultaneously* a realization of indefinitely many other dispositional properties. If the molecular structure that realizes a glass's fragility were exposed to extreme heat or an acid, the molecular structure that would result, the realization of the new property, would be different from that which would have resulted from its being struck. Thus, the molecular structure that realizes the glass' fragility also realizes indefinitely many other dispositional properties. Which of these countless dispositional properties is *actualized* depends upon what conditions that selfsame molecular structure is subjected to.

The model for unconscious belief advanced here, more generally, unconscious mental states, is analogous to what was just said about dispositional properties: One and the same brain state is *simultaneously* a realization of any number of unconscious mental states. Given that brain state, various conscious states may subsequently be realized; which one is realized depends on how the agent is prompted. The parallel to dispositions is not exact but a heuristic device. Ultimately, my model for unconscious mental states is based on chaos theory and, therefore, unlike dispositions, is not stimulus driven, though the stimulus, together with the structure of the brain and its history, will determine whether there is a burst to an attractor state and, if so, to which one. When there is a realization of one of these attractor states, the agent has a conscious state, and which conscious state is determined by the attractor state. (See chapter 4.)

The neuronal realizations of unconscious mental states should be further distinguished from the broader class of neuronal states that have nothing to do with cognition—say, those involved in digestion or respiration. The value of categorizing some non-conscious states as "unconscious *mental* states" is to indicate the existence of relations between them and various conscious mental states—relations that other non-conscious states do not share. Certain states, the unconscious mental states, will enter into dynamical patterns terminating in a certain strange attractor. Having the latter results in some particular conscious state (see chapter 4). Other brain states, those that are not conscious and not mental states, never enter into such dynamical patterns, by definition. In spite of such relations that exist between conscious and unconscious mental states, my position is that *all* unconscious mental states are *non*-intentional, *non*-representational.

Obviously my view is at direct odds with computational, causal, and other third-person models of cognitive behavior, all of which rely heavily upon the idea of unconscious representation. On this point, my view is even in opposition to John Searle's theory of mind, with which my theory shares a good deal, as Searle too holds that unconscious beliefs are representational.[36] Searle's argument is straightforward, and it is shared by many who would reject his theory of mind: It relies on Leibniz's Law.[37] The argument goes as follows: One of John's beliefs is that asparagus is a vegetable. It is the same belief that John has, whether John is consciously entertaining it or whether he is asleep, otherwise unconscious, or conscious but thinking about other things entirely. When in any of these latter states, it is correct to say he still has the selfsame belief that asparagus is a vegetable. His conscious belief is intentional. Therefore, the argument goes, *this* belief when unconscious is intentional.

The appeal of this argument turns on the reification of beliefs. While it is correct to hold that one "has" the same belief, whether it is consciously or unconsciously had, it is not some identical *thing* that one has on either occasion. It is not some little "nugget" tucked away somewhere in the brain. The chaotic theory of beliefs (even more simply, the dispositional model) advanced above undercuts treating belief as a thing. Thus, the application of Leibniz's Law as a basis for an objection to my view fails, for the realizations of conscious and unconscious beliefs are different. Although for convenience we speak of the "same belief" whether consciously or unconsciously had on a given occasion, it is not the selfsame *thing* in the agent, though one and the same sentence may be used to express it in either manifestation. To say (as above) that John has the belief that asparagus is a vegetable when not consciously entertaining it is to make a pragmatic claim about what conscious belief John would have, or what he would do or say when prompted in various ways. How the belief is "had" is explicated as how it is realized, and conscious and unconscious realizations may well have different properties. On my theory they definitely do.

Now the representational nature of conscious beliefs plays a clear role in the analysis of intentionality and opacity of conscious beliefs. But it is not at all clear how representation could be involved in talk of *unconscious* beliefs realized in the brain.[38] Recall that on my view a single sentence expresses both the conscious and the unconscious belief; the sentence bears the burden of the identity. Any opacity questions that may arise regarding unconscious mental states are reducible to the opacity of *sentences* that express those unconscious states; they just do not apply to the realizations of the unconscious mental states, since these are non-representational.

Even if Searle's argument were sound, however, it would provide no help as to *how* unconscious beliefs or mental states *could be* intentional. There appear to be enormous conceptual and methodological problems in answering this "how" question. This is another version of the "how possibly" question already discussed in chapters 3 and 4. Searle himself denies that that the neurological facts are themselves sufficient to infer aspectual shape, even though on his view belief states are caused by and realized in brain states.[39] He argues that no matter how complete the behavioral or even the neurophysiological evidence, there would still be an inference from these facts to the aspectual facts. Behavioral or neurological facts cannot, he says, constitute aspectual nor intentional facts.[40] Given this, it would seem preferable to avoid this "how" question altogether. Obviously, the question is avoided on my account. Unconscious beliefs do not have aspectual shape, are not intentional—they are not representational on my theory.

Why should we avoid this question as applied to unconscious beliefs or representations? One reason relies on what Searle himself has argued: that behavioral or neurological facts are not sufficient for intentional facts. Unfortunately, this point wipes out too much, as it would seem to pose an equally formidable problem of explaining how *conscious* states could be intentional or representational. It turns out that this is another version of the traditional explanatory gap problem, now applied to the gap between brain states and non-phenomenal contentful states. This new problem, along with a framework for closing both the gaps was presented in chapter 4; it did not commit us to unconscious representations. But there are further grounds for treating conscious and unconscious states differently with regard to their representational nature.

Hardly anyone would dispute that at least some conscious human mental states are representational. From the first-person perspective there is no doubt that we sometimes have conscious representations. This is a crucial point imbedded in methodological chauvinism. Still, this leaves open just what enables the fact that we have such states. (Compare the earlier discussion about conflicting intuitions as to what is required for a representational state.) Of course, there can be no non-inferential awareness of any "unconscious representation," and so the evidence regarding the representational nature of unconscious states is certainly different and less compelling. What is the evidence?

It is generally assumed in cognitive theories that a system's successful adaptive behavior is dependent on its having inner representations of its environment. Just how these inner representations are explicated varies considerably from theory to theory, but it is almost universally held that adaptive systems have unconscious representations. To the extent that unconscious representations are argued for at all, the arguments are based on whatever success the theories that employ them enjoy. A kind of move familiar to scientific realism appears to be operative. It is as if the locution 'unconscious representation' were a theoretical term in a theory, and when such theories meet with some measure of predictive success one concludes there are unconscious representations.

Such reasons for holding that unconscious representations exist should be contrasted with existence claims of conscious representations, already discussed. The latter do not depend on the successful application of this or that theory but simply on our being non-inferentially aware that a certain item represents something to us. (Compare theorists A–D, and other examples discussed in chapter 1.) Because of this rather different evidential basis for conscious and unconscious representations, one might well wonder whether a univocal sense of 'representation' is being employed in these different expressions. Obviously a difference in evidence does not show that there is a difference in what the evidence is for; by the same token, however, the success of such theories does not establish that an unequivocal sense is involved. One must not presuppose that there is no equivocation either.

What would undermine the claim that there are unconscious representations, when the support for that claim relies on its use in theories that have had some predictive success? Suppose that, in fact, the production of adaptive behavior can be explained by, say, non-representational brain activity, and there is an adequate theory that explains this behavior without appeal to unconscious representations. This would undercut support for the existence of unconscious representations when that support relies largely on theories that employ the disputed concept, for it would show that the work can be done without that concept. Moreover, if there are no unconscious representations, whatever is designated in the brain by successful theories of adaptive behavior that use the term 'unconscious representation' must be something other than what the face value of that term would suggest, Therefore, the sense of 'representation' in 'unconscious representation' would be different in those theories than is understood by that term in 'conscious representation' when the latter term is applied on the basis of non-inferential evidence.

The theory described near the beginning of the previous paragraph would also be a theory based in neurophysiology that would support my claim that unconscious beliefs are not intentional, not representational. Such a neurophysiological model exists in the work of Walter Freeman, already discussed in chapter 4. Commenting on that work in relation to representation, Christine Skarda argues that "the patterns of neural activity responsible for behavior do not 'represent' anything, that brains do not 'read' them, and that 'neural representations' need not play a role in the production of behavior in animals" (1987, p. 189). Skarda maintains that Freeman's research on the olfactory bulb disconfirms the assumption that inner representations of the environment are required for adaptive behavior. For Freeman, as we saw in chapter 4, the brain is a self-organized system. Such systems are not input driven; indeed, according to Freeman, the input gets "washed out"—there is no representation of it that undergoes transformations. If representational theories here rejected were correct, this should not happen.

My purpose in citing these results here is to remind the reader that the idea of representation is not required to explain adaptive behavior, even in humans; an active empirical research program denies that the behavior of a system is dependent on the system's internal or neuronal states' *representing* the environment. I do not presume to decide scientific questions between Freeman's theory and the theories of others. I do wish to point out that there is a viable alternative hypothesis to that usually employed in explaining an organism's successful adaptive behavior—one that does not require positing unconscious representations. So the existence of unconscious representations does not follow from the fact that there are relatively successful predictive theories that posit them. These results should, at the very least, make us hesitant to conclude that unconscious states are representational in the same sense as are our conscious states. In any case, though my contention that there are no unconscious representations is unorthodox, it has both philosophical and empirical support.

Further support for this conclusion is garnered from Kathleen Akins (1996). She challenges the strategy by which naturalists (read "strictly third-person methodologists") attempt to give an account of the "aboutness relation," the basic idea of intentionality. Akins identifies four common assumptions of diverse naturalists' programs and argues in considerable, persuasive, and informative detail why one of these is misguided. The assumption she challenges is "that the simple perceptual case is in some sense 'basic,' that it constitutes the most likely starting point for such a theory [of "aboutness"]" (341). The naturalists hold that we can build on this "base" aboutness relation to analyze more complex intentional relations.[41]

Why, according to Akins, is this assumption misguided? The plausibility of the assumption is based on the traditional view of sensory perception, and this view of perception is "not universally or even generally true" (344). Akins zeros in on the following feature of the traditional view of perception:

The senses show the brain, otherwise blind, how things stand, "out there," both in the distal world and in its own distal body. . . . The receptors, we think, must react with a unique signal, one that correlates with a particular [for example] temperature state. Thus, the brain gains information about what it is like "outside." . . . Sensory systems must be veridical in some sense of the word. (342)

After discussing in some detail the sense of 'veridical' at issue, she thoroughly examines the case of thermoreception and conclusively shows, among other things, that thermoreceptors do not correlate with any particular temperature, not even with any particular temperature change. (I pass over her fascinating discussion here, including her rebuttal of various objections a naturalist might raise in support of the traditional view of perception, but it is highly commended to the reader.) In short, the sensory systems, according to Akins, are "narcissistic." She uses this term to characterize the fact that the receptors respond in a particular way to information that affects them rather than veridically reflecting the corresponding sensory property in the world. In particular, thermoreception is a result of four different types of receptors, each of which, in both its static and its dynamic functions, reacts to stimulation in a surprising and variable way. These reactions, not expected on the traditional view of veridical sense, belie any correlation to environmental temperature or other sensory properties.

Driven by such results that find a variable divergence between an external property (such as temperature) and the receptor states that respond to it, on the one hand, and how we perceive stable objects or properties in our environment, on the other, Akins distinguishes the ontological project from the sensory-motor project:

. . . aboutness constitutes something like an ontological "capacity," an ability to impose stability, order, and uniformity upon a conception of the world (and sometimes the world itself) on the basis of stimuli that do not themselves exhibit these properties. . . . [For example, at a simple level and additional to the divergences already mentioned, as you move about there are dramatic changes in the stimuli received and in the receptor states but, typically, not in your awareness of the objects or properties represented.] That none of these changes in the stimuli matters to your perception is a remarkable fact. . . . That you come to glean this stable ontology, of particulars that instantiate types, of particulars that occupy stable places in the world, is an outstanding capacity. . . . To conceive of types and tokens, places and objects as existing at all, given our sensory access to the world, is a fantastically difficult task. Call this the *ontological project*.

On the other hand, there is that small task, assigned to sensory systems, of getting the job done, of directing motor behavior. For the most part, this is not an ontological project . . . because sensory systems encode information symbiotically with motor needs, the similarities and differences, uniformities and discontinuities that the senses "record" need not exist in the world. . . . Call the narcissistic encoding of this type of information the *sensory-motor project*. (368–370)

Therefore, the ontological project involves representations of stable objects or properties in the environment but the sensory-motor project does not. Akins observes that there is a rather large "gap between the needs of the sensory-motor project and the demands of the ontological project" (370) The gap, she rightly insists, requires explanation: ". . . how exactly does the information provided by our sensory systems co-exist with, form a whole with, the ontology imposed by a representational system?" (370–371) She concludes: "Trace out the causal path between the object of perception, the stimulation of the receptors, and whatever neural events that thereafter eventuate [sensory-motor project] and this alone will not *explain*, in the required sense how *genuine representation* arises [ontological project]." (372, last emphasis added)

The idea is that, whatever occurs in the sensory-motor system, there is no straightforward interpretation of it such that it represents, or even correlates with, the stable objects in the environment that are projected in the ontological project, the objects of which we are conscious. There are no reliable correlations between types of physiological states and kinds of stimuli originating in the agent's environment. This, we already saw, is a conclusion that Freeman also drew, but it adds independent support for the non-existence of unconscious representations, since Akins' arguments to the same conclusion do not presuppose that the dynamics of the sensory systems is chaotic, as Freeman does.

Akins is not mounting an anti-naturalist campaign. (Nor, of course, is Freeman.) She is arguing that a core strategy in the naturalist's endeavor to explain representation will not work, so the overall strategy must be altered. I, too, do not advance an anti-naturalist campaign, at least so long as naturalism is compatible with the employment of the first-person perspective, as I think it is.[42] My argument is that all current naturalists' strategies designed to explain the mind will fail insofar as they employ a strictly third-person perspective; naturalism must incorporate a first-person perspective to succeed.

Akins' argument is quite different from mine, though our arguments may share some very close relations. The nature of the problems concerning the gap I discussed in the previous chapter between brain states and what I called 'minimal content consciousness' seem to parallel the problems concerning the "gap between the needs of the sensory-motor project and the demands of the ontological project" (370) that Akins speaks of. In fact, Akins' work reveals two gaps: a gap between the narcissistic properties and the deliverances of ordinary perception (similar to the usual phenomenal/brain state gap) and a gap between the narcissistic properties and the properties or things in the world (such that the former fail to even correlate with, let alone represent, the latter). Akins' compelling case for the latter is one thing that is important and new in her paper. Moreover, though Akins does not explicitly address conscious/unconscious representation issues,[43] her talk of "genuine representations" involved in the ontological project, as opposed to the information obtained via the sensory-motor project, would seem to support my position. Clearly the information available in the sensory-motor project is not available in the same—conscious—way to the agent as are the representations of the ontological project. My distinction between genuine representational states and merely informational ones seems to align rather neatly with Akins' distinction between the ontological project and the sensory-motor project.

One might object that the "narcissistic" nature of the information gleaned in the sensory-motor project does not show that the states of the sensory-motor system *themselves* are not representational. It could be maintained that these states *do* represent; it is just that *what* is represented is different from what is represented in the ontological project and at the conscious level.[44] The objection itself is more powerful against me than it is against Akins, since all she argues is that certain traditional approaches to naturalizing aboutness that take the sensory-motor system as the basic aboutness relation will fail, whereas I maintain the much stronger thesis that unconscious states of such a system simply do not represent. Period. Nevertheless, if one cannot get to the ontological project from the sensory-motor project, as Akins' work suggests, then at the very least, *if* "representations" are involved at the sensory-motor level, *they are of a very different sort than that at the conscious level*. That may be all I need.

Now, to talk of "genuine representation," as Akins and I have done, always raises suspicions as to what is so "genuine" about one's favorite analysis. But the point can be made innocently enough. What is important is not the word used, but the fact that "representations" in the sensory-motor project appear, at best, to be significantly different from those in the ontological project, and there seems to be no way of going from the former to the latter, for they are not even reliably correlated. If the gap and the significant differences between the two senses are real, then the common practice of using the same term to cover both is a grossly misleading equivocation. Better to reserve application of the term 'representation' to those items where there is widespread agreement that they are representational, the conscious ones. Those items that appear to be representations from a third-person perspective but lack the critical conscious aspect may be called *information bearers*.[45]

Earlier I argued that consciousness is clearly sufficient for representation and probably necessary. I have now argued that there are no unconscious representations. If that is correct, then, clearly, consciousness is also necessary for representation.

I have also argued for an analysis of unconscious beliefs that allows them no intentionality, because there are no unconscious representations. If I am right on all this, it would go far in explaining why there has been so much success in studies of cognition that ignore consciousness, even if consciousness is necessary for representation. These studies succeed when they focus on unconscious processes. Their successes turn on the fact that the processes studied do not involve representations at all, but only information-bearing states. Having assumed that the latter are representations, they think representation can be studied apart from consciousness. It is a grave error, however, and one that is frequently made, to infer from such successes that the results that obtained for "*un*conscious beliefs" or "unconscious representations" (which are in fact merely information-bearing states) are transferable to *conscious* beliefs and representations, or that consciousness itself is epiphenomenal and not central to representation and cognition. This error stems from the deeply flawed but widely held assumption that the sense of *belief* and *representation* employed in discussions of conscious and unconscious states is the same as that deployed in the study of non-conscious cognitive processes. If I am right, this assumption is false.

Does a First-Person Methodology Force the Results to Be Subjective?

Scientific theories generally have no use for the first-person perspective. My theory, and in particular methodological chauvinism, does. Is my view unscientific? No. A theory that is concerned with intentionality, representation, or phenomenal states—in short, a theory of mind—should include a first-person methodology; it does so without diminishing its objective or scientific status. I have already argued that we can have an objective theory, which includes a first-person perspective, of subjectivity (chapter 3), but I now want to identify another important reason why this is so. Specifically, I wish to explain what distinguishes the use of a first-person methodology in the study of mind from its use in the study of other domains of nature. With respect to our own intentional, representational, or phenomenal states, we sometimes have the privilege of the first-person perspective. Importantly, this is a perspective we never have with regard to, say, light, matter, or a human cell. This difference in accessibility to the subject matter is precisely why first-person folk theories of the latter types are inadequate and why they result in unwarranted anthropomorphism. Given this difference, however, we should expect that a theory that includes a first-person methodology should succeed in domains where we have *some* privileged access, at the same time uniformly failing in those where we have none.[46]

Dennett (1987, p. 9), among many others, does not agree. He quotes, with approval, an attack on folk psychology by Patricia Churchland: "So long as the brain functions normally, the inadequacies of the commonsense framework can be hidden from view, but with a damaged brain the inadequacies of theory are unmasked." (Churchland 1986, p. 223) The suggestion is that the inadequacies clearly present in the treatment of the abnormal are also present, though "masked," in the normal domain. There is, however, a significantly different reading of these inadequacies of folk psychology, one consistent with my position. Our first-person perspective (for most of us, and by definition) does not extend into the realm of seriously abnormal behavior. Thus, we should not expect the success of folk psychology or our first-person perspective to be informative regarding abnormal mental states any more than we expect it to be useful in, say, physics. None of us has a first-person perspective regarding the domain of physics, and most of us lack this perspective regarding seriously abnormal mental behavior. Acknowledging this, however, in no way implies that the inadequacies of the first-person perspective in the study of abnormal human behavior would also be manifest in the study of normal behavior, a domain where we clearly have the privilege provided by the first-person perspective.

My limitation on the domain of applicability and usefulness of the first-person perspective may appear (on a careless view) to be subject to a criticism advanced by Paul Churchland in "Theory, Taxonomy, and Methodology" (in Churchland and Churchland 1998). There he criticizes (in his colorful way) any defense of a theory that relies on restricting the domain. He maintains that "any hangdog theory . . . so long as it has some paltry success for some benighted purpose within some sheltered domain" (23) could be defended in this way. But I am not "sheltering" my claims of the value of the first-person perspective from refuting cases, I am simply limiting it to those cases where in fact we have a first-person perspective. To apply it elsewhere would be sheer folly. To dismiss the results it delivers in the domains where it applies because of its lack of value in areas where it does not apply would be nothing short of absurd. One does not denigrate hammers because they are, oh, so inadequate to drive screws.

Restricting the domain of applicability of a theory or a method to avoid refutation or criticism is unacceptable only if the character of the theory or methodology is such that, if correct, it *ought to apply* to a wider domain. But nothing in the nature of the first-person methodology I have advocated and applied would suggest that it should be applicable to the study of, say, physics, or even abnormal psychology. Though I have argued that it is essential to employ this methodology in the study of mind, there is no suggestion that it should or could be applied to everything we wish to investigate regarding the mind. In particular, nothing I have said would suggest that it should or could be applicable to abnormal minds.[47] This is no failure of the method.

Folk psychology is undoubtedly incomplete, and even in areas in which it is successful the success certainly does not depend on the employment of the first-person perspective alone, whatever that might amount to. I am not advocating a "pure" first-person approach. I am arguing that the *exclusion* of a first-person approach will prohibit an adequate understanding of the human mind, not only when the subject is qualia or phenomenal consciousness but also, just as importantly, when non-phenomenal intentional or representational states are at issue. Ironically, it is the exclusive employment of the third-person perspective that generates an anthropomorphic view by encouraging premature attribution of representational states to non-human systems. Undoubtedly, many of these systems have content of some sort and do respond in ways that appear to be intelligent and purposeful to us (i.e., from the third-person perspective). Such organisms and devices may be mere information bearers, however. Some of these information bearers, no doubt, also have representational states, but we must not prematurely project to them representational states simply on the grounds that they are information bearers.

Summary

My reluctance to attribute representational states to non-humans is based on several facts. First, if anything is a representer, we are. Second, we do not yet know in virtue of what we have this ability. Third, there are systems so structured that, when their motions are observed from a strictly third-person perspective, they appear to have representational systems, but this appearance is contrary to fact. Fourth, we *never* have access to other types of systems' states as we *sometimes* do to our own. Fifth, that subjective access both alerts us to the existence of representational states and informs us that we have the capacity to be a value of the third variable in the representation relation. Sixth, and most important, it is in virtue of that subjectivity that we are able to successfully represent a particular object, to distinguish representers from information bearers, and to accommodate the fundamental fact of representation. Finally, since there are no unconscious representations, consciousness is not only sufficient but also necessary for representation. Thus, we must follow the counsel of methodological chauvinism and include a first-person methodology in a basic way in the study of mind. The ironic result is that the use of this methodology purges anthropomorphism from the study of representation.

6 Minimal Content and the Ambiguity of Sensory Terms

The distinction between minimal content and objective content is particularly salient and has a distinctive application in the analysis of sensory terms. The reason it is so distinctive is that in this domain minimal content and objective content *can never be correctly identified with one another*. This is in marked contrast to the case of thought, since what is signaled by the minimal content and the objective content of a thought can be, and frequently is, identified. The reason for this difference is that the use of sensory terms is itself ambiguous between indicating something *as it appears to the agent* and something *as it is in the external environment*—that is, between a subjective and an objective referent. In chapter 3, the former was identified as phenomenal minimal content; the latter is what answers to the correlative concept of objective content for phenomenality. My claim that sensory terms are ambiguous will be argued for largely independent of my theory of minimal content and objective content, but the fact that my theory provides a theoretical foundation for the ambiguity is one of its strengths.

The various terms for specific colors, smells, tastes, sounds, and tactile qualities (including solidity and liquidity, and texture terms) are what I call *sensory terms*. I argue that sensory terms are ambiguous between identifying (1) objective features of bodies that are external to the perceiver, features whose existence is independent of the perceiver, and (2) subjective features that are dependent on the perceiver and are internal. I hasten to add that these very subjective features are indisputably presented to the perceiver *as though* they exist apart from her and *as* actual features of external bodies, even though things are not this way. The ambiguity is genuine: (1) and (2) are distinct features. Failure to keep these different features clearly in focus has led to confusion in the arguments over phenomenal properties, either by begging questions against opposing positions or talking at cross-purposes. Recognizing the ambiguity resolves some of these disputes and clarifies what is really at issue in others.

Holding that sensory terms refer to these distinct features neither presupposes nor commits one to a dualistic ontology. It is simply to recognize that the referred to features are significantly different from one another, just as are many other features in the physical realm. Attempts to reduce or identify the one with the other are misguided. They must be recognized as playing important but different roles in the philosophical and scientific study of perception. Along these lines, I will provide reason to see that the classical identities, such as heat = mean kinetic energy of molecules and lightning = atmospheric electrical discharge must be cast in a new light, one that reflects this ambiguity. But the ambiguity also has consequences for how we should understand theses of mind-brain identity.[1]

Common Sense and Galileo

The thesis that there is the sort of ambiguity in sensory terms just indicated confounds common sense. The uncritical common-sense view, both ancient and modern, holds that, say, color and heat terms are univocal. In addition, the color and heat of the flame *are really in the flame*. These two common-sense beliefs draw their strength from the indisputable fact that our experiences vividly present such features as being features *of* external objects, not as effects on our sensory apparatus or some internal mental item or feature. To common sense, 'heat' and 'color' are understood as applying to . . . you know, what we see and feel *out there*. The "feel" of heat is crucial to something's being heat, and the heat we feel is *right there in the fire itself*; the color of the flame is just the color expanse that we *see out there*. They are "indwelling properties of some external body."[2] If you doubt these things, just look at and reach out and touch the flame, then you'll know. Or so one might argue on the common-sense view.

It is well known that this common-sense view of colors, heat, etc. has not been universally held. Democritus may have been the first in the Western tradition to challenge it. A more sustained challenge began in the work of Descartes and Galileo, with Boyle, Locke, and others following.[3] Galileo states that, with regard to qualities such as extension, shape, and motion, "by no stretch of imagination can I conceive of any [corporeal] body apart from these conditions." These "conditions" are what he comes to call "objective qualities"; they are co-extensive with those we now call "primary qualities." But with regard to those he called "subjective" and which we now call "secondary," Galileo says this:

. . . these tastes, odors, colors, etc., so far as their objective existence is concerned, are nothing but mere names for something which resides exclusively in our sensitive body (*corpo sensitivo*), so that if the perceiving creatures were removed, all of these qualities would be annihilated and abolished from existence. (1623/1960, pp. 27–28)

As we saw in chapter 4, Galileo offers a fascinating and rather detailed proposal of how various combinations and actions of objective or real qualities could cause or give rise to the various subjective qualities we experience, and he explicitly rejects the idea that heat, color, odor, etc. are "indwelling properties" of ordinary external objects. At one point, he claims to have "now shown how such affectations, often reputed to be indwelling properties of some external body, have really no existence save in us, and apart from us are mere names" (30–31). The qualities that external bodies have are not at all like the subjective qualities of color, heat, etc. Thus, Galileo explicitly denies the common-sense beliefs on these matters and speaks of two kinds of properties: the subjective and the objective. In contrast, the common-sense view has no need of this subjective/objective distinction in discussing (say) color and shape, because it takes color, heat, odors, etc. as having the same standing as did shape, motion, number, and the rest—all were thought to be intrinsic ("indwelling") features of ordinary bodies.

Objectivists, Subjectivists, and Instruments

In recent times, there have been advanced objectivist and subjectivist accounts of secondary qualities. The objectivist, like the early common-sense view just sketched, tends to identify, say, color with some external objective feature; nevertheless, the modern-day objectivist's view is significantly different from the common-sense view, as the objective features picked out are not at all like the phenomenal features that common sense attributes to the external bodies themselves, since the objective features of heat or color are, e.g., mean molecular kinetic energy or spectral reflectances. This view holds that the visual sensory apparatus detects some objective feature of bodies, downplaying the subjective features as merely a means, ours, for detecting these objective features.[4] The subjectivist, on the other hand, tends to identify colors and such with the features presented in sensory experiences, internal subjective features of the perceiver or his experiences, distinguishing these from any external causes. Subjectivist accounts subscribe to a "massive error theory" of perception, since the external objects and features do not, on this view, resemble the way sensory experiences present them; objectivists, on the other hand, seek to avoid this consequence by identifying color, taste, etc. with some objective features.

Let us explore the objectivist's idea that our sensory experiences are how we detect various objective features in our environment through an analogy already used to a simple detecting device (chapter 3), but now examining claims about the "reality" or nature of the internal states of such devices. Voltage in a cable can be measured by a voltmeter; this device changes its states in response to variations in voltage applied to it. Disconnect the voltmeter and those states disappear, though the voltage applied to the cable may still be present. No mystery here. One readily grants this without the slightest temptation to say that the voltmeter states are not real and "apart from the instrument are mere names" (to paraphrase Galileo). Clearly, there is also no need to posit some non-physical stuff that has the voltmeter states.

Just so, I suggest, for our experiences. When we think of sentient beings as, in part, complicated multi-purpose detecting devices, states produced in such "devices" by various objective events will cease when devices of that type (sentient beings) are removed, just as Galileo held. But this should no more commit one to the denial of the reality of our internal (subjective) states than we are committed to the reality the voltmeter's internal (objective) states. Nor does the claim that such states of sentient beings are real commit one to the existence of some non-physical stuff as the medium for them any more than it does in the case of an ordinary instrument, such as a voltmeter. That these states are essentially dependent on the existence of a certain sort of detecting device (say, a human being or a voltmeter) does not imply that the states of the body that are produced when it detects some objective feature in its characteristic way are themselves unreal, nor that such "states of detection" require a special medium.

Nor is it true that recognizing these distinctive subjective, phenomenal features commits one to an act-object analysis, where one is aware of some internal image that represents or resembles an external object or feature, as some have argued.[5] It is simply to recognize that they are indisputable occurrences that certainly are causally related to a variety of objective physical events. They are *data* that require analysis. To insist on their status as data that require explanation is not to subscribe to any particular theory of them. Nor does it commit us to any particular methodology.

The sense-data theories of the twentieth century were attempts to explain such data. Their proponents were unable to provide an explanation of these incontrovertible appearances largely because they took the appearances to be *objects* or *individuals* somehow inspected by the perceiver on an internal screen. (Compare my discussion of the "phenomenological fallacy" below.) The appearances, however, could not support this heavy theoretical baggage imposed upon them by the sense-data theories. The failure of sense-data theories to explain the appearances in no way undermines the need for an explanation of the appearances, however.

The appearances at issue are the phenomenal aspects of our experiences, and I take the term 'qualia' simply as a label for such starting points, a kind of recalcitrant data.[6] In contrast, the sense data of sense-data theories may be, and have been, viewed as theoretical entities of those theories. As such, one might demand evidence for *positing* them—for example, do they increase explanatory power? The "qualia" at issue, viewed as incontrovertible data, are not thereby taken as either entities or posits of some theory. Therefore, one cannot reject them on grounds that they do not increase explanatory power, or that they do not have causal powers. These appearances are starting points for theorizing. Any theory of mental states must explain why they appear to us as they do, regardless of their ultimate ontological status. To paraphrase Descartes in another context: *That* we are presented with appearances (colors, warmth, and so on) in experience cannot be doubted; still, we must inquire as to *what* they are. There is no requirement that any such analysis involves a spectator examining objects on an internal screen.

There is also no good reason to deny the reality of subjective states that arise in creatures like us when stimulated by various objective features. As Searle has emphasized, it is an objective fact that we have such states. So, the reality of our internal states and that of, say, a voltmeter, are on a par. There is no more reason to deny the realty of one than the other.

There is, however, a much more recalcitrant problem than that of the reality of our internal states, one that goes to the "how possibly" question raised in chapter 3. This problem results from an important dissimilarity between our internal states and those of simple instruments. In our own case, the internal states in question have certain distinctive features; they are subjective and have "what it is like" aspects. But since the objective events that produce our subjective states are radically different in character from what they produce, the idea that the former give rise to the latter seems unfathomable, at least to many.[7] It is important to realize for present purposes, however, that to deny the reality of these subjective aspects is a mistake.

The Subjective/Objective and Real/Unreal Distinctions Compared

If what has just been argued is so, then the failure of sense-data theories to account for qualia does not trump the need for explanation of subjective states and their features in a non-dismissive manner. One way to be dismissive with regard to these subjective features has already been argued against; it is to deny that they are real. Galileo did this. Not only did he draw the distinction between the objective and the subjective properties, he denied that the latter were real. I do not question the appropriateness of the subjective/objective distinction, but I have already challenged the further claim that the subjective features are not real. I now add to that challenge. What is gained by this denial? Given that there exist causal relations between the objective, real features of external bodies and the subjective experiences of sentient beings, why deny that the subjective experiences are real? Can real causes have "unreal" effects? Galileo's reasons for denying their reality are, I think, clear enough: Remove sentient beings and the colors and the rest of the subjective features disappear, while the shaped particles in motion remain. But this difference is already clearly marked by the subjective/objective distinction. What further point is made by utilizing the vague real/unreal distinction? None. It marks nothing more than what is already indicated by the former distinction.[8]

Galileo himself thought that subjective experiences were caused by objective features, and he advanced fascinating explanations of how the objective features could give rise to the particular qualitative features we experience.[9] But if subjective experiences are caused by objective properties there can be no good reason to hold that the causes are real and the effects not. I think a more accurate way to portray Galileo's intent would be simply to state that he meant to put the subjective experiences aside as not properly in the domain of physics. The dependence of secondary qualities on sentient beings, no longer a surprising claim to many of us, was a radical claim in his time and still conflicts with the "common-sense view." But it is a claim that can and should be made without denying the reality of the subjective features.[10]

The Ambiguity in Sensory Terms and Why Talk of Real Essences Should Be Dismissed

A subtler way of dismissing the subjective features is to identify the quality in question with some objective feature external to the sentient being—say, molecular kinetic energy, spectral reflectances, dispositions of external bodies, or even brain processes. Often, when they claim that there are such identifications, modern-day theorists think they are stating what is the "true nature" or "real essence" of color, heat, or whatever.[11] One thing that is wrong with such approaches is that they presuppose that there is a *single* thing that it is, say, "color" or "heat," and that the job is to find out just what that one thing is. The world might have been this way; however, given what science has taught us about such phenomena, our experiences of them, and how sensory terms are embedded in discourse, this is not how things are.

What I mean by the phrase "how sensory terms are embedded in discourse" may be clarified by an example. As already noted, common sense has held for centuries that heat is *in* the fire. You feel it—the heat *in* the fire—as you approach it. The flame is *itself* hot. Heat is a simple intrinsic property of various things, which we may detect by touch. On a (naive and early) common-sense view, the word 'heat' indicates a univocal feature of external bodies. Had there been no kinetic theory of heat, or some such theory, the word might have continued to have a univocal sense—one indicating an external and intrinsic qualitative property of some bodies. Enter the kinetic theory and things change.[12] Heat is now identified with mean molecular kinetic energy, an objective, non-phenomenal property, which many claim to be the "true nature" or "real essence" of heat.

The introduction of the kinetic theory of heat is a critical juncture. In earlier times, mean molecular kinetic energy was unknown, though people felt heat. What became of the felt heat upon the discovery of molecular kinetic energy? Although Galileo told us it is not real, we have seen reason to think that this assertion amounts to simply saying that it is not an objective feature of the world, insofar as it depends on beings such as ourselves. Though such subjective features are not properly in the domain of physics, as Galileo saw, they and their relation to objective features are properly in the domain of philosophical and psychological investigations; moreover, such investigations may be conducted without compromising the objectivity of the analysis. (See chapter 3.)

The word 'heat' may be taken to refer to the molecular kinetic energy *or* the subjective feeling of heat, for the latter has not disappeared upon discovery of the former. In discourse, 'heat' is, in fact, used in both senses,[13] though often it is only implicit.

So it is with all the sensory terms on my view—they all have this systematic ambiguity between features in the world, external to a perceiver, that typically cause certain states in creatures like us, and the subjective, phenomenal features themselves that are typically caused in this way. When I maintain that there is this systematic ambiguity, I am not merely appealing to the tendency to conflate the two senses; rather, I am arguing that in fact the two senses pick out different, though related, features, each of which is of independent interest. The phenomenal features are not, *as such*, features *of* external bodies.[14] Moreover, insofar as perception presents these very features as features *of* external bodies, it is systematically in error. There are, however, *other* features—features that are *of* external bodies that causally interact, under the right conditions, with creatures such as us so as to produce the phenomenal qualities.[15] The error is based on a failure to distinguish between detecting states and their features, on the one hand, and what is detected, on the other. Both mark important real phenomena in nature, requiring further investigation, but arguments between the subjectivist and objectivist would seem to exclude one or the other of these.

The subjectivist sometimes argues that, since we experience, say, color as a homogeneous, "grainless" simple, an objectivist's account that attributes a great deal of structure to color is incompatible with this homogeneous presentation and, therefore, the objectivist cannot have it right. The objectivist, in response, coins a fallacy that she accuses the subjectivist of having committed in this argument, something called the "fallacy of total information." This fallacy, it is alleged, results from the Cartesian idea that our perceptions are completely and infallibly known by us; they have no hidden features. Once it is recognized that this fallacy is operative in the subjectivist's reasoning, the objectivist continues, there is no bar to accepting the objectivist's account of color—an account that uncovers the hidden features of color. Similar arguments on both sides can be run for the other sensory modalities.

This pointless dispute illustrates the dangers of not explicitly recognizing and adopting the ambiguity of sensory terms. The objectivist, in effect, changes the subject in this dispute. Even if one grants that there is more to color perception than is revealed in some "grainless" experience, and thus that color perception does not give total information of "color," still *the fact that there is a grainless experience is itself "information" that requires explanation*. It is just that information that the subjectivist wants explained. In short, for perception to pose a problem for the objectivist it need not be supposed that one has total information in perception, or that one has complete knowledge of what is known in perception. The so-called fallacy of total information is not what drives the subjectivist's problem.

The subjectivist's point is that what the perceiver experiences in perception, call it x, demands explanation. This x cannot be identified with properties of external bodies, micro-physical or otherwise. The x here, as I see it, is what was identified in chapter 3 as *phenomenal minimal content*. It is the *phenomenal aspect* of the perception *as perceived* by the perceiver, just as minimal content is the *subject* of a thought *as conceived* by the thinker. The uniform colored expanse that the agent is aware of need not exist as a feature of material bodies any more than phlogiston need exist for a thinker to have it as the minimal content of her thought. (See chapter 1.) On my theory, there is no danger, therefore, of turning these appearances into troublesome objects or sense data that the perceiver inspects on some "inner screen."

Explaining something other than x—say, dispositions or the microphysical structure of external bodies—does not address the subjectivist's problems, no matter how emphatically one insists that color *just is* this micro-physical structure, or whatever. The shortcomings of the objectivist's account here vis à vis the subjectivist's concerns would not be altered a bit were she to add the claim that this particular micro-structure is the "essence" of color. But, by the same token, the subjectivist would not diminish the objectivist's claims regarding color were she to insist that the phenomenal aspect of color experiences is the "essence" of color. For, just as a complete analysis of thought requires two kinds of content, so too does perception. A complete analysis of phenomenality requires not only phenomenal minimal content but also a corresponding objective content. It is the latter that the objectivist is getting at in these disputes. Though the subjectivist and the objectivist both are free to propose what is the "essence" of color, neither can substantiate his claims. Both the subjective and objective features are real and important phenomena; they each require explanation, as do the relations between them. Subjectivist or objectivist accounts are inadequate to the extent that they exclude one of these.

The general claim that all sensory terms are ambiguous in the way just described is simply to recognize the fact that, when there is talk of sense experience, sometimes the topic of discussion (the focus, or what is at issue) is the phenomenal features as experienced by perceivers, and sometimes the topic is the external causes of those experiences. Which is at issue is too often unclear. Sometimes there is an imperceptible shift from one to the other in a single discourse, and sometimes they are simply conflated. Both are important, and the relations between them can and should be examined. Nothing is gained and something is lost in our understanding of perception by ignoring either one. Neither should be denigrated or dismissed because of any alleged discoveries of the "true nature" or "real essence" of color, and similarly for the other sensory modalities.

Generally, I find talk of real essences as gratuitous and distracting additions to substantive matters. For the case at issue, it is important to recognize that, even if one were to grant real essence talk as useful for some purpose, whether the objectivist or the subjectivist were to have gotten it right, what the other investigates remains important and relevant to our understanding of color. We require further knowledge of each and their relations to one another. Suppose an objectivist were right about the real essence, in some sense, of color, heat, etc. It would not follow that there is *nothing more* to be said about various associated phenomena—the subjective experiences, typically caused by the identified objective features, that sometimes are the referent of the corresponding sensory term. All that would follow from this assumption is that these subjective experiences are not germane to the alleged real essence. This is certainly compatible with phenomenal states' having (many) other features that are of immense independent interest.[16] A similar conclusion follows if we replace 'objectivist' with 'subjectivist' in the above, with appropriate other changes. Such moves in no way give reason to doubt the described ambiguity in sensory terms; our linguistic practices support the claim.

Traditional Claims of Identity and Reduction in Light of the Ambiguity

Here I offer a plausible account of the use of the word 'heat' that fits the facts and is in accord with the conclusion that the word is ambiguous between the objective and the subjective. Given that parallel facts obtain for the other sensory modalities, the conclusion also is in accord with the ambiguity of terms for these modalities. This has consequences for some traditionally held identities and reductions, to which I now turn. These alleged identities are typically, but mistakenly, advanced as giving the "essence" or "true nature" of the left item of the identities.

A number of identities have been advanced as successful reductions. Consider the following "reductions"—call them f-reductions, the f standing for 'feature':

heat = kinetic energy of molecules

light = electromagnetic radiation

lightning = electrical discharge in the atmosphere

water = H_2O.

Contrast the f-reductions with the following reductions—call them t-reductions, the t standing for theory[17]:

thermodynamics to statistical mechanics

ray optics to wave optics

wave optics to electromagnetic theory.

With t-reductions, we have "reductions *within* physical science. These reductions are inter-theoretic reductions, reductions of one theory to another, both of which are within physical science. For example, and with simplifications, when various statistical assumptions about the behavior of molecules are made, one can deduce that the pressure they exert on the containing walls is proportional to the mean kinetic energy ($p = 2E/3V$, or $pV = 2E/3$). When we compare this result with the Boyle-Charles law ($pV = kT$), we see that the latter could be deduced from the various statistical assumptions about the behavior of molecules and the laws of mechanics, "*if* the temperature were in some way related to the mean kinetic energy of the molecular motions." Thus a postulate is introduced: "$2E/3 = kT$, that is, that the absolute temperature of an ideal gas is proportional to the mean kinetic energy of the molecules assumed to constitute it." (Nagel 1961, pp. 344–345)

My point here is that 'T', temperature, is a concept that has been regimented within scientific theory, and it is *that* concept that is then reduced. Its regimentation is via the various techniques devised to measure it and the role it plays in the scientific theory—for example, in the Boyle-Charles law. We thus obtain certain identities of the corresponding theoretical elements. In this case, the approximate identity is of temperature and mean kinetic energy of molecules.

To my mind, reducing temperature, in its technical, theoretical sense, and in the way indicated, is some significant distance from reducing "heat." It is temperature, not heat, that gets reduced. Prior to this t-reduction, the term 'temperature' is regimented by a scientific theory. I accept the various t-reductions and resulting identities. There are, however, serious problems with the f-reductions and the alleged identities. Whereas in t-reductions the terms on *both* sides of the various identities have been antecedently regimented within some scientific domain, in f-reductions the left-hand member of the identity is embedded in ordinary discourse.[18]

A reason, I submit, that so many have endorsed the alleged identities based upon the f-reductions is that they tend to conflate them with corresponding t-reductions. This is unacceptable. First, the 'heat' of ordinary discourse is not quite the 'T' of the Charles-Boyle law, with similar remarks for the other f-reductions. Second, the alleged f-reductions are attempts to reduce a folk concept or term—a concept or term not in a scientific theory—to a concept or term that is in a scientific theory. In view of the different roles that ordinary and scientific terms play, particularly, concerning their relative preciseness, and the very different settings in which they are embedded, this is peculiar at best. Even with the inter-theoretic t-reductions, where both terms occur in scientific theories, certain "bridge principles" are required (the postulate quoted from Ernest Nagel above, for example). Since 'heat' is a term from ordinary discourse, not a term regimented by a scientific theory and not involved in a t-reduction, whatever bridge principle is proposed, it will inevitably be far less precise. Any attempt to identify or (f-) reduce a folk term with a theoretical term is far more suspect than an identification or (t-) reduction of two scientifically regimented theoretical terms.

Well, then, just what exactly do these identities based upon f-reductions assert? My contention is that in all these cases there is no identity, there are *two* features here, and nothing is causally "reduced," though there often is a causal connection between the two. This is not how the situation is usually understood, however. Consider this passage in John Searle's 1992 book *The Rediscovery of the Mind*, hereafter cited as *RM*:

In general in the history of science, successful causal reductions tend to lead to ontological reductions. Because where we have a successful causal reduction, we simply redefine the expression that denotes the reduced phenomena in such a way that the phenomena in question can now be identified with their causes. (p. 115)

Now many, including those who have serious disagreements with Searle on closely related issues, would agree with this statement. I do not, despite the orthodox view to the contrary.

Let me forestall an obvious objection based on a possible misunderstanding of my claim that there are two features (subjective and objective) involved and not a reduction. The objection might go as follows: "Look, although the *experience of heat* is not reduced to kinetic energy of molecules, *heat* (usually said with great emphasis) is thus reduced." I am well aware that the early identity theorists Place and Smart were much concerned with distinguishing *heat* from an *experience of heat*, *color* from an *experience of color*, and so on, and they thought by doing so they showed that certain objections were misplaced. That may be, but it does not blunt my objection, as it is not based on such a confusion.[19] Rather, my objection here is that in the case of heat (but similarly for the other sensory terms) *nothing* is reduced, causally or otherwise, and so not to the kinetic energy of molecules either.

First, there is an oddity in claiming that a causal reduction leads to an identity. Aside from some believers in God, most would deny that anything is self-caused. 'A causes B' implies 'A is *not* identical to B'. So, it is, or at least borders on, semantic nonsense to talk of identifying an effect with its cause.

Second, there is, I think, a subtler confusion that grounds the belief that a reduction has occurred or that an identity claim is in order. To unravel this confusion and to expose the emptiness of the identity claim, consider an alien being with radically different sensory apparatus than ours, yet capable of having experiences and with enough cognitive ability to also discover a theory of the kinetic energy of molecules. Suppose that this being can detect the kinetic energy of the ambient air, not by having heat experiences as we do, but by having certain subjective experiences radically different from any we have. Call them "Zeat-experiences." There is no obstacle to supposing that the alien would say, analogously to our own case, that Zeat = mean molecular kinetic energy and, although *Zeat-experiences* are not thus reduced, *Zeat is* (said with great emphasis on 'Zeat').

But just what is this Zeat that is allegedly reduced? Well, we know what mean molecular kinetic energy is, but, by hypothesis, we would not have a clue what Zeat is. Unfortunately, we have no more an idea of what heat is— apart from our experience—when it is said (again emphatically) that *heat is reduced* than we know what Zeat is in the expression *"Zeat is reduced."* Of course, we and the aliens know what heat or Zeat *experiences* are like, respectively, but it is *not these* that are reduced. What is reduced?

When we say that heat is reduced, either (i) our understanding of 'heat' in that statement trades on our understanding of 'the experience of heat' and the claim is then false, since all parties agree that the experience of heat has not been thus reduced, or (ii) it is understood as mean molecular kinetic energy, in which case there is no reduction, since something "reduced" to itself is no reduction (except in a technical mathematical sense that has no bearing on the matters at hand). There is no third candidate. We delude ourselves into thinking we are saying something significant when we say (with emphasis) that, although heat experiences are not reduced, *heat* is.

In short, *nothing was reduced—something new was discovered*, which we happen to naturally detect in a certain rough, qualitative way. As a result of this discovery, a new domain of discourse is introduced involving the kinetic energy of molecules; the term 'heat' is now applied within the new domain, while retaining—in a modified way—its earlier application, namely, to the feel of heat.[20] This is the crucial initiation point of the systematic ambiguity in the term.

This new placement of the original domain referred to by the term 'heat', away from external objects and into the subjective realm, is, perhaps, what Searle has called "carving off" the subjective. Searle also speaks of redefinition of terms such as 'heat' "in such a way that the phenomenon in question can now be identified with their causes" (*RM*, p. 115). Such "redefinitions" allegedly involve the identification of the phenomenon with the newly discovered objective events, such as molecular kinetic energy, though Searle is also careful to point out that "this redefinition does not eliminate, and was not intended to eliminate, the subjective experiences of heat (or color, etc.) from the world. They exist the same as ever." (120) Thus, although Searle does not explicitly talk about ambiguity in sensory terms, what he says about "carving off" (the subjective) and "redefinition" of the term (the objective) so as to apply to what is really a property of external bodies implicitly recognizes the subjective/objective ambiguity of sensory terms. But if the reading of Searle that I have suggested is correct, he should abandon talk of "causal reduction" in this context, for the reasons already indicated.

The much-heralded f-reductions based on identities of the sort "heat = mean molecular kinetic energy" trade on the ambiguity in the sensory terms at issue. But 'heat', in its pre-scientific sense, is not thereby reduced nor, as I have just argued, is anything else. Once science has uncovered certain objective features—features that are, and have been, imprecisely detected by means of certain of our subjective experiences—it is easy to see how (in a confused way) we are tempted to think that there is a reduction of the latter to the former. This false belief is forcefully abetted by the fact that the pre-scientific sense of 'heat', and other sensory terms, was such that the subjective phenomenal features associated with these terms *were thought to actually reside in the external bodies*. The persistent common-sense grip of this misconception makes it an easy though confused and mistaken step to the claim that a reduction or an identity has been determined. What we mistakenly thought was out there gets identified with or reduced to the kinetic energy of molecules, the new discovery. But what we thought was out there isn't there and never was, despite the appearances to the contrary. Instead, certain peculiarities of our own experiences were mistakenly projected as intrinsic properties of the external bodies. Once this is appreciated, talk of reduction or identity in these contexts is seen to be pointless and without merit.

Such scientific developments in fact warrant the claim that it is just false to project the phenomenal features that we experience onto or into the external bodies themselves. Distinct objective features that typically cause certain subjective experiences have earned their right to be the referents of sensory terms, but this does not usurp the distinctive subjective features' claim to the same role. By not explicitly recognizing the resulting ambiguity, it is obscurely and falsely presumed that some sort of reduction has occurred. I have argued that these scientific developments support neither claims of causal reductions nor identities of the sort discussed. They do support the claim that sensory terms are ambiguous between objective and subjective features.

I think there are pragmatic consequences here of some import to what philosophers have said about such reductions. A number of misleading or false claims have been made, the source of which can be traced back to ignoring the ambiguity in sensory terms. In particular, I think the failure to keep the ambiguity clearly in mind goes to the core of the dispute between objectivists and subjectivists. To put it in the baldest terms possible, as I see it, the objectivists are engaged in efforts to establish that the various features ("color," "heat," etc.) *just are* the corresponding regimented features science has uncovered, while the subjectivists are at pains to establish that "color," "heat," etc. *just are* the residual features (what the initial unambiguous folk term mistakenly attributed as intrinsic properties of external objects). I will return to this dispute in the last section of this chapter, but for now the important point is that even though philosophers may recognize the ambiguity in words such as 'color' and 'heat' *they are not minding the lesson*. Again to put it baldly: If one accepts the ambiguity, it is pointless for the objectivist to argue that, say, color is spectral reflectance *and* that the subjectivist is wrong, as it would be pointless for the subjectivist to similarly argue, with corresponding changes in the theses.

Of course, all of this implies that we must reevaluate the point of some traditional and hallowed identities that are deployed in philosophical discussions: sound = compression waves, light = electromagnetic radiation, lightning = electrical discharge, and even water = H_2O. If what I have said is correct, all of the left terms of these alleged identities are ambiguous. I will examine the lightning case in detail in the next section. The structure of the identity claim for lightning that is there developed and argued for is seen to be different from its usual portrayal. Its formulation codifies some of the issues regarding identity and reduction of heat raised above. The structure advanced is the pattern that all the other alleged identities should follow, if they are to be justified.

Of particular note is my extension of the above claims to ordinary things, for I include the alleged identity of water with H_2O. Debates about the real essence of water are also beside the point on my view. The term 'water' is ambiguous between its ordinary observational sense (a transparent, tasteless, odorless, colorless, liquid) and its objective realization (H_2O). As above,

I deny that there has been a reduction of water to H_2O, and for similar reasons.[21] A virtue of this proposal is that it provides a theoretical underpinning of the point that Eddington was making with his "two tables" and Wilfred Sellars with his contrast between the manifest and scientific images, and it does so within a general theory of mind.

The Importance of the Preceding for Mind-Brain Identity Claims: A Case Study

The early identity theorists in the philosophy of mind U. T. Place and J. J. C. Smart relied on such alleged identities (f-reductions) as those considered above as a kind of model for the identities they proposed in the philosophy of mind. They thought they had shown that, much in the way that one can establish that lightning = electrical discharge in the atmosphere, it was possible to establish that sensations = (a certain kind of) brain process. In this section, I detail their failure to take cognizance of the ambiguity of sensory terms and show how this renders their identity thesis misleading or false. I present what the justified structure of the relevant identity claim should be.

Place first illustrated the relevant kind of identity claim with the example that a cloud is a mass of water droplets in suspension.[22] Water droplets (or other particles) in suspension constitute a cloud; it is "nothing else" (1956/2000, p. 79). Place recognized that we are able to experience both a cloud and water droplets (as we move into the cloud) in the same way. Because this is not true of sensations and brain processes,[23] he sought a closer analogue for sensation–brain process identity:

The operations required to verify statements about consciousness and statements about brain processes are fundamentally different [in contrast to statements about clouds and water droplets in suspension]. To find a parallel for this feature we must examine other cases [than the cloud/water droplets identity] where an identity is asserted between something whose occurrence is verified by the ordinary processes of observation [as are sensations] and something whose occurrence is established by special scientific procedures [as are brain processes]. (ibid., p. 81)

Place holds, further, that the relevant parallel is found in the identity of lightning and electrical discharge:

As in the case of consciousness, however closely we scrutinize the lightning we shall never be able to observe the electric charges, and just as the operations for determining the nature of one's state of consciousness are radically different from those involved in determining the nature of one's brain processes, so the operations for determining the occurrence of lightning are radically different from those involved in determining the occurrence of a motion of electric charges. (ibid.)

For Place, then, occurrences of lightning and electric charges are determined in fundamentally different ways; the former are "verified by the ordinary processes of observation," while occurrences of the latter are "established by special scientific procedures" (ibid.). The reader may well ponder that I made much of something just like this in the previous section: each side of the pair of occurrences of heat and molecular motion, color and reflectance triplets, etc., are determined in fundamentally different ways, and just the different ways that Place cites for lightning and electric charges.

Place further recognizes that the basis for the identity claim cannot be merely systematic correlation of two sets of observations, as this would fail to distinguish it from causal relations (or accidental generalizations). Here is his response to this problem and its application to the case of lightning:

. . . we treat two sets of observations as observations of the same event in those *cases where the technical scientific observations set in the context of the appropriate body of scientific theory provide an immediate explanation of the observations made by the man in the street.* Thus we conclude that lightning is nothing more than a motion of electric charges, because we know that a motion of electric charges through the atmosphere, such as occurs when lightning is reported, *gives rise* to the type of visual stimulation which would lead an observer to report a flash of lightning. (p. 81, all emphases added)

This is an important and complicated point. According to Place, the two sets of observations that are correlated are (1) what an ordinary observer would report as an occurrence of lightning, which would be based on her unaided observation of a flash of light in the sky, and (2) observations resulting from scientific procedures that determine the occurrence of electrical discharge in the atmosphere. There is a subtlety in (2) that is typically overlooked. Because of this, I will treat the issues in some detail, detail that may appear to be tedious but which is required to tease out some important points, usually ignored, that pertain to the ambiguity of sensory terms.

The *observations* indicated in (2) are not of electrical discharge in the atmosphere as such, for, as Place correctly states in a passage quoted above, "however closely we scrutinize the lightning we shall never be able to observe the electrical charges." The observations indicated in (2) are the "technical scientific observations" Place mentions, and these are various instrument readings set in the context of the appropriate scientific theory. It is on the basis of these that we are able to determine that there are electrical discharges in the atmosphere. The latter determination requires the application of some relevant theory for both the gathering and the interpretation of the technical observations of (2). Once the occurrence of electrical discharge is thus determined, a crucial element comes into play before an identity claim may be made. It must be shown that "the technical scientific observations set in the context of the appropriate body of scientific theory provide an immediate explanation of the observations made by the man in the street," as quoted above.

Place is explicit on the necessity of this last step to establish the identity in question, for without it we cannot "treat the sets of observations [those of (1) and (2)] as observations of the same event" (as above). Moreover, the situation is no different in this respect for the sensation–brain process identity claim. For Place says that if what he has just said about lightning and electrical charges is correct, then "it would be necessary to show that introspective observations reported by the subject can be accounted for in terms of processes which are known to have occurred in his brain" (p. 81, emphasis added).

As far as I can tell, the introspective observations reported play the role of the ordinary observations ((1) above), and the brain processes play the role of the electrical discharge. But to continue the parallel, the brain processes themselves are not directly observed, they are not reported as observations of type (2); we no more observe brain processes, as such, than we observe electrical discharges. In both these cases certain technical scientific procedures are applied that result in certain (scientific) observations (say, instrument readings) which, in conjunction with a relevant theory, provide the basis for saying certain events (electrical discharges or brain processes) have occurred.

If what I have said is correct, the usual ways of formulating the familiar identities is misleading at best. We do not have an identity between sensations (lightning) and brain processes (electrical discharge); rather, there is an identity between what is indicated by the corresponding two sets of observations. The unobserved cause ("referent," if you like) of these two sets of observations is established to be the same.

The latter character of the identity claims at issue is obscured by talk of "the true nature" (essence?) of lightning , sensation, or whatever. This is exemplified by the following quotation from Smart:

This, it is now believed, is what the true nature of lightning is [electrical discharge in the atmosphere]. Note that there are not two things: a flash of lightning and an electrical discharge. There is one thing, a flash of lightning, which is described scientifically as an electrical discharge to the earth from a cloud of ionised water molecules. (88)

Of course, Smart has a point: Whenever there is an identity claim, there are not two things but one. I certainly do not dispute this; my point is that we must be careful as to how the identity claim is expressed because of the ambiguity in sensory terms. Smart continues:

. . . the "look" of lightning, may well in my view be a correlate of the electrical discharge. For in my view it is a brain state caused by the lightning. But we should no more confuse sensations of lightning with lightning than we confuse sensations of a table with a table. (89)

Now, the "look" of lightning is a flash of light. So, on Smart's view, the difference in 'flash of lightning' and 'lightning' is that between a sensation of lightning and lightning. These are not identical, since electrical discharges in the atmosphere "give rise to" (cause) flashes of lightning, and causes cannot be identical to their effects. Thus, if the identity in question is true, it must be that *flashes of lightning* differ from *lightning*.[24] Given what was established in the last section, we have what by now should be a familiar problem: if the look of lightning (flash) is distinct from lightning, just *what* is it that is said to be identical to electrical discharge in the atmosphere? By divorcing *flashes of lightning* from *lightning*, we are robbed of the *initial* content, the pre-scientific content, of the latter term. Do not say that it is just electrical discharge in the atmosphere, for then there is no point to the identity claim. 'Electrical discharge in the atmosphere = electrical discharge in the atmosphere' is trivial, analytic and uninformative, while 'lightning = electrical discharge in the atmosphere' appears to be none of these. So we need an explication of the content of the left term of the latter identity.

What Smart misses, and Place did not miss, is that the identities are between two sets of observations which are claimed to be of the same event. To establish such a contingent identity, we must show how we may treat two sets of observations obtained in fundamentally different ways as observations of *the same event*. Place provided an answer: The scientifically determined event (based on observations of set (2)) causes or gives rise to the ordinary observation, that of set (1) discussed above.

Is Smart just availing himself of this last point? I think not. I think Smart's statements evince certain confusions on this fundamentally important point. To see this, let us first ask whether the "look" of lightning is irrelevant to the discussion of the identity in question (as Smart, but not Place, maintains). Suppose that it is irrelevant. Then how exactly is the term 'lightning' used in the identity? Smart appears to give us an answer:

> . . . to forestall irrelevant objections, I should like to make it clear that by "lightning" I mean the publicly observable physical object lightning, not a visual sense-datum of lightning [the "look" of lightning]. (88)

I say that Smart *appears* to give us an answer because just what the "publicly observable object lightning" is anything but clear. Smart (ibid.) has maintained that the "true nature of lightning" is electrical discharge in the atmosphere. (88) But *this* "true nature" is *not publicly observable*, for *it is not observable at all*, and Place agrees with me on this ("however closely we scrutinize the lightning we shall never be able to observe the electric charges"). What if anything here is publicly observable here are the results of the applications of the appropriate scientific procedures Place alluded to: the instruments and their readings (set within the appropriate theory) used to detect electrical discharge.

So, if the look of lightning is irrelevant, as Smart maintains, and the motions of electric charges are not publicly observable, *nothing of relevance* is publicly observable on Smart's view, contrary to his claim.[25] It appears that the appeal to "the publicly observable physical object lightning" is at best evasive and at worst vacuous.

Flashes of lightning are determined to occur by "ordinary observation"; they may be observed with the unaided eye. Electrical discharge cannot be so observed; electric charges are theoretical entities. There is no reason to review here the long history of the observational/theoretical distinction in the philosophy of science. The upshot of that history is that there is no sharp distinction between observational and theoretical entities, but a continuum, with theory intruding to varying degrees throughout. Still, certain occurrences fall closer to one end of the continuum than the other, from ordinary observations to scientific observations. For example, the observation of a white track of a certain shaped in a cloud chamber is publicly observable in one sense—there is inter-subjective agreement on the appearance of such a track—but the electron whose motion through the chamber caused the ionization of molecules that appear as the track is not publicly observable. It is metaphorical, at best, to say that one "observes" the electron when one observes the track. Just so for the case of lightning: Motions of electrons through the atmosphere cause the flashes we observe. Neither in this case nor in the case of the cloud chamber are *electrons* publicly observable. What, if anything, is publicly observable in these cases are tracks and flashes—not motions of electrical charges. But the publicly observable track and flashes amount to no more than inter-subjective agreement on the "look" of electric charges in motion in these different circumstances. Thus, Smart is wrong in denying the relevance of the look of lightning to the identity claim.

Smart makes a further error. He obscures the critical fine points Place specifies regarding the important placement of the ordinary observations in the context of a scientific theory. Place recognizes the importance of explaining how certain scientific entities or processes give rise to the two sets of observations. Smart obscures this by abandoning the "look" of lightning, which is the means of obtaining one of the sets of observations in the identity claim. We have seen that this left no publicly observable lightning, despite Smart's claim to the contrary. Since Smart provides no explication or candidate for just what is supposed to be publicly observable on his view, his contention "by 'lightning' I mean the publicly observable physical object lightning" is vacuous.

I am in strong agreement with Place's statements that I have quoted, but I think they force a different formulation of the identities at issue:

(i)   lightning = electrical discharge in the atmosphere.

This identity claim is confused because of the ambiguity in 'lightning'. One sense of the word is that of the subjective flash of light that we may, and do, mistakenly project onto external events, the look (as with heat, the feel was projected). Call it 'lightning$_s$'. The other sense is the actual external event that has since been discovered. Call it 'lightning$_o$' (which we normally detect in a subjective way). Now, while the term 'lightning' has two senses, the expression 'electrical discharge in the atmosphere' does not; it has a univocal and objective reading. Thus, (i) has two readings:

(ia)   lightning$_s$ = electrical discharge in the atmosphere
(ib)   lightning$_o$ = electrical discharge in the atmosphere.

That (ia) is false is clear; moreover, (ib), though true, is trivial, analytic, and uninformative, as we saw above. We need a different formulation.

Recall that Place starts with two sets of observations, the ordinary, subjective ones and the scientifically determined ones. For brevity, let us call the ordinary and scientific observations OO and SO, respectively. The latter are neither electric charges nor observations of them; they are instrument readings that form the basis for verifying the discovery that electrical discharge has occurred. The idea behind the identity claim is that the observations of the sets OO and SO are determined by same event, which we may express as

(ii)   OO = SO.

This quite roughly captures an idea often expressed by advocates of identities such as (i) when they say that the terms of the identity have different senses but the same reference. However, this is rather odd when applied to (ii), because the crucial element of the identity that it is supposed to represent is not reference; rather it is that the same event *causes* or determines *both* sets of observations, and this is left out.

What to do? Well, in line with Smart's claim that we have discovered the "true nature" of lightning, we might say the following:

(iii)   What is going on in the atmosphere at t = electrical discharge in the atmosphere.

This characterizes the discovery that has been made, but the left term of the identity lacks specificity. How we normally pick out the *what* of (iii) is through ordinary observation, so a more precise specification of (iii) might be

(iv)   What "gives rise to [is a cause of] the type of visual stimulation that would lead an observer to report a flash of lightning" (as Place put it) = electrical discharge in the atmosphere.

I think what (iv) asserts is far clearer and more defensible than (i). I do not think Place confused (i) and (iv), given his careful statements as to how the two sets of observations are so differently determined, though caused by one and the same event. Indeed, for Place, unlike Smart, the "look of lightning," which is implicated in (iv), is not irrelevant to establishing the identity. It plays an essential role because it is the result of ordinary observation and is an element of one of the correlated observation sets.

The kinetic energy of molecules, compression waves in a medium, or even H_2O molecules are no more publicly observable when one feels heat, hears sound, or looks at a glass of water than is electrical discharge when one looks at a stormy sky. Nor are they publicly observable in any other way—these scientific entities are not observable. Such entities and processes are scientifically determined to occur, and they are what typically cause or gives rise to what we do sense under certain conditions. One might argue (A) that the "true referents" of the sensory terms such as 'heat', 'sound', 'water', and 'lightning' are the scientific entities just mentioned or (B) that what one means by those terms is the "true nature" of the relevant phenomena, as Smart does, but in either case that is quite different from holding that such alleged true natures are publicly observable.

Now, (i) is a much more exciting-sounding claim than (iv), for it suggests that a reduction of one thing to another has occurred—that we have discovered the "true essence" or "true nature" of *lightning*—whereas (iv) makes no such suggestion or implication. Having said that, I should make it clear that I do accept (iii) above and can accept claims that we have discovered the true nature (appropriately understood) of *what is going on* in the atmosphere on these occasions. My point is that, even granting all that, one cannot simply say that one has discovered the true nature of *lightning*. 'Lightning' has two senses, and electrical discharge captures only one of them. Once we are clear on the ambiguities involved and the exact nature of the identities warranted, we see that talk of "true natures" or "real essences" adds nothing.

Indeed, all the discussions of the various scientific identities touted in discussions of issues in the philosophy of mind are presented as if they demonstrate past successes of reductions. What I have tried to show in this section and the previous one is that these clear scientific successes are not successes of reduction, and that the formulations of the alleged identity claims are importantly misleading. *There is no reduction, and the identities suggested by the usual formulations* (for example, (i)) *are at best misleading*. I have made this point explicitly with regard to lightning here, and earlier I made it with regard to heat.

The argument clearly applies to all of the classical identities cited in these contexts. The scientific successes referred to are the discoveries of objective phenomena or processes, which can cause in us certain sensations. Before those discoveries, we mistakenly projected the subjective features that we experienced as objective features of external objects and applied terms such as 'heat', 'color', 'sound', and 'lightning'. But the features that were projected are not what gets identified with the newly discovered phenomena. Instead, something much less determinate—"what is going on," or "what is out there," things not open to ordinary observation as are the subjective features—is identified with the newly discovered scientific process or entity.

If this is correct, the traditional scientific "identities," as usually formulated, cannot serve as models for an identity between sensations and brain processes, for they are either specifications of new discoveries, as with (iii), or they are vacuous, as shown in the discussion of Smart and in the previous section regarding heat. Thus, without denying any of the identities (when properly formulated), we recognize that there has been no reduction of the subjective to the objective in these cases, only that our projections were in error and what typically causes the subjective has been discovered.

These results raise another point that has not been adequately appreciated. When sensation–brain process identity was first proposed, one of the touted virtues was that it removed concerns over the explanatory gap: The problem of how brain states or processes could give rise to phenomenal states would evaporate if they were not two things but one. This superficial resolution should never have been accepted. At best, it shows that if there is mind-brain identity the explanatory gap has a solution; it does not provide the solution. Anyone who was initially concerned with the explanatory gap would not be relieved on being told "Don't worry; they are in fact identical." Such an individual still would be concerned with how this could be so, even while accepting the identity.

Place correctly specifies what is required to establish that two sets of observations that are differently determined are observations of the same event. In making this point, Place is implicitly acknowledging the ambiguity of sensory terms and the correctness of (iv). Therefore, if brain-mind identity is to be modeled upon various scientific identities, the model is (iv), not (i). But this raises the explanatory gap again, this time even more seriously than just indicated. If Place is right regarding what is required to establish such identities, the sensation–brain process identity claim presupposes a solution of the explanatory gap. Compare (part of) the passage already quoted above:

. . . we treat two sets of observations as observations of the same event in those cases where the technical scientific observations set in the context of the appropriate body of scientific theory provide an immediate *explanation* of the observations made by the man in the street. (81, emphasis added)

In this case, one set of observations are the ordinary sensory ones we make when we look, feel, taste, and so forth. The other set of observations consists of readings of instruments connected to brains. Simply being told that the sets are identical (as above with OO = SO) does not provide the explanation that Place himself correctly says is required. Without that explanation, the subjective remains intact and no more tractable on the supposition of mind-brain identity.[26]

The "Phenomenological Fallacy," Topic-Neutral Sentences, and the Explanatory Gap

I now turn to Place's assessment of a problem that was raised by the early-twentieth-century physiologist Charles Scott Sherrington. I think Sherrington was raising the explanatory gap problem. Place's discussion of him illustrates the point made at the end of the previous section: that Place, in advancing mind (sensation)–brain identity, left out the crucial explanation that he recognized was required for similar identity claims. Place quotes Sherrington:

... there follows on, or attends, the stage of brain-cortex reaction [the physiochemical] an event or set of events [the psychical] quite inexplicable to us, which both as to themselves and as to the causal tie between them and what preceded them science does not help us; a set of events *seemingly incommensurable* with any events leading up to it. The self "sees" the sun; it senses a two-dimensional disc of brightness, located in the "sky". . . . Of hint that this is within the head there is none. Vision is saturated with this strange property called "projection," the unargued inference that what it sees is at a "distance" from the seeing "self." Enough has been said [though not quoted either here or by Place] to stress that in the sequence of events a step is reached where *a physical situation in the brain leads to a psychical, which however contains no hint of the brain or any other bodily part.* (82, emphasis added)

According to Sherrington, the psychical "attends" the physical, "projects" outward, "contains no hint of the brain," and is "seemingly incommensurable" with it. This is clearly an early expression of the explanatory gap problem, though Place does not recognize it as such. Indeed, Place is blind to the problem that Sherrington raises and claims to find in it a logical mistake:

This logical mistake, which I shall refer to as the "phenomenological fallacy," is the mistake of supposing that when the subject describes his experience, when he describes how things look, sound, smell, taste, or feel to him, he is describing the literal properties of objects and events on a peculiar sort of internal cinema or television screen, usually referred to in the modern psychological literature as the "phenomenal field." (82)

Central to what Place characterizes as a mistake is the idea of a subject describing properties of *objects* on some *internal field*. Did Sherrington use these ideas in the passage quoted? I find no evidence of it. I understand Sherrington to be saying that our experiences, described from the first-person perspective (that is, what we apparently sense, the "psychical") are "seemingly incommensurable" with and certainly radically different from descriptions of brain processes (the "physiochemical") that they "attend." There is no talk here of objects on some internal phenomenal field. What Place describes as a mistake does not occur in the passage from Sherrington, as far as I can tell. There is not the slightest suggestion on Sherrington's part that the subject is examining properties of objects on some internal field and then projects them to the external world. On the contrary, the projection is (psychologically) immediate.[27] The claim that it is a projection and that the external bodies do not themselves have the properties we experience rests on other considerations, largely scientific; these considerations, though clearly operative, are not discussed in the passage quoted by Place. It is uncontroversial that in experience we see objects as though they were at a distance without perceived inference ("unargued inference," to use Sherrington's phrase), and that we do so because of events in our brains, although the former gives "no hint" of the latter. It is just as uncontroversial that experiences and brain events, at the very least, *appear* radically different in character. Maintaining these things does not require objects on some internal field, no phenomenological fallacy committed here.

Sherrington, however, goes on to draw a questionable conclusion:

The supposition has to be, it would seem, [that there are] two continuous series of events, one physiochemical, the other psychical, and at times interaction between them. (82)

I agree with Place that this does not follow logically from the considerations Sherrington offered. Nor is it true. But clearly the falsity of a conclusion does not imply the falsity of the considerations from which it is drawn. It seems to me that Sherrington, in keeping with scientific practice, put the supposition forth by way of offering a hypothesis to explain certain facts mentioned in the previous quote, which I summarize as follows:

(1)   Our experiences present no hint of anything going on in our heads.

(2)   The projection is immediate ("unargued inference").

(3)   These experiences appear to have radically different features than those of brain processes.

Place himself endorses (3). He holds that the "operations for determining the nature of one's own state of consciousness are radically different from those involved in determining the nature of one's brain processes" (81).[28] He also describes them as "fundamentally different" on the same page. I take it to be evident that Place would endorse (1) and (2) too. In consequence, putting aside the "supposition" that there are two series of events (the psychical and the physical), we must still contend with (1)–(3). Describing properties of objects on an internal field, the core idea of the "phenomenological fallacy," is not operative in the inference ("two continuous series of events," already put aside). More important for present purposes, it is certainly not needed to support (1)–(3). Sherrington mentions neither objects nor properties on an internal field, and what he says does not presuppose them. Indeed, Sherrington talks throughout of *events*, and he does not mention "internal fields" or anything that would correspond to such.

There remains the question whether the facts (1)–(3) pose a problem for the identity theory. I think that they do in a way that Place does not see. The apparent incommensurable character of our experiences and the events that go on in our brains is precisely what make it seem utterly (to use Sherrington's word) *inexplicable* that the one can give rise to or be identical with the other. The problem Sherrington points out is none other than what has come to be known in recent times as the "explanatory gap problem" (discussed in chapter 4).

Since Place apparently misses the force of Sherrington's version of the explanatory gap problem, it is ironic that in more recent times one of the much-touted advantages of Place's identity theory is the claim that it eliminates the explanatory gap problem, since there can be no gap if there are not two events but one. As we saw at the end of the previous section, this is much too facile a resolution, however, since what drives the explanatory gap problem is the *radically different* character of brain states and sensory states. Simply being told not to worry because there is an identity does not begin to address the problem as to how they *could possibly be* identical; rather, it makes one suspicious of the alleged identity.[29] Contrary to Place, this problem does not turn on any presupposition of examining objects in an internal field, the so-called phenomenological fallacy. Apparently both Place and Smart failed to see the force of this problem.

I suspect that what led Place astray here was the preoccupation of Anglo-American analytic philosophers with sense-data theories throughout the first half of the twentieth century. Sense data often *were* thought of as non-physical *objects* on an *internal screen*, and physical objects in the external world were to be "constructed" or "inferred" from these. Sherrington, however, was not advancing a sense-data theory. In support of my claim that Place subsumed Sherrington's view to that of the sense-data theorists, consider the fact that Place, immediately after introducing the "phenomenological fallacy" as the error in Sherrington's view, presents an argument on his behalf, one that sense-data theorists of the time typically offered:

. . . when a subject reports a green after-image he is asserting the occurrence inside himself of an object which is literally green, it is clear that we have on our hands on an entity for which there is no place in the world of physics. In the case of a green after-image there is no green object in the subject's environment corresponding to the description that he gives. Nor is there anything green in his brain. . . . Brain processes are not the sort of things to which color concepts can be properly applied. (82)

Place responds to this argument as follows:

The phenomenological fallacy on which this argument is based depends on the mistaken assumption that because our ability to describe things in our environment depends on our consciousness of them, our descriptions of things are primarily descriptions of our conscious experiences and only secondarily, indirectly, and inferentially descriptions of the objects and events in our environment. (ibid.)

This criticism of the argument concerning after-images that a sense-data theorist might offer is well taken. I have no desire to support a sense-data theory. Insofar as sense-data theories are committed to non-material objects or entities, their position is difficult to support, if not indefensible. But we already saw that the psychical events of which Sherrington spoke were not objects or entities on a "peculiar sort of internal cinema or screen." Sherrington addressed the fact that the undeniable experiences we have— undeniable from the first-person perspective—are "seemingly incommensurable with any of the events leading up to it," the neuronal events. Place simply ignores this.

Another manifestation of Place's and Smart's failure to appreciate the force of the explanatory gap is their unjustified and inflated sense of the power of "topic-neutral statements," which had been introduced to avoid certain objections to the early identity theory.

Place introduced the idea of a topic-neutral sentence in his discussion of the after-image case (83), though I believe it was Smart (in his reply to "objection 3" on p. 90) who introduced the term 'topic-neutral'. Here is what Place says:

> . . . when we describe the after-image as green, we are not saying that there is something, the after-image, which is green; we are saying that we are having the sort of experience which we normally have when, and which we have learned to describe as, looking at a green patch of light. (83)

Smart says:

> When a person says, "I see a yellowish-orange after image," he is saying something like this: *"There is something going on which is like what is going on when* I have my eyes open, am awake, and there is an orange illuminated in good light in front of me. . . ." Notice that the italicized words, namely, "there is something going on which is like what is going on when," are all quasi-logical or topic-neutral words. (90)

Such a description of what is "going on" is intended to be "neutral" between the mental and the physical, and it is. The relevant and important question, however, is whether such a description of troublesome cases addresses the problem Sherrington raises or whether it directs our attention away from that problem. As no doubt you have surmised, I think it is the latter—an irrelevant diversion. Here is why.

Consider how Place applies the idea of topic neutrality to another case:

> When the subject describes his experience by saying that a light which is in fact stationary, appears to move, all the physiologist or physiological psychologist has to do in order to explain the subject's introspective observations, is to show that the brain process which is causing the subject to describe his experience in this way, is the sort of process which normally occurs when he is observing an actual moving object and which therefore normally causes him to report the movement of an object in his environment. (83)

Just so for the after-image case: the brain process that occurs when one has a green after-image is of the sort one has when looking at a green patch of light.

It is important to realize that this solves the problems posed by the apparent moving light or after-image (and generally for cases of illusion) only relative to a solution of the normal case. *Only if the problem has been solved for the normal case are topic-neutral analyses helpful. No such solution has been offered.* It has *not* been shown in the normal case how brain processes could give rise to, let alone be identical with, experiences of (say) green. Shifting to abnormal cases and explaining them in terms of the normal ones is an advance of sorts, but it neither solves nor addresses the problem for the normal case—it presupposes a solution to it. Sherrington's framing of the problem did not rely upon the abnormal cases; it relied on the normal ones. Seeing green under normal circumstances is, in his terms, a psychical event that attends physical events in the brain, but the former seems not to be explicable in terms of the latter. The two kinds of events are seemingly incommensurable. Importantly, I note that the force of the problem posed does not depend on the characterization of the experiences as "psychical events." All that is required is that it is an event that has features radically different from those of brain processes. Sherrington's problem, a version of the explanatory gap problem, remains an obstacle to the identity theory of Place and Smart because it raises the "how possibly question." Place and Smart fail to notice, let alone address, this problem. Talk of topic-neutral sentences is simply an irrelevant diversion.

An Argument on Behalf of the Subjective Side of the Ambiguity

Let us return to the thesis of the ambiguity of sensory terms. An important reason in support of the claim that the subjective side of sensory experience deserves investigation apart from and in addition to external objective features is the well-known fact that colors and apparent instances of the other sensory modalities occur in dreams, in hallucinations, under hypnosis, and during electrical stimulation of the brain by a knowledgeable neuroscientist. In such cases, the typical external causes—what the colors, heat, etc. are usually "identified" with—are absent. This issue cannot be put aside by simply distinguishing, say, the experience of color from color, because in both the veridical and the non-veridical cases these sensory effects may be *indistinguishable* from the first-person perspective. Though this is not news, it is important. The subjectivist wants to describe both the veridical and the non-veridical events as 'experiencing heat', 'experiencing red', etc. An objectivist, however, takes exception with these descriptions. She might respond that what one has in, say, a dream is a *representation* of color, not an *experience of* color.[30]

These differences illustrate my earlier point that these discussions are often conducted in a question-begging way, for both the objectivist and the subjectivist are presupposing their respective views of color to make their points. The subjectivist assumes that, since the veridical and the non-veridical events are indistinguishable from the first-person perspective, they are both experiences of heat, or red, or . . . . The objectivist assumes that since the objective property identified with a given sensory modality is not present when the non-veridical events occur, they cannot be described as an experience of, say, heat or red. This question begging on both sides is a consequence of each of them implicitly endorsing just one side of the ambiguity in sensory terms.

Suppose that the real essence of color is spectral reflectance and that what one has in color dreams *is just a representation* of, say, spectral reflectance, *not an experience* of color (spectral reflectance), as some objectivists would have it. Even if this is supposed, there still appears to be an undeniable, familiar, but important fact: "What goes on" in an individual when she has a "representation of color" in a dream (that which is alleged by the objectivist not to *be color*, nor colored) may not be distinguishable perceptually or qualitatively from the color experiences one has when awake, when considered from the first-person perspective. Though the locution 'what goes on' is vague, it is a neutral way of expressing the relevant fact. (The reader may want to think of Place's and Smart's use of 'topic-neutral sentence', discussed above. Smart similarly used the locution 'what goes on'.) In short, from the first-person perspective the veridical and non-veridical states may be indistinguishable, relative to their phenomenal aspects.

My analysis provides for the facts of these cases. The phenomenal minimal content for both the veridical and non-veridical states would be the same; that is, the phenomenal aspect as perceived by the perceiver would be the same in both circumstances, though the objective content would be different.

What can the objectivist say? If we grant the objectivist her claim that in the one case the agent *just* has a *representation of color*, while in the other she has an *experience of color*, it is safe to conclude that in the latter case the agent also has a representation of color. The difference in the two cases is a result of the difference in the causes of the representation. On certain objectivist views, one has an experience of color only if the cause of the representation is a reflectance triplet.

Clearly, the representation of color is distinct from objective color, say, a spectral reflectance triplet that it represents. Moreover, the spectral reflectance triplet *itself* lacks the phenomenal character of "what goes on" in an individual who has an experience of (objective) color, such as one has in a "color" dream. The scare quotes are used by way of respecting the objectivist account. For on that view the phenomenal character of "color" is, well, what? It certainly is not the reflectance triplets.[31] Science teaches us that spectral reflectances are not themselves "colored" in the way that we experience color when we have an internal representation of a spectral reflectance triplet.

Therefore, not only is the objectivist begging the question against the subjectivist, she is also changing the subject when she identifies a sensory modality with some objective feature that lacks the phenomenal aspect that is experienced by sentient beings, at least humans. Furthermore, even if there is an objective physical property to be identified as the referent of color, as Hilbert and others argue,[32] it is a different referent than what was initially at issue, namely, the *phenomenal character* of color experience. The latter may be indistinguishable whether spectral reflectances are the distal causes (as when we are awake) or there is some other cause (as when we have color dreams).[33] The initial referent, the phenomenal character of experienced color, what is for me the perceptual analogue of minimal content, is the same in both situations.

To put my point within the objectivist framework presented, the *having of a representation* of color in the veridical and non-veridical cases is indistinguishable from the first-person perspective. Even if the representation is itself some neuronal structure (as Lycan would hold), *the having* of this neuronal structure is something different. This kind of "having" is what I characterized and argued for as a new fact in Jackson's Mary case (chapter 3). What results from our having such representations is itself worthy of independent investigation. Even though common sense had it wrong in holding that external objects themselves have the intrinsic phenomenal character that results from our having these representations, what is thereby subjectively picked out is of great philosophical interest, quite apart from its being a means of detecting certain micro-physical properties (be they properties of external physical objects or of the brain).

Generally, the subjectivist emphasizes the phenomenal character of experience. Replacing that topic with another can in no way give satisfaction to the subjectivist's concern. To do so is simply to change the subject; it does not solve problems associated with phenomenal aspects. It simply diverts attention from the phenomenal character, as did Place and Smart with their topic-neutral sentences.

David Hilbert begs the question by, in effect, appealing to what he takes to be "colors themselves" (the "real essence"), thereby changing the subject of investigation. It is a well-known empirical fact that certain objects with very different reflectances can appear to have the same color in normal circumstances. Such objects are known as *metamers*. It is generally recognized that this poses a prima facie difficulty for the objectivist's view that color just is surface reflectances. Hilbert responds to this difficulty by noting that people are sometimes "epistemically off": " . . . color perception and language give us anthropocentrically defined kinds of colors and *not colors themselves*" (27, emphasis added)

Now, I have no problem with examining color as spectral reflectances. Nor do I have any problem (in one sense) with the claim that, although our detection of spectral reflectances does not track their variations well, this in no way counts against the claim that color (in one sense) is spectral reflectances. All that is one possible, even plausible, outcome of investigating *the objective side* of color terms. But I do have a serious problem with the claim that this tells us about the *colors themselves*, as this involves an utterly unsupported essentialism regarding color, implicitly denies the ambiguity of sensory terms, and begs questions against the subjectivist. I also have a problem with the dismissive attitude toward the subjective side of color that is suggested by the characterization of our "inadequate" tracking of reflectances as a defect. This characterization presupposes that tracking the objective features is the "essence" or the sole function of the subjective side of perception. Though I do not deny that this tracking is *a* function, there is simply no reason to hold either that it is the essence or the sole function; thus, the dismissive attitude is not warranted.

Hilbert continues as follows:

Perception does not reveal the whole truth about colors and the truth it does reveal is delimited by the characteristics of our perceptual systems. Human perception of all properties, not just colors, is indeterminate in the sense that it only delivers partial information about the fully determinate qualities that objects possess. (27)

I am inclined to say to all this "Of course, of course." But to point out that human perceptual systems present information in certain delimited ways *is not to say that the character of the perceptual information they do present is of itself of no philosophical or psychological interest* in the study of perception. It is not to say that the information delivered by our visual sensory systems has nothing to do with "color," or even with "colors themselves." (Compare my criticism above of the so-called fallacy of total information.) My point has been that the subjective phenomenal character of our experiences of color, heat, taste, and so forth are themselves worthy of investigation, as is the objective side of these experiences. There is nothing to be gained by denigrating, dismissing, ignoring, or diverting attention away from one side of the ambiguity in favor of the other, and nothing to be gained by appealing to essences.

In a much broader sense, there is another point of agreement between my view and Hilbert's, though again we make quite different things of it. "My defense of the objectivity of color is relative," Hilbert states, "in the sense that I take my task to be showing that there are no problems facing the objectivity of colors that are not equally problems for the objectivity of primary qualities such as shape." (27) His strategy, obviously, is to rely on the widespread acceptance of the objectivity of the primary qualities, despite certain problems, and to show that the objectivity of the secondary quality of color is no worse off; therefore, he concludes, there should be no bar to accepting an objective account of color, given that we accept the objective account of primary qualities.

Part of this is familiar: Accounts of the primary and secondary qualities are confronted with quite similar problems. It is a point that George Berkeley made much of in the eighteenth century, though clearly to a different end than Hilbert. The orthodoxy then, stemming from the work of Galileo, was that the primary qualities are objective, mind-independent qualities, and that various widely accepted arguments showed the secondary qualities to be subjective, mind-dependent qualities. What Berkeley did was argue that the very same problems that led thinkers to the conclusion that the secondary qualities were subjective applied with equal force against the mind independence of primary qualities. Berkeley then concluded that both the primary and the secondary qualities were mind-dependent, subjective.

Berkeley subsumed the primary to the secondary, regarding both as subjective. Hilbert subsumes the secondary to the primary, and concludes that both are objective. I say "A pox on both their houses." While many of the problems for both primary and secondary qualities are largely the same, this does not drive us to either conclusion. Quite the contrary, sensory terms are and should be ambiguous between the objective and the subjective. Nothing is gained but something is lost in excluding either. There is ample evidence and reason to acknowledge that the true statements we make using sensory terms are properly analyzed sometimes by the one construal and sometimes by the other.

These same points stand if the objectivist weakens the identity to supervenience, for if that is not to be vacuous she must give an account of what the *determining* relation is between the subvenient and the supervenient properties. (Compare my criticism of certain applications of supervenience in chapter 4.) Either way, subjective phenomenal experiences themselves still pose recalcitrant problems. I maintain that progress here is more likely to be achieved when we forthrightly recognize the ambiguity in sensory terms, give each its due, and thereby avoid changing the subject when problems arise. Various pointless disputes regarding true natures are also avoided.

If the above is right, then the view that the representational content *exhausts* phenomenal content, a view currently advocated by a number of notable philosophers,[34] is wrong. For, in effect, I have argued that the having of such representations is of interest with respect to the phenomenal features experienced, quite apart from what they may or may not represent. The having of such representations results in, or gives rise to, new features of interest and importance apart whatever it is that the representations themselves may represent. First, they do have, or give rise to, such other features, if for no other reason than that *any* representation, even an arbitrarily concocted one, will have features other than its representational ones. Second, with regard to the case in point, these other features are of special interest and importance, for external objects are presented as though they themselves have these features when in fact they do not have these phenomenal features—a significant puzzle. Third, the use of sensory terms that indicate such features is entrenched. Further, there is the well-known explanatory gap problem of explaining how brain states, lacking these phenomenal features, nevertheless somehow give rise to them. It is a vexing and fundamental difficulty. Its solution is crucial to any complete philosophy of mind.

Most objectivists' accounts are motivated in part by desire to avoid an error theory,[35] to preserve somehow the common-sense intuition that external bodies "really" are colored and the prima facie datum that external objects are presented *as* colored. Not only is it a mistake to try to support this, but one consequence of what I have argued is that objectivists, to the extent that they succeed in this, have changed the subject. It should, however, be clear that I oppose a strictly subjectivist account as strongly as I oppose an objectivist one; both are incompatible with the ambiguity of sensory terms.

Concluding Remarks

There is a great divide in philosophy of mind between intentionality and phenomenality. With regard to the first, we saw the importance of recognizing the ambiguity in the locution 'the subject of a thought' between minimal content and objective content. With regard to phenomenality, there is a corresponding ambiguity between the phenomenal minimal content and an objective content; the latter signals features that are distinct from but typically cause what is signaled by the former. The concepts of minimal content and objective content provide a common framework for understanding both sides of the great divide. This unifying theme is, I think, a distinct strength of my theory of mind.

The subjective side of the ambiguity was seen to be primary in the analysis of intentionality (the fundamental intentional state). It is similarly and much more obviously fundamental for the analysis of phenomenality, as phenomenal states have traditionally been the very paradigms of subjectivity. In the next chapter, I return to thought content and argue that a widely accepted externalist theory of it fails to undermine the primacy of the subjective that I have argued for. In chapter 8, I will press the primacy of the subjective into new territory by arguing for its necessity in the domain of linguistic meaning. Still, I have endeavored to show that, although subjectivity is fundamental to all of these topics, it is consistent with an objective account of all of them.

7 Rethinking Burge's Thought Experiment

It has been more than 25 years since Tyler Burge first published his famous thought experiment.[1] The literature that followed is immense. Burge has responded to some of his critics and has developed the anti-individualist view presented in the original article. In this chapter I will not attempt to address this literature. Instead, I will focus on serious problems in Burge's argument that have been overlooked.

My theory of mind, developed in earlier chapters, is clearly internalist or individualist. Burge's is clearly externalist or anti-individualist. Because our theories are incompatible, and because Burge's view has gained such widespread support that it has virtually become the orthodox position on thought content, it is important for me to show why I think Burge's arguments fail. The ensuing criticisms of his position do not simply juxtapose our opposing positions. I argue that there are some debilitating problems in his discussion of his thought experiment, and that he ultimately begs the question against the individualist. Once this is shown, it is evident that his argument fails as a criticism of internalism and does not establish anti-individualism of thought content.

The Thought Experiment

Burge maintains that a person's mental states or events may vary with certain changes in the environment while the person's body remains the same. This is the crux of his anti-individualism with respect to mental content. The basis for this stems from his famous thought experiment. I will argue that the most that Burge's experiment shows is that the *truth values* of certain of the thinker's *utterances* will be different in the actual and the counterfactual cases because the words uttered have different meanings. At best the thought experiment is inconclusive with respect to the question of whether the thinker's *beliefs* or his *thoughts' contents* are the same or different in the two situations. I argue on independent grounds that the thinker has or could have the same belief contents in the two situations. If I am right, Burge's thought experiment, contrary to the usual analysis, does not support an externalist or an anti-individualistic view of thought content.

Of primary interest are the propositional attitudes—cases where a person has a psychological attitude (believes, desires, fears, etc.) toward a state of affairs or a proposition. It should not be assumed that the propositional attitudes are necessarily or essentially linguistic; at least this must not be initially presupposed. Thus, some non-human animals without any linguistic capabilities may have propositional attitudes. Burge would agree with this—see pages 96, 114, and 115 of his 1979 paper. We may, however, express any alleged propositional attitude linguistically, be it our own, another human's, or some non-human creature's. The sentence "Willard believes that gold is a natural kind" expresses what we take to be one of Willard's propositional attitudes. This mentalistic idiom has an embedded sentential clause. Burge calls such embedded clauses "content clauses" or "that-clauses." He says that they "provide the *content* of the mental state or event" (74). There is a potentially dangerous equivocation lurking here between that-clauses, which are the publicly observable expressions of the mental contents of attitudes, and the contents themselves. The equivocation is abetted by the fact that we speak of both the contents of statements and of thoughts.[2] Later, I will show how Burge is guilty of just such equivocation.

Burge does not give an account of mental contents or notions, as such. This is unfortunate since his thought experiment crucially relies on the concept of a notion (specifically, whether or not a counterfactually considered individual has the same notion of arthritis as he has actually). He does assert that mental contents do have some internal structure, at least partly parallel to that of the that-clauses that express them:

Just as whole that-clauses provide[3] the content of a person's attitude, semantically relevant components of that-clauses will be taken to indicate notions that enter into the attitude (or the attitude's content). (75)

Notions, then, are components or elements of mental contents; thus, it follows that an individual who has different notions in two situations will also have different contents. Just how semantically relevant components of that-clauses "indicate" the notions that Burge tells us they indicate is a different and crucial point. I will address this later; for now, it will suffice to keep clearly in mind that we have contents and notions on one side (the mental) and that-clauses and terms on the other (the linguistic).[4]

Burge presents his now-famous thought experiment in three steps:

(I) A person is considered who "has a large number of attitudes commonly attributed with content clauses containing 'arthritis' in oblique occurrence." Some examples are that this individual has had arthritis for years and that it is better to have arthritis than cancer of the liver. This stage is completed with the important remark that "in addition to these unsurprising attitudes [true ones], he thinks falsely that he has developed arthritis in his thigh." (77)

(II) "The person might have had the same physical history and non-intentional mental phenomena while the word 'arthritis' was conventionally applied, and defined to apply, to various rheumatoid ailments, including the one in the person's thigh, as well as to arthritis." (78)

The final step is the critical one, and the one with which I take exception:

(III) "In the counterfactual situation, the patient lacks some—probably *all*—of the attitudes commonly attributed with content clauses containing 'arthritis' in oblique occurrence." (78)

Burge concludes from his thought experiment that "the patient's counterfactual attitude contents differ from his actual ones" (79).[5] But by (II) there is no bodily difference in the individual, so the crux of anti-individualism, Burge thinks (79), follows from this: "The difference in his mental contents is attributable to differences in his social environment."

Each step of the experiment is supported, Burge thinks, by "common practice in the attribution of propositional attitudes" (88). All that he thinks might be disputed is whether the steps of the experiment should be interpreted literally, as he does. This question is raised only with respect to (I). He examines, at great length, four versions of "reinterpretation strategies." He then examines what he calls three philosophical arguments for reinterpretation. Each reinterprets the patient's belief, in particular his notion of arthritis, when he says that he has arthritis in his thigh. I think the thrust of Burge's response to all of these is correct, so I will not discuss this issue further: it is literally correct to attribute to the patient in the actual situation the belief that he has arthritis in his thigh. Burge thinks that (II) and (III) are intuitively plausible, unproblematic, and independent of any particular theory.

My Analysis—First Stage

Most who have challenged Burge's interpretation of his thought experiment appear to agree with him on (II) and (III), since they challenge only (I). I agree with (I) but argue that (III) is a misstep. I will show that the thought experiment does not support (III), that the conclusion that the subject has different attitude contents in the counterfactual situation is false, at best unsupported. Therefore Burge's thought experiment does not support anti-individualism.

When the patient described in (I) has the belief that he might express by the sentence "I have arthritis in my thigh," what shall we make of this? I assume that a person cannot have a single belief. Each belief a person has involves implicitly, but essentially, a number of other beliefs. These other beliefs normally do not require explicit mention for the agent to be understood; nor does the believer typically entertain them, even when he is explicitly entertaining some target belief (say, that he has arthritis in his thigh). Nonetheless, they are beliefs that analysis makes explicit. Some of them are, in a sense, "part of" the target belief (call these *component beliefs*); others, though not strictly part of the target belief, are presupposed by it (call these *background beliefs*).[6] For purposes of the analysis of the thought experiment, some of these beliefs must be made explicit. In ferreting them out, I will appeal to what is, to quote Burge (88), "common practice in the attribution of propositional attitudes." Thus, I will employ the same methodology that Burge has avowed in presenting the thought experiment, though I will come to a different conclusion. The justification of the appeal to ordinary intuitions or practices here is that his objective, as is mine, is "to better understand our common mentalistic notions" (87). Since we come to different conclusion using this methodology, I will argue for other substantive considerations on behalf of my position.

What are the relevant beliefs that analysis yields for a case such as that described in (I)? If an individual has a belief that he expresses, or would express, by uttering the sentence "I have arthritis in my thigh," this belief implies that he believes the following:

(1) Sometimes my thigh aches.

(2) These aches are caused by some disorder.

These beliefs may be viewed as resulting from a decomposition of the target belief (component beliefs). Furthermore, that the patient expresses (or would express) his target belief with the sentence "I have arthritis in my thigh" implies that he has another belief:

(3) The term that applies to this disorder in my speech community is 'arthritis'.

This may be considered a background belief. To call it a background belief is to acknowledge, among other things, that the subject need not entertain it explicitly. For (3) is not, while (1) and (2) are, part of the content of the target belief. It is a background belief because it is a condition for express-ing the content of (1) and (2), and hence for expressing the target belief. That (3) is implied by the target belief is in keeping with Tim Crane's insightful argument (1991, p. 18) that the subject of Burge's thought exper-iment must have certain beliefs about the appropriate use of words[7]: Not only does the subject have the belief *I have arthritis in my* thigh; he also has the belief that "I have arthritis in my thigh" is the right sentence with which to express the former belief. And later Crane correctly states that "it is true that one needs no beliefs about meaning, truth or reference in order to think [as Burge argues]; *but to express one's thoughts in words, it is not pos-sible that one should lack beliefs about these things*" (20, emphasis added). If the subject is sincere, it is clear that he would not use the sentence he does to express his (target) belief unless he also believes (3).

So (1)–(3) are necessary conditions for having the target belief in the cir-cumstance described by the experiment. Furthermore, given that an indi-vidual has beliefs (1)–(3), it would be in keeping with "our common practices of content attribution," the methodology that Burge endorses, to attribute the target belief to him. It strains (my) credulity to think that one would refrain from attributing the target belief to someone who had beliefs (1)–(3).[8] What grounds could there possibly be for withholding such an attribution according to our common practices? I, therefore, hold that beliefs (1)–(3) are jointly sufficient for the target belief in the actual cir-cumstances specified in the experiment.

Belief (3) deserves more thorough discussion.[9] Since my analysis requires it, my analysis may seem to be a metalinguistic approach. Burge argues extensively against such approaches to his thought experiment. Since I endorse these arguments of his, something appears amiss. Another related objection to (3) is that it explicitly contains a linguistic term, and this seems contrary to what I stated at the outset: that we must not presuppose that mental contents are linguistic. We must allow that non-linguistic animals are at least candidates for having mental contents.

Consider the second problem first. (I have already addressed this in part in my appeal to Crane 1991.) We infer what a non-human's contents are from its behavior. The same is true in assessing another human's contents, but the range of behavior relevant to this purpose in the human case is significantly different from that available with non-human animals. In the human case, the linguistic behavior of an individual is a primary factor in such endeavors. Certainly, it is in large part because of this sophisticated linguistic behavior that we are able to have such varied and detailed mental contents. While we surmise that non-linguistic creatures have mental contents (hence, notions), we are confident that theirs must be far more rudimentary than ours simply because they lack this capacity.

Arthritis is a sophisticated notion. It is implausible that a non-linguistic creature would have this notion. Such a creature may well have the disease arthritis and be aware of the aches and pains it experiences and so have, in some sense, notions of aches and pains; nevertheless, it would be grossly wrong to attribute to such a creature the notion arthritis. It would seem that a necessary condition for having a sophisticated notion, such as arthritis, is that the creature have linguistic capabilities, while a necessary condition for attributing a sophisticated notion to another is that she exhibit some relevant linguistic behavior. Since the patient in Burge's thought experiment has a sophisticated notion, he has linguistic capabilities. If we are to attribute this notion to him, he must exercise these capabilities; we would not attribute such a notion to an individual unless he exhibited verbal behavior that could serve as evidence for such an attribution. To implement these capabilities, he must have various beliefs, if only implicitly, that pertain to linguistic items. In particular, he uses the word 'arthritis' and has various beliefs as to how that word is used in his speech community (as is exemplified in his use). If the patient thinks he has arthritis in his thigh, this is a thought he might express by the sentence "I have arthritis in my thigh," assuming that he does not wish to mislead us as to what his beliefs are. Utterances such as these would serve as some of our evidence that he has the notion *arthritis*. Of course, a good number of his utterances involving the word 'arthritis' would also have to be true, as is specified in the experiment, if we are to attribute to him the notion *arthritis*. Thus, belief (3) is warranted as a background belief that is appropriately part of the analysis of the target belief.

The point is not that anyone who has the notion *arthritis* has a belief about the use of the English word 'arthritis'; rather, anyone who has the sophisticated notion arthritis must also have a belief about the use of some appropriate word in his speech community. If one runs an analogous thought experiment in a German-speaking community, a member of that community, Hans, might express his target belief with the sentence "Ich habe Gelenkentzündung in meinem schenkel." We could still unpack Hans' belief by (1)–(3) in English (or, for that matter, any other language) but with one important change: Whatever language we formulate (3) in, the word in quotation marks must be the corresponding word for arthritis in the language of the speech community of the subject of the experiment. So Hans, who is similar to the subject in Burge's experiment, would also have beliefs (1) and (2), but (3) would be replaced by (3G): The term that applies to this disorder, in his speech community, is 'Gelenkentzündung'. Nevertheless, (3) and (3G) reflect the fact that in either case *the subject believes that he is using the right sentence (hence, the right term) to express his belief* as to the condition of his thigh. (See my discussion of Crane above.)

Another reason for objecting to my analysis might be that emphasizing the conditions for knowing that another person has the notion *arthritis* seems unduly epistemological. I have two responses. First, if I am right that linguistic ability or behavior is a necessary condition for having or attributing a sophisticated notion, and I take *arthritis* to be such, then it is false that the above is epistemological in its thrust. Second, if one ignores consideration of what the patient would say or says, and merely stipulates what his content is, then it is hard to see how the thought experiment *shows* anything, other than *how* anti-individualism would work *if it were true*. Obviously, an experiment thus conceived could *not* be used to argue that individualism is false. (Later I will show how Burge does in fact beg the question.) Additionally, since according to Burge our common practices of content attributions are to play a role in deciding what the contents are and whether they are the same or different in the two cases, *it is impossible to see how such practices could even be brought into play in these cases, if the patient did not exhibit relevant verbal behavior as a basis for such attributions*. So what the patient says, or would say, is relevant evidence; therefore, under the circumstances of the experiment, belief (3) must be reckoned as a relevant background belief and thus as an element in the analysis of the target belief.

Still, there is the question whether my analysis is metalinguistic, given that (3) is among the necessary conditions for the target belief. This question is important because Burge has argued extensively against such views, and I have endorsed them. So it might seem that I endorse a refutation of my analysis. I think it is fair to say that, since (3) is an element of my analysis, my analysis does have a metalinguistic component. Whether having such a component makes the analysis itself metalinguistic is debatable, but ultimately it is not very important. What is important is that *Burge's rebuttals to metalinguistic analyses of the thought experiment do not apply to my analysis, for my analysis does not require any reinterpretation of the content attributions*. In contrast, all the metalinguistic approaches discussed by Burge do require reinterpretation of the content attributions, and they do so in a way that is critical to them. Importantly, all of Burge's counterarguments to metalinguistic approaches rest on his attack on their common claim (which Crane shares) that a reinterpretation of that-clauses in the attribution of attitudes to the subject is required. Because reinterpretation is central to them, Burge states that "these methods must not only establish that the subject held the particular attitudes that they advocate attributing; they must also justify a *denial* of the ordinary attribution literally interpreted" (93). He repeatedly argues that they fail in this. I accept Burge's arguments to the conclusion that it is wrong to hold that reinterpretation is required in the cases considered, and that no justification has been offered for a denial of the ordinary attributions. But *my analysis nowhere depends on any reinterpretation*. Therefore, whether my analysis is metalinguistic or not, Burge's (existing) rebuttals do not apply.

Deeper Issues—Second-Stage Analysis

Let us return to the analysis of the patient's belief, and let us call the subject Bert. We may assume both that Bert is sincere when he expresses this belief and that he intends to communicate with members of his speech community, rather than mislead them. Thus, it is reasonable to attribute (3) to Bert, and it is obvious that Bert believes (1) and (2). As argued above, the conjunction of (1)–(3) is both necessary and sufficient for the target belief in the actual circumstances stipulated. I do not think that there is any violation of our common practices of propositional-attitude attribution in maintaining that the subject has these three beliefs, given that he has the target belief. (1) and (2) are in accord with the facts of the case, as they are judged by these practices, and (3) accords with what I have argued is required for having a sophisticated notion. Exactly similar considerations apply to Bert's target belief in the counterfactual case, however. Bert, actually and counterfactually, certainly has many other thoughts about arthritis, some of which may be relevant to a complete analysis of the target belief. However, given Burge's description of thought experiment and our common practices of content attribution, I do not see that any further belief beyond (1)–(3) is required to attribute the target belief to Bert. Again, the conjunction of (1)–(3) is sufficient. (More on this below.)

As with Burge's analysis, none of this requires any reinterpretation of the word 'arthritis'. In the actual world, Bert literally believes he has arthritis in his hands, and he literally believes he has arthritis in his thigh.[10] He is correctly expressing his literal beliefs, but his belief that he has arthritis in his hands (and his expression of it) is true, while his belief that he has arthritis in his thigh (and his expression of it) is false. In view of what I have argued and the conditions of the experiment, Bert would not even have the latter belief unless he had belief (3). Furthermore, Bert's target belief is false because (3) is false: The term in his speech community that applies to the disorder in his thigh is not 'arthritis'. On the other hand, since (3) is true in the counterfactual situation, as are (1) and (2), counterfactual Bert's target belief is true.

Consider Burge's conclusion that "the patient's counterfactual attitude contents differ from his actual contents" (79). Something is different in the two cases, but Burge has misdiagnosed the difference when he asserts that it is the notion *arthritis* that is different. The analysis I have offered of Bert's content of his belief in the actual case is an analysis that accords with common practices of content attribution, and it yields content that is or need be no different from the content that Bert has or could have counterfactually. At the same time, my analysis accounts for what is different in the two cases. According to my analysis, what the thought experiment establishes as different is simply the counterfactually assigned *truth value* to belief content (3) and the sentence expressing it, and it is this difference that accounts for the differences in the truth values of the target beliefs. Importantly, this does not show that the contents of the target beliefs are different. Specifically, it does not show that that the *notion* component, *arthritis*, is different qua *thought* content.

One might think something is amiss here: One may plausibly hold that a difference in truth value is sufficient for a difference in content. But if one also holds, as I do, that the truth values of the target beliefs are different in the two situations, then my claim that Bert actually and counterfactually has or could have the same mental content appears to be false. On the face of it, this seems right, but only if one ignores the difference between mental and semantic content. What is right about this is that when *sentence structures* of the same type have different truth values assigned they must have different *semantic* content, but this in and of itself does not exclude the possibility that there can be variance between semantic content and mental content. I will argue below that when the difference in truth value is due to a difference in the meaning of the same word (i.e., typescript or utterance) in the two worlds, *and* if the notion an individual associates with a word may deviate somewhat from the community's notion (hence, from the word's meaning) but still count as "the same notion," Bert actually and counterfactually can have the same notion, even while an utterance or sentence (containing the term expressing his notion) has a different truth value than a sentence of the same sentence structure evaluated in a different community. As a result, in cases like those under consideration, where both a belief and the sentence expressing it specifically turn on word meanings (as with (3) and therefore also with the target belief), their truth values will depend on the language community indexed and may diverge; nevertheless, the mental content may still be the same.

The linguistic practices of a community are emphatically and uncontroversially anti-individualistic. But granting this in no way advances the claim that an individual's *belief contents* are similarly independent of the individual. Clearly, what the community's linguistic practices are will be a determining factor as to whether (3) is true or false for the indexed community. All this shows is that the truth value of (3) will vary with the linguistic practices of the community. Whether the word 'arthritis' applies or not clearly depends on the definition of the word in the relevant community. What it emphatically does *not* show is that the mental content, the notion of the believer who uses the word, will vary with those social practices. Advocates of anti-individualism must establish that the social practices alter *mental contents*. Burge's thought experiment, I argue, does not establish this.

Diagnosis and More Criticism

Why has it been widely believed that Burge's experiment supports anti-individualism? I think that in the support that Burge offers there is a very subtle conflation of the *term* 'arthritis' and the *notion* it indicates. Such conflation is invited by several factors, as discussed earlier. Unfortunately, Burge says very little about the identification of notions, other than what has already been indicated:

(*)   Semantically relevant components of embedded that-clauses in belief ascriptions indicate notions that are elements of mental contents, and the attribution of propositional attitudes via the ascription of that-clauses is to be governed by common practice. (1979, 75)

The appeal to common practices is of limited value when the contending parties make opposing claims. Thus, in part, I must leave it to my reader to decide which of us departs more seriously from common practice. But I do not leave it at that.

The difference between Burge and me turns on far more than differing claims about what contents common practices would attribute in the actual and counterfactual cases. It is crucial to explain how the patient's understanding is at once somewhat deviant from the understandings of others in his community, even though he shares with them, in some sense, the same notion of arthritis. While I agree with Burge that in the actual case Bert has the same notion as does his language community, I give a significantly different account of his deviation.[11] Our differences go to the very heart of what mental notions are and how they relate to the linguistic items used to communicate them. Burge apparently is content with a kind of identity between "relevant components of embedded that-clauses in belief ascriptions" (linguistic) and "notions that are elements of mental contents" (mentalistic), as is suggested by (*), and he explains Bert's deviance against that background and other factors that I discuss below. I am not content with that.

Burge and I can agree that, whatever mental notions are, any specification of them will be linguistic. But Burge claims that "however we describe the patient's attitudes in the counterfactual situation, it will not be with a term or phrase extensionally equivalent with 'arthritis'" (79). Why so? Burge explains that it is because "the word 'arthritis' in the counterfactual community does not *mean* [emphasis added] *arthritis*" (79). This last claim is true by stipulation and is not in dispute. The question is whether it implies that we cannot describe the patient's attitudes in the counterfactual case using "a term or phrase extensionally equivalent with 'arthritis'." Surely there is a close empirical connection between the meanings of words and the notions they indicate, and this gives some point to Burge's further claim that "it is hard to see how the patient [counterfactually considered] could have picked up the notion of arthritis," for the meaning of 'arthritis' is different in the actual and counterfactual cases. *If counterfactual Bert could not pick up our notion*, this would support the inference that I just called into question, viz., that "however we describe the patient's attitudes in the counterfactual situation, it will not be with a term or phrase extensionally equivalent with 'arthritis'." The problem is that it is not evident that the linguistic stipulations in the counterfactual case would prohibit his picking up our notion unless, that is, one ignores the distinction between a term (or its meaning) and an individual's notion.

Talk of counterfactual situations is always subject to incompleteness and indeterminacy of detail. Perhaps we *could* fill out the case so that Bert just could not get the notion arthritis, but we are not compelled to do so, and Burge's counterfactual specification does not force it. What *is* forced is that the *word* 'arthritis' has a different counterfactual *meaning* than it actually does. So if Bert, counterfactually considered, did somehow get our notion, then his understanding would deviate, to a certain degree, from that of others in the counterfactual community. This certainly can happen, and it is precisely what does happen in the actual case. Bert's actual understanding of arthritis deviates from that of his fellows, and it leads him, on occasion, to misapply the word 'arthritis' in his actual community. The degree of Bert's actual misunderstanding is exactly the same degree that the counterfactual meaning of 'arthritis' deviates from the actual meaning of the word.[12] Since by hypothesis this degree of deviation occurs in the actual situation, there is no bar to someone's acquiring a notion which deviates to that extent from that of the rest of his community, *despite the assumed linguistic restrictions*. For *if Bert could not deviate to the specified extent in the counterfactual case, he could not do it actually either*. But in the latter case, Burge's thought experiment would be deflated from the onset. Therefore, it must be allowed that Bert, in the counterfactual case, could have picked up our notion of arthritis, and Burge's claim that it is hard to see how Bert in the counterfactual case could have picked up our notion of arthritis has no force. Thus, we may correctly describe someone's attitudes in a counterfactual situation by using a term or a phrase that is extensionally equivalent to one used in the actual world, even though there is no extensionally equivalent term in the counterfactual situation.[13]

I have just argued that Bert, counterfactually considered, could have the same content as he does actually, despite some restrictive linguistic assumptions and despite Burge's claim to the contrary. But if I am right in maintaining that the implicit beliefs (1)–(3) correctly unpack Bert's target belief, it is not implausible, and certainly not impossible, to attribute (1)–(3) to Bert counterfactually, given the specified counterfactual circumstances. Therefore, we could have grounds for holding that Bert *does* have the same content both actually and counterfactually. Either way, however, once it is established that counterfactual Bert could or does have the same content as he does actually, it follows that Burge's thought experiment neither establishes anti-individualism nor refutes individualism.

Have I merely assumed that Bert has the same content in the two situations? I think not. I offered an explication of the content of Bert's (actual) belief that he had arthritis in his thigh in terms of three other beliefs. These three beliefs are not claimed to provide an exhaustive analysis of all of Bert's thoughts concerning arthritis. I have argued, however, that they exhaust what is relevant to the particular belief content of Bert's vis à vis the thought experiment, and that they are in accord with our common practices of content attribution. Earlier I argued that (1)–(3) are necessary and sufficient for the target belief in the specified *actual* circumstances. If there is some differential content that Bert has or must have in the counterfactual case, this must be demonstrated. I fail to see it. It will not do to insist that Bert counterfactually has a different notion *because the word 'arthritis' has a different counterfactual meaning*, for I have demonstrated that Bert counterfactually could deviate from his counterfactual community just as he does from his actual community, despite this linguistic difference; moreover, I have shown that the extent of the difference is exactly the difference that is required in the actual case before the thought experiment can even get started. I have also argued that "our common practices of content attribution" do not provide the requisite differential content for the two situations.

Burge has not offered any specific candidates that I might seek to rebut. Until a candidate is offered, my charge stands. Rather than provide a candidate, Burge argues that, since the word 'arthritis' has different meanings in the two cases, the patient's notions (hence, his contents) are also different. I will now elaborate on this faulty inference.

Community Notions versus Individual Notions

For convenience, I introduce an abstraction: the *community notion*, namely the notion that exactly fits the community's definition of the term used to indicate it. In the counterfactual case, Burge would stipulate that Bert's notion of arthritis is strictly identical to the meaning of 'arthritis' in that community—to the community's notion. In that situation, 'arthritis' does not have the same meaning it has in the actual case. Thus, the notion that individuals who get it right would associate with 'arthritis' in the counterfactual community differs from what those who get it right in the actual community would associate with it.

What notions and meanings are, and what relations exist between them, are difficult questions that will not be fully addressed here. The relation between meanings and community and individual notions will be addressed in chapter 8.[14] Burge says very little of the relations between them beyond what is contained in (*) above. But the idea of a *community notion* fits with, and indeed may be viewed as a partial explication of, Burge's claim that semantically relevant components of embedded that-clauses indicate notions. A new question emerges, however—a question that pertains to what the relation is between an individual's notion and his community's notion.

Define an *ideal agent* as one whose notions are exactly congruent with those of her community's. These community notions are just those indicated exactly by the meaning of terms. So, the notion indicated by a term is identical to the notion that an ideal agent would associate with it. When we have a slightly deviant agent, such as Bert, there is some sort of slippage between an individual's notion and that of an ideal agent or the community notion. The question is where to locate the source of this slippage. Since speakers often do not know the exact definitions of the words they use to express contents, such slippage must be widespread. Bert's (mis)understanding is not so great that we should say that the word he uses indicates a *different* notion; hence my earlier agreement with Burge in saying that Bert has the same notion as his fellows: No reinterpretation is required, despite the deviance.

It may be instructive to think of the "slippage" just referred to between an individual's notion and the community notion in relation to my basic distinction between minimal content and objective content. Recall that this distinction was introduced to accommodate the fact that 'the subject of an agent's thought' is ambiguous between the subject of the thought as conceived by the agent and the subject of the thought that an objective observer of the agent would attribute to her. That the individual's notion may deviate from the community's notion reflects the fact that the agent's conceptions may differ from what an objective observer (the community) would take it to be. The current discussion provides reason for thinking that the ideas driving the distinction between minimal content and objective content would be similarly fruitful in discussion of notions. Indeed, the distinction already drawn between community notions and individual notions reflects this. These new concepts will come into play in the next chapter.

Though I agree with Burge that Bert has "the same notion" of arthritis that his community has, we disagree on why this is so. Burge's analysis of Bert's deviance presupposes a divide between the meaning of the term that indicates the notion and the individual's collateral understanding of what is designated by the term. When Burge holds that actual Bert has the same notion as others in his community, he means that it is exactly similar to that of others in his community. That is, Bert's *notion* of arthritis has *exactly the same content* as the *word* 'arthritis'. Where Burge locates Bert's deviance is in his *collateral* understanding of that selfsame notion.[15] In contrast, I deny that Bert's notion must be exactly similar to his community's in order for it to be truly said that he has the same notion as they do; therefore, the content of an individual's *notion* need *not* exactly match the content of the word's definition. This is a central point of contention between Burge and me.

When we turn from an individual's notions to a community's notions or to the meanings of words, things are radically different. A word's meaning indicates the community's notion; it is the notion one should have when one uses that word to indicate a component of the content of one's thought. (This is simply a consequence of how I have defined 'community notion'.) According to Burge himself, Bert's particular deviation in the actual case is not sufficient to hold that Bert has a different notion. In important contrast, precisely the same degree and kind of deviation when applied to word meaning is sufficient to hold that the word 'arthritis' means different things actually and counterfactually; hence, the respective community notions differ. This is as it should be. It makes sense to say that an individual has the same notion as the community, even when the individual deviates somewhat from the community norm, but it makes no sense to speak of the community's notions' deviating from the community's norms. Changes in the community's norms are not deviations; they are establishment of new norms.

Given this large difference in sensitivity to such slight deviations from norms (depending on whether it is an individual's or a community's notion that is at issue), and given that the deviations are important to the very formulation of the thought experiment, we must be wary of transferring what might be truly said of a community's notion (or a word's meaning) to an individual's notion. In particular, while there can be little doubt (I have none) that the meaning of terms is anti-individualistic and, thus, community notions are also anti-individualistic, *these results do not clearly transfer to an individual's mental contents and notions*. I think it is, in part, the plausibility of anti-individualism applied to terms and community notions, coupled with Burge's tendency to pass back and forth between word meanings and notions and his failure to distinguish individual and community notions, that has made his view appear plausible.

Shifting between notions and terms or their meanings is unobjectionable so long as ideal speakers or community notions are in play, since community notions and meanings are definitionally identical. A similarly tight connection between an individual's notions and a community's notions and meanings is neither to be found nor to be desired. There is some significant latitude in how far off one's notion may be and yet still be correctly described as "the same notion" as the community's notion. No doubt there are difficult borderline cases; however, given our varied learning histories and variations in the degree to which we know the exact meanings of the terms we use, I would not be surprised if some such latitude for individuating a person's notions is a necessary condition for communication.

Burge's inference from words' having different meanings to an individual's having different thoughts with different contents and notions would be valid if we added the premise that all agents are ideal, so that their individual notions would be strictly identical to their communities' notions. This would be of no help in establishing the truth of Burge's conclusion, however, since this additional premise is clearly false. More important, it would be of no help to Burge, since *the very structure of the experiment requires that the agent is not ideal.* When an individual's notions or contents are at issue, and the individual is slightly deviant, such transitions between word meanings and notions cannot be allowed.

Individuation of an Individual's Notion

Without some independent argument, one is not warranted in holding that differences in the linguistic content of a word in different worlds establishes that individuals correctly using the term in those different circumstances would *thereby* have different notions. (Below I will consider a passage in which Burge explicitly makes this illegitimate move.) To my knowledge, no one has offered such an independent argument. Even if such differences in linguistic content typically indicate differences in notions on the part of those using the term, this does not always hold. I have argued that it does not hold in the experiment. The point is that if we are not to beg the question here we must allow for at least the possibility that there may be some deviation between an individual's notion and a community's notion. That is, we cannot exclude a priori the possibility that the content of the individual's notion is not exactly similar to the semantic content of the term used to indicate her notion in her community, and that despite such deviation it is correct to hold that she has "the same notion" as her community. The community notion itself is completely determined by the meaning of the corresponding word in that community. It is not obvious, however, that an *individual's notion* is completely determined by the linguistic content.

The idea that an individual is somewhat "off" from her community is crucial to the experiment. I agree with Burge that, at least in some such cases, the individual has the same notion as does the community, in spite of such deviations. There are two crucial divides between Burge and me regarding the analysis of these facts upon which we do agree. The first is a difference as to how we individuate notions. I do it narrowly, via the agent's own conceptions, and allow for something less than exact similarity between these and the community's associated notions. Burge does it broadly and in a way that strongly implicates the meanings of words in the agent's speech community. Moreover, he insists that there is strict identity of notions in the thought experiment, though there is some deviation between the agent's and the community's notions. Of course, this divide turns on nothing less than whether one is an individualist (internalist) or anti-individualist (externalist) regarding mental content. I offer this chapter as whole, and much of the rest of this book, in support of my position.

The present argument, however, does not simply juxtapose my opposing position; rather it is directed at the specifics of the second divide, alluded to in the previous paragraph. This divide concerns *where the deviation is located* when, as Burge and I agree, the subject (such as Bert) is somewhat off. Burge holds that Bert does have strictly the same notion, but his understanding is incomplete. I argue below that Burge is not justified in partitioning the error in this way. In contrast, I hold that while Bert's notion itself is not exactly similar to the community's notion, it is still the same notion. Either way some slack is needed. Burge maintains the notion is exactly identical to that indicated by the definition of 'arthritis', and he locates the required slack in the actual case in the subject's understanding of collateral information. I locate the slack in the identity conditions for the same notion when the topic of discussion is an individual's, as opposed to a community's, notion. For me these identity conditions blur with what Burge characterizes as understanding of collateral information. I will now explain what I mean by "blurring."

When I hold that Bert has "the same notion" as the community in the actual case, the locution 'the same' is not to be understood as 'exactly similar'. This is supported by our common practices of notion attribution. Often, perhaps typically, an individual simply does not know the exact definition of a word. So long as the individual is not seriously wrong (as in the experiment), we would still attribute to him the community notion, a notion expressed by the exact definition. That is, we would maintain that the individual's notion is the same as his community's *despite this deviation*. (Compare the related discussion earlier in this chapter.) If strictly the same notion or exact similarity were at issue, we would be in error in doing this, but no error is committed in such cases. Since the claim that an individual's notion is strictly the same notion as that indicated by the definition of a term used to express her notion in oblique context is contrary to this, it is wrong.

More deeply, Burge's construal seems to presuppose some precise analytic-synthetic distinction, as if one could first exactly specify an individual's notion via the definition of a term used to ascribe a notion in oblique contexts and then go on to explain that the individual is a bit off because her understanding of collateral information is incomplete. This suggests that the information provided in a definition can be neatly distinguished from other, collateral, information related to understanding the term or what it applies to.

Now, Burge, along with many others, does not think that such a distinction can be clearly drawn. In fact, on page 88 he explicitly endorses Quine's view, as I do too, that we cannot distinguish mistakes about concepts themselves (definitions) from mistakes in our empirical knowledge or understanding of those concepts (collateral information). But in spite of this, Burge goes on to claim that his arguments "seem to me to remain plausible under any of the relevant philosophical interpretations of the conceptual-ordinary-empirical distinction." I do *not* think his arguments remain plausible. The claim that there is a strict identity between an individual's notion and the notion indicated by the definition of a term flies in the face of the rejection of the conceptual/factual distinction. It implausibly presupposes that in certain types of situations, such as those described in the experiment, all the error can be placed on the understanding or collateral information side, apart from the concept or notion itself.

The upshot is that, in questions pertaining to the identity of an individual's notion relative to a community's notion, we must not require that the notions be strictly similar; correlatively, we must oppose locating the slack entirely in the subject's incomplete or mistaken understanding of collateral information, as Burge does. We must recognize that the conditions for holding that an individual's notion and his community's notion are the same are labile. At the same time, we may agree that strict identity or exact similarity is applicable in discussion of either linguistic content or community notions. It is only when an individual's notion itself is at issue that the sameness conditions must be relaxed.

Burge's Equivocation

The surreptitious and illegitimate transition from word meanings to an individual agent's notions is the operative principle in Burge's argument to the conclusion that the patient's counterfactual contents differ from his actual contents. A variant of this principle, applied to extensions of terms, is advanced early in his paper in a section innocently titled "Terminological Matters." Acknowledging that there can be different views of 'content' depending on one's theory, Burge makes the following claim:

(A)   In cases where we shall be counting contents different, the cases will be uncontentious. (75)

He continues by endorsing the following principle, which he obviously holds to be evident:

(B)   On any systematic theory, differences in the *extension*—the actual denotation, referent, or application—of counterpart expressions in that-clauses will be semantically represented, and will, in our terms, make for differences in content.

If (B) were true without qualification (linguistic or mental content), then Bert's notion of 'arthritis' would be clearly different in the actual and counterfactual cases, and his respective contents would be different too. Is the principle true without qualification? I have repeatedly noted the potential for equivocation on the term 'content' because it applies to both linguistic and mental items. (A) opens with a clear reference to mental contents, whereas (B)—insofar as it is evident and uncontentious—applies to linguistic expressions. Thus, although the closing claim of (B) (that such differences in extension "make for differences in content") indisputably applies to linguistic contents, it cannot be applied, as Burge intends, to mental contents— not without further argument. No such argument has been given.

Note also that (B) obliterates any variation between an individual's notion and a term correctly used to express it: differences in the extensions of terms imply differences in the agent's associated notions (hence, of contents). That's it. Given this principle, Bert counterfactually considered *must* have a different notion of arthritis, since the extension of the term is by stipulation different in the two situations. (In a sense, the individual drops out altogether; if this were the case, the name for the view, 'anti-individualism', is especially apt.) This, or something very close to it, may be true, *if* anti-individualism is true; however, this cannot be presupposed in an argument *for* anti-individualism, not without begging the question. I have argued at length that what is said of words should not be automatically transferred to an individual's notions. Thus, in contrast with (A), (B) is quite contentious when applied to mental contents. Furthermore, if I have rightly applied our "common practices of belief attributions" in concluding that Bert's relevant contents, both actually and counterfactually, are represented by (1)–(3), then I have shown that Bert has or could have the same content and arthritis notion when considered actually and counterfactually. Therefore, the thought experiment itself does not warrant any anti-individualistic thesis.[16]

An Independent Source of Difficulty for Burge

There is another source of difficulty for Burge, one that I have not pursued here. If different extensions can be read as different applications, as Burge suggests in the quoted passage, and differences in the extensions of terms imply differences in the mental contents an individual associates with them, then sameness of mental content implies sameness of extension or application. This raises a problem with Burge's formulation of the thought experiment. Burge maintains that, in the actual case, the patient has the same notion of arthritis as do the rest in his community. But the patient *applies* the term more widely than do the others. In some sense of extension then, the extension for the patient is different from the extension for others in his community and, given (B), it follows that *he cannot have the same notion as the rest.*[17] But having the same notion in such a case is a main point of Burge's, one that he argues for at great length. Apart from the objections already raised, this illuminates a new question as to whether Burge can consistently maintain both (B), which he mistakenly advocates as unproblematic, and that the patient has the same notion (strict identity) as the rest in the actual case. If he cannot, then this is yet another way to show that the thought experiment does not support the thesis of anti-individualism.

Answer to an Objection

Anthony Brueckner, in "Defending Burge's Thought Experiment" (2001), purports to show that my argument against (III) fails.[18] I will show two things: Brueckner's objections are ineffectual, and that his discussion addresses only a very small part of my argument.[19]

The part of my argument that Brueckner does address pertains to my claim that if in the actual world a subject (say Bert) were to sincerely utter the target sentence "I have arthritis in my thigh" it would be in keeping with our ordinary practices of content attribution in oblique context to hold that Bert has (at least) three other beliefs: (1)–(3) above. I hold not only that (1)–(3) are necessary for the target belief but also that they are sufficient. Although Brueckner apparently has reservations about the necessity claim,[20] he waives them and focuses on the sufficiency claim. Here is what he says:

> The sufficiency claim seems obviously false. Suppose by analogy, that Kurt and Kim both believe that there is smoke in their neighborhoods, that the smoke is caused by a disorder, and the term that correctly applies to this disorder in their respective speech communities is 'fire on the bank'. Suppose that Kurt expressed a belief about his local financial institution by uttering 'There is a fire on the bank in my neighborhood'. It obviously does not follow from our assumptions (which parallel (1)–(3)) that Kim expresses the same content as Kurt's by uttering the sentence in question. He might well live near a river bank where leaves are burned. (389)

This purported counterexample is not at all analogous to my case. What Brueckner's case turns on is the *use of an ambiguous word in the actual world*. In Burge's thought experiment, the word 'arthritis' has different meanings in the actual and counterfactual situations, but it is *univocal in each*. For any given world where there are practices of content attribution in oblique context that rely on an agent's use of a word, these practices surely factor in whether an operative word is ambiguous or not, requiring more information where there is ambiguity. Since 'bank' is ambiguous in the world Brueckner considers, the practices as applied to this case would reflect that fact, therefore, they would not justify the claim that Kurt and Kim have the same content based simply on what Brueckner advances as parallel assumptions. Indeed, given the ambiguity, more information would be required before *any content* is attributed to either Kurt or Kim.

Thus, the alleged counterexample fails in two ways. First, the parallel assumptions are *not sufficient to attribute any content*, let alone the same content, to Kim and Kurt, because an important word is ambiguous. Second, Brueckner's case is not parallel to the Burge case because 'arthritis' is univocal in the actual and the counterfactual cases. Nothing I have said commits me to the sufficiency of the parallel assumptions that Brueckner presents for a content attribution in his purported analogy, and it is simply false that common practices would attribute the same content to Kurt and Kim under the conditions specified by Brueckner, more information would be sought.

So I deny that Brueckner's case is relevantly analogous—it is no counterexample. Let no one say that his case is analogous because the word 'arthritis' has different meanings actually and counterfactually, for this does not an ambiguous word make. If, contrary to fact, it did, then we would have to make the utterly ridiculous claim that *every* word is ambiguous, multiply so, as it could have any number of different meanings in any number of possible worlds. Moreover, the common practices of content attribution in oblique context are world-bound; they are not altered in one world because a word has a different meaning in another possible world.

Brueckner has evidently conflated the idea of a word having different meanings in different worlds with that of an ambiguous word in a given world. This, we have seen, is a mistake. One can see, however, that were one to confuse these, it might block one from seeing the sufficiency of (1)–(3) for the target belief in the actual world. Once this confusion is eliminated, we recognize that 'arthritis' is univocal in this world, and we rely on our common practices of content attribution in oblique contexts, I fail to see any plausibility to the claim that we would attribute beliefs (1)– (3) to an agent in the actual world and demur in attributing the target belief to her. (With these clarifications in mind, I invite the reader to reconsider the sufficiency of (1)–(3) for attributing the target belief to someone in this world.)

In any case, you will see (below) that I do not, and did not in my 1999 paper, leave my case at the level of conflicting intuitions, despite the impression to the contrary conveyed by Brueckner's paper. Importantly, my claim that Bert has the same notion *counterfactually* depends on other, different factors—I did not make this claim until these other factors were developed.

Even before Brueckner presents his alleged counterexample, he begins his attack with the following (mis)representation of my argument:

With the sufficiency claim in hand, Georgalis' argument against (III) is simple. Bert in the counterfactual situation will again have beliefs (1)–(3), by the necessity claim. But then Bert in the counterfactual situation will again have the target belief that is expressed by his utterance of (A) in the actual situation, by the sufficiency claim. So Bert's belief contents do *not* vary between the actual and the counterfactual situation, contrary to Burge. Anti-individualism, then, is not established by the thought experiment, given a proper understanding of it. (388–389)

This is a simple argument but not mine. Brueckner apparently, but mistakenly, thinks that at this stage in my argument I hold that (1)–(3) is sufficient for Bert's having the same content actually *and counterfactually* and that my argument against III rests entirely on this. While I do hold that (1)–(3) are rather simply implicated in the sufficiency claim for the actual case, things are much more complicated for the counterfactual case. I discuss these complications, but Brueckner ignores what I say. The points that I make in that discussion are also required for my argument against (III). Brueckner, however, continuing in the vein of the passage just quoted, grants that Bert counterfactually has beliefs (1)–(3), but says the following:

> It seems obvious that it does not follow that Bert in the counterfactual situation has the target belief that he has arthritis in his thigh. His belief that the achy disorder in his thigh is properly called 'arthritis' simply leaves it wide open whether his word 'arthritis' expresses the concept of arthritis or tharthritis. (388)

As I have just indicated, I agree that it would be too quick to conclude that *counterfactual* Bert had the same notion as he does actually, based simply on his having the beliefs (1)–(3), but I did not make this quick move.

For starters, although my claim that (1)–(3) is necessary and sufficient for the actual case occurs on page 148 of my 1999 paper, I do not even mention the counterfactual case until page 152. This is important because, to repeat, though I think that the sufficiency of (1)–(3) for attribution of the target belief is obvious in this world, it is a far more delicate matter to make the corresponding claim in the counterfactual world without begging the question against Burge. Much that is relevant to the relation between a mental notion and linguistic practices is argued for in the intervening[21] and subsequent pages (see below). All these complications are as critical to my claim that (1)–(3) are sufficient for the target belief in the counterfactual situation (and that therefore Bert has the same notion in both situations) as they are to my argument against (III).

Another mistake in Brueckner's paper, one related to the mistakes and oversights already mentioned, occurs when he claims that the issue between Burge and me is whether one may ignore the difference in meaning of 'arthritis' in the two situations. This comes out in his rebuttal of a proposal he concocts as a possible defense of my position against his objections. The defense he offers requires holding the circumstances fixed between the two situations, which he proceeds to interpret as ignoring the difference in meaning of 'arthritis' in the two worlds. In rejecting this possible defense, he says:

> Whether this change in "specified circumstances" [difference in meaning of 'arthritis' actually and counterfactually] can be ignored in attributing beliefs to Bert is exactly what is at issue between Georgalis and Burge. (389–390)

That Brueckner identifies this as an issue between Burge and me implies that he thinks that I hold that one can ignore the difference in meaning, for Burge certainly relies heavily on the difference in meaning in the two worlds to obtain his conclusion, but it is simply false that I held or hold that the difference in word meaning can be ignored.

Specifically, I introduce two new concepts, *community* and *individual notions*, and discuss at length the relations between these and word meanings in different speech communities and different worlds; I then go on to apply these results to the thought experiment. This occurs on pages 154–158 of my 1999 paper. In addition, I discuss the relations between individual notions and word meanings on pages 158–160. All of this was to disarm Burge's conclusion to different mental notions in the two situations that is somehow based on differences in meaning. These arguments are extensive and complicated—they may well contain errors—but the charge that I *ignore* the important difference in the meaning of 'arthritis' in the actual and counterfactual situations is completely without merit.

Both Brueckner and I have noted that I—following Burge's lead—appeal to common practices of content attribution in oblique context. But I recognized the limitation of such a methodology when parties disagree. After noting (pp. 151–152) points of agreement and difference with Burge, here is what I said in my 1999 paper:

The appeal to common practices is of limited value, when the contending parties make opposing claims. So, in part, I must leave it to my reader to decide which of us departs more seriously from common practice. But I do not leave it at that. *The difference between Burge and me turns on far more than differing claims about what contents common practices would attribute in the actual and counterfactual cases.* The key problem is to explain how it is that the patient's understanding is at once somewhat deviant from others in his community, even though he shares with them, in some sense, the same notion of arthritis. While I agree with Burge that in the actual case, Bert has the same notion as does his language community, I give a significantly different account of his deviation than does Burge. One that goes to the very heart of what are mental notions and how they relate to linguistic items used to communicate them. (152, emphasis added)

As I said, I do not leave it at conflicting intuitions of what content common practices would or would not warrant. Instead, I address (153–162) what I identified as "the key problem" in the passage just quoted. The argument that occurs in those pages is complicated, introduces some new notions, gives grounds for rejecting Burge's claim that the agent has different notions actually and counterfactually *despite the differences of meaning in the two situations*, criticizes Burge's contention that they could not be the same, supports my contention that the subject of the thought experiment may well have the same notion actually and counterfactually, and meets two possible objections that one might raise to my view. (The latter occurs in the next section of the present work, but it was on pages 160 and 161 of my 1999 paper.) All of this is critical to my rejection of (III). Brueckner addresses none of it.[22]

Brueckner proceeds as though my argument against (III) relied entirely on the claim that our common linguistic practices would judge (1)–(3) sufficient for the target belief both actually *and* counterfactually, as if much that I just enumerated did not play a role in establishing the sufficiency claim in the counterfactual case, and as if all of it was not integrally part of my rejection of (III). Therefore, not only does Brueckner's defense of Burge's thought experiment fail because his alleged counterexample does not work; aside from that, he has attacked a severely truncated version my argument against anti-individualism. My objections to Burge's thought experiment and anti-individualism remain intact.

Answers to Possible Objections

Before closing, I will examine two possible objections to my argument that Bert has the same notion in the actual and counterfactual cases, and that we literally attribute the arthritis notion to Bert in the actual situation. These two claims may seem inconsistent for the following reasons. If we literally attribute our community's notion of arthritis to Bert in the actual case, and this notion of arthritis is different from that of the counterfactual community's, but Bert in the counterfactual community operates with that community's notion, then it seems to follow that either Bert does not have the same notion in the two situations (as Burge maintains), or we must *reinterpret* Bert's notion in the actual case. But Burge has argued against the latter and I agreed. So, Bert must have different notions actually and counterfactually, contrary to my claim. Another line of objection might go as follows: Since the counterfactual community's notion is no different from Bert's (counterfactually considered) and, by my own admission, Bert (actually considered) has the same notion as we do, it would seem to follow on my view that the counterfactual and actual communities do share the same arthritis notion. Clearly, they do not. Can these apparent shortcomings of my analysis be avoided?

These problems dissolve once it is recalled that the conditions for 'the same notion' are labile when applied to an individual. Strict identity is appropriate when comparing community notions, since a community notion is an abstraction and is defined to be exactly indicated by the definition of the term used to express it. Thus, too, it follows that two communities whose definition for a term differs, will have different community notions. Period. Things are different when an individual's notion is compared to either another individual's or to a community's notion; here we must relax the conditions for being the same notion, as exact similarity is not required. Such difference in the construal of 'the same notion' depending on whether or not an individual's notion is in question is supported by two claims that both Burge and I accept: (1) that there is no strict conceptual-factual distinction and (2) that it makes sense to say that an individual has the same notion as do other members of her community, even when she deviates somewhat from them or from the norm of her community. In contrast, it makes no sense to speak of the community's notion deviating from the community's norm. Thus, I am not committed to the claim that the community's notions actually and counterfactually are identical. Thus, the second objection is met.

By adding the following to this last point, I can show how the first objection to my view is also avoided. The counterfactual community intends a certain notion to be associated with their term 'arthritis'. The community's notion is different from ours because the meaning of the word 'arthritis' is stipulated to be different. That is just how community notions and word meanings are related. In important contrast, while Bert in the actual world is somewhat deviant, this is not tantamount to either Bert's *meaning* something different by the term or having a different notion associated with it than does the rest of his actual community. Strict similarity criteria are not applicable in comparing an individual's notion with another individual's, or when his notion is compared with the community's notion. So the community notion associated with the term 'arthritis' differs in the actual and counterfactual cases, and while the community does not have the same notion in both cases, Bert does. Individualism remains unscathed.

8   Minimal Content, Quine, and Determinate Meaning

In previous chapters I argued that ignoring the first-person concept of minimal content led to false results and quandaries regarding the mind. In this chapter I will do the same for language. I will start by introducing several new concepts—concepts that are based upon that of minimal content.

The new concepts are *intended reference, intended interpretation*, and *objective reference*.[1] The first two are first-person concepts; the latter is a hybrid first-person and third-person concept. In spite of their first-person aspects, objective knowledge of intended reference and intended interpretation is possible, as is the case with minimal content. I will demonstrate how these concepts shed light on meaning and reference by exploring how they alter our understanding of W. V. Quine's famous theses of Indeterminacy of Translation and inscrutability of reference. I will argue that without these first-person concepts Quine's thesis of Indeterminacy of Translation is vacuous and reference is nonsense. Quine was aware that reference was at risk of being reduced to nonsense on his view, but he thought he eliminated that risk. I will argue that he failed to protect reference from nonsense, and I will expose the vacuity of Quinean Indeterminacy. (I attempted to show this in my Ph.D. dissertation. At that time I had only a most inchoate idea of minimal content and, thus, certainly no independent support for it. In consequence, my arguments against Quine's theses were not as compelling as they could have been. I believe the earlier deficiencies have been at last corrected in this book.)

Nevertheless, I will argue that there is something of great philosophical importance in Quine's theses of Indeterminacy of Translation and inscrutability of reference, once they are understood in the light of intended interpretation and intended reference. Of course, and alas, these are not alterations of which Quine would approve. In chapter 9 I will argue that consequences of deep significance for ontology and realism result. In this chapter, in anticipation the next chapter, I will introduce a fourth concept: *ontic reference*. It is decidedly not a first-person concept.

The New Concepts

I turn first to an exposition of intended reference and intended interpretation. Help is obtained from Quine's notion of *theory form* and his notion of a *model*:

> We may picture the vocabulary of a theory as comprising logical signs such as quantifiers and the signs for the truth functions and identity, and in addition descriptive or non-logical signs. . . . Suppose next that in the statements which comprise the theory . . . we abstract from the meanings of the non-logical vocabulary and from the range of the variables. We are left with the logical form of the theory, or, as I shall say, the *theory form*. Now we may interpret this theory form anew by picking a new universe for its variables of quantification to range over, and assigning objects from this universe to the names, and choosing subsets of this universe as extensions of the one-place predicates, and so on. Each such interpretation of the theory form is called a model of it, if it makes it come out true. (Quine 1969,[2] pp. 53–54)

This, of course, is just the usual way of obtaining what in mathematical logic is called a formal theory and then considering alternative models for it. The ideas of formal theories and alternative models were utilized in chapter 1 in the discussion of the various number and set theorists. The concept of *interpretation* includes that of *model*, as it drops the requirement that it makes the theory come out true. Thus, all models are interpretations, but not conversely. Those ideas have been applied to languages; here the concept of interpretation is more appropriate than that of a model, as we are concerned with the semantics of sentences regardless of their truth values. Consider a formal language as a vocabulary plus syntax. The vocabulary is a set of sign types specified as an alphabet and a list of primitive "words" (not necessarily recursively specified). The syntax consists of the rules of formation that enable one to construct well-formed "sentences." The syntax, then, will include various functors and punctuation marks. "Words" and "sentences" are enclosed in quotation marks in the preceding since they are not meaningful in the semantic sense since they are elements of a formal language. They become semantically meaningful on specification of an interpretation.

As is well known from Quine's work, changing the interpretations of the individuative apparatus (definite and indefinite articles, plurals, pronouns, identity, and related linguistic items) is central to giving alternative translations of a language, and this is part of the syntax; thus the functors in a formal language are also left uninterpreted. With this in mind, given a meaningful language, we may abstract from it the language form (or formal language) in a similar fashion as Quine indicated for the obtaining of a theory form from a theory. (In fact, to specify a formal theory one must first specify a formal language to express the formal theory.)

The *intended reference* (IR) of a formal expression of some formal language will depend on the interpretation at issue. It is the object or the kind (set) of objects assigned *under some one interpretation*. In the first instance, it will be an individual referring expression, and in the second it is a general referring expression. I will speak of the *intended interpretation* (II), as opposed to the intended reference, when I wish to speak more broadly of a sentence or a language and not just its referential parts. Though II and IR are distinguishable, they are inseparable. The referring parts of language are not separable from the individuative apparatus, hence, not from II. Thus, when I explicitly speak of just one of these it should be understood that the other is implicit. I will often use the abbreviations II and IR not so much for brevity as in the hope of minimizing the possibility of accreting extraneous features associated with the expression 'intended' from the vernacular.

I argued in chapter 5 that for there to be a representation it was essential that a *particular* mapping be employed by (or, when explicit, selected by a conscious agent). I dubbed this the *particularity requirement* and the problem of doing so the *particularity problem*. There is a related particularity requirement for securing a *single* interpretation for a language. We will see that the satisfaction of the particularity requirement for language also requires a first-person perspective, a subjective point of view, and, hence, a conscious agent. The term 'intended' is employed to reflect the role of a conscious agent, as well as the fact that the purported referent is a *particular* object (or a *particular* set of objects); it is not merely any of the several possible referents which a referring term could have if compensatory adjustments were made in the interpretation of the individuative apparatus. That such compensatory adjustments can be carried out is the crux of Quine's theses—this I do not dispute. What I argue below is that Quine's view lacks the resources to handle this "particularity requirement" because he eschews the subjective.

It is important to realize that both of the concepts IR and II have dual and related application: I apply these concepts to both individual agents and language communities. They are generic ways of identifying a *purported* word-world relation for either a particular agent or for a particular community. When the individual's determination of the word-world relation is at issue and the word is a singular term, the IR is specified by the individual's minimal content; when the word is a general term, the IR is the extension of the agent's individual notion. When the community's determination of the word-world relation is at issue, this amounts to questions about the standard extension of the linguistic sign, and it will express either the objective content or the community notion, depending on whether the term is singular or general. In such cases, I speak of the community's intended reference. Of course, an individual agent strives to have her IRs match those of her community's, to be non-deviant. That is one major thing she tries to achieve as she learns the language of her community.[3]

While the concepts of *intended reference* and *intended interpretation* are word-world relations involving either an individual or a community, there is an implicit mind-word relation in these concepts, since they specify *purported* objects via the mapping intended by the individual agent. This last point radically divides me from Quine's view. It also brings out the relation between minimal content and these new concepts that are based on it. The solution of the particularity problem for representation depended on that of minimal content, the subject of a thought as conceived by the thinker. Intended reference is the correlative concept when language rather than thought is under discussion. The concept of intended reference is ultimately rooted in the concept of minimal content, and it plays a similar logical role. When a speaker utters or writes a sentence, there is a legitimate and quite restricted sense in which she constitutes its interpretation. I will explain this restricted sense below; we shall see that the constitution at issue falls far short of constituting meaning. As with minimal content, a speaker non-inferentially knows her IR and her II. The possibility of her being in error regarding which interpretation or reference she intends makes no sense. As before with minimal content, this does not imply that a speaker cannot be wrong regarding what is in the world, nor does it guarantee that her intended reference or interpretation matches that of her linguistic community.

My discussion of what a speaker intends to refer to will for the most part be confined to standard situations; I will not be concerned here with cases of mistakes or slightly deviant uses on the part of the speaker. Not that these are unimportant; Burge-type cases are deviant in this way, and they were discussed in chapter 7. These cases are not, however, germane to the issues surrounding the indeterminacy of translation.

I digress here to explore yet a different kind of mistake, but only to put it aside and to add some further clarity to the notion of intended reference. When a speaker intends to refer to a rabbit (as we and she, being English speakers, would understand the term), but when what prompted her utterance was not what we would call a rabbit but some other kind of creature, we have a case of mistaken reference. Mistakes (and deviant uses), unlike the relevant Quinean cases, can be exposed on behavioral grounds. Consider such a case of mistaken reference: A furry animal scurries by and I say "Did you see how quickly that rabbit moved?" My friend points out that it was not a rabbit but instead a groundhog, and he takes me to a trap in which the animal has (conveniently) been caught. I acknowledge my mistake and say "Well, I thought it was a rabbit, I thought it was one of those"—as I point to a rabbit that has (again, conveniently) been watching us. Here both my friend and I, despite my mistake, have our intended references in line with one another's, and they match our community's notions of *rabbit* and *groundhog*.

In the above situation, the speaker knew what he intended to refer to with his uses of 'rabbit'. Though his individual notion did not deviate from the community's notion, he was mistaken as to what prompted his utterance. This is an ordinary kind of mistake that has no bearing on any ultimate ontological question or any other philosophical issue. When we say he was mistaken, we are not saying that the object in question was *really*, in some ultimate sense, a groundhog, but only that in ordinary contexts the kinds of stimulations that were presented are the ones members of our community, including the speaker, ordinarily associate with the type of object that we call a 'groundhog', not a 'rabbit'. There is inter-subjective agreement that the second object referred to was a rabbit and the first was a groundhog.

This inter-subjective agreement is important. Where there is this agreement on the referent of a term, I will call it *objective reference*. Objective reference is the linguistic analogue to the *objective content* of an agent's thought, introduced in chapter 1; it is also the extension of a community notion (chapter 7). Recall that the objective content indicates the subject an objective observer of the agent would ascribe as the subject of the agent's thought.

In this sense, 'objective reference' pertains to (assumed if not actual) inter-subjective agreement on, to put it in Quinean terms, the parsing of stimulus meanings. Ordinarily, and often philosophically, we uncritically assume that language is public to this extent. That is, when others use words in a manner similar to the way in which I use them, I take them to be intending to state (refer to) what I would intend to state (refer to) by using that sequence of words.[4] Normally, we assume that our intended references and our individual notions match the objective references and the community's notions. In the interest of effective communication, we strive to make them match.

The objective reference of 'rabbit' in English is just the object that most of us *take to be* the cause of the appropriate stimulations (the affirmative stimulus meaning). This notion of reference, then, is the usual *purported* denotation of a referring expression.[5] It encompasses the objects that are ordinarily thought to exist; thus, 'objective' in 'objective reference' turns on inter-subjective agreement; it accords with common practices of making and attributing references to things. We may meaningfully ask whether one's intended reference matches the objective reference in this sense. IR, then, is in part a function of a given speaker (but not completely independent of her community), whereas objective reference depends on the IRs of a community of speakers and expressions. In specifying these concepts of reference, I used the words 'purported' and 'intended' to prohibit any presupposition that one has actually succeeded in referring to objects of a certain sort, i.e., that the objects in the world are really—independent of us, independent of how we parse the stimulus meanings—of the kind we talk about. That is, there is no claim built into the notions *intended reference* and *objective reference* that we are right about the objects in some deep ontological sense.

The latter brings us to another level at which we may be tempted to apply the term 'objective reference,' viz., when we want to say that the object in the world is *really* of a certain sort, independent of any knowing agent, and over and above the fact that we usually take there to be objects of that sort answering to the expressions in question. Here is a strictly ontological use of 'reference' that goes beyond the above-indicated inter-subjective agreement on the propriety of assent to or dissent from sentences under given stimulation conditions. When the expression is used in this way, we are talking, or trying to talk, at the transcendental level. Call this attempted use *ontic reference*.

Intended reference is the root semantic concept; it ultimately depends on the concept of minimal content. The latter is the root mental concept. An individual agent's thought has a minimal content that she may express with some word that in turn expresses her intended reference. Objective reference is a generalization over individuals' IRs of a given language community based on a presumption of identity of IRs from one individual to another, barring evidence to the contrary. It is the extension of either the objective content or the community notion, depending on whether the term is singular or general, respectively. One may move from either intended reference or objective reference to ontic reference by taking the additional step of claiming that the purported objects are the actual objects in the world in some strong ontological sense. Thus, we see how readily what the more traditionally minded philosopher wants to say about ontology—what there *really* is apart from us—is accommodated in the above. What I have said thus far in this chapter does not exclude talking this way. I think it is ultimately meaningless to do so; I will argue this in the next chapter.

Intended Reference and Quine's Theses

Quine would not countenance my notion of intended reference, since it is based on a first-person methodology. Even so, Quine himself is forced to rely on a similar concept, sometimes implicitly and sometimes explicitly. Consider his discussion of suggestions that have been made for tests to determine the divided reference of the infamous expression 'gavagai'. Quine claims that such tests must be unsuccessful because the stimulus meaning is identical for a variety of possibilities. Thus, he concludes, "the purpose (of such tests) can only be to settle what *gavagai* denotes for the native as a term" (1970, p. 181).[6] That is, such tests cannot settle what the divided reference of the term 'gavagai' *itself* is but, as he says, only what it is *for the native*. Talk of the divided reference of an expression "for a native" sounds, at least superficially, like an appeal to some concept very much like that of intended reference. Occasionally, Quine even talks explicitly of intended references; for example, after stating how more than one model can satisfy a given theory form, he says: "Which of these models is *meant* in a given actual theory cannot of course be guessed from the theory form. The *intended reference* of the names and predicates have to be learned rather by ostension or else by paraphrase in some antecedently familiar vocabulary." (*OR*, p. 54; emphasis added)

How are we to understand Quine's use of the locutions 'which of these models is meant' and 'intended reference'? Is it which of these is meant by the *user* of the theory form, or is it which of these does the *theory itself* (interpreted theory form) mean, apart from any users? Is it the intended references of some user of the names and predicates ("for the native"), or is it the intended references of the names and predicates themselves? For Quine—though not for me—these differences amounts to naught. Though Quine avails himself of the concept of intended reference, ultimately he denies that such talk is meaningful.[7] For he says that we can do no better regarding the divided reference of the term for the native than we can for the term itself, as the native's individuative apparatus is similarly subject to the indeterminacy of translation as is the language itself (1970, p. 181).

The obstacle to determining the divided reference of a term arises, on Quine's view, because the individuative apparatus of the language itself is subject to the indeterminacy of translation; I wholeheartedly agree. I also agree that the native's individuative apparatus—when viewed from the third-person perspective and the data Quine has stipulated—is similarly subject to the indeterminacy of translation. The last result trivially follows from the former, for from the third-person perspective and the stipulated data nothing of the individuative apparatus "for the native" is revealed that is not already revealed in efforts to determine this apparatus for the language itself. The most that this shows, however, is that, so long as we are limited within Quinean constraints, one can no more determine the intended references for the native than one can for the terms themselves. It does not establish that there is no intended reference for the speaker distinct from a term's reference. We saw in chapter 1 a number of reasons for accepting the first-person concept of minimal content, as distinct from objective content. But if we accept minimal content, there is no automatic bar to accepting the first-person concept of intended reference that is based on minimal content and is supported by similar relevant data from the first-person case.

Quine is certainly right in saying that the intended references cannot be decided on the basis of the theory form and that appealing to ostension and paraphrase in some antecedently familiar vocabulary cannot resolve this. Of these means of settling the intended references he says:

But the first [ostension] of these two ways has proved inconclusive, since, even apart from indeterminacies of translation affecting identity and other logical vocabulary, there is the problem of deferred ostension. Paraphrase in some antecedently familiar vocabulary, then is our only recourse; and such is ontological relativity. . . . It is thus *meaningless* within the theory to say which of the various possible models of our theory form is *our* real or *intended model*. (*OR*, p. 54; emphasis added)

The problems of ostension and paraphrase do apply when one is trying to determine *another's* IR, but they are purely epistemic problems.[8] To the extent that Quine suggests that one needs to learn one's own intended reference by ostension or paraphrase, he is quite wrong. An individual is not in the position of having to *learn* which interpretation *she* intends, as another observer of her may well have to, and this for exactly the same reasons one is non-inferentially aware of one's own minimal content (chapter 1), as I argue in the next section. Strictly third-person methodologies are misleading on this point, because they impose artificial constraints. They require turning a blind eye to the first-person perspective, so certain concepts and points remain invisible to it.

Deferred Ostension and Paraphrase: Asymmetry of the First-Person and Third-Person Cases

As a result of Quine's refusal to countenance a first-person perspective, he is forced into the artificial position of maintaining that one must learn one's own intended references by ostension or paraphrase *because* that is how we must do it to ascertain *another's* intended references, i.e., from a third-person perspective.[9] The difficulties that arise from deferred ostension and paraphrase are not applicable to the first-person case.

Consider first the case of deferred ostension. If I point to a gas gauge to indicate the relative volume of gas in the tank, I am non-inferentially aware that this is what I am doing and that I am not indicating anything about the gauge itself. Of course I may not be explicitly aware of this in the sense of thinking (quite artificially), while pointing, "I am now pointing to the gas gauge to indicate the relative volume of gas in the tank, and my main concern is the amount of gas, not anything about the gauge, except insofar as the gauge is related to my main concern." But just as I *am aware* of the subject of my thought as I conceive it (my minimal content), I am aware of my intended reference in ostension in the sense that, if asked, I do not have to infer what it is, nor do I have to *learn* it by any subsequent investigation (be it further ostensions, paraphrase, or whatever). Similar results obtain in more abstract cases of deferred ostension. Thus, if I point to a Gödel number, my intended reference being the correlated formula, there is no question *for me* whether I intend to refer to the Gödel number or to the formula; this is not something I must learn, though another may well have to make some queries of me to learn what is my intended reference. Moreover, in each of these cases I can switch back and forth between the intended references (say, Gödel numbers and formulas) and be non-inferentially aware of which I intend to refer to on any such occasion.

The discussions of the battle diagram and theorist D in chapter 1 made the same point at the level of thought. I could contemplate the battle diagram and switch what was signaled by the Xs and Os, or theorist D could have her minimal contents (and hence her symbols) now represent numbers, now sets. Such switching can be achieved without any change in one's overt behavior; so, another would have to make queries of me or D to ascertain this fact. Such queries would no doubt involve ostensions and paraphrase, with all the usual attendant problems. However, neither I nor D must resort to such means, as we know straight out what is represented in such cases. Our awareness in such cases is direct, but from a third-person perspective it is invisible. Quine constrained to a strictly third-person methodology mistakenly thinks that the problems of ostension and paraphrase apply to oneself, as they do to others.

Each of us has a similar special access to our own intended references, but none of us is in this privileged position with respect to another's intended references. When the issue is another's intended references, each of us is in the position of having to learn what they are. Of course, in practical situations there are contextual clues concomitant with the ostensions that aid one in attempting to learn another's intended reference. For example, if I am driving with a friend and she asks me if we have enough gas to arrive at our destination, and I point to the gauge, she may safely conclude, assuming that I am not perverse, that my intended reference is the amount of gas in the tank and not, say, the pleasant blue light of the gauge. We are not, however, here concerned with the extent to which such epistemic problems of another's deferred ostension may be circumvented (dealt with later), but only with the difference in applicability of some of those problems to the first-person and third-person cases.

The asymmetries between the first-person and third-person cases also apply when we turn to paraphrase. For a wide range of cases, if I make an utterance that employs a referring expression, the intended reference of that expression is again something I am aware of without any need for subsequent learning; typically, there are no inferences that I must make based upon the evidence of my behavior. The "something" I speak of being directly aware of is not the object itself, if there is such a thing; that would be ontic reference, and nowhere will I make such a claim. The "something" may not even be the objective reference, as my intended reference may not match the extension of the community notion. Rather, it is the speaker's awareness of what object(s) she takes there to be and to be speaking of when she makes her utterance—that is, the intended object of her referring expression, objective and ontic reference aside. When I make an utterance involving a referring expression, there is no need for me to paraphrase that utterance in "some antecedently familiar vocabulary" to determine what I intended to refer to by that expression. If there were such a need, we would be in a fine fix, for what vocabulary is more familiar to us than the one we have used for years?[10]

Quine, restricting himself to third-person methodologies, focuses on the words themselves. Regarding the words themselves, there is no difference between the first-person perspective and the third-person perspective, even when stimulus meanings and the speaker's behavior is brought into play. As a result, he entirely misses the asymmetries indicated above and thinks the same problems apply to the first-person case as apply to the third-person case. He has a point when one is asking about the references of the words themselves or of another speaker, but the problems of paraphrase and ostension that apply when considering these cases evaporate in the first-person case. The data from the first-person case, argued for in earlier chapters, are perfectly admissible, and they are required to avoid a truncated and distorted theory of mind. We now begin to see that a restrictive third-person methodology also distorts a theory of meaning and reference.[11]

Of course, an individual may have to paraphrase into an antecedently familiar vocabulary to learn what her intended references ought to be for some terms. This happens when she is trying to get the community notion or objective reference of a new (for her) term, or when she becomes aware that her intended reference associated with a familiar word may not fit exactly that of others. (Her individual notion may be somewhat different from her community's notion, as in a Burge-type deviation.) In the first instance, an individual just learning physics, for example, may have to paraphrase terms such as 'force' and 'electron'. But once physics is learned this is no longer necessary unless, as with the second alternative just mentioned, there is a realization that she has not yet got it just right. But Quine, in making the above claims, is not restricting his attention to sophisticated new terms or to somewhat deviant cases; he is including the most mundane terms, such as 'rabbit'. In any case, once the speaker is adequately educated, she is immediately aware of her intended references—that is, of the objects she is purporting to talk of in making her utterances (regardless of whether there really, in some ultimate sense, are such objects, ontic reference). This awareness is achieved without recourse to ostensive definition or paraphrase.

I am not suggesting that in learning one's first language one has all one's intended references in mind, and that all one has to do is learn how to express them with the linguistic marks of one's language community. Surely there is a complex interplay between the (rudimentary) thoughts of an individual learning her first language and the language used by the community in which she finds herself, an interplay that continues in complex thought processes throughout her adult life. (Compare the case with 'electron' above, or my discussion of sophisticated concepts in chapter 7.) This is not the kind of learning that is in question. Even though Quine sometimes considers this sort of situation, his purpose is not to make any point about actual language acquisition but about meaning.[12]

I conclude, then, that the statement "The intended reference of the names and predicates have to be learned rather by ostension or else by paraphrase in some antecedently familiar vocabulary" (*OR*, p. 54) is false when applied to oneself. Even so, Quine is right to raise the problem of deferred ostension and paraphrase regarding the determination of another's intended reference, though subsequently I will show that the situation is still not quite as bad as Quine would have us think even in this instance. Once intended reference in my sense is admitted, there is objective evidence that counts toward determining which of the interpretations is intended by another.[13] Still the important point now is that the alleged indeterminacies arising from deferred ostension and paraphrase do not materialize in the first-person case of intended reference and interpretation.

Quine's Quandary, Reference Frames, and the Problem of Particularity

Quine's efforts at making sense of reference in the face of indeterminacy of translation and the inscrutability of reference can succeed only if intended interpretation is introduced, notwithstanding the fact that II is not determinable by strictly third-person methodologies. So much the worse for such methodological scruples as applied to meaning and reference, and so much the better for II, IR, and the root mentalistic concept of minimal content.

After arguing for indeterminacy of translation and inscrutability of reference even as applying to oneself, Quine says:

We seem to be maneuvering ourselves into the absurd position that there is no difference on any terms, interlinguistic or intralinguistic, objective or subjective, between referring to rabbits and referring to rabbit parts or stages; or between referring to formulas and referring to their Gödel numbers. Surely this is absurd, for it would imply that there is no difference between the rabbit and each of its parts or stages and no difference between a formula and its Gödel number. Reference would seem now to become nonsense not just in radical translation but at home. (*OR*, pp. 47–48)

Quine goes on to give two different ways of rescuing reference from this quandary: one involves the notion of a background language, the other that of a reference frame or a coordinate system. The former purports to give sense to expressions in the object language by paraphrase or description in the background language. The reference-frame approach does not involve an appeal to another (background) language; rather, it involves taking the words of the language in question "at face value." Thus, there is in general a difference between making sense of reference in terms of background languages and doing so in terms of frames of reference or coordinate systems. The differences in these two approaches are later reflected in the "theoretical" and "practical" resolutions of the problem of infinite regresses of background languages.[14]

Reference in the background language, Quine argues, can itself be made sense of only relative to yet another background language, which in turn requires yet another background language, but "in practice we end the regress of background languages, in discussions of reference, by acquiescing in our mother tongue and taking its words at face value" (*OR*, p. 49). While the theoretical resolution (of the problem of infinite regress) comes from a relational theory of what the objects of a theory are, "it makes no sense to say what the objects of a theory are, beyond saying how to interpret or re-interpret that theory in another . . . no ultimate sense in which that universe [i.e. of some theory] can have been specified" (*OR*, p. 50). In short, we must paraphrase in another language. I argue that on Quine's own terms neither the former nor the latter succeeds in rescuing reference from nonsense.

Consider the frame-of-reference approach. Quine writes:

[Picture] us at home in our language, with all its predicates and auxiliary devices. This vocabulary includes 'rabbit,' rabbit part,' 'rabbit stage,' 'formula,' 'number,' 'ox,' 'cattle'; also the two-place predicates of identity and difference, and other logical particles. In these terms we can say in so many words that this is a formula and that a number, this is a rabbit and that a rabbit part, this and that the same rabbit and this and that different parts. *In just those words*. This network of terms and predicates and auxiliary devices is . . . our frame of reference, or coordinate system. Relative to it we can and do talk meaningfully and distinctively of rabbits and parts, numbers and formulas. (*OR*, p. 48)

On the frame-of-reference approach, we have that, relative to our frame of reference, we "can and do talk meaningfully and distinctively of rabbits and parts, numbers and formulas" (*OR*, p. 40); we can do so by "acquiescing in our mother tongue and taking its words at face value" (*OR*, p. 49). But what is it, on a Quinean view, to take words at face value? For light on this, let us look again at an excerpt from the passage just quoted:

In these terms [i.e. within English] we can say in so many words that this is a formula and that is a number, this is a rabbit and that a rabbit part, this and that the same rabbit, and this and that different parts. *In just those words*.

Granted, one can *say* these things, use "just those words," but to do so is of no help if those words do not have some particular meaning and reference. The appeal to the locution 'just those words' will help only if the expressions 'rabbit' and 'rabbit part', in English, have their usual denotations, viz., rabbits and rabbit parts. Then, and only then, can *those words* be used to express a *particular* difference.

When we concentrate just on sequences of words uttered under various (verbal and non-verbal) stimulatory conditions, ignoring any subjective states of those who utter the words, this is truly to give the expressions a life of their own. But we then find, given the indeterminacy of translation, that there are no unique answers to what expressions themselves refer to. They can be said to refer to any of a number of different kinds of things so long as appropriate adjustments are made elsewhere in the language. But this is precisely why the reference-frame approach that Quine offers will not eliminate the quandary over reference, for, as was observed earlier, we can assert a difference between rabbits and rabbit stages, in "just those words," only if those words have a particular (at least a purported particular) reference. But how is this to be done on a Quinean view? If the "words" are words qua elements of a formal language, they are meaningless. (My first efforts to develop this point against Quine's views appeared in my thesis (1974). Yalçin (2001) develops this point independently; unlike me, he does not exploit the first-person perspective.)

The point is that the *face value* of the words cannot be the sign or phonemic types, for as marks or sounds they clearly do not and cannot fix any interpretation. So it must be "words" as they appear in some *particular interpreted* language. But how are we to know *which* interpretation—which, so to speak, face value? How is a particular interpretation to be fixed so that the expression 'the face values of words' is significant? In my discussion of representation (chapter 5) there was a problem similar to the one just entertained. There I dubbed it *the problem of particularity*. I use the same locution for the current manifestation of the problem. My contention is that the Quinean view fails to provide the resources to solve this problem. This ultimately undermines Quine's efforts to rescue reference from nonsense on the frame-of-reference approach.

Given the indeterminacy of translation, the words themselves have neither particular meanings nor references—*words themselves have no face value.* The different phonemic or inscriptional types are neither necessary nor sufficient to secure differences of meaning or reference, and Quinean strictures prohibit an appeal to my first-person concept of intended reference (or, more generally, that of intended interpretation). Intended interpretation does provide the resources to meaningfully talk of the "face value of words": the usual denotations and meanings that are associated with the expressions via the intentions of the speakers of the language on a *given* interpretation. From a first-person perspective we know that a particular interpretation can be fixed in one's own case, which one is intended by the agent, though this is invisible from a strictly third-person perspective of the agent. From the latter perspective, it could be any of the permissible alternatives established by Quine. Thus, without II (IR), the face value becomes any of a number of values, *but no one in particular.* Quine's appeal to the "face value" of the words is either empty (as when a formal language is at issue) and of no use to the problem at hand, or it is a disguised appeal to objective reference (in my sense), but the latter is ultimately based on the first-person concept of intended reference. Thus, the face value of words is secured at the price of abandoning a strictly third-person methodology. Quine's unwillingness to pay this price results in his failure to make sense of reference using the "reference frame approach."[15]

One may well point out that the reference-frame approach—taking words at face value—is, for Quine, the practical resolution of the problem over reference; at least this is what he says of the approach when applied to the problem of infinite regress. Admitting intentional idioms to this extent would be acceptable for Quine, since he acknowledges the practical utility of the idioms in question (cf. Quine 1960,[16] p. 221). I have argued that it is more than that, and I will now add to that argument: Quine cannot get off so easily.

I have argued that, with inscrutability and indeterminacy and without intended interpretation, the expression 'take words at face value' is empty. I now reinforce this result by examining what Quine takes there to be involved in knowing a word. Presumably, knowing a word is both necessary and sufficient for being able to take a word at face value. Quine claims there are two parts to knowing a word: (1) a phonetic part—being familiar with the sound of it and being able to reproduce it, and (2) a semantic part—which he explains as knowing how to use it (*OR*, pp. 27–28). These two conditions do obtain in the mother tongue—e.g., for the word 'rabbit', I am familiar with its phonetic component and I know how to use it. Quine tells us that this is sufficient for my knowing the word. Does it provide a basis for taking words at face value so as to resolve the quandary over reference just considered? No. It is sufficient for knowing the syntactical features of a word, but reference is more than that. The *use* of a word is in large part a function of the theory or language *form* where it finds its home and not that of the various interpretations; otherwise different interpretations could not be used for the same language form without behavioral detection. According to Quine, I do not know when I use (correctly) the word 'rabbit' whether I am speaking of rabbit stages, undetached rabbit parts, or rabbits. Use does not discriminate these possibilities. Importantly for Quine, my utterances could be construed as any one of these *without altering the use of the term 'rabbit'*. Thus, the conditions on *knowing the word* that Quine presents cannot help solve the problems lately raised. They do not fix a face value for a word. Here is another way to see the last point: We all recognize that the properties of rabbits are different from the properties of rabbit stages, and that what is true of one is not, in general, true of the other. But if 'rabbit' may be construed as referring to either of these different kinds of objects, certainly *we must take the inscription type 'rabbit' as a different word type under one construal than it is under the other*—the analytical hypotheses would be different. (All this is so in spite of the fact that phonetically and typographically it is the same word and no behavioral criterion would distinguish the different construals.) Since the conditions stated for knowing a word are not sensitive to these different construals, they are not sufficient for knowing a word. The alleged "face value" is ultimately no semantic value on the Quinean view. Quine's discussion of the "face value" of a word does not resolve the quandary over reference—it evades it.[17]

The last point stands even if I am dead wrong about intended reference. All that was needed for the above is the realization that distinct alternatives are required and the indeterminacy of translation. Thus, neither taking words at face value nor appealing to reference systems is sufficient, within Quinean constraints, to save reference from nonsense. It is insufficient because within Quinean constraints the notion *taking words at face value* cannot solve the particularity problem. We have seen, though, that once we allow IR we may then meaningfully speak of the face value of expressions, and that only then can the reference-frame approach be used to extricate us from the quandary over reference that issued from other quarters. Thus, a Quinean must either accept IR or provide another reading of 'taking words at face value'—one that does not presuppose IR. Of course, acceptance of IR also implies the rejection of the indeterminacy of translation applying to oneself, the rejection of first-person indeterminacy. Alternatively, a Quinean could stand fast, reject intended interpretation, and—implausibly—simply hold that reference *is* nonsense.

Quine's Quandary, Background Languages, and the Problem of Particularity

Let us now examine whether Quine's reliance on a background language fares any better in rescuing reference from nonsense. First notice that any background language will itself be indeterminate in precisely the same way as is the object language; i.e., alternative denotations and interpretations for the expressions of the background language will also be possible, any one of which would accommodate all speech dispositions and not be contradicted by any of all possible stimulations, and thus would be equally legitimate. Thus, the background language itself requires interpretation in some background language and similarly for the latter. This Quine explicitly recognizes and labels "the problem of infinite regress." Waiving this problem and keeping the background language fixed—still, if we are to make sense of reference, it cannot be achieved by appeal to a (fixed) background language *within* which we may formulate several incompatible models *and for which it makes no sense to say we mean (intend) one particular model rather than another.*[18] I stress that having multiple models is not, in itself, the devastating blow to making sense of reference in this way. I argue that reference is nonsense only if we go further and deny we can mean (intend) or be aware that we mean (intend) one of these interpretations as opposed to the others. Once the latter is done, as Quine does (the inscrutability and indeterminacy applying to oneself), Quine's attempt to save reference from nonsense fails. For as long as one does not know in terms of *which* of the possible models in the background language the object language is to be paraphrased—and, again, one does not with indeterminacy and inscrutability as applied to oneself—then one has not succeeded in giving a particular meaning and reference to the object language.

Let it not be thought that what is here being argued is merely that Quine's appeal to a background language to make sense of reference merely postpones difficulties; again that is just the problem of infinite regress, and I waived that problem. Rather, I argue that not even a postponement is achieved. What Quine has done by appealing to a background language is purport to resolve (and relativize) the indeterminacy of the object language to a background language; but even assuming that the given background language is fixed, *more than one model can be formulated within it that is an adequate interpretation of the object language,* and since he has precluded our first-person awareness of *which* is intended, *no resolution is achieved—not even relatively.* Once again, the particularity problem has exacted severe damage.

Obviously, if what I have argued in previous sections is correct, one cannot hope to appeal to the "face value" of the formulated model to resolve this problem. What is involved here is one aspect of the doubly relative character of ontology (*OR*, pp. 54–55). That is, we need to know which background language the object language is relativized to and also how the object language is to be interpreted into the given background language—that is, in terms of which model. What has been said above pertains to the second aspect. (In fact, the same problems apply to the first aspect too, in addition to the infinite regress problem acknowledged by Quine, but, as I have said, I put that aside.)

To extricate ourselves from this manifestation of the *problem of particularity,* we need to be able to meaningfully single out, intend a *particular* model among those that we may formulate in the background language and which satisfy the object language. Without this the quandary remains; merely specifying a theory form is, for reasons already indicated, not sufficient.

My contention here is even stronger than any I have advanced thus far: The very notion of an *alternative* translation is itself *without sense* unless we have intended interpretation. Given the indeterminacy of translation, if I can conceive or speak of two or more alternatives, then I must be able to differentiate one from the other beyond their different orthographic or aural types. I must be able to intend one of them as opposed to another, to intend one of them in particular. Without this capacity, the very meaningfulness of talk of two or more alternatives (beyond alternative phonemic or inscriptional types) is lost. To say that some translation is a possible alternative is to say that *that particular* translation is an alternative. But if that translation T can equally be taken as some allegedly different translation T' *and we do not know which is which*, then how can we even conceive of T and T' as different alternatives? (Compare chapter 5, where the problem of particularity played a similarly crucial role in my discussion of representation.) If we take seriously Quine's indeterminacy of translation and inscrutability as *applying to oneself*, one can never be assured that when she speaks of T (interpreted, say, as a "thing" translation) she is not speaking of T' (interpreted, say, as a "stage" translation) and vice versa; indeed the very cogency of saying that we are talking about T rather than T' is brought into doubt. Indeed, the case is worse than just indicated, for a locution such as 'interpreted as a "thing" translation', as used above, would not even be available. These considerations force the conclusion that indeterminacy of translation without intended interpretation is simply vacuous.

Earlier I argued that Quine presupposes and makes implicit use of something like the idea of IR or II. If I am right in the above, he *must* do so for his theses to even make sense. Of course, Quine may avail himself of locutions regarding speakers' intentions or meanings as a practical matter, which he claims to do on several occasions. I am not criticizing his view on the ground that he avails himself of the vernacular for practical reasons. My criticism concerns whether his theoretical formulation of his theses can be sustained without the deployment of some first-person concepts. If what I have argued is correct, this cannot be done; but since he excludes first-person concepts from his theoretical formulation of his theses of indeterminacy of translation and the inscrutability of reference, the status of these are uncertain at best. I maintain that this, coupled with some additional augmentation, shows both that the thesis of Indeterminacy of Translation is vacuous and that reference is nonsense on his view.

To make some of this more concrete, consider another example of Quine's implicit use of intended interpretation in his discussion of alternatives. In discussing an exchange between an immaterialist and a materialist, Quine says the following: "When we come to the immaterialist and we tell him there is a rabbit in the yard, he will know better than to demur on account of a known holophrastic relation of stimulus synonymy between our sentence and some sentence geared to his different universe." (*OR*, p. 99) And later he says that the immaterialist would agree with our statement about a rabbit in the yard "just to convey agreement on the stimulus content or even out of habit carried over from youth" (*OR*, p. 103). But if the immaterialist did not think that the materialist intended to refer to something other than what he himself intended, there would be no question of his demurring from our statement regarding a rabbit.

It is clear that unless the materialist and the immaterialist knew their own intended references, knew what they each intended to refer to and thought that it was different from what the other is (probably) purporting to refer to, these quoted passages would be utterly without significance and could have no point, for the materialist in uttering 'rabbit' could equally "mean" (with appropriate adjustments elsewhere) *rabbit stage*, and similarly for the immaterialist. Such first-person shifts in intended references would not be ascertainable from a third-person perspective and are not allowed by the Quinean methodology We have already seen that appeals to just the face value of the phonemic or inscriptional types are of no avail if a difference in semantics is to be secured. The expression themselves cannot fix the semantics; they themselves have no face value. The only option to fix a particular interpretation appears to be the intentions of the agent(s) using those marks or sounds. This, in turn, requires that the agent know her intended interpretation. None of this is possible without augmenting Quine's methodology with a first-person one. Without concepts based upon this expanded methodology, Quine's discussion of the interchange between the materialist and the immaterialist would be nonsense.

What sense is there in speaking of a rabbit (thing) language if one cannot distinguish—even for oneself—intentions to refer to rabbits from rabbit stages? What sense would there be to the dispute between the materialist and the immaterialist if neither intended a particular interpretation of her utterances, and if the expressions themselves lacked particular (semantic) face values? What is being said does not require that one actually be able to correctly determine another's intended interpretation, but only that she has one and it is available to her, from her first-person perspective. At the same time, I recognize that neither one's own nor another's II is behaviorally determinable, nor is it determinable from any strictly third-person method- ology. My argument is that our first-person perspective assures us that we each have an II when we use language and there are reasons for thinking we know another's. (I will examine the grounds for objective knowledge of another's II in a later section.)

What is important to secure the meaningfulness of talk of alternative interpretations is a speaker's ability to intend a particular interpretation. Intended interpretation is required for the expressions to have some seman- tic face value and to solve the problem of particularity. I repeat and stress that it is only *which* interpretation that is determined or constituted by the agent—she does not thereby determine meaning or reference.

Alternative Interpretations, Genuine Hypotheses, and the Vacuity of Quinean Indeterminacy

Perhaps Quine would view the above-mentioned difficulties of fixing a par- ticular interpretation with equanimity, for, as I have already noted, he sometimes suggests that there is in fact no difference between possible translations. Let us examine this claim further. Quine states that "two systems of analytical hypotheses are, as whole, equivalent so long as no verbal behavior makes any difference between them; and, if they offer seemingly discrepant English translations, one may again argue that the apparent conflict is a conflict only of parts seen out of context" (*WO*, p. 78). Thus, for Quine, the alleged alternative translations are *not genuine alterna- tives*; because as a whole they are empirically equivalent, they are not really different. They appear to be different when we look at individual sentences; however, when we look at the total corpus, the differences, Quine tells us, disappear.[19] Indeed, Quine claims, this result "helps to make the principle of indeterminacy of translation less surprising . . . [it] requires notice just because translation proceeds little by little and sentences are thought of as conveying meanings severally (*WO*, p. 79). It would follow from this not only that the indeterminacy of translation would be "less surprising" but that it would be non-existent—there would *only be an illusion of indeterminacy* so long as the translation was incomplete.[20] All the alternatives would amount to on this view would be alternative systems of linguistic forms (verbal or written). Similarly, the alleged ontological alternatives would not, insofar as they go beyond the empirical content provided by the method of stimulus classes, be genuinely different alternatives. For with respect to just their empirical content, provided by the method of stimulus classes, they are equivalent. Thus, again, all we would have is alternative phonemic or inscriptional forms. But with regard to *these*, there can be *no indeterminacy*, as the differences in phonemic or inscriptional forms *show* themselves. This, however, could be the "face value" only in a trivial and empty sense.

From a theoretical point of view, the Indeterminacy of Translation would be vacuous. Claims to the effect that one does not know what another (be he a foreigner or a neighbor) means and refers to, or that one does not know such things with respect to oneself, lose all effect. With no genuine semantic differences between alternatives, there is then nothing to mean and refer to, save the stimulations that count as the empirical evidence that Quine allows. At best, these claims may be viewed as a misleading way of putting the point that individual sentences do not have meaning *and* that the *only* meaning systems of sentences have lies in their empirical content as determined by the method of stimulus classes.

This point about the content of individual sentences, familiar from Quine's "Two Dogmas of Empiricism," continues in his discussion in "Ontological Relativity" of the empiricist's treatment of statements about the external world. Having gone through the failures of trying to deduce such statements from sensory evidence and logico-mathematical auxiliaries, and the weaker attempt of just translating truths about the world into the latter, Quine tells us that the empiricist concedes that "the empirical meanings of typical statements about the external world are inaccessible and ineffable" (*OR*, pp. 78–79). The explanation Quine offers for this inaccessibility and ineffability is simply that "the typical statement about bodies has no fund of experiential implications that it can call its own" (*OR*, p. 79).[21] Sentences have meaning and experiential implications only by virtue of being contained in a larger theory or language.

To say the latter, however, is not to say that the meaning of sentences is exhausted by the stimulations—those stimulations are compatible with the theory or language as a whole. That is, it does not follow that a sentence—as part of a larger theory or language—does not itself have a particular intended interpretation and reference. It may still, in virtue of the individual's or language community's intention, have some particular interpretation and, thus, say something about particular objects other than stimulations. This is so even if *what* it says is not ultimately separable from the rest of the theory (interpretation) or does not itself, apart from the language of which it is a part, have a separate fund of empirical content. So the meaning holism appealed to, which I endorse, does not preclude particular meaning and reference of individual sentences that are embedded in the language.

Quine's claim that these alternatives are equivalent is closely related to the view that the analytical hypotheses are not genuine hypotheses. To make this out, Quine contrasts analytical hypotheses with hypotheses about stimulus meanings. He takes the latter to be genuine hypotheses. The matching of stimulus meanings, he tells us, is an objective matter:

'Gavagai' and "There's a rabbit"[22] have stimulus meanings for the two speakers, and these are roughly the same or significantly different, whether we guess right or not.

Not so for analytical hypotheses:

. . . no such sense is made of the typical analytical hypothesis. The point is not that we cannot be sure whether the analytical hypothesis[23] is right, but that there is not even . . . an objective matter to be right or wrong about. (*WO*, p. 73)

Clearly, if we preclude the possibility that a speaker intends his utterances to be construed in some particular way, there is nothing to be right or wrong about in constructing analytical hypotheses so long as they conform to the method of stimulus classes. I have already argued against this, but Quine wishes to preclude this possibility, and thus his denial that analytical hypotheses are genuine is not surprising. This reinforces his claim that the alternatives are equivalent, for "so long as no verbal behavior makes any difference between them" *and* there is no intended interpretation we would have no grounds, behavioral or otherwise, for distinguishing them. I conclude (once more) that if Quine is right in holding that the appearance of alternative translations is just a result of "parts seen out of context," and that there is no objective matter concerning which "grand synthetic" analytical hypothesis is the correct one for a given speaker or language community, then not only is indeterminacy of translation "less surprising," as he holds; it is vacuous.

Evidence from the first-person perspective establishes the falsity of a claim that denies that an individual can intend a particular interpretation (or, at the very least, it poses a problem for the claim, a problem that cannot be simply dismissed without begging the question). Once this is acknowledged, we can generalize over the IRs (IIs) of members of the language community to ground a particular interpretation for that community, which we can get right or not. Errors are possible regarding another individual's IR (II) or the generalization over the community. But if there is IR (II), then there is the possibility of getting it right. There is a fact of the matter.

An Answer to a Quinean Counter

Quine marshals seven causes to explain why some fail to appreciate his claim that there is no objective matter to be right or wrong about regarding the choice among workable sets of analytical hypotheses. My arguments to the contrary may be viewed as closely tied to the reason he considers to be the major cause for such failures (the fourth); an examination of this cause may be instructive. I quote at length:

[There] is a stubborn feeling that a true bilingual surely is in a position to make uniquely right correlations of sentences generally between his languages. This feeling is fostered by an uncritical mentalistic theory of ideas: each sentence and its admissible translations express an identical idea in the bilingual's mind. The feeling can also survive rejection of the ideas: one can protest still that the sentence and its translations all correspond to some identical even though unknown neural condition in the bilingual. Now let us grant that; it is only in effect his private semantic correlation—in effect his private implicit system of analytical hypotheses—and that is somehow in his nerves. My point remains; for my point is then that another bilingual could have a semantic correlation incompatible with the first bilingual's without deviating from the first bilingual in his speech dispositions within either language, except in his dispositions to translate. (*WO*, p. 74)

Does this support Quine's view as opposed to mine? I think not. In fact, given a plausible assumption that I will identify below, this passage supports my view and counters Quine's. What I have said about intended interpretation allows that two bilingual individuals could have different intended interpretations (that is, different correlations), yet neither bilingual will deviate from the other "except in his dispositions to translate." If I had argued that the expressions themselves had some unique interpretations, independent of the person that uses them, then this case would count against that claim, but that has never been my position.

According to me, it is important to realize that there are two ways to understand the question "Is there a *correct* translation?":

(1)   Do the words themselves have a unique meaning and reference?

(2)   Does the speaker, in making utterances, intend them to have some unique meaning and reference?

I agree that Quine's bilinguals show us, as does the indeterminacy of translation, that the answer to (1) is negative. Quine thinks that the second question is based on confusion or false presuppositions regarding meanings, but neither the case of the bilinguals nor indeterminacy of translation establishes this.

Quine, overly impressed by the startling fact that he has uncovered, namely that we cannot distinguish the alternative translation manuals using a strictly third-person methodology, concludes they are not really different.[24] Unable to determine in this way which alternative is the correct one, he gives up on the idea of there being a correct translation manual. In doing so he either ignores (2) or conflates it with (1), a tendency on his part noticed earlier. Either way, it is a mistake that can only be justified by heavy-handed application of a strictly third-person methodology.[25]

When Quine says "there is a stubborn notion that we can tell intuitively which idea someone's sentence expresses, our sentence anyway, even when the intuition is irreducible to behavioral criteria" (Davidson and Hintikka 1969, p. 304), his intent is clear; it is that we are mistaken in persisting in this stubborn notion. But in defending an affirmative answer to (2), I have nowhere argued that one can tell *intuitively* which idea someone else's sentence expresses, and I certainly have not argued that one can have privileged access to someone else's intended interpretation. I have argued that in the first-person case one is non-inferentially aware which interpretation ("idea") one's own sentence expresses. (Whether or not one counts the latter as "intuitively" telling in one's own case is irrelevant.) Quine, without doubt, would not see this as an improvement and, therefore, could not abide an affirmative answer to question (2). I do not rehearse my arguments for that claim here. My present point is simply that Quine's bilinguals do not show us that he is correct here; indeed, they indicate that he is quite wrong on one side of this issue, the one that pertains to (2) above. Here is why: If two bilinguals have different semantic correlations, and their correlations are realized in their nerves, as Quine suggests, then we would have every reason to expect that these neuronal realizations would themselves be different from one another. This is the plausible assumption alluded to earlier. In view of what was developed in chapter 4, they would be manifested by two different dynamical transitions to different attractors in the bilinguals' brains.[26] Not only would this support the claim that each bilingual intended a particular interpretation; in addition, given a fully developed neuroscience, we could determine that they were different by examining their brains.[27] Indeed, we can consider a single bilingual who alternates between translation manuals, as our number theorist D (in chapter 1) did between models for sets and numbers. When the bilingual intends a "thing" translation, his burst states would be different than when he intends a "stage" translation. In any of these cases, that there is one burst state rather than another would clearly be an objective fact of the matter, determinable from a strictly third-person perspective. What one could not determine from this perspective is *which* manual or model the instanced burst state is correlated with; thus, third-person indeterminacy is preserved.

Nothing that I have said opposes indeterminacy of translation as applied to another; thus, correlating the bilingual's 'rabbit' utterances with certain types of her burst states and 'rabbit stage' utterances with different burst states of hers could not settle which is which for her, nor does this conflict with anything I have said. On the arguments I advanced in chapter 4, I hold that which interpretation is intended is realized in the brain of the bilingual as certain burst states, and that different interpretations are realized by different bursts. That a particular burst state occurs in *her* brain, that *she has it*, is what enables the first-person perspective that makes her non-inferentially aware of which manual is operative at the time. This is an additional fact at the level of intentionality that parallels the additional fact at the phenomenal level argued for in chapter 3 (the Mary case). As before, analyzing these burst states from a strictly third-person perspective does not reveal these additional facts.

Quine's denial that there is a correct answer, and the consequent denial of II, follow from his claim that the indeterminacy of translation applies to oneself (first-person indeterminacy), for this implies that one is not aware which interpretation one intends. If there were no data supporting the contention that one is aware of intended interpretation in one's own case, one would be hard pressed to make the case for it. Surely, there would then be no reason to think that one's neighbors had it. But the claim that the indeterminacy of translation applies to oneself blatantly disregards the first-person data, and it already presupposes that there is no such thing as intended interpretation. Thus, that thesis could not be used as a basis for rejecting II without begging the question. I have already argued that without intended interpretation the thesis of indeterminacy of translation is vacuous. I conclude that there is no first-person indeterminacy of translation.

Meaning over and above an individual's overt behavior is, of course, something Quine would like to banish. I have argued of late that the Quinean framework itself requires some intentional notion, in its theoretical and not merely in its practical formulation, if indeterminacy of translation is not to be vacuous and reference is not to be reduced to nonsense. Thus, despite Quine's desires, the intentional notion of II is required. It is worth repeating that adopting the concept of II does not make *meaning* determinate in one's head, though *which* meaning is thus determined.

Intended Reference, Mentalism, and Privacy

Once the concepts of intended interpretation and reference are deployed as essential elements of an underlying theory of mind and language, there are consequences that appear to conflict with two further central and related proposals of Quine's—proposals that many others who endorse an exclusively third-person methodology would support:

(1)   a rejection of any form of mentalism in semantics

(2)   a rejection of any sort of private language.

I will examine the degree of mentalism my theory introduces into semantics and whether it brings in its wake a private language.

With respect to (1), Quine says the following:

[With] a naturalistic view of language and a behavioral view of meaning, what we give up is not just the museum figure of speech. We give up an assurance of determinacy . . . according to the museum myth . . . the meanings of the words are supposed to be determinate in the native's mind. . . . When on the other hand we recognize . . . that "meaning . . . is primarily a property of behavior,"[28] we recognize that there are no meanings, nor likenesses, nor distinctions of meaning, beyond what are implicit in people's dispositions to overt behavior. (*OR*, pp. 28–29)

The primary objection persists even if we take the labeled exhibits not as mental ideas but as Platonic ideas or even as the denoted concrete objects. Semantics is vitiated by a pernicious mentalism as long as we regard a man's semantics as somehow determinate in his mind beyond what be implicit in his dispositions to overt behavior. (*OR*, p. 27)

Quine's reliance on a strictly third-person methodology is, of course, the basis for these remarks.

Independent of Quine, I have made a case for the first-person concept of minimal content and for intended reference, the consequences of which are in direct opposition to Quinean scruples. Of course, I am not denying that behavior also plays a prominent role with regard to meaning. Having said that, I need not argue as to whether the role behavior plays is of such a magnitude as to make meaning "*primarily* a property of behavior," for aside from this quibble there remains an immense difference between Quine and me.[29] My theory—in a specific restricted way—is resolutely committed to regarding "a man's semantics as somehow determinate in his mind beyond what be implicit in his dispositions to overt behavior." Thus, according to Quine, I am committed to a "pernicious mentalism." While I enthusiastically embrace the commitment of my theory to the very limited "mentalism" required by the concepts of intended reference and interpretation, I categorically reject the charge that it is "pernicious."

First, any mentalism involved in my theory is a direct result of the fact that IR and II are first-person concepts. I have argued extensively for the necessity of augmenting any third-person methodology with such concepts for the study of mind and language. Second, the reason that I say that this mentalism is limited regarding semantics is that it is only required to determine *which* reference or meaning, not reference or meaning itself. This limited mentalism is of the utmost importance, for, among other reasons, it solves the particularity problem in its various manifestations, and it saves the Indeterminacy of Translation thesis from vacuity and reference from nonsense. It is imperative to realize that the notions of IR and II do not force us to identify reference or meaning with anything mental, nor have I made any attempt to do so. What I hold is much simpler: What is fixed in the mind(s) of the language user(s) is just *which* interpretation (semantics) she is deploying. This is quite different from holding that the *interpretation* or *semantics* is itself determined in the mind. This is the limited mentalism and the resulting determinacy that IR and II yield.

But do acceptance of the first-person concepts of IR and II and the limited mentalism that such acceptance entails commit us to a private language?

Whatever publicity there is to language on a Quinean view is a result of stimulus meaning, or more broadly, the method of stimulus classes, which also includes dispositions to overt behavior. The method of stimulus classes is a strictly third-person methodology. This serves as a constraint on the permissible analytical hypotheses, though not a sufficiently strong constraint, as Quine himself argues, to determine uniquely a single translation manual. With this I agree; nevertheless, analytical hypotheses must be introduced, for central to Quine's theses is the point that the method of stimulus classes and dispositions to behavior is inadequate for determining the divided reference of terms; indeed, we cannot even determine that an expression is a term without analytical hypotheses. Moreover, there is no avoiding analytical hypotheses, for to speak of "language" without including referring terms would be a severely mutilated and inadequate sense of 'language'; thus, Quinean or not, we must go beyond stimulus meaning and, thus, beyond strict publicity provided by the method of stimulus classes.

It is easy to see that, whatever publicity stimulus meaning provides, we still have when intended interpretation is introduced. This is so because II pertains to the *choice* of analytical hypotheses—not the range of possibilities, but *which one* is operative. Stimulus meaning is a constraint on the range of possible choices for Quine and for me; it operates as a constraint independent of the speaker's choice, her intended interpretation. Still, the difference between Quine's theory and mine on intended interpretation is huge and has already been noted: I allow, while Quine denies, the significance of questions as to which theory or set of analytical hypotheses an individual intends. There is on my view the possibility of getting it right. Whatever "privacy" there is on my theory, it is limited to this "which question" and, therefore, to the limited mentalism that I have argued for.

In concluding this section, let us consider the following passage:

What [indeterminacy of translation] does occasion . . . is a change in prevalent attitudes toward meaning, idea, proposition. . . . [But] a conviction persists, often unacknowledged, that our sentences express ideas, and express these ideas rather than those, even when behavioral criteria can never say which. This is why one thinks that one's question 'What did the native say?' has a right answer independent of choices among mutually incompatible manuals of translation (Davidson and Hintikka 1969, p. 304).

Whether II would reinstate proposition, idea, and meaning I have not determined. I have been careful to stress that intended interpretation *does not constitute meaning or reference*, however these are ultimately construed. The conviction that persists for me is not the one that Quine opposes, namely that our sentences express ideas. Rather, it is that our sentences do express some particular interpretation but they do not do this on their own. Whether they express one interpretation rather than another is determined by an individual's mental act, or by a generalization over such mental acts of the members of the speech community, inferring that they generally intend the same interpretation. Indeed, the very idea of an alternative interpretation requires intended interpretation, as I argued above.

Whatever "privacy" of language there is on my theory concerns *which* interpretation the speaker intends; importantly, this is directly known from the first-person perspective. This is a far cry from holding that there is a private language of the sort that Wittgenstein and others have objected to. The only objection that could be raised against it is that it requires something other than a strictly third-person methodology. Certainly, I have addressed such concerns. I believe that I have laid them to rest.

Objective Knowledge of Another's II or IR

There is some empirical room, and certainly some logical room, for doubt as to the identity of intended interpretation from speaker to speaker; still, there is evidence that may be utilized in attempting to determine a neighbor's II (IR).[30] Given (a) that language is propagated by imitation and feedback, (b) the syntactic isomorphism of another's utterances and one's own, (c), our common culture, and (d) our common biological makeup, it is plausible to suppose another's II is the same as one's own, barring evidence to the contrary. The objective character of (a)–(d) gives reason to hold that we can have objective knowledge of another's II, once the first-person reasons are recognized for holding that there is II in one's own case. If I am aware that I have it, there is no positive reason to deny it to others. The concepts of II and IR are based on that of minimal content. Once we have minimal content, there is no credible reason to deny II and IR. But then there is every reason to suppose that others must have it too, and, just as we have reason to think that we can have objective knowledge of another's minimal content, so too can we have objective knowledge of another's II or IR.

Of course Quine would recognize neither minimal content nor II. Restricting what can count as objective data to the method of stimulus classes, he takes the inability to determine what another's II is on the basis of this method as reason to reject the idea of another's having an intended interpretation. He then goes much further: If another has no II, then I do not either, since if I had II, *another* utilizing a strictly third-person methodology could not determine what it is. It would follow on his view that I would have a private language, but Quine excludes the latter. So, he concludes, neither oneself, nor another has intended interpretation.[31] This reasoning is of a piece with rejecting first-person methodologies.[32] Quine has got things seriously reversed.

Having passed the heady days of old Vienna, why would one think that all that is objective, all there is, and all that is significant, is what can be determined in the strict way that Quine recommends? Claims about one's neighbor's intended interpretation are empirical claims that go beyond one's own experience. As with any other such claims, we can do nothing but base them on the best possible evidence. The theoretical possibility that your neighbor's intended interpretation is different from your own cannot be denied, but this is slim reason to preclude its existence. It certainly is no reason to ignore what is manifestly present from the first-person perspective. Moreover, in the face of the objective reasons provided by (a)–(d) above, it is a good conjecture that not only is another's II typically the same as one's own, such judgments are objective.

Knowledge of a foreigner's II (IR) is not as straightforward as the case of a neighbor's, given the absence of (a), (b), and possibly (c). Though any foreigner can be relatively confident that each of her neighbors has the same II as she does by considerations precisely analogous to the preceding, our relation to a foreigner differs from our relation to one another. For us to obtain knowledge of her II (IR) we would have to construct various tests, e.g., of the kind alluded to in "On the Reasons for Indeterminacy of Translation." Quine does acknowledge that such tests may provide "an indirect hint as to which of various analytical hypotheses regarding . . . [the individuative apparatus] . . . might in the end work out most naturally."[33] I submit that it would be in keeping with good scientific practice (objective empirical research) to take the "naturalness" of the translations guided by these indirect hints as grounds for claiming that the resulting divided references are the ones intended by the foreigner, i.e., the divided reference for-the-native, and correlatively, a certain interpretation of other native linguistic constructions.

Notice that I used 'practice' rather than 'practical' above. Though practical considerations sometimes play a role in science, the doing of science is not itself practical. Thus, when I say that it is in keeping with good scientific practice to base our conclusions about a foreigner's intended references on such evidence, I am not saying, as Quine might, that from a practical point of view we may project certain intended references to the native, even though she does not, in a strict sense, have them. That is, I am not saying that it is merely convenient to speak *as if* the native had them. Rather, I am claiming that the foreigner *does indeed have intended references*, just as my neighbors and I do, and we are doing the best we can to determine what they are, though we may be wrong. The evidence supporting most claims in science is indirect. It is just so for determining another's II, be she foreigner or neighbor.[34] This is no reason to deny the existence of instantiations of first-person concepts, particularly when the first-person data are compelling in one's own case and when their denial leads to unacceptable consequences. Once II and IR are admitted, there is no reason to deny that we can have objective knowledge of them, whether it be one's own, one's neighbor's, or a foreigner's II and IR.

Summary Comparison of the Two Methodologies

The methodological difference between Quine and me is stark. Quine rejects the idea that the translation relation is objective *because* it is indeterminate in principle relative to the totality of speech dispositions. More generally, the translation relation is indeterminate relative to all evidence obtainable from any strictly third-person methodology. On the other hand, once the methodology is expanded to include the first-person perspective, as I recommend, the translation relation is readily determinate in the first-person case, is recognized as objective (in my expanded sense of chapter 3), and is determinable in the case of another (modulo the usual empirical uncertainties in such matters).

Quine, however, holds that the translation relations that I endorse are themselves of no scientific value: "Such postulation promises little gain in scientific insight if there is no better ground for it than that the supposed translation relations are presupposed by the vernacular of semantics and intention." (*OR*, p. 29) If the only basis for such relations were the vernacular of semantics and intention, this would be slim justification for the position.

I have not relied on the vernacular. I have offered different and important reasons for incorporating subjective intentional idioms for the philosophical study of mind and language. First, I have independently argued for the existence of first-person awareness of minimal content and that recognition of such awareness is necessary for an adequate account of mind. Minimal content is the foundation for IR and II. Second, I have shown that successful talk of particular interpretations and the ability to rescue reference from nonsense require—without appeal to the vernacular—intended interpretation. Third, and in consequence of the latter, I have argued that without intended interpretation the Indeterminacy of Translation is vacuous. Fourth, I have shown, using Quine's own example of the bilinguals, how different semantical correlations could be reflected in different objective facts of neuronal conditions in the speaker's brain. (Though from a third-person perspective we could detect the difference, we could not determine which is which.) It follows, then, that we must allow that analytical hypotheses are genuine hypotheses. The alternatives are not semantically equivalent, and the speaker does intend her utterances in some particular way. Fifth, I have given a general argument (in chapter 3 and in the last section of chapter 5) that the use of a first-person methodology in these matters does not diminish the objective character or the scientific nature of the findings. I have applied that reasoning to knowledge of another's intended interpretation. Sixth, since which interpretation a speaker intends is invisible using a strictly third-person methodology, a very limited but innocuous "privacy of language" is allowed.

Which methodology should be adopted? According to my arguments, without incorporating the first-person perspective one cannot meaningfully talk of *particular* interpretations, and without this, Indeterminacy of Translation is vacuous and reference is nonsense. These consequences of Quine's methodology, together with the independent support for the expanded methodology earlier advanced should, I hope, make the choice clear.

One last important general conclusion remains to be made explicit. If what I have argued is correct, it follows that:

1. The *very idea* of a *particular* interpretation requires the idea of an agent determining this one rather than that one.

2. The agent's act of determination is itself constitutive of *which* interpretation is at issue.

3.   An agent can non-inferentially know his own particular intended inter-pretation, his II, but others cannot know his in this way

4.   When someone tries to determine another's II, the thesis of the Indeter-minacy of Translation comes into play.

When we add the seemingly uncontroversial assertion that the meanings of sentences of a language are a function of the particular interpretation of the sequences of marks or sounds of the language, and when we recognize that 1–3 decidedly turn on the subjectivity of the agent, it follows that *meaning itself is ultimately grounded in the subjective.*

9   Ontology Downgraded All the Way

I have argued at length against Quine's claim that there is no correct answer as to what an individual intends to refer to or which interpretation she intends. Nevertheless, I wholeheartedly endorse his ingenious arguments as to how compensating adjustments in the individuative apparatus of a language can yield competing alternatives of references and interpretations—alternatives that are neither discriminable by the method of stimulus classes, nor by any strictly third-person methodology. My objections have not been directed against this last point, which I accept. I have argued that intended reference and interpretation are required so that the thesis of Indeterminacy of Translation is not vacuous and reference is not nonsense. Once these concepts are introduced, the consequences of the Indeterminacy of Translation and the inscrutability of reference are different than Quine thought. Among other things, there is no first-person indeterminacy, though third-person indeterminacy remains. I argue in this chapter that even when these theses are understood in light of intended interpretation and reference, there remain very deep consequences for ontology.

Indeterminacy of Translation and Transcendental Metaphysics

There is a crude but informative picture of mind, language, and the world that I wish to exploit. It is crude because I do not enumerate the numerous qualifications that would have to be made for the picture to be accurate. It is informative because even without the qualifications it highlights certain salient and uncontroversial relations between mind, language and the world. The simple picture turns on the fact that language may be used to convey an agent's thoughts and to indicate items or states of affairs in the world—language points to the mind and it points to the world. My purpose in presenting this crude picture is to make explicit a possible ambiguity in the thesis that the Indeterminacy of Translation applies to oneself. I call this *first-person indeterminacy*.

First-person indeterminacy may be construed as the claim that it ultimately makes no sense to hold that an individual intends one translation as opposed to some other, seemingly different one when the two translations are empirically equivalent, since there is no fact of the matter regarding which of the two is the correct translation of the speaker's utterances. This is Quine's position, against which I argued in the previous chapter. But since Quine's thesis of the Indeterminacy of Translation is closely linked with the inscrutability of reference and with his thesis of Ontological Relativity, there is a distinctly different way of reading the claim that indeterminacy applies equally in the first-person and third-person cases: An individual is in no privileged position regarding the determination of which of the possible alternative translations of her utterances *is the one that matches or corresponds to what and how things are really in the world*, no matter how determinately she non-inferentially knows which is her intended interpretation. On this second construal, I will argue that there is no fact of the matter and that differences between first-person and third-person perspectives are, unlike the case for the first construal, nonexistent.

The claim that some one translation describes the way the world actually is would be not only an (interpreted) word-world relation; it also would be an attempted transcendental application of the translation. The term 'ontic reference' was introduced for just such purposes. If we were to speak of transcendental objects, then we might as well speak of their relations and properties and, thus, of transcendental uses of whole sentences. I mark such uses with the locution 'ontic interpretation', which is analogous to 'ontic reference'. Ontic interpretation and ontic reference are equally indeterminate from one's own point of view as from another's. It does follow from Quine's arguments that there is no asymmetry of the first-person and third-person perspectives regarding which translation matches or corresponds with the way the world "really" is. Each of the acceptable translations divides the reference of terms differently. Thus, the objects qua objects purported to be in the world are different for each translation manual, their respective references go beyond the stimulations, and they cannot be uniquely determined on that basis. The reason for this lack of unique determination is that the individuative apparatus of a language is not immune to the indeterminacy of translation and, so, we have the extraordinary consequence that reference or extension is no better off than meaning or intension. Quine tells us that the indeterminacy of translation "began as a challenge to likeness of meaning. . . . Of two predicates which are alike in extension, it has never been clear when to say they are alike in meaning and when not . . . Reference, extension, has been the firm thing; meaning, intension, the infirm. The indeterminacy of translation now confronting us, however, cuts across extension and intension alike. . . . Reference itself proves behaviorally inscrutable." (*OR*, p. 35)[1] He goes on to explain (same page) why extension or reference has seemed to be "firm": Within our own language we think of the apparatus of individuation as given and fixed.

The last point is pertinent to a central result of my theory. On my theory there is an important ambiguity in the use of the terms 'reference' and 'extension'. By the 'extension' or 'reference' of a term we may legitimately indicate (i) the intended reference, (ii) the objective reference, or (iii) the ontic reference.[2] Why these ambiguities are not normally noticed may be explained by the fact that typically when 'extension' or 'reference' is used it is in a context where the operative understanding corresponds to what I have called objective reference. The latter has built into it inter-subjective agreement among members of the community. Moreover, since objective reference is a generalization over the intended references of members of a community with a presumption of identity, there is typically no reason to distinguish intended from objective references in such contexts. Add to this the fact that Quine observed, namely, that the individuative apparatus is normally presumed fixed, and there is no reason to think that intended and objective reference can come apart; hence, typically no reason to distinguish them. Add further the realist tendencies of many philosophers, and there is an implicit presumption that objective reference is ontic reference.

If one accepts Quine's argument to the conclusion that the indeterminacy of translation applies to our home language and accepts my arguments for introducing and distinguishing three senses of reference, then the practice of ignoring the differences is unacceptable. In light of this, consider a famous passage: " . . . the inscrutability of reference is not the inscrutability of a fact; there is no fact of the matter" (*OR*, p. 47). Having discussed three notions of reference, I will examine this claim as applied to each of them.

First, is it true of intended reference? This is basically a mind-word relation, and insofar as my arguments are sound we do have first-person awareness of intended interpretation and, a fortiori, of intended reference; thus, there is no inscrutability of intended reference in one's own case, no first-person inscrutability of reference (nor of intended interpretation). With respect to another person, the case is different, but since there is support for hypotheses about another's intended reference there is no inscrutability of another's IR.[3] Therefore, intended references are not inscrutable in either the first-person case or the third-person case. I have, in effect, already considered Quine's claim at the level of objective reference in discussing the claim as applied to IR in the first-person and third-person cases, for objective reference is just the generalization of intended reference over the speakers of a language community with a presumption of identity. If each speaker has intended reference, then we are right or wrong in presuming an identity of these across speakers, and there is a fact of the matter for objective reference that is not inscrutable. Things are quite different for ontic reference and ontic interpretation; with regard to these, there is no fact of the matter.

The reading of the claim that the thesis that the indeterminacy of translation applies to oneself that I do not accept is the reading in which this claim is understood in the transcendental way: The translation matches or corresponds to the way the world "really" is. So understood, however, it is compatible with the admission of intended interpretation and first-person determinacy regarding it. For certainly an individual's being aware—in a privileged way—of which translation she intends (her II), does not help her (or anyone else) in the least in determining whether that interpretation characterizes the world as it actually is, even when there is inter-subjective agreement on the II of the language within a community. Ontic reference or interpretation concerns an (interpreted) word-(ultimate) world relation which is cognitively and epistemically well beyond that of objective reference.

My case for first-person determinacy regarding II (IR) does not imply anything like an Aristotelian intuition of real essences. What we directly know is which interpretation each of us intends, hence, too, what our own intended references are. We certainly do not thereby directly know which, if any, interpretation fits the world (beyond the stimulations), and certainly not the ultimate ontology; moreover, there are no indirect means to favor one over another, as there is in the case of determining another's intended interpretation or reference. Therefore, we cannot know how the world is in any ultimate sense. With II the relation between mind and language is at issue; the world comes in only indirectly as what the agent thereby *purports* there to be in the world.

IR and II do not imply, and should not suggest, any special powers of the mind to grasp (alleged) ultimate objects, true essences, properties, or relations of things in the world, even in the ordinary sense of things. It is perhaps the belief on Quine's part that the alternative to a naturalistic view of language (as he conceives this) is an intuition of real essences, in some Platonic or some non-abstract realm, that drives him to his excesses. Once the different senses of reference and interpretation that I have introduced are recognized, we see that we need accept neither intuition of real essences nor first-person indeterminacy and inscrutability of intended interpretation and reference. On the other hand, Quine's claim that "the inscrutability of reference is not an inscrutability of fact; there is no fact of the matter"— when understood at the level of ontic reference—is a claim I wholeheartedly endorse. No first-person perspective comes to the rescue here. The objects we usually talk about are *merely* the results of *our* parsing the stimulus meanings, somewhat arbitrarily, if Quine is to be believed, in one of several theoretically possible ways, and that is the best we can do.

Now, one might want to maintain, with Quine, that the method of stimulus classes cannot in principle adjudicate between competing ontologies (as I do), while still maintaining that there are determinable objects in the world independent of us (as I do not); we just cannot determine what they are, and thus separating the epistemic from the ontological matters. That would be to say that although it is a fact that such and such objects exist and that there are facts about these objects (i.e. the properties they have and the relations they stand in) there are ultimate limitations in principle on our knowledge of these things and facts, and hence to claim an epistemic inscrutability of fact but to allow that there is some ultimate fact of the matter.

The previous paragraph would appear to leave open the *possibility* of there being a fact of the matter, of there being objects in the world, even if we are in principle precluded from knowing what they are. I think this is a mistake. Such claims that depend upon the epistemic/ontic distinction presuppose that we can speak of objects in the world independent of any theory or background language, i.e. objects, on the one hand, and theories about them, on the other. I think Quine is right when he denies this: Our talk of theories and ontologies must be relative to a "background theory with its own primitively adopted and ultimately inscrutable ontology" (*OR*, p. 51).[4] But if it is not possible to speak of objects apart from theories, then there can be *no significance* to talk of ontology apart from a background theory.[5] If this is so, then it also would make no sense to hold that the limitations discussed above are *merely* epistemological.

It is at the level of ontic reference that inscrutability of reference cuts deepest, however, through the bone, as it were. In contrast to the cases of intended and objective reference, there is no evidence as to ontic reference, what objects "really" exist (as opposed to certain acceptable alternatives), and we cannot even talk of objects apart from background theories. Importantly, with regard to ontic reference there is no asymmetry of access between the first-person and third-person perspectives, as there is with intended reference. It is that asymmetry that ultimately allows us to hold that there is a fact of the matter with respect to the correct translation, which interpretation is intended by a given speaker, and what are her intended references. Thus, I reject first-person indeterminacy under the first construal above. But since there is no asymmetry of access to ontic reference, no talk of objects apart from their background theories, and no Aristotelian intuition of "real essences," the inscrutability of reference can bring into doubt the very significance of talk of ontic reference and should lead us to deny that there is a fact of the matter at this level. Thus, I endorse first-person indeterminacy under the second construal above.

Exactly what Quine's position is on the epistemic/ontic issue is confusing, however. There is, on the one hand, his stark claim that "the inscrutability of reference is not an inscrutability of fact; there is no fact of the matter." Quite apart from his point that ontology is always relative to a background theory, this unqualified, bold statement certainly would suggest that he is not merely making an epistemic claim and that he is rejecting ultimate ontological claims. On the other hand, there is the vexing fact that he frequently makes statements that endorse realism. This ambivalence is partly responsible for obscuring the devastating consequences of his ingenious arguments for traditional ontology. Instead of embracing the latter, he repeatedly and persistently endorses a certain kind of realism.[6]

As I see it, Quine erred on both sides of the "double directedness of language." He erred in thinking that there is no correct answer regarding which translation or reference a speaker intends, as I have argued in the previous chapter, and he erred in thinking that his position is compatible with realism, as I argue in the remaining sections of this chapter. I will detail the tension between Quine's avowed realism and his view of ontology and show that the more defensible view is the rejection of realism and, more broadly, that talk of transcendental or ultimate ontology is meaningless.

The Epistemology of Ontology[7]

To my mind there has always been a fundamental tension in Quine's work between his commitment to a kind of scientific realism, on the one hand, and his frequent employment of proxy functions and the rejection of transcendental metaphysics, on the other. Quine has defended his brand of scientific realism and naturalism (1992a). He has expanded his defense (1993, 1996), utilizing observation sentences in their holophrastic guise (Quine 1993). He has argued (1993) that the latter bear "significantly on the epistemology of ontology" and that they provide for the commensurability of theories. I argue that they fail in all these tasks. Further, Quine's long-standing commitment to a kind of scientific realism, on the one hand, and his frequent employment of proxy functions and the rejection of transcendental metaphysics, on the other, constitute an untenable position. A consistent Quinean must abandon scientific realism and ontology. I also argue that, insofar scientific realism is a robust ontological thesis, we all must abandon it, along with traditional ontological talk, for it is meaningless.

Quine (1993) tells us that when observation sentences are taken *piecemeal*, i.e., when component terms of observation sentences in their referential capacity is at issue, they are theory laden, but when they are treated *holophrastically*, linked as a whole to the current stimulations and independent of any possible subject matter, there is no theory dependence. It is in the latter capacity that observation sentences are pure, pristine, "the child's port of entry into cognitive language" (1993, p. 109). And later, "Holophrastically . . . the observation sentences are anchored to sensory neural intake *irrespective of their theoretical subject matter*" (1993, p. 110, emphasis added). Quine praises the virtues of observation sentences in their holophrastic capacity. He maintains (1993, pp. 110–112) that they serve as common reference points for incommensurable theories and advance the epistemology of ontology, among other things.

Subsequent to his 1993 paper, Quine has given up the claim that holophrastic observation sentences are independent of theory. In a response to a series of earlier versions of the present chapter, Quine came to agree that the relevant holophrastic observation sentences are theory dependent.[8] Nevertheless, Quine appears reluctant to accept the fact that this concession undermines the alleged virtues of observation sentences just mentioned. In what follows, I detail the theory dependence of an important class of holophrastic observation sentences to show how this forces a rejection of Quine's realism.

In *Word and Object*, Quine spoke of units geared as wholes to stimulations,[9] which I will call *one-word observation sentences*. Holophrastic observation sentences correspond somewhat to these, but only somewhat; as we shall see, holophrastic observation sentences go beyond one-word observation sentences in a crucial way. The piecemeal treatment corresponds to what Quine earlier described as the move to accepting certain analytical hypotheses, which enabled parsing sentences into terms and dividing the reference of the latter (*WO*, pp. 68–73, 90–95).

A small part of the problem with Quine's discussion of observation sentences in his 1992 and 1993 papers is that he conflates two distinct dimensions pertinent to talk of observation. The dimensions are (1) degrees of observationality and (2) whether a sentence is taken piecemeal or holophrastically. Quine "rescinds" degrees of observationality in his 1996 paper, but the way he does so does not obviate the problems spelled out in this chapter. Quine tends to identify sentences treated holophrastically with those of high degree of observationality.

A more serious problem is the conflation of the earlier idea of a one-word observation sentence with the idea of a sentence taken holophrastically. This problem and its consequences will be examined in detail in what follows.

To see how holophrastic observation sentences go beyond one-word observation sentences, I will divide the observation sentences Quine considers in his 1993 paper into a series of levels, epistemic considerations determining the level of a given observation sentence. It is the fact that some holophrastic observation sentences go beyond one-word observation sentences that disables them from performing the epistemic tasks Quine assigns them. (The one-word observation sentences are also inadequate to the tasks but for different reasons.)

Note first that Quine's point in praising observation sentences is to provide an intermediate ground between classical epistemology, with its foundational view, and the anti-foundational views found in the works of N. R.

Hanson, Paul Feyerabend, and Thomas Kuhn. Quine suggests that the move from phenomenalism to physicalism was due at least in part to the realization of the inadequacy of the idea that there is a phenomenalistic conceptual scheme somehow given from which we can posit the physical world (1993, p. 107). For Rudolf Carnap, Otto Neurath, and Moritz Schlick, the issue became one of specifying what sentences to count as "protocol sentences." Quine asserts that "subsequent physicalists were impatient with even this" and that "they shelved the whole notion of epistemological starting point, and therewith the last remnant of epistemology" (ibid., p. 108). He thinks they gave up too easily, for he tells us that what to count as protocol "becomes clear, if one is both single-mindedly physicalistic and single-mindedly epistemological" (ibid.).[10]

Quine seeks to reactivate, in modified form, the notion of "epistemological starting point," a notion abandoned by earlier physicalists. He thinks his notion of holophrastic observation sentence can play that role and can provide an intermediate ground between the classical epistemological foundationalists and the contemporary anti-foundationalists. He states that "the protocol sentences [which he subsequently calls "observation sentences"] should be the sentences most closely linked causally to this neural intake [the impact of molecules and light rays on our sensory receptors] . . . , sentences like 'It's cold', 'It's raining', 'That's milk.'" (1993, p. 108) He recognizes an obvious objection to such sentences serving as an epistemic foundation is that *they already assume knowledge of the external world* and so they are of dubious evidential support for such knowledge. He seems think he meets this objection. I argue that he is unsuccessful.[11] To this end, I now introduce the first of the levels of my epistemic classification of Quine's observation sentences, the purest form of observation sentences, level 1: "Observation sentences—as I call them—can be conditioned outright to distinctive ranges of sensory intake, or as physicalists let us say neural intake. The child can be conditioned simply to assert or assent to the sentence under some distinctive stimulation. . . ." (Quine 1993, p. 108) Such sentences avoid the objection just noted. However, if observation sentences are to be powerful enough to do the *epistemological* work that Quine has in store for them, he recognizes he must broaden the class further. In addition to observation sentences such as these, there are others, which I place in level 2: "We learn some of them from other ones by analogy, recombining their parts. We learn to form compounds of simple ones, using grammatical particles." (ibid.) Not even this is enough. Observation sentences must encompass even more. Level 3: "As adults, we learn many more *through the mediation of sophisticated theory*. Thus, take the sentence 'There is some copper in the solution'. We understand it by construction from its separate words, but it becomes an observation sentence for a chemist who has learned to spot the presence of copper by a glance at the solution." (ibid., emphasis added)

Why does Quine count sentences of what I have called levels 2 and 3 as observational? We are told that "what qualifies sentences of both sorts as observational, for a given individual, is just his readiness to assent outright on the strength of appropriate neural intake, irrespective of what he may have been engaged in at the time" (ibid.). This criterion for a sentence's being observational is relative to an individual and, to borrow an expression from Feyerabend, is "quickly decidable." Whether a sentence is taken as a unit or parsed with terms taken in their referential capacity is irrelevant to its being quickly decidable for a given individual (or for an entire community). Such matters, however, are *not* irrelevant with respect to the question whether knowledge of the world is already assumed. Quine must contend with the latter if he is to establish the epistemic virtues of his observation sentences.

In my classification, for a sentence to be of level 1 it must be treated as a one-word observation sentence. Such sentences, of course, are not intrinsically one-word observation sentences—no string of marks or sounds is intrinsically a one-word sentence; a sentence may be parsed and treated non-holophrastically, *but when so treated it is no longer a level-1 observation sentence*. Thus, while both level 1 and level 3 may be quickly decidable and holophrastically considered, these features are not sufficient to qualify a sentence as a one-word observation sentence. Level-1 sentences are restricted to the latter.

There are many ways one might partition Quine's class of observation sentences, depending on one's purposes. My levels 1 and 3 are chosen so as to highlight an epistemological point, one that exposes the inadequacy of the class of Quine's observation sentences to do the epistemic work he sets for them. In particular, level 1 is restricted to one-word observation sentences to isolate those and only those that do not presuppose knowledge of the world. Sentences that I place in level 3, however, are those that Quine tells us are learned "through the mediation of sophisticated theory." As such, they do not qualify as one-word observation sentences, even though they can be treated holophrastically and are (often) quickly decidable. Being treated holophrastically and being a one-word observation sentence are, for these reasons, importantly different.

Quine's inclusion of level-3 sentences among the observational is necessary, however, if one is to have any hope of obtaining a basis for knowledge of the world—level-1 sentences by themselves are too weak. But including the level-3 sentences undermines his attempt to meet the obvious and fundamental objection he recognized to the initial protocol sentences offered by early positivists: Knowledge of the world is assumed. For example, a chemist's response "There is copper in it" to seeing a green precipitate is clearly dependent on the chemist's (assumed) knowledge of the world.[12] This is in no way contravened by the fact that on various occasions it is holophrastically treated or quickly decidable. Level-1 sentences avoided this objection by remaining unparsed; they are by stipulation one-word observation sentences, each geared to some distinctive stimulation. No knowledge of the world is presupposed; such sentences are not parsed into terms that refer. In saying this I am not holding that it is impossible to parse them. No one claims that any utterance or string of marks intrinsically constitutes a one-word observation sentence. The point is simply that, given the epistemic partitioning of the class of observation sentences that I have offered, when a level-1 sentence is parsed it ceases to be a level-1 sentence—by that very fact. Parsing unavoidably introduces assumptions about the world, whether they are widely held assumptions (such as that there are medium sized physical objects) or assumptions of some specialized group (say, chemists).

The idea of a one-word observation sentence, a level-1 sentence, is importantly different from both the idea of a holophrastic observation sentence and the idea of one that is quickly decidable; Quine uses the latter feature to warrant sentences of level 3 as observation sentences. But some sentences of level 3 are subject to the initial objection; they assume knowledge of the external world. That level-3 sentences may be quickly decidable or holophrastically treated in no way circumvents this objection. The *epistemic differences* between level-1 and level-3 sentences are obscured when Quine emphasizes their common holophrastic treatment. Important consequences of these points for ontology will be specified below, but first more must be said about Quine's treatment of observation sentences.

For Quine, observation sentences are "Janus-faced." Facing inward, the subjective side, "the neural intake is keyed to the sentence as a monolithic

whole, no matter whether the sentence was first acquired by simple ostension [level 1] or by excursion through theory in the manner of the chemistry example [level 3]" (1993, p. 109). The last clause of this quote makes it
evident that Quine allows for the holophrastic treatment of level-3 sentences. This is certainly permissible. Whether doing so avoids the charge of
assuming knowledge of the world is a separate question. I am arguing that
it does not. We can see the same point in another light if we examine the
other face of these two-faced sentences.

Quine tells us that observation sentences also face outward to their subject matter. This is their objective side, and thus construed "the sentence
figures not holophrastically, but piecemeal word for word" (1993, p. 109).
Furthermore, *observation sentences in their outward guise* are also, he tells us,
"the vehicle of evidence for objective science, intersubjectively attested"
(1993, p. 109). Since it is in their outward guise that observation sentences
are the "vehicle of evidence for objective science," it is at level 3, not at level
1, that sentences play this role. But level-3 sentences presuppose knowledge
of the world, unlike level-1 sentences. The epistemic neutrality of level-1
sentences is not transferred to level-3 sentences, even when the latter are
recognized as Janus-faced, treated holophrastically, or quickly decidable.

The degree of objectivity of the outward-facing observation sentences is
further compromised by what Quine says is "the further requirement for
our definition, [viz.,] that assent to the sentence and dissent from it must
command agreement of all competent witnesses" (1993, p. 109). Who will
count as competent? *Those who have the requisite knowledge.* In the chemistry
example, it is obviously those who have knowledge of the relevant chemical theory and, therefore, the knowledge to interpret the green precipitate
under the appropriate conditions as indicative of the presence of copper.
Never mind that the sentence "There is copper in it" is quickly asserted or
assented to and is keyed to the stimulation as a monolithic whole and thus
treated holophrastically. An observer would not, and could not, quickly
assert or assent to such a sentence, holophrastically or otherwise, without
the appropriate knowledge—knowledge that goes far beyond the immediate stimulations.

Importantly, it is also clear that observers lacking the requisite knowledge
would not even count as competent observers. (Of course, lacking that
knowledge, an individual might well quickly respond "It turned green," but
that is another matter entirely.) To provide an "epistemic starting point"

not subject to anti-foundational criticisms, as Quine wishes, the candidate observation sentences must not assume knowledge of the world. That the sentences can be treated holophrastically does not circumvent this problem; holophrastic treatment of these *presupposes* prior parsing, for they are learned through the mediation of theory; thus, there are attendant assumptions about the world. Their subsequent holophrastic treatment does not eliminate the assumptions required that such treatment presupposes.

In response to an earlier (July 1993) version of the present chapter, Quine reports that he attaches "importance to a distinction quite close to that between your [i.e., my] levels 1–2 and level 3; namely, in my case [i.e., Quine's], between sentences that are observational relative to the whole community of normal speakers of the language and ones that are observational only relative to a trained subclass. I shall call them the primitive and the professional observation sentences." He further notes that, though both "serve as checkpoints in the experimental method," persistent questioning force the scientist ultimately to rely on the primitive observation sentences. But whether the primitive observation sentences coincide with those of levels 1 and 2 turns on how broadly based the community of normal speakers of the language is taken to be. If, for example, a sentence pertaining to medium-size physical objects is observational for the whole community of normal speakers of the language, then, while such a sentence would count as primitive, it would not count as a sentence of levels 1 and 2. It could not be included since it assumes knowledge of the external world; the references of its terms are divided. So, in general, our distinctions are not co-extensive.

As I stated earlier, the point of the classification of level 1 is that for sentences in this level *no knowledge of the world is assumed*. The point was *not* that there was general agreement on them. Nor was the point that no sentence of level 1 could be parsed—they all *can* be (as I have repeatedly stated). However, when this occurs, assumptions about the world are made, and the sentence so treated no longer counts as a level-1 sentence. I will call sentences of levels 1 and 2 *proto-observation sentences*. It is clear that Quine's notion of a *primitive observation sentence* is, in general, more inclusive in its extension. It is also worth repeating that widespread agreement on the primitive observation sentences does not imply that they lack any built-in assumptions about the world. Because the primitive and the proto-observation sentences differ in these ways, truly persistent questioning of a scientist would force him to rely on the latter, not the former.

If the above is correct, Quine's argument against incommensurability is called into question. He says that observation sentences are "shared reference points for the two theories," and that "comparing the responses of the two theories to these shared checkpoints, then, should afford traces of commensurability insofar as the two theories are under empirical control at all" (1993, p. 111). He notes that this requires that the observation sentence in question be learned holophrastically. But how such sentences are learned or used is not as critical as what they presuppose in the relevant epistemic context. Whether such sentences are learned or used holophrastically is a red herring. The real point is that for sentences to serve as epistemically neutral checkpoints they must do their epistemic work *as one-word observation sentences*, with no assumptions about the external world. Only proto-observation sentences will do, if any will.

The sentences *themselves* of levels 1 and 3 may be treated holophrastically or not, but a fundamental difference between the levels is that level-3 sentences epistemically presuppose a great deal of theoretical knowledge *from the very beginning*, regardless of whether they are holophrastically treated or not. Therefore, level-3 or primitive observation sentences (insofar as the latter go beyond proto-observation sentences) are disqualified as impartial arbitrators between theories. The foundational epistemic burden, if it is to be borne at all, must go to the one-word observation sentences, *as* one-word observation sentences. Proto-observation sentences may serve to force revision or rejection of a theory inconsistent with them—they may serve as "negative check points" (Quine 1993, p. 111). What they cannot do is discriminate between empirically equivalent theories, for being consistent with the same range of proto-observation sentences is a necessary condition for the theories' being empirically equivalent.[13] Observation sentences that can discriminate are not epistemically basic; they are parsed, and they presuppose some ontology. Thus, the intermediate epistemological ground between foundationalism and anti-foundationalism, which Quine sought to secure with his Janus-faced observation or protocol sentences, has slipped away.[14]

Holophrastic Observation Sentences and Realism

Let us now examine these results in relation to Quine's realism. His long-standing position is that science tells us what there is and what what there is does. (See my discussion of (3) below.) We have just seen how, according to Quine, holophrastic observation sentences play an important evidential role in science; furthermore, Quine states that the holophrastic role of observation sentences "bears significantly on the epistemology of ontology" (1993, p. 112). Having said that, he continues, as he has so often done in the past, in a rather odd fashion:

(*)   Their association with neural intakes, being holophrastic, is *unaffected by any reassigning of objects to the terms involved*. But also the logical relations of implication that connect scientific theory with observation categoricals [i.e., pairs of observation sentences combined into generalizations such as 'When it snows, it's cold'] are unaffected by one-to-one reinterpretation of terms; all that matters to logical structure is identity and difference. We conclude that *the sensory evidence for science is indifferent to what things science says there are*, so long as identity and diversity among them is preserved. . . . *So far as evidence goes, objects figure only as neutral nodes in the logical structure of our total theory of the world.* (1993, p.112, emphasis added)

Certainly holophrastic observation sentences play an important evidential role in science, and science tells us *how* the world is. Given (*), however, it seems impossible for science to tell us *what* there is, i.e., for it to have any bearing on ontology. If the objects assigned to the terms and predicates of a theory are mapped one-to-one to different objects to preserve the logical structure of identity and difference, then we have two interpreted theories, though only one formal theory. Clearly, the formal theory could not be a candidate for telling us what is in the world. By hypothesis, the interpreted theories have different ontologies, though the evidential support for them is the same. Which is the correct ontology? If, as Quine says, "so far as evidence goes, objects figure only as neutral nodes in the logical structure of our total theory of the world" (1993, p. 112), the evidence cannot adjudicate here. This, however, is what they must do if their holophrastic role is to bear significantly on the epistemology of ontology, as Quine claims (ibid.). Though in other kinds of cases the holophrastic observation sentences may serve as "negative checkpoints," as indicated above, this has no direct bearing on the positive question as to what there is.

If one is to eschew transcendental metaphysics, as Quine counsels, there is a tension between the claims of scientific realism, endorsed by Quine, and the claim that the bodies assigned to terms of a theory can be swapped without affecting the observation sentences which support the theory. This is a deep tension, one that I think is traceable back through many of Quine's writings. Here I will cite only a recent occurrence of this conflict.

Drawing on his earlier writings, Quine challenges the objectivity of our idea of an object:

(1)   The very notion of an object at all, concrete or abstract, is a human contribution, a feature of our inherited apparatus for organizing the amorphous welter of neural input. (1992a, p. 6)

In the same article, Quine makes the point he made in (*), one which he has made repeatedly over the years by appealing to proxy functions, viz.,

(2)   . . . if we transform the range of objects of our science in any one-to-one fashion, by reinterpreting our terms and predicates as applying to new objects instead of the old ones, the entire evidential support of our science will remain undisturbed. . . . Once we have an ontology, we change it with impunity. (8)

Quine recognizes that this view "may seem abruptly at odds with realism, let alone naturalism" (9), but he explicitly rejects this conclusion and makes the following assertion:

(3)   The world is as natural science says it is, insofar as natural science is right. . . . (9)

I have no quarrel with (1) and (2). Jointly, they provide support for abandoning transcendental metaphysics or, simply, ontology. My point is that all this also compels the rejection of any robust reading of (3).

I just noted that Quine recognizes no conflict between his acceptance of (2) and (3), despite the appearance to the contrary. How does he purport to resolve the conflict? He says this:

Naturalism itself is what saves the situation. Naturalism looks only to natural science, however fallible, for an account of what there is and what there is does. (9)

Science itself, Quine tells us, must use man-made concepts and man-made language, "but we can ask no better. The very notion of object, or of one and many, is indeed as parochially human as the parts of speech; to ask what reality is *really* like, however, apart from human categories, is self-stultifying. . . . [This is essentially the point of (1); however, he continues:] But early positivists were wrong if and when they concluded that the world is not really composed of atoms or whatever. The world is as natural science says it is, insofar as it is right. . . . (9)

If the only reservations to holding the claim that natural science tells us what there is were (a) that science is fallible, (b) that our concepts and language are man-made, and (c) that the very idea of an object is also man-made, I would have little trouble embracing (3), so long as (3) was understood in light of (a)–(c). But it is (2), the point of proxy functions, together with the inadequacy of observation sentences to the epistemic tasks that Quine wishes to put them which ultimately undermines (3), as argued above.[15]

There is an anemic reading of (3) that dissipates all conflict between it and (1) and (2). On this reading, "the world is as natural science says it is" amounts to no more than the claim that a certain set of *words* is used in science, rather than some other possible set. This is a reading consistent with Quine's attempt to rescue reference from nonsense in "Ontological Relativity" (pp. 26–68). In chapter 8, I argued at length that these attempts by Quine to rescue reference from nonsense fail. I will not rehearse the details of those arguments here, except to show that Quine's considerations already challenged fare no better in preserving his brand of realism.

Having argued that inscrutability of reference applies to oneself, Quine seeks to avoid the apparent nonsense this makes of reference by "picturing us at home in our language, with all its predicates and auxiliary devices. . . . In these terms we can say in so many words that this is a formula and that a number, this is a rabbit and that a rabbit part. *In just those words*. This network of terms and predicates and auxiliary devices is, in relativity jargon, our frame of reference, or coordinate system. . . . Reference *is* nonsense except relative to a coordinate system. In this principle lies the resolution of our quandary." (ibid.) He goes on to tell us that it is meaningless to ask what our terms *really* refer to: "It is meaningless to ask this absolutely; we can meaningfully ask it only relative to some background language." (1969, p. 48) Relativizing to a background language, Quine also notes, gets us into regress of background languages, and this is cut off in practice by "acquiescing in our mother tongue and *taking its words at face value*" (1969, p. 49, emphasis added). Thus, "taking words at face value" not only is critical to rescuing reference from nonsense and terminating the regress of background languages; it also plays a central role in explaining the sense in which the world is as natural science says it is.[16]

Though reading (3) along these lines eliminates the inconsistency with (1) and (2), it is a most anemic reading. A customary understanding of scientific realism is that the presumed referents of the terms of a successful scientific theory *actually* exist. Granted, 'realism', even 'scientific realism', has a number of distinct construals, but when the term is used in the same context as 'ontology', then the suggestion, if not the implication, is that the realism at issue is that the terms of our best scientific theories refer to real objects in the world. In contrast, the anemic reading suggested presents an ontology in name alone. It is reminiscent of Carnap's rejection of ontological questions in the external sense.

Carnap argued early on that when there is no empirical difference between linguistic frameworks (theories), questions as to what there is really, apart from such theories, what he dubbed "external questions," are meaningless (1956, pp. 205–221).[17] Thus Carnap downgraded ontology all the way. He contrasted external questions with internal questions, which were meaningful existence questions that could be answered within the linguistic framework (theory). However, Carnap did not hold that one would then be a realist with respect to the accepted theory except, perhaps, in the most diluted form that his analysis of internal existence claims allowed. The external questions are within the realm of transcendental metaphysics, which both Quine and Carnap reject. The anemic reading of (3) is in accord with restricting questions of existence to internal ones. If this is all scientific realism comes to, however, it is misleading to call it *realism*. Better to abandon all talk of ontology, downgrade it all the way, as Carnap did.

There is, however, an important difference between Carnap and Quine on this score. To my knowledge, Carnap never made much, if anything, of what Quine calls "proxy functions." Nor did he take into account the points, as expressed in (2) above, which may be made by appeal to such functions. It was the fact that Carnap did not utilize proxy functions and did not make realist claims that enabled him to speak of internal existence claims without the difficulties that Quine gets into. Carnap rejected external existence questions outright and deliberately trivialized the internal ones. Quine rejects external existence questions too,[18] for he eschews transcendental metaphysics. But it is Quine's use of proxy functions that significantly contributes to the tension between (2) and (3). This is most evident when (3) is asserted in the context of ontological issues, as Quine typically does.

My point is that either (3) must be given an ontologically anemic reading to be consistent with (1) and (2), or (3) must be rejected. But in either case, ontology is downgraded all the way. If Quine restricts himself to the anemic reading, then he does downgrade ontology all the way and, in that case, it would be better to drop all misleading talk of *scientific realism*. Quine, however, appears as reluctant to abandon talk of scientific realism as he is to go all the way.

An Apparent Way Out Fails

Support for a more robust realism may be sought along different lines, but within Quine's naturalism. I pursue this path only to show its inadequacy. Consider some things Quine maintains in "Epistemology Naturalized" and in "Natural Kinds."[19] One might reason that we may rely on the man-made categories of natural science to tell us what there is because these categories naturally evolve from our inquiring interactions with nature; there is no higher court of appeal. Furthermore, the "similarity determined by scientific hypothesis and posits and constructs" is based on and a development from a more "immediate, subjective, animal sense of similarity" (Quine 1969, p. 134). The latter is a result of an innate standard of similarity, an "innate qualitative spacing of stimulations." So, there would seem to be a more or less direct line from what stimulates us and the categories of science.

The innate-similarity standard might, in some sense, provide a basis for saying what there is (shades of classical empiricism, no doubt), but only in a weak sense, and one which is ultimately inadequate to the task. The innate qualitative spacing of stimulations could at best account for one-word observation sentences. When it comes to dividing the reference of terms, and thus to imposing categories of objects, such innate quality spaces are not fine-grained enough to do the job. So, innate quality spaces can offer no grounds for some particular kind of objectual reference. Thus, it offers no grounds for holding that science tells us what there is.

This attempt to rescue Quine's realism meets more obstacles. Similarity classes determined by science are even more remote from the stimulations at our surface than are those resulting from our "animal sense of similarity." Any hopes one might have had along this line are further dashed when it is realized that as science develops the similarity standard itself becomes superfluous, for the relevant phenomena are defined in virtue of their underlying structures, as Quine himself points out. Now add to this the crucial fact, expressed in (2), that the categories of our science pertaining to that underlying structure can be mapped one-to-one to different categories, while still being true to the observation sentences. Once again, it appears that (3) must be jettisoned along with the rest of the metaphysical flotsam.

The Dilemma for Holophrastic Observation Sentences

The problems that I argued plagued Quine's conception of observation sentences reflect problems that epistemologists of the first half of the twentieth century faced. Quine, of course, is acutely aware of those problems. He notes that one important aspect of Carnap's Aufbau project was of a piece with that of "the old phenomenalist epistemology [which] inspired a project of rational reconstruction, the derivation of natural knowledge from sense data" (1993, p. 111). A problem, perhaps the central problem, for any such reconstruction was that if the sense data were taken narrowly enough so that they could serve as a safe neutral epistemic foundation, one could not get back to physical objects, let alone our natural knowledge of them. Alternatively, if the basis was taken more broadly to overcome such meager and debilitating beginnings, then the basis itself was called into question; it no longer was epistemically neutral. Among the others involved with versions of these problems were Bertrand Russell, C. I. Lewis, and A. J. Ayer.

Quine's attempt to find an intermediate ground between classical epistemic foundationalism and recent anti-foundationalism confronts a similar dilemma. His observation sentences must be pared all the way back to level 1 to be epistemically neutral. Thus, they are not referential, and they are silent on what there is. They themselves are not sufficient to secure objects in the world, and theories with different ontologies are consistent with them. Piecemeal, they are no longer neutral adjudicators between radically different but empirically equivalent theories with different ontologies. So in neither orientation can they resolve incommensurability or ontological issues.

Closely related to the classical project of constructing physical objects out of sense data was the equally Herculean task of establishing the meaningfulness of theoretical statements or terms on the basis of observation statements or terms. Again, Carnap led the way and many followed. These massive efforts also failed.[20] This series of failures—essentially the downfall of Logical Positivism—resulted in the abandonment of the observational/theoretical distinction, the rejection of the idea that anything was "given" in sense perception that could serve as a foundation for knowledge or meaning, and the realization that the very idea of a pure observation was illusory. What emerged was the belief that there is a continuum from the more observational to the more theoretical, theory intruding in varying degrees throughout. Moreover, it was realized that the orientation of the line of the continuum itself varies depending on which theories are accepted. These outcomes were among the things that led to the various anti-foundationalist positions.

It is anti-foundationalist programs based on such results that Quine hopes to derail in resurrecting the observation sentence. He is, of course, keenly aware of the problems the epistemologists of the first half of the twentieth century faced. He mentions, in particular, the fact that observation sentences are theory laden as a serious source of misgiving as to their being up to the foundational tasks the early epistemologists of this century wished to put them. It is precisely this problem that he hopes to circumvent by treating observation sentences holophrastically, for he locates the problem in taking observation sentences piecemeal.

Holophrastic Conditioning versus Holophrastic Treatment

In his 1996 paper, Quine contrasts his earlier views on observation sentences (in *Word and Object*) with his more recent views, such as those put forth in his 1993 paper. In the earlier work, he recognized degrees of observationality as a function of how much theory or collateral information intruded. This is in accord with the development of the Positivists' view of the matter, recently sketched herein. But Quine maintains the following:

. . . in later writings I held observationality as absolute, based on immediacy of assent, and then I accommodated the intrusion of theory by contrasting the *holophrastic* conditioning of the observation sentence to neural intake with the *analytic* relations of the component words to the rest of language. The sentence figures holophrastically both in the infant's first acquisition of it and in the scientist's immediate assent to it when testing a theory. (1996, p. 162)

I have argued that the immediacy of assent is not sufficient to secure "observationality as absolute." There are crucial epistemic differences between an infant's first acquisition of a sentence and a scientist's immediate assent to a sentence. Here we have immediate assent marking the holophrastic use for the scientist. But if I have argued correctly, this holophrastic use, the immediate assent to a level-3 sentence by a scientist, does not warrant giving it the same epistemic status held by level-1 sentences, the one-word observation sentences. Though the immediate assent may mark that the sentence figures holophrastically, it does not circumvent in itself the analytic relations between the words of the sentence. The immediate assent to a sentence is not sufficient to deny the intrusion of theory, but it is just this lack of intrusion that is the hallmark of level-1 sentences.

There is also an important difference between the acquisition of a sentence by holophrastic *conditioning* and the holophrastic *treatment* of a sentence (already acquired) marked by immediate assent. Typically, level-3 sentences are not holophrastically *conditioned*, though we will see below that they may be. In contrast, level-1 sentences can only be acquired by holophrastic conditioning. A child's first acquisition of certain sentences (e.g., 'Mama') fits here whereas a level-3 sentence such as "There is copper in it" is typically learned through the analytic relations of its word parts, i.e., through the intrusion of theory. Even so, it may be immediately assented to by a scientist given the appropriate stimulation and so, in Quine's sense, figure holophrastically. This, however, does not make it holophrastically conditioned, nor does it eliminate the intrusion of theory. On the other hand, one who has learned the appropriate theory can holophrastically condition *someone else*, someone ignorant of all the relevant theory, to immediately assent to or assert the sentence under appropriate stimulation. For an ignorant individual thus trained (and it matters not how many are thus trained), "There is copper in it" is a one-word observation sentence, but it is not a one-word observation sentence for the trainer or for the community in the know, even when they immediately assent under appropriate stimulation. The point is that the trainer, in order to carry out such holophrastic conditioning, must already have mastered the relevant theory.[21]

So, I repeat, while one can immediately assent to or have holophrastic uses of level-3 sentences, this cannot serve as a basis for treating "observationality as absolute," contrary to Quine's claim (1996, p. 162) These characteristics of sentences do not in themselves have any bearing on their roles as adjudicators for competing theories or for establishing scientific realism. Immediacy of assent or holophrastic treatment is not to the epistemic point. Only one-word observation sentences (of level 1) could play these epistemic roles—the sentences that are holophrastically conditioned without the benefit of someone's knowledge of the relevant theory. (Of course, although these are candidates, they are not adequate to these tasks.)

Recapitulation of Some of the Main Points

Observation sentences taken piecemeal are certainly theory laden, and I have argued against Quine's claim that treating them holophrastically can transform them into objective arbiters between competing theories and ontologies. Just why this result obtains turns on the fact, argued above, that level-3 observation sentences are theory laden even when they are immediately assented to or taken holophrastically: Holophrastic or not, level-3 sentences assume knowledge of the external world. It is only the level-1 observation sentences, the one-word observation sentences, that are not theory laden. Level-1 sentences—as a condition of membership—can only be treated holophrastically. Once parsed, they no longer count as level-1 sentences, and the initial objection of assuming knowledge of the world applies. In contrast, level-3 sentences may or may not be treated holophrastically, but their holophrastic treatment, unlike that of the one-word observation sentences, is no sign of their epistemic neutrality. As was argued earlier, the ability of those in the know of the relevant theory to immediately assert or assent to the sentence under appropriate stimulatory conditions is necessarily based on their possession of the relevant theory. Therefore, holophrastic observation sentences of level 3 are theory laden in spite of any immediate assent to them and cannot objectively resolve epistemic foundational issues or ontological questions, except negatively, as indicated earlier.

Two Dimensions of Observation Sentences

I now turn to the two distinct dimensions pertinent to Quine's treatment of observation sentences mentioned at the onset; I will show how their conflation contributes to Quine's belief that observation sentences can do more than I have argued they can. For convenience, I take the continuum of observationality, degrees of observationality, to be one with that of the most observational to the most theoretical.[22] The elements of this continuum, however, do not match the holophrastic/non-holophrastic distinction. As we have seen, whether a sentence is holophrastic or not has to do with its circumstances of use, how much one knows, and how one was trained, and not with its epistemic status. Thus, it is not only sentences of highest observationality that can be treated holophrastically; we may so treat sentences right up the scale, well into the heavily theoretical area, if not all the way to the end. Where do the one-word observation sentences fit on this continuum? They are off the scale to the left of the most observational. The epistemic gap between the one-word observation and the most observational sentences on the scale is due to the fact that the latter may still be taken piecemeal and remain highly observational. One-word observation sentences, *as* one-word observation sentences, are never taken piecemeal. Doing so changes their status.[23]

Quine (1996, p. 162) tells us that he retains "the absolute notion of an observation sentence as simply an occasion sentence that commands the subject's immediate assent, however fallible and revisable. Fallibility is then accommodated in a separate dimension, *theoreticity*, which invests observation sentences in varying degrees." He comes to this conclusion after reflecting "further on the bipolarity of the holophrastic and analytic perspectives, as against the gradualism [degrees] of observationality in *Word and Object*" (ibid.).[24] Whether one speaks of degrees of observationality or of immediate assent, the following question remains: Can the observation sentences do the epistemic and ontological work they are assigned?

The subject's immediate assent does not pick out a distinct dimension for "the absolute notion of observation sentence," as Quine claims (1996, p. 162). Fallibility is not the fault that I press here, rather it is the work that the proxy functions do. Immediate assent is too broad a net for the absolute notion of an observation sentence, as it encompasses both level-1 and level-3 sentences; theory intrudes significantly in level 3 but not in level 1. If I am right, it is only the one-word observation sentences that are absolute in Quine's sense, and they are not adequate for the epistemic and ontological tasks that have been under discussion.

What is important for present purposes is that the high degree of observationality of sentences such as "There is a cup on the desk" does not in any way depend on their being treated holophrastically: They remain highly observational sentences even when treated piecemeal. The latter does not detract from their high degree of observationality. At the other end of the scale, the fact that many, perhaps all, sentences of level 3 can be treated holophrastically does not transform them into epistemically neutral sentences. Conflating the idea of observation with the idea of a sentence's being treated holophrastically obscures this last point. Only one-word observation sentences escape theory dependence, and thus only they are epistemically neutral. These sentences, however, are not sufficiently robust to have any positive epistemic bearing on ontology. Nor, as argued earlier, are they able to positively resolve conflicts between competing global theories.

By focusing on the possibility of treating sentences holophrastically and invoking the idea of quick decidability or immediate assent, levels 1 and 3 are conflated. For some purposes such common grouping of these levels may be desirable. I have tried to show that for positively resolving issues around the competition of theories and the epistemology of ontology such common grouping is intolerable. Ontology must be downgraded all the way.

Epilogue

So there it is. Consciousness and subjectivity are broader than the phenomenal. They permeate both the intentional and the phenomenal, and they are crucial to linguistic meaning. I hope by now you are convinced that the concept of minimal content provides a unified foundation for both a theory of mind and a theory of language, whereas the orthodox, strictly third-person methodologies applied to these areas have inherent flaws. My theory corrects those flaws by recognizing the primacy of the subjective in a way that does not immerse us in a "touchy-feely" morass of subjectivity. Why has this plain, immediately accessible datum of minimal content been overlooked? The answer is simple. Minimal content is invisible to the orthodox methodology.

What accounts for this debilitating methodological restriction and the consequent failure to recognize the primacy of the subjective? I speculate that there have been two main sources, both rooted in a careless extension of the orthodox methodology from domains in which it properly applies (those in which there is no privileged first-person perspective, such as the study of cells) to domains in which we do have a first-person perspective: consciousness. First, the Positivists articulated a detailed view of scientific method that they forcefully and persuasively advanced. For them the only way to objectivity was through a strictly third-person methodology. Their view of scientific method had tremendous influence in philosophy and beyond. Arguably, it had a tremendous impact on psychology as psychologists endeavored to be scientific by positivists' lights. The result was Behaviorism. Part of the significance of this was that virtually any talk of consciousness became suspect, as it was not amenable to study by the favored methodology. As the inadequacies of Positivism and Behaviorism became evident, they were eventually abandoned; nevertheless, the firm grip of the idea that a strictly third-person methodology is necessary for any objective study remained. It continues today, usually under the guise of "naturalism." Second, Wittgenstein's private language argument reinforced this aversion to the subjective and the use of first-person methodologies. I have argued that the limited privacy of language found in my theory is not pernicious. Indeed, it is essential.

The primacy of the subjective in the study of mind and language is unavoidable. Importantly, it can be accommodated without compromising the objectivity of our results or burdening us with dubious ontological commitments.

Notes

Chapter 1

1. In chapter 3, I will explain why these theories separated these two aspects.

2. Without suggesting that they all hold exactly the same view, I will note that those advancing the idea of phenomenal intentionality include David Chalmers (1996), Terence Horgan and John Tienson (2002), David Pitt (2004), Charles Siewert (1998), and Galen Strawson (1994).

3. I will argue in chapter 3 that this strategy rests on a mistake.

4. This feature depends only on the fact that we sometimes know without inference part of what our thoughts are about in some sense. It is not that we know all of it in this way. It is not that we always non-inferentially know part of it. It is not even that we need explicitly entertain what that content is. To make my case, it is enough if the agent has been, or could become non-inferentially aware of part of the content of his thought in some sense; I do not need that he is always so aware. These restrictions will become clearer below. Nor is the claim that we have special access to our own minimal contents to be confused with maintaining a private language or anything like that. The special access is not due to the "privacy" of minimal contents; others are not precluded from having knowledge of another's minimal contents. It is just that their knowledge of mine must be inferential, whereas my access to my minimal contents can be non-inferential. Compare the discussion of one's forming an image or drawing a diagram and other cases discussed below. (Also compare Davidson 1984, 1987.) How and why we can have objective knowledge of another's minimal contents is discussed in chapter 3 and the last section of chapter 5. The extent to which my theory commits me to the privacy of language (hardly at all, and without pernicious consequences) is discussed in chapter 8.

5. David Armstrong (1963) argues against the claim that *all* introspective reports are incorrigible. Even if his argument for this is sound, it does not refute my claim that *some* introspective knowledge is incorrigible. Moreover; Armstrong's arguments assume that incorrigibility claims must be confined to a "perceptual instant," but

none of my arguments for infallible knowledge of minimal content are contingent upon this assumption. Similarly, R. Nisbett, T. Wilson, and A. Gopnik (see McGeer 1996, p. 496) argue that psychology rejects the presumption that first-person reports should be accepted, barring good reason to override; they appeal to various evidence in support of this. Here too the kinds of error they find are irrelevant to my concept of minimal content, defined below, and our infallible knowledge of it.

6.   Shoemaker (1990) attempts to provide for a limited privileged access that is neither infallible nor transparent but which is available to the externalist. Donald Davidson (1987, 1984) argues for the importance of first-person authority and points out that some ignore or dismiss it, while others fail to see the seriousness of the problem it poses for externalist views of mental content. He notes (1988) that, while Burge (1988) acknowledges first-person authority, he does not adequately show how such authority can be reconciled with his view. (See my discussion of Burge in chapter 7, where I show this failure undermines his famous thought experiment.) Though the problem is serious, Davidson argues that first-person authority can be reconciled with an externalist view of content. In chapter 2, I argue that Heil's (1988) attempt to advance a Burgean view of first-person authority or privileged access is unsuccessful in reconciling first-person authority with externalism. I also argue there that any externalist account must fail, including those like Davidson's, which appeal to the natural history of the agent. The asymmetry of access that I argue for is like that upon which Davidson's bases first-person authority in that it turns on the agent's non-inferential knowledge of the content of one's thought, but the content that I argue for which is governed by first-person authority is much narrower than Davidson's. For him, there is special access to our occurrent beliefs, desires, and other propositional attitudes as these are ordinarily understood (1987, p. 447), what is often referred to as wide content. The content that I argue we each have privileged access to is a "narrow content." We shall also see that it is not to be identified with what is normally referred to as narrow content.

7.   Although the example is Heil's (1988, p. 248), I exploit it in ways he would not endorse.

8.   There is a reading of the word 'subject' in the locution 'subject of the intentional state' that is legitimate but is not my intended usage, viz., as the individual who has the intentional state. My usage concerns a restricted part of the intentional content of the intentional state. For example, if I believe that Mary is beautiful, Mary is the "subject" of my intentional state, not me, not the thinker. Scare quotes are used here because it is this use of 'subject' that I argue has two readings: as minimal content and objective content.

9.   Holding this does not entail that whenever I am in a state that can be said to have minimal content that I must also be explicitly aware of that minimal content on that occasion. (See my warning in an earlier note.) The awareness spoken of here is simply the non-inferential knowledge of what is represented by the minimal con-

tent, not the noticing of some special feature of the state or its minimal content. And that's a good thing, for it would seriously count against my view. As to why this is so, see, e.g., Kripke 1982, especially the latter part of part 2.

10.   Though Searle's most extended account is to be found in his 1983 book *Intentionality*, a particularly clear discussion of the differences between intrinsic intentionality and derivative or metaphorical intentionality appears in Searle 1984. It is worth noting that acceptance of Searle's framework for an analysis of intentionality, as he presents it in the early chapters of *Intentionality*, does not commit one to the acceptance of the causal account of intentionality he gives in the final chapter. Too often arguments against the latter are mistakenly thought to argue against the former.

11.   This move, a shift of types, has parallels with Frege's identification of the referent of an expression in oblique contexts with its customary sense. On my view this shift to a new type of referent is not required. More on the relations between Frege's view and mine later.

12.   A recent view that is motivated by this line and differs with Searle on this point is advanced in Crane 2001. In a paper under review, I argue that Crane fails in this and that Searle's view is superior.

13.   This way of putting it is borrowed from Searle (1983, p. 6). The decomposition of this schema discussed immediately below goes beyond Searle.

14.   One might think that the same rational that leads to distinguishing m and o would force recognition of a similar distinction for Φ. This is not so. The point in making the distinction between minimal content and the objective content is that there are compelling grounds for analyzing the 'subject of the agent's thought' in two different ways. For purposes of analysis, there are no similar grounds for holding that Φ should be similarly analyzed. When the agent is "off" regarding the attribution of Φ, it typically is a result of a deficiency in her *understanding* of Φ. The difference between understanding and awareness will be introduced in the next section and will be discussed further elsewhere in the book.

15.   It is interesting, if not surprising, to garner some support for something like my distinction between minimal content and content objective content from a paper by Willard Van Orman Quine (who undoubtedly would have protested the use of his distinction in support of mine). Quine's 1994 paper also brings out an additional advantage of treating intentional states as I do, viz., a basis is provided for accommodating the treatment of sentences expressing intentional states, decomposed as (i) and (ii) , within the syntax of predicate logic. Quine is not alone when he asserts that "no theory is fully clear to me unless I can see how this syntax [that of predicate logic] would accommodate it" (ibid., p. 144). My proposal may be viewed as a suggestion that also enhances the clarity of our understanding of intentional states in this regard, one that is different from Quine's quotation-based solution that he offers

in the mentioned paper. Quine attaches great importance to the subject's point of view in the treatment of propositional attitudes in the paper cited. For example, he notes that the failure of substitutivity in belief contexts stems from the fact that "the subordinate clause of the construction is uttered *from the subject's point of view* . . . and . . . the subject . . . didn't know the things were identical" (ibid., p. 145, emphasis added). My formulation differs from Quine's, but it is the same kind of distinction at play. On my theory, the subordinate clause expresses the thinker's minimal content and requires an instantiation of $\Psi(\Phi(m))$ rather than of $\Psi(\Phi(o))$, and the thinker may not know that m and o signal the same thing. Additionally, Quine notes that the "quantification $\exists x$ (Ralph believes that x is a spy) raises an ontological problem of the value of 'x'" (146). I agree, as I do with his diagnosis that "the difficulty, again, is just discrepancy between the real world, to which the outlying '$\exists x$' relates, and the empathized world—Ralph's—in which the recurrence of 'x' is trapped" (146). I suggest a different resolution of this problem raised by Quine: Employ expressions for the objective content when the real world is at issue, and employ expressions for Ralph's minimal content when it is a question pertaining to the "empathized world," for in the empathized world, the subject of the thought as conceived by the agent is at issue, not the subject that an objective observer would ascribe.

16.   Talk of "actual objects in the world" is to be understood here, and throughout, as simply those objects upon which there is inter-subjective agreement within a given community. No deep ontological claim is being made. The reasons for this and some of the consequences will be apparent in chapters 8 and 9.

17.   Someone may object at this point and insist it is not clear that the content is numbers in one case and sets in the other, since it is not even clear what numbers and sets are apart from the role they play in a theory. (See Benacerraf 1965 or Resnik 1981.) If the question were "What does the objective content indicate?" I would be inclined to agree, but that is not the question. There is a clear sense in which what A and B *conceive* their respective objects to be is distinct. No matter how that difference eventually gets cashed out, and no matter what the ultimate nature of numbers and sets—as minimal contents they are distinct. Taking the position that numbers and sets are nothing apart from the relations that they enter into (and, thus, insofar as they enter into the same relations, they are the same contents) is to give a theoretical account of the *ontological* status of numbers and sets, one that might even be right. Similarly, if one holds that numbers are ultimately certain kinds of sets, that there are no numbers. Thus, such considerations bear on our *understanding* of numbers and sets; they do nothing to explain the appearance of awareness of minimal contents, and different ones at that.

18.   I suggest that minimal content can be useful in an analysis of *fictional objects*. Normally, an agent attempts to have her minimal contents signal the same subjects as do the objective contents of her thoughts; whenever she learns they do not match, she aligns her minimal content so that it does. Things are otherwise with fic-

tional objects. A fictional object is simply the subject of a thought as conceived by the thinker, her minimal content represents an object that she *knows* does not exist, she knows the objective content of her thought is empty, so *efforts toward realignment are deliberately excluded.*

19.   To challenge this one would have to give an extremely strong holistic account of meaning. One that would have as a consequence that the content of 'number' is different for our theorists A and C because of their differing ability to manipulate the symbols. If we were to accept this, we might wonder whether two individuals ever could have the same content, inasmuch as it is doubtful that two individuals would ever actually have identical symbol-manipulating abilities. (The unrealistic assumption that A and B have identical symbol-manipulating abilities was made strictly for the sake of argument.) The results here further support the importance of distinguishing explicating and individuating. (Compare below.) See my discussion of Burge in chapter 7, where I discuss the conditions for saying two individuals have the same concept even when there is not an exact match between their conceptions.

20.   The 'pre' in 'pre-axiomatic' should not be understood temporally. Perhaps a more accurate prefix would be 'extra.' It may well be questionable whether the objects are grasped apart from *any* theory or background language whatsoever (see chapters 8 and 9), though I do not think that Rota et al. are making such a strong, unrestricted claim.

21.   They state: "Since there is no one group, but groups come in incredible variety, such a pre-axiomatic grasp of the notion of group cannot be attributed to familiarity with a single group. One could argue that such an understanding is derived from familiarity with several groups and their 'common' properties, but this would amount to begging the question, since familiarity with more than one group presupposes an unstated understanding of the concept of group that permits one to recognize several instances as being instances of the same general mathematical structure." (Rota et al. 1989, pp. 381–382)

22.   In chapter 7, I will show how this point can be used to undermine Burge's famous thought experiment, which he offered on behalf of anti-individualism. How it bears on meaning will be discussed in chapter 8

23.   The uniqueness of minimal content in this regard will also provide for the resolutions of some problems regarding representation (chapter 5) and some others I will raise for Quine regarding his theses of Indeterminacy of Translation and the inscrutability of reference (chapter 8).

24.   This regress problem is not always noticed by those who employ a strictly third-person methodology. David Armstrong is an exception. I discuss the problem in the context of giving an analysis of representation and Armstrong's (unsuccessful) attempt to block the regress with his appeal to a claim that simple concepts are

intrinsic representations in chapter 5 and show how the fundamental intentional state solves this problem.

25.   I am grateful to John Bickle, whose persistent (stubborn) resistance several years ago to my claim that consciousness is required for representation contributed to my development of the idea of a fundamental intentional state.

26.   This kind of indeterminacy problem is discussed in detail in chapter 8 in conjunction with Quine's thesis of the Indeterminacy of Translation. The latter thesis undergoes a radical modification in light of the results herein.

27.   To the extent that appropriate symbol manipulation is a component of understanding, to that extent it would be correct to speak of such programs as instantiating understanding of number theory, and some instantiating a better understanding than others. Whether the sense in which such programs "understand" is anything more than metaphorical is another question, because whether appropriate symbol manipulation is merely a measure of understanding, is actually partly constitutive of or sufficient for it has yet to be determined. On the distinction between metaphorical and intrinsic intentionality, see Searle 1984. Here we are also touching on problems raised by Searle in his famous Chinese Room, discussed below.

28.   Compare Dretske's statement that "unless the symbols being manipulated mean something *to the system manipulating them*, their meaning, whatever it is, is irrelevant to evaluating what the system is doing when it manipulates them" (1985, pp. 27–28). I agree with Dretske that the important and relevant case is that in which the symbols mean something for the system processing them, though I disagree with him on what this amounts to or whether his approach can adequately deal with it. In addition, I prefer to put the point in terms of the system's privileged access to its minimal content. For Dretske's more recent development, see his 1997 book *Naturalizing the Mind*. The exact nature of my disagreement with him is made explicit in chapter 5, where I argue that his account of representation is seriously defective.

29.   The capacity to have access to one's minimal content is closely related to an item having any content *for* the system, human or otherwise, that deploys the item. The idea of a symbol having content for a thinker is developed further in chapters 5, 7, and 8.

30.   In contrast to the minimal content, the objective content is objective and, in this respect, it is more like a Fregean sense, or rather a truncated Fregean sense, for unlike the latter, it only indicates objects, not states of affairs. Of all the concepts that I have employed, however, it is probably that of representative content, understood with an objective content rather than with minimal content, which is closest to a Fregean sense.

31.   One might argue that my distinction between minimal content and objective content aligns somewhat with Descartes' distinction between objective (sometimes

translated as 'presentational') reality and formal reality, respectively. See *Meditation 3*. Confusingly, what is translated as 'objective reality' denotes, in Descartes, something more like what we would now think of as subjective.

32.   The latter alternative holds, since minimal content is just a component of the representative content, R, on one of its decompositions, $\Phi(m)$.

33.   This is developed in Searle 1980. The case somewhat simplified is essentially as follows: An English-speaking person is locked in a room and provided with a large ordered store of sequences of Chinese characters together with a set of elaborate syntactic transformation rules. The latter are formulated in English, but operate on strings of Chinese characters. The individual in the room does not understand Chinese. However, given new strings of Chinese characters from someone outside the room, he is able to apply the transformation rules to the received strings so as to produce new strings that he then passes out of the room. A Chinese-speaking person on the outside is passing meaningful Chinese sentences to the man in the room, and the latter, unknown to himself, is returning meaningful and appropriate Chinese responses.

34.   Compare my discussion of Galileo in chapter 4. Galileo also attempts to explain certain common-sense appearances that seem to conflict with his view.

35.   It is reported that Johnson uttered "Thus, I refute Berkeley" while kicking a stone.

Chapter 2

1.   Armstrong (1968, 1980), Lycan (1987, 1992), and Rosenthal (1986, 1990, 1991) advocate higher-order theories of consciousness. Armstrong and Lycan build their theory on a perceptual model, a higher-order theory of perception (HOP). Rosenthal's theory of consciousness appeals to higher-order thoughts (HOT). My argument stands against either version.

2.   All page references here are to Heil 1988. Heil strongly relates self-awareness to second-order intentionality, though he only takes the latter to be one way of being self-aware. Of the latter he says: "I shall use the expression 'self-awareness' in what is perhaps a non-standard way. I am concerned here only with the capacity to 'introspect' on mental states and goings-on, not anything more elaborate. I shall not address, for instance, the ability sometimes ascribed to human beings to focus inwardly on an ego, self, or other mental substrate." (242, n. 7) This use of the locution is widespread. However, I think it is misleading to call it '*self*-awareness', since it seems only to involve awareness of (one's own) mental contents, and so awareness of "*self*" indirectly, at best. I will continue to call it 'awareness of content' or 'privileged access to content'; I use the latter when the emphasis is on the asymmetry between first-person and third-person access. I continue to refrain from using 'self-awareness'. A further word on 'content': Heil does not hold that one is always

aware of the content of one's thought, nor do I. Nor does either of us hold that one is ever aware of all the content of' one's thought. It is enough that one is sometimes aware of at least part of the content of one's occurrent thought. I made these qualifications in chapter 1. For Heil's qualifications, see pp. 238–242 of his 1988 paper.

3.   This formulation is Heil's. It is taken from some correspondence we had before the publication of my 1990 paper, which criticized his 1988 paper. I am grateful to him for the correspondence.

4.   Still, they may not be all that different. In all three cases, one might identify the external condition determining the content to be some neural state, and one distinct from that determining the corresponding thought having that content. We may have some reason to think that there is such a state. However, this much 'externalism' would not seem enough to satisfy most externalists; the key to externalism is to incorporate features of the environment external to the subject's body. In any case, establishing this would still leave one open to the charge that it is the sign rather than the content that is determined.

5.   I discuss this point regarding the particularity of a representation in considerable detail in chapter 5.

6.   See note 4 for a candidate, though for the reason given in that note it is not helpful to externalism.

7.   Regrettably, it is not uncommon for philosophers to equivocate on "intentional content" and "intentional object." This leads to conundrums when what the intentional state is about does not exist (and others), conundrums that can be avoided by resolutely distinguishing the two, as both Searle and I, in my extension of Searle's theory, do.

8.   My discussion of Van Gulick's views on understanding, semantic transparency, and just how phenomenal consciousness figures in an account of them is restricted to his 1989 paper. (I first criticized these views in my 1996 paper.) He has, however, presented these views in several other essays (e.g., Van Gulick 1988, 1993).

9.   As we will see, it is not clear that Van Gulick thinks phenomenal representations are separate from *human* understanding, though it is clear that he thinks they are separate from *understanding*. The distinction between understanding and human understanding reflects the functionalist position that whatever has the right functional relations, human or non-human, will exhibit understanding. Van Gulick entertains the possibility that phenomenal representations may be contingently tied with human understanding, though not a feature of understanding, generally.

10.   The issues concerning particular contents are of fundamental importance. They have been discussed some already, but a thorough discussion occurs in chapter 5.

11.   I am grateful to Henry Jacoby for raising the objection to a much earlier version of this argument.

12.   Not that no one is trying. The deepest and most sustained effort of which I am aware is that of Zenon Pylyshyn (1986). Pylyshyn plausibly maintains that a program meant to model some psychological phenomena should be *strongly equivalent* to it and takes important steps toward providing an account of strong equivalence. In brief: "In my view, two programs can be thought of as strongly equivalent or as different realizations of the same algorithm or the same cognitive process if they can be represented by the same program in some theoretically specified virtual machine. . . . The formal structure of the virtual machine—or what I call its *functional architecture*—[is] the sort of functional resources the . . . [system] makes available. . . . Specifying the functional architecture of a system is like providing a manual that defines some particular programming language. Indeed, defining a programming language is equivalent to specifying the functional architecture of a virtual machine. Thus the way I address the issue of the appropriate level of comparison between a model and a cognitive process—or the notion of strong equivalence of processes—is to provide a specification of the functional architecture of a "cognitive virtual machine." (91–92) The determination of the *functional architecture* of the brain is crucial to Pylyshyn's overall project, as he himself stresses; indeed, he argues that "*any* notion of correspondence stronger than weak equivalence [i.e., simply input/output equivalence] must presuppose an underlying functional architecture, or at least some aspects of such an architecture" (92). One of the reasons for this is that any program that models cognitive processes must not merely *emulate* the way the brain does it (see, e.g., 98–99), but the basic operations used in the program must be the same as the basic operations used by the brain, if they are to be strongly equivalent. If it is to be a model of cognitive activity, it must *execute* the program in the same way as does the brain. However, "since . . . there is no well-developed theory of algorithmic equivalence in computer science, these ideas must be developed without benefit of an existing body of analysis" (115). This is not as damaging to the project as one might at first suspect since, as he stated earlier, "the relevance of formal criteria [for algorithmic equivalence] to cognitive-science goals is marginal (we are not concerned with the task of comparing two *programs* but with comparing a program and a set of empirical phenomena); the pursuit of strong equivalence in computer science is of interest because it reveals underlying conceptual issues" (90). Of course, one such issue is the importance of the distinction between the functional architecture and the cognitive process so as to assess strong equivalence claims (260). Pylyshyn's work is probing, rich, and important. He is defining a research program for the study of cognitive processes. One of the *goals* of the program is to develop a notion of strong equivalence. Since the models are not merely to emulate the cognitive processes, he further requires an empirically based criterion for determination of the functional architecture of a system. He plausibly argues for two independent empirical criteria for zeroing in on the functional architecture of a system, what he calls *complexity equivalence* and *cognitive impenetrability*, but he also notes that "there

is no way to guarantee in advance that both criteria pick out the *same* level of functional architecture" (114). It is worth repeating that the relatively precise and rigorous field of computer science lacks a "well-developed theory of algorithmic equivalence" (115). Pylyshyn certainly does not think that the criterion for strong equivalence in cognitive science is an accomplished task. So, in spite of the importance and fruitfulness of Pylyshyn's work, it cannot be offered in rebuttal to my claim that there is (now) no principled criterion of functional equivalence. Should his or a similar project come to successful fruition, my argument that depends on the fact that there is no principled, non-ad-hoc criterion of functional equivalence, would need restructuring. Until then, my argument cannot be rebutted by appeal to a possible assumed principled criterion of functional equivalence. The *possibility* of such a criterion certainly cannot by used to claim that two *specified* systems, such as A and B, are not functionally equivalent, for it would beg the question.

13.   See Carnap 1966, pp. 131–133.

14.   Some of these same points against the functionalist can be made, somewhat surprisingly, by appealing to Quine's theses of the Indeterminacy of Translation and the inscrutability of reference. I discuss these in chapter 8.

15.   Further possibilities that result by reversing the causal or logical relations or holding that the content and verbal disposition are independent need not detain us here, since they block, rather than advance, my objector's case.

16.   In chapter 4 I do this for brain states and mental states, states that appear to be of radically different kinds. Hence, I avoid a similar criticism of my theory when I later claim that having a conscious state is the same as having a certain sort of brain state.

17.   This appearance is of a different type than the one discussed in the previous paragraph. On what is involved in explaining this sort of appearance, see the last section of chapter 1.

18.   There is an important issue here that often is overlooked. When it is said that a causal interaction between the system or creature and its environment is required to determine or individuate content the proponent of such a claim is usually silent as *to whom* the content is thus determined. I examine this crucial point in detail in chapter 5. See also what I have said about "determining the content" earlier in this chapter and about individuating content in chapter 1.

19.   It should be obvious, though, that what I am here characterizing as minimal content is distinct from what is often considered to be narrow content, i.e., conceptual or inferential role. While one might reject minimal content, one certainly cannot identify it with this sense of narrow content. For the classic discussions of narrow and wide content and of Twin Earth, see Putnam 1975. An important issue surrounding the concept of narrow content is whether it is required for psychological explanation. Brian Loar (1988) and Ned Block (1986) argue, contrary to Burge,

that narrow content is required for psychological explanation and that the main challenge to this view is to "find a non-arbitrary way of constraining the relevant connection, so that each psychological state can turn out to process a determinate narrow content, and to explain how this constrains its truth conditions" (Loar 1988, p. 8). Here "relevant connection" refers to a concept's inferential connections to other concepts, in accordance with both Loar's and Block's concept of narrow content, which is distinctly different from my narrow concept of minimal content. If my arguments are thus far correct, inferential connections, functional role semantics, lacks the resources to determine a *particular* content. I develop different arguments to the same conclusion in chapters 5 and 8, and I also show there how my concept of minimal content is a determinate narrow content that does constrain it truth conditions. I am not here directly concerned with the question as to whether the notion of wide content is itself adequate for a science of psychology, or whether one also needs some notion of narrow content for such purposes. There are many issues pertaining to this important question that I do not address in this book; nevertheless, I do think psychological explanation does require some concept of narrow content, and I think minimal content can make a contribution here. In particular, it is uncontroversial that to understand an individual's behavior we must know how *she conceives* things, since she deliberates about things and acts (seeks or avoids) in accordance with how she thinks things are. Knowing how she conceives things is especially important when there is divergence from how things are objectively. Behavior that is aberrant to objective observers is sometimes driven by just such divergences.

20.   In saying this I am not holding that the identity of concepts, or the meaning of terms are ultimately determined by the individual. See my discussion of Burge in chapters 1 and 7 and my discussion of Quine in chapter 8.

21.   The differences between explicating and understanding content, on the one hand, and individuating content, on the other, were discussed in chapter 1.

22.   See Burge's discussion of his arthritis example (1979) and Davidson's criticism of it (1987). Although I have many points of agreement with Davidson on these and related issues, the fact that he ultimately bases his points on the causal histories of the agents undermines, in my opinion, his conclusions, or so I argue below. For my discussion of Burge, see chapter 7.

23.   Some years ago John Heil raised this objection in response to a paper of mine that presented this argument.

24.   Of course, an individual's knowledge may change in time so that his minimal contents represent the different entities in his new environment (say, when he is transported to Twin Earth and learns of XYZ) or correctly represent what was always in his environment (say, when the phlogiston chemist learns the oxygen theory of combustion). But when this happens, surely his thoughts are different than they were. Although his minimal content and objective content would now signal the

same entity, this has no bearing on their earlier divergence. So, when the phlogiston chemist gets converted to the oxygen theory of combustion, his new thoughts about burning objects will have both his minimal content and objective content signaling the same entity, without altering the fact that in his earlier thoughts, while causally interacting with an environment similar to the current one, his minimal content and objective content diverged in what they signaled.

25.   Davidson (1987, p. 455) makes a similar point. Whether I am right about these views on content sharing an ancestry with classical empiricism is quite immaterial to my other points.

26.   Typically, of course, we take the objects our minimal contents represent to actually exist. This is an additional belief, however, one which is independent of our having minimal contents, of our conceiving our thoughts to be about this or that. That our thoughts have minimal content is in no way dependent on this further belief about them. Moreover, when we discover that there is no corresponding objective content or that it is different from our minimal content, we abandon that minimal content and attempt to align our new minimal content with the objective content. However, we do not always do this: when I contemplate a fictional object, I know that the minimal content and the objective content do not match—that is the point of a fictional object.

27.   In chapter 8, however, I will argue that sentence or word meaning ultimately depends upon minimal content.

28.   Compare my discussion of Johnson's purported refutation of Berkeley in the last section of chapter 1.

Chapter 3

1.   Horgan and Tienson (2002, p. 520) have dubbed this division *separatism*.

2.   Searle is an important exception here. His Chinese Room thought experiment is very explicit in its focus on *understanding*. Unfortunately this has not stopped others from recasting Searle's case in terms of *phenomenal* consciousness. See, for example, Van Gulick 1989 and my discussions of that paper in Georgalis 1996 and below.

3.   See chapter 2, where I argue that functionalism has not even succeeded here and reasons are provided as to why it cannot do so.

4.   Certainly phenomenal states are or can be conscious, but it is not as clear that every conscious state is or can be phenomenal. I have argued (chapter 1) that there are non-phenomenal conscious states, pace Tyler Burge (see below), and that this is of importance in showing the role consciousness—without phenomenality—plays in intentionality.

5.   See, for examples, Dretske 1995; Harmon 1990; Lycan 1996; McDowell 1994.

6.   Of course, insofar as the representationist is willing to countenance my analysis of intentionality, then that would be quite another matter. I would then be open to her position, though I think certain other problems do arise for this view, even if this augmented view of intentionality were adopted. I do not go into these other problems here.

7.   Among other reasons for this is that Block defines the latter functionally. See chapter 2 for why a functional analysis will not work here.

8.   Mentality is in fact a broader concept than (genuine) intentionality, contrary to the suggestion in the quoted passage. A generalized pain or anxiety is mental without being intentional. (Searle and others have made this point.) This aside, the first premise, even as stated by Van Gulick in his reformulation of Searle's argument, does not assert that semantic transparency is *required* for the broader notion of mentality; however, as stated, it does for the narrower notion of genuine intentionality. In any case, Van Gulick's recasting of Searle's concept of genuine or intrinsic intentionality in terms of semantic transparency is not a reformulation that he would accept.

9.   Though I did not employ the locution 'semantic transparency', I did speak of symbol manipulation, and one of my points was that there could be a great deal of sophisticated (and rapid) symbol manipulation without there being any phenomenal content.

10.   Without suggesting that they all hold exactly the same view, I note that those advancing the idea of phenomenal intentionality include David Chalmers (1996), Terence Horgan and John Tienson (2002), David Pitt (forthcoming), Charles Siewert (1998), and Galen Strawson (1994). Horgan and Tienson, for example, explain it as follows: "*Phenomenal Intentionality*: There is a kind of intentionality, pervasive in human mental life that is constitutively determined by phenomenology alone." (520) They offer what the they claim is a sharper formulation: "There is a kind of intentional content, pervasive in human mental life, such that any two possible phenomenal duplicates have exactly similar intentional states vis-à-vis such content," where "two creatures . . . [are] *phenomenal duplicates* just in case each creature's total experience, throughout its existence, is phenomenally exactly similar to the other's" (524).

11.   We saw above that Davies and Humphries do identify Nagel's "the something it is like" with phenomenal consciousness.

12.   Sometimes the WIL is extended in a third, more general, way: what it is like for a conscious being on any given occasion to be in some occurrent intentional state—a combination of attitude with content. Authors who agree that there is a WIL experience to intentional states may still differ as to which of these different extensions (attitude, content, or combination thereof) of the restricted sense is operative. I will largely ignore such differences in my discussion, as no new issues are raised by these variants.

13.   The qualification to *this sort* of WIL is made because, as I will argue below, there is a sense of WIL that is operative, one that is connected to our first-person awareness of our minimal contents but which in no way implicates the phenomenal.

14.   To say this is not to deny the existence of what Galen Strawson has called "understanding-experience" involved in intentional states, of which he says: "To talk of understanding-experience, then, is not to commit oneself to the implausible view that there is some single qualitative type of experience that anyone who has understanding-experience must have. It is not to commit oneself to the view that particular qualitative experiences invariably go with understanding particular sentences." (1994, p. 7) Indeed, he seems to be in explicit agreement with my denial that the WIL of intentional states delivers any uniform phenomenal feature, as he further states: " . . . we need to allow that a particular case of understanding-experience can involve a specific cognitive experiential content while overcoming the tendency of the words 'specific experiential content' to make us think only of distinctions like those found in sensory experience." (13) I am in complete agreement with him on this, as I am with his claim that it is of the utmost importance to recognize the fact of understanding-experience. But Strawson thinks that the concept is "elusive" and there is little hope of doing anything theoretical (11) because it "evades description" (12). I disagree with his expressed pessimism. While I have not previously used the locution 'understanding-experience' I believe that what I have said in chapters 1, 5, and 8 does address in considerable theoretical detail the issues raised by the concept of understanding-experience.

15.   I thank Natika Newton for raising this objection, which prompted the response that follows.

16.   Saying this is not to deny that some phenomenal aspect or another is associated with an occurrent intentional state, but when it is, it is only contingently associated with it—unlike minimal content. I argued above for the contingency claim.

17.   The idea that there is something non-phenomenal that is *for* an agent is also crucial to my theory of representation, see chapter 5.

18.   Commenting on the expression "what it is like," Nagel says that "it does not mean 'what (in our experience) it *resembles*,' but rather 'how it is for the subject himself'" (1980, n. 6). I think the use of 'how' here is appropriate and informative for phenomenal states, but in keeping with my suggestion in the text, I suggest '*what* it is for the subject himself' when propositional attitudes are at issue. Though clearly in saying the latter, I am not appealing to what it *resembles*.

19.   I recall David Chalmers commenting, in a conversation, that he uses these terms interchangeably, and even adding 'consciousness' to the list. (I extend my apologies to him if this report is inaccurate.) Horgan and Tienson begin their 2002 essay by asking "What is the relationship between phenomenology and intentionality?" and proceed to discuss "phenomenal aspects." They also state the theses of

"The Intentionality of Phenomenology" and "The Phenomenology of Intentionality" in terms of "phenomenal character"; moreover, they then proceed to explain "Phenomenal Intentionality" using the word 'phenomenology'.

20.   For it turns on applying what I called the unrestricted sense of the WIL locution, and this fails to deliver a type-identifying uniform phenomenal feature of intentional states. The case is no better for the application of the unrestricted sense of WIL to uncover a "phenomenological" aspect of intentionality, and for the same reasons. More on this below.

21.   Compare note 14 above, in which Strawson is quoted admonishing us to accept a different reading of the locution 'specific experiential content' than that found in sensory experience.

22.   One might object that since others can think the same *thoughts*, they are in fact objective. This objection, if it were sustainable, would prove too much. For the case is no different for phenomenal experiences: When I am cognizant of a green apple on the table because of my perceptual experience, the subjectivity of this experience is not threatened because others can be cognizant of the same thing. Here as in the case, say, of the thought that two is a prime number, others may think the same thoughts as I do without undermining the fact that there are subjective aspects to both of these thoughts. I have assumed here that my minimal contents and objective contents signal the same things. When this is not so, the subjectivity of my thoughts, whether perceptual or non-perceptual, is even more evident. In both the phenomenal and the non-phenomenal cases, *what* is experienced, in one sense, may be objective without affecting the subjectivity of the experience itself.

23.   I will extend the analysis I have given of intentionality to that of phenomenality in chapter 6: both require minimal content and objective content.

24.   Of course, Mary's task is far more difficult than this suggests. Often we use a color term in the absence of any thing of the color of which we are speaking—e.g., "My car is green" in the absence of any green thing. This exacerbates Mary's problem, though it does not preclude obtaining correlations of brain states with actual color perceptions.

25.   This claim may draw support from no less authority than Ernest Nagel. In his classic book, before closing his discussion of state descriptions, he states: "One final point of considerable importance should be noted. A definition of the 'state of a system' suitable for a given empirical subject matter, cannot be supplied *in advance* of an adequate "causal" theory for that subject matter." (1961, p. 292) Nagel further explains that he understands a theory to be causal "if it relates time-rate of changes in some set of magnitudes with other magnitudes." The set of magnitudes is the set of relevant variables that I referred to above.

26.   See my chapter 5. There I also examine a related issue concerning the conditions for saying that a non-human has representational states.

27. There is some reason to think that Nagel would agree with my earlier claim that we can have objective knowledge of subjective states and the claims made in this paragraph and those regarding Sally, for consider the following passage: "There is a sense in which phenomenological facts are perfectly objective: one person can know or say of another what the quality of the other's experience is. They are subjective, however, in the sense that even this objective ascription of experience is possible only for someone sufficiently similar to the object of ascription to be able to adopt his point of view—to understand the ascription in the first person as well as in the third. . . ." (Nagel 1980, p. 163)

28. Though, of course, the objectivity just referred to is not one restricted to an exclusively third-person methodology. In the last section of chapter 5, I will argue that a third-person methodology that also incorporates a first-person perspective for the study of subjectivity can be objective in a legitimate sense of that word; moreover, failure to incorporate the first-person perspective in the philosophical or psychological study of the mind leads, contrary to what might be expected, to anthropomorphism. I also introduce a methodological principle, methodological chauvinism that encapsulates the points made herein.

29. I am very grateful to Bill Lycan for his generosity with his time, both in conversation and correspondence. Though I am sure he does not agree with what I say in this section, he was able to eliminate some of my misunderstandings of his view. No doubt some remain. (My comments on Lycan are based on the manuscript of Lycan 2003.)

30. Compare my discussion of nomic and non-nomic properties in chapter 5 in connection with the role consciousness plays in representation.

31. Lycan explains that this premise, coupled with the hypothesis that Mary knows every physical fact about color experience prior to exiting her color deprived room would entail that materialism or physicalism is false, since Mary appears to learn a new fact upon release. Hence, he is concerned to deny that Mary learns a new fact. In contrast, while I argue that Mary does learn a new fact on release from the room, I draw no ontological conclusions from this, nor do I think that any follow. As to my aversion to ontological matters, see chapter 9.

32. I would like to thank Michael Veber for his resistance in conversation to my claim that that Mary learns a new fact, as the presentation below is better than it would have been otherwise.

33. Mary can consider what it would be like because she is not deprived of all subjective experience, though she has of yet had no color perceptions

34. It is actually an empirical matter whether Mary would straight-away see colors when released. Nevertheless, as the thought experiment is usually discussed, including by those who advocate an ability hypothesis, it is taken for granted that Mary does see colors straight-away upon release.

35.   David Chalmers (1996, p. 118) also holds this. He argues in a similar vein that some explanation of how this comes about is required, if we are to seriously treat the proposal. But I also show in the next chapter wherein I disagree with his arguments and the conclusions he draws, and I propose my own solution to the problem.

36.   There is also an additional problem for feature (2) of the Inner Sense Theory being of any help in resolving the "how possibly" question, if what I argue regarding representation (chapter 5) is correct. For then what Lycan calls 'representation' in feature (2) falls short of being representation.

37.   I hasten to add that Lycan (1996, 1999) has addressed the "how possibly" question; indeed, he thinks that he has answered it. I do not examine his interesting proposals here. I think he fails primarily for two general reasons. Higher-order perception theories are no better off than higher-order thought theories with regard to accounting for our first-person, first-level awareness of content, and I have already argued against the latter theories. Secondly, the very idea of representation already requires the concept of consciousness, as I argue in chapter 5; so, it cannot be used to explain consciousness

38.   Nagel may or may not agree. As to why he may agree, see the quotation in note 27.

39.   In addition to what I have already said in support of this, I explain that this does not make the investigation unscientific in the last section of chapter 5.

40.   It is well known that David Chalmers (1996) is credited with coining the former expression and Joe Levine (1983) the latter.

Chapter 4

1.   It is important to stress this ordinary observational sense of the term. David Chalmers objects to this analogy, used in a distant ancestor of this chapter. His objection is based on a different interpretation of 'liquidity'. His objection goes as follows: " . . . the water case is not a useful analogy for you, because in that case it's clear that what needs to be explained is structure and function—we explain the liquidity, transparency, etc. and it's obvious that those are the sort of structural/functional matters that are wide-open to physical explanation." (email, December 13, 1998) For it to be "obvious" that these properties are open to a structural/functional explanation, one must presume, at the least, that these properties are understood in a physio-chemical way, rather than in the way I recommend here, a way that corresponds to our ordinary observation of liquids. I will have more to say about the role of structure and function in these matters below. In chapter 6 I will argue that these two interpretations of 'liquidity' reflect a wide spread and systematic ambiguity in all sensory terms.

2.   Similarly for solidity of ice, where much stronger intermolecular bonds keep the individual molecules in fixed position relative to one another; in the case of water vapor, the individual molecules have such high energy that they are unable to form intermolecular bonds and move freely with respect to one another.

3.   Searle utilizes the molecule/liquidity case in an attempt to show that there are no metaphysical obstacles to an account of our intentional states as causal features of our brains. He claims our mental states are genuine biological phenomena that are both "caused by and realized in the brain," a claim that, among other things, seems to introduce a notion of mental-physical causation. He has been widely criticized on this point. My aim here is neither to review these criticisms nor to defend Searle on this matter. Instead, I will examine one of the ways that Searle does try to dispel the air of mystery, as my case is similar though different from his. The difference is important. Searle illustrates the idea of something being caused by and realized in something else by making an analogy to how liquidity is both caused by a kind of molecular motion and realized in that molecular behavior. In fact he cites the analogy as one that is parallel to Leibniz's famous case of imagining a giant machine that could think, feel and perceive. One so large, that we can walk into it as though it were a mill. On so doing we would find parts that interact with one another, but never find perception or any other mental state. Similarly, in the case of a liquid we would not find the liquidity at the level of the molecules. Searle holds that "in both cases we would be looking at the system at the wrong level. The liquidity of water is not to be found at the level of the individual molecule, nor are the visual perception and the thirst to be found at the level of the individual neuron or synapse. If one knew the principles on which the system of H_2O molecules worked, one could infer that it was in a liquid state by observing the movement of the molecules, but similarly if one knew the principles on which the brain worked one could infer that it was in a state of thirst or having a visual experience." (1993, p. 268) What we have in all these cases is that certain macro-phenomena are caused by and realized in certain micro-phenomena. This may be so, but the trouble is that right now it is difficult to see how the firing of neurons or the passing of chemicals across synapses *could* give rise to intentionality in a way analogous to how we can see how non-liquid molecules and certain sorts of bonds between them *can* give rise to liquidity. (Searle has mentioned to me that Thomas Nagel has raised a similar objection to his use of the analogy.) I offer a resolution to this objection below and also have something to say about mental/physical causation.

4.   The concept *comprehensible to us* is itself a subjective concept. This may be another reason why so many physicalists imbued with a strictly third-person methodology eschew or downplay the problem of the explanatory gap. See below.

5.   I raised these points in criticism of John Heil's treatment of supervenience in my 1995 review of his 1992 book. Apparently, he now agrees, for in the conclusion of his 1998 paper he states: "I have argued that the concept of supervenience as standardly formulated provides little in the way of ontological illumination. . . .

Supervenience is not explanatory. . . . Supervenience claims hold, when they do, because the world is a particular way. *What we need to be clear about is what that way is.* Different cases yield different results." (emphasis added) The emphasized passage is what I argued for in my 1995 review and held that without it supervenience claims are uninformative and useless.

6.   As to the competition between options 1 and 2, one is reminded of one of Kuhn's claims. Often when a given scientific paradigm, say, the current network of neurophysiological practices and theories, is under pressure because of its apparent inability to solve some outstanding problem, those strongly committed to it are willing to postpone work on this problem. They are confident that new techniques, methods, or information, all compatible with the existing paradigm, will be obtained that eventually will allow solution of the problem. They would endorse option 1. Others see the problem as refuting the existing paradigm, preparing the way for a new paradigm. They would endorse option 2. (Despite what I just said, I do not hold that there is a single paradigm in contemporary neuroscience).

7.   Colin McGinn (1989) has argued for such a pessimistic conclusion.

8.   These physicalism/anti-physicalism "wars" ultimately presuppose an untenable view of substance, or so I believe, but I cannot argue for that here.

9.   One reason someone might think they are necessary is if the explanatory gap problem is confused with a reduction of phenomenal states to brain states and one accepts the classical model of reduction one kind of entity to another. I think it is a mistake to view the explanatory gap problem as a reduction problem, regardless of the model of reduction. See chapter 6 for more on the issue of reduction in this context.

10.   In discussing this analogy earlier, my emphasis on the point that liquidity must be understood in its ordinary observational way rather than any physio-chemical sense of that term was to preserve the parallel between the first-person and third-person aspects that we find between subjective states and brain states.

11.   Galileo thinks he has resolved the problems associated with his view of the subjective qualities of four of the senses, but he has nothing substantive to say about sight and the attendant qualities of color and light, though he offers some inchoate speculations on the latter. One quaint aspect of his presentation, not presented here, is how he attempts to further ground each sense for the subjective qualities in the four basic elements of fire, air, earth, and water.

12.   Just as Berkeley did—see the section titled "Explaining the Appearance" in chapter 1. As we will see in chapter 6, Place and Smart failed in this respect.

13.   At one point, with regard to heat, Galileo explicitly states how his view is contrary to common sense: "From a common-sense point of view, to assert that that which moves a stone, piece of iron, or a stick is what heats it, seems like an extreme

vanity." (1623, p. 32) I will further discuss the common-sense view of secondary qualities and its relation to Galileo's view in chapter 6.

14.   True, the whole may function differently than the parts can individually but, for all that, the whole is not itself qualitatively different from its parts. Functionalists generally, though not without exception, admit their inability to reduce qualia, phenomenal states, to functional states. In chapter 2, I argued that they are also unsuccessful in reducing intentional states to functional states.

15.   Fred Dretske (e-mail, August 27, 2000) has objected to my claim that we need a new dynamics: " . . . the old dynamics provides everything you say the new (non-linear) dynamics provides. We take a gas, hydrogen, and burn it. The ash is water. Bingo, something completely new. So we are already familiar with the process in which you can take ingredients, combine them, and get something with an alto-gether new property (gas + gas = liquid)" I might add, in the spirit of his objection, that we do this utilizing the "old dynamics." What this objection misses is exactly similar to what David Chalmers' objection to my molecule/liquid analogy also missed. (For my response to Chalmers, see note 1.) It is at the ordinary observational level that an altogether new property occurs, (observed) gas + (observed) gas = (observed) liquid; observed liquids are certainly qualitatively rather different from observed gases. But, as in my response to Chalmers, at the physio-chemical level we do not get something new or radically different. $2H_2 + O_2$ molecules combine to yield $2H_2O$ molecules, molecules + molecules yield more molecules, albeit different molecules and with different strengths of inter-molecular bonds, but *qua* molecules and this micro level of explanation, *just more of the same*. So, Dretske's case shows nothing (radically) new and different when we restrict ourselves to considerations at the physio-chemical level, to the standard dynamics, to the "old dynamics." It is at the level of ordinary observation that the change from a gas to a liquid is radi-cally different. This difference in ordinary observations is not explained by an exclu-sive physio-chemical explanation at the micro level. The terms 'gas' and 'liquid' in the physio-chemical explanation have to do with differences in inter-molecular bonds, and as such, it is more of the same. It does not, without further ado, reflect on the ordinary observational (phenomenal) differences between that of "gas" and "liquid." (See my discussion regarding the ambiguity of such terms between our sci-entific and ordinary understanding of them in chapter 6.) At the physio-chemical level there is nothing substantially new. Similarly, as argued earlier, the molecule/liquidity case is only an analogy for the explanatory gap problem, when characterized in terms of inter-levels and when 'liquidity' is understood in its ordi-nary observational sense.

16.   Self-organization is a characteristic of chaotic systems. See the appendix to this chapter for a brief explanation of some central concepts of chaos theory.

17.   J. A. Scott Kelso (1997) lists among the conditions for a self-organized system that there must be a large number of elements with nonlinear interactions. He

points out that this requirement constitutes a major break with Sir Isaac Newton, whom he quotes as holding that "the motion of the whole is the sum of the motion of all the parts" (Definition II, *Principia*). In contrast, Kelso holds that "for us, the motion of the whole is not only greater than, but *different* than the sum of the motions of the parts, due to nonlinear interactions among the parts or between the parts and the environment" (16). Feedback models are sometimes thought to account for self-organized behavior. In counter to this, Kelso (9) appeals to the work of W. Ross Ashby, who proved feedback models are inadequate for complex systems with a large number of elements. He also argues that a feedback (linear) analysis is also precluded by the fact that there are no reference values with which the feedback may be compared.

18.   Detailed discussion of Freeman's work supporting the role of chaos in brain processing of information is found in the papers by Chris King, Carl Anderson and Arnold Mandell, Earl MacCormac, and David Alexander and Gordon Globus in MacCormac and Stamenov 1996b. Others have also successfully applied chaos theory to brain activity. For a fascinating and clear account of other successful applications of chaos theory to brain activity, see Kelso 1997.

19.   See, for example, Freeman 1996, 1991, 1992, and 1995—a sequence that goes, roughly, from simpler to more technical works.

20.   An issue here is related to what is known as the "binding problem." This problem is how the outputs from the different supposed feature detectors are connected. A proposed solution, one which Freeman, himself, had a hand in, is that the feature neurons fire synchronously (40 hertz). Freeman now rejects this as a pseudo-problem, for it is based on the idea of feature detector neurons in each of the sensory cortexes. Freeman rejects the idea of feature detector neurons because it is observer relative, and what is significant for the brain is the global activity of the neurons. Aside from the difficulties with feature detector neurons, the "40-hertz solution" is now rejected by him, since the frequency distribution in the visual and olfactory systems is not synchronized but broad spectrum, as Freeman has demonstrated. On the question of feature detectors, see the next note.

21.   Compare Akins' (1996) discussion of heat, where no single correlation is found between the heat stimulus and the various resultant changes in physiological states. The nonexistence of such correlations may well further indicate the need to examine more global properties of the brain through the use of chaos theory, as Freeman found in study of smell. I discuss Akins' work in chapter 5.

22.   A further fact that supports the contention that the system is chaotic is that the bulb and the olfactory cortex excite one another so that neither settles down, nor do they agree on a common frequency of oscillation. (If the connection is severed between the two, they become stable and quiet.) This competition between the two increases sensitivity and instability and contributes to chaos. The importance of this connection between the olfactory bulb and cortex when understood in the light

of another biological fact leads to a rather startling speculation. Here is, what I understand to be, the other biological fact. (I thank John Bickle for bringing this fact to my attention.) As the cortex increases in mass it takes on more functions, functions that in lower animal forms that have less cortical mass are performed by brain systems other than the cortex; this is particularly true of sensory systems. Suppose, in accordance with the mind/brain theory that I advance, which draws heavily upon the work of Freeman, that the *having* of phenomenal or contentful experience is a direct result of *one's own brain* undergoing a burst to a strange attractor, and that these burst states involve the cortex. Assuming that oscillations between the olfactory bulb and the olfactory cortex that occurs in humans does not occur in some lower animals whose cortex is not involved when their sense organs are appropriately stimulated, the speculation is that such lower animal forms *simply lack qualia, contentful states, or conscious states—they do not have subjective experiences.* In light of what I argue in the next chapter, such animals would be information bearers but not representers.

23.   If brain dynamics is chaotic then superficially, at least, this last feature would seem to go far in explaining why, although we can frequently give an ad hoc explanation of someone's behavior, we are not as successful in predicting what someone will do, despite *similar*, even empirically indistinguishable but not identical, initial conditions.

24.   This passage is clearer than it might otherwise have been if it were not for Ümit Yalçin's refusal to accept the idea that one could have a deterministic system whose states were not in principle predictable.

Chapter 5

1.   For an example of a violation of this stricture, see Macphail 1987. Macphail examines possible differences in intelligence from species to species without prior analysis of representation in humans. Vauclair (1990, p. 395) criticizes Macphail for not paying sufficient attention to the concept of representation. Vauclair takes a step in the right direction in offering a definition of representation. However, Vauclair does not go far enough, for he offers neither evidence nor argument that his concept of representation is that operative in the human performance of intelligent tasks.

2.   To the extent that I am right in maintaining the importance of the first-person perspective and the consequences I have drawn from it for an analysis of intentional states, I am also right in denying Dennett's claim that being able to take an "intentional stance" toward a system is sufficient for that system to have intentional states. The last claim requires further support in that Dennett (1987) would require, in addition to our being able to take an intentional stance toward a system, that the system itself exhibit a certain objective feature which he calls a 'real pattern', if the system is to have intentional states. (See e.g. Dennett 1987, pp. 25–26. For an

extended treatment of his idea of a real pattern, see Dennett 1991.) Consideration of whether talk of real patterns in this connection can avoid the problems the first-person perspective poses for Dennett's kind of analysis of intentional states will have to wait for another occasion, though my discussion of the distinction between representers and information bearers, below, independently supports the rejection of intentional stance type theories.

3.   The specific views examined are those of Churchland and Churchland (1983), developed further by Paul Churchland (1979), Fred Dretske (1985, 1995), and Ruth Millikan (1984, 1989).

4.   This is discussed further in the next section. See also Beckermann 1988.

5.   One anonymous referee who read the article version of this chapter did raise this objection.

6.   The reader is reminded that insisting on the conscious aspect of representations does not commit me to holding that when s is occurrently aware that r represents t, her awareness consists in her noticing some peculiar feature of either r or her occurrent state. And that's a good thing, since if it did, that would seriously count against my view. See e.g. Kripke 1982, especially the latter portion of section 2, for a discussion of why it is a mistake to look for such a feature. I am not sympathetic to views that associate a phenomenal aspect with intentional states for reasons already presented in chapter 3. Kripke's arguments here give further support for this rejection. For an example of the contrary position, see Siewert 1998.

7.   Searle (1979) notes that Wittgenstein and Kenny have argued that an intentional state and its object have some "internal relation" to one another. Searle agrees and holds that an intentional state *is* internally related to its object: "Because an intentional state contains a representation we can now give a clear sense to the notion that it is 'internally related' to the object it represents: Any representation is internally related to its object in the sense that it could not be *that* representation if it did not have *that* object." (184) He realizes that much depends on how this relation is explicated. My explication, given below, is in accord with this and is in terms of minimal content.

8.   Dretske and Millikan do not speak of "intrinsic representations," but they do attempt to eliminate indeterminacies regarding what is represented; so they do address in effect the particularity requirement. That they fail in this will be argued in a later section.

9.   Armstrong adds that not all concepts are selective capacities, and some non-simple concepts are selective capacities, but all simple concepts must have selective capacities.

10.   This is argued by Heil (1980). See especially pp. 164–167.

11.   If one is aware of the minimal content of one's thought then one is at least implicitly aware of a certain mapping. Alternatively, if one is aware of a particular mapping, one is also aware of a certain minimal content, the object of the thought as conceived by the agent. So whether we speak of mappings or objects here is a matter of convenience determined by the context.

12.   On my view, one can be a physicalist and still accommodate the first-person perspective. In the last section here, I indicate how the result may nevertheless be, in a worthwhile sense, objective. See also chapter 3.

13.   Indeed, the very idea of doing something for a purpose is one that presupposes the notion of representation in accordance with my (partial) analysis of representation, and as distinct from *information bearing*. This last concept and how it differs from representing will be explained below. A later section will examine in detail the failure of teleological theories of representation.

14.   The exact role conventions play in determining relevant mappings and just how an individual may deviate from those conventions is addressed in more detail in my discussion of Burge's thought experiment in chapter 7.

15.   Compare the section "Understanding, Explicating, and Individuating" in chapter 1. The reader is also reminded that on my theory, minimal content does not have ontological significance; it is merely a moniker for the subject of an agent's thought as she conceives it.

16.   We will see in chapter 8 that these results will have important consequences for Quine's Indeterminacy of Translation thesis.

17.   Compare my discussion of Dretske and Millikan below, where I charge that they do assume this claim.

18.   This is a standard notion of *information*. See, for example, Van Gulick 1990, p. 109. Nothing that I say turns on this exact formulation.

19.   In "object of attention" I mean both 'object' and 'attention' to be understood from a first-person perspective.

20.   In chapter 2 and in my 1996 paper, I argue that functionalism generally and Van Gulick's specific version of it (1988) fail to account for the special access we have to our own minimal contents. As to the inadequacy of teleological accounts of representation, see the section below titled "Clarification of the Scope of the Arguments."

21.   Nagel (1980, p. 161 and n. 5) makes similar points.

22.   On a more optimistic note: If it turns out that consciousness is necessary for representation, as I hold, it is not implausible to suppose that at some stage of scientific development we could objectively identify what feature enables consciousness in us. (For a hypothesis as to a candidate for the sort of brain state that is

promising in this regard, see Georgalis 2000 and chapter 4 of the present volume.) We would then be able to determine which non-human animals also have this feature and, therefore, assuming that certain other factors that are in play when we represent are similarly realized, have strong grounds to hold that they also have similar representational states.

23. An advocate of an exclusive third-person methodology who holds this view is Ruth Millikan.

24. Some variant of the appearance to which I refer is recognized and confronted by a number of authors. For example, even Dennett (1987), who wants a unified theory of all manner of representations, is concerned to explain the appearance of a difference in how we represent and how, say, thermostats do. He does so in terms of the kinds of connections to the environment and degree of complexity, to over-simplify a bit. Just how seriously Dennett takes the distinction is subject to interpretation, but that need not detain us. He revisits something like the distinction in "Real Patterns" (1991). Fred Dretske (1985, 1995) focuses on an item having meaning in a *system's cognitive economy* versus its being *assigned* meaning by us. I certainly do not mean to suggest that Dretske and Dennett draw the same distinction, or that mine is the same as either of theirs. Indeed, it is not. The point is simply that they recognize the need to address *some* such distinction. Whether they are successful in drawing the distinction in a principled way that can address the points I identify as crucial to my distinction is another matter. In a subsequent section I will argue that Dretske's and Millikan's manner of distinguishing information from representation are inadequate.

25. Clearly, on my view information-bearing states are representational simply in a metaphorical way that is parasitic on the genuine sense. Compare Searle 1983, 1992. As is well known, Searle distinguishes intrinsic intentionality from both derivative and metaphorical intentionality. My debt to Searle on this and other matters is great.

26. We can, for example, account for the mere appearance that the sun revolves around the Earth. What accounting for such appearances comes to is explained more fully in chapter 1 of the present work and in my 1990 and 1994 papers.

27. A very early version of this section was presented in March 1993 at the University of Dayton at a colloquium on Recent Debates in the Cognitive Science Literature. Paul Churchland and Alvin Goldman were the invited speakers. I am grateful to both of them for their comments on my presentation and to the University of Dayton for the opportunity.

28. The Churchlands make this move frequently. (In their 1983 paper, see the opening paragraph and passages on pp. 7–8, 11, and 14.) Such a move, in fact, turns on an equivocation between information-bearing creatures and ones that represent but, as I argue, it is a mistake to identify them.

29.   The Churchlands offer a somewhat more precise account of calibrational content: "A state S of a system O contains the calibrational content P if and only if O would not be in S unless P, with some high degree of probability n/m." (1983, p. 14). Paul Churchland develops this idea in his 1979 book.

30.   The Churchlands think that an advantage that calibrational content offers is that it provides for non-sentential models of content. Thus, it greatly expands the class of information bearers, as it admits as possibilities creatures who have no linguistic capabilities. This is as it should be. Having said that, I also point out that while a system need not bear information that is sentence-like, it does not follow that representation need not be sentence-like. For it does not follow that the information bearer has *any* representations, is ever in a representational state. Still, I am *not* arguing that representation *must be* sentence-like; rather I am pointing out that the Churchlands' argument to the contrary depends on the (mistaken) presupposition that an information bearer is, also, a representer. (The Churchlands also hold that an information-bearing creature is an epistemic one. But if I am right in arguing that there is a significant difference between information bearers and representers, then we should not be quick to agree with the identification of information bearing creatures with epistemic ones either.)

31.   Their apparently differing treatment of the shell creature example (as though hard-wired) from that of the snake (as if it had a genuine representational system), seems to conflict with this last result. The appearance of a difference in their evaluation of the two cases results primarily from the fact that in discussing the former they are concerned with exposing what they take to be a defect of the computationalist view, viz., its inability to provide a hookup between the representational system and the environment, a defect they maintain calibrational content corrects. I have argued that it corrects this problem only if calibrational content is identical to representation, but then their view is disabled from making the important distinction between representation and information bearing.

32.   Paul Churchland was in the audience when I presented a very early version of this section. He acknowledged my criticisms and the need to draw the distinction. He suggested that he could do so by bringing complexity considerations to bear. I am dubious that this can be done so as to avoid the criticisms I have raised. In any case, I am not aware of his having proposed any such account that goes beyond this general assertion. Note that "the complexity stratagem" that he suggests is similar to Dennett's (1987, 1991). Any such strategy must face the question why "more of the same" can yield something distinctly different. It is not enough to simply appeal to the evident greater complexity of systems that do represent, as it advances no understanding of how this could be. Compare the discussion of the gap problem in chapter 4.

33.   I am grateful to Reinaldo Elugardo for providing me with this way of formulating the issue.

34.   Interestingly, the polarity of the magnetosome is different depending on whether the bacteria in which they reside are in the northern or southern hemisphere. If this were not so, the bacteria in one or the other hemisphere would have died off, since they would be pulled in the wrong direction, toward oxygen-rich water.

35.   For example, for each number in the sequence 1, 2, 3, . . . , whenever I am not attending to it, I still have the unconscious belief that it is a natural number.

36.   My debt to Searle is great, and I think he is profoundly right about intentionality. Still, I think he is wrong in holding that unconscious beliefs are intentionality, but abandoning this claim does not, I think, necessitate wholesale changes in his view.

37.   In arguing for the connection principle, Searle (1992, pp. 156–162) advances his claim that unconscious beliefs have aspectual shape in some detail. He has confirmed in conversation that something like the short argument here presented captures the thrust of the point contained in the larger argument to the broader conclusion.

38.   Since on my view there are no unconscious intentional states, the above would seem to totally undermine what Searle (1992, p. 156) calls the connection principle: " . . . all unconscious intentional states are in principle accessible to consciousness." My differences with Searle here are not as great as they may seem. I think there are two central points that Searle wants to advance with the connection principle. The first is that some, but not all, non-conscious states are importantly related to conscious states. The second is that all non-conscious states that are unconscious *mental* states are in principle accessible to consciousness. I am in complete agreement with the first; it is the point I attempt to capture with the unconscious/non-conscious distinction, which Searle used before me. I also accept a modified form of the second. Modified because I think that once we have a science of cognition (again, no matter whether it is based neuronally, computationally, or in some other way) it is highly implausible to think that *all* non-conscious states will be in principle accessible to consciousness though, undoubtedly, many will be. What their "accessibility" comes to on my view is that the structure and dynamics of the brain activity is such that given certain stimulations, it will undergo a burst to an attractor state, the latter is a manifestation of the conscious state and is qualitatively different from the preceding brain states. If this is so, it is misleading to speak of accessibility to the states that are prior to burst states. These states are designated as 'mental' because they lead to the relevant burst states but are not themselves accessible to consciousness. But as argued earlier, and as opposed to Searle, such unconscious mental states are not representational, not intentional. In contrast, those states that are *both* non-conscious *and* non-mental states do not lead to such bursts. (See chapter 4 and its appendix for further explanation of the role of burst states.) I cannot here discuss all of Searle's reasons for making the more general claim, but a

large part of why he is driven to do so is, I think, his holding that unconscious beliefs, *being beliefs*, must have aspectual shape. This, I have argued should be denied. Once denied, the connection principle must be reformulated, since there are no unconscious intentional states; still, if the two central points of the connection principle are as I have just stated, then the first and a modified form of the second is preserved. Thus, I claim that at least the spirit of the principle is preserved, even if Searle still wants more.

39.   The aspectual shape of a mental state is determined by its representational nature. One might hold a belief under one representation, but disavow it under an extensionally equivalent representation.

40.   Searle (1992, p. 158) thinks this because "we would still have to have some law like connection that would enable us to infer from our observations of the neural architecture and neuron firings that they were realizations [for example] of the desire for water not of the desire for H_2O."

41.   For different reasons, I argued in chapter 3 that it is a mistake to approach intentionality, aboutness, on a perceptual model.

42.   Compare my claim that we can give an objective account of subjective states, while utilizing, in part a first-person methodology. See chapter 3 and the next section.

43.   However, Akins does say that "the distance between the neurophysiologist's view of sensory systems and our first-person perspective on conscious perception should raise a genuine puzzle . . . about representation" (1996, p. 367). Indeed it does, and I am pressing that puzzle as hard as I can.

44.   Of course, if Freeman is right, this reply is a non-starter.

45.   It is worth noting that insofar as the properties that Akins has called 'narcissistic' fail to correlate with distal properties, then they may not even count as information-bearing ones.

46.   For a similar line, see Nagel (1980, pp. 162–164) on the contrast between objectivity and subjectivity, and on the importance of the first-person point of view in the study of human experience. See also Nagel 1986, pp. 32–37 and 60–66.

47.   To the extent that one is abnormal, to that extent one's first-person perspective would be informative of others' subjective states that share the abnormality in question, assuming that certain other cognitive/rational faculties are in place.

Chapter 6

1.   These results also have an affinity to some issues A. S. Eddington posed with his famous "two tables" and those that Wilfred Sellars raised when he contrasted what

he called the manifest and the scientific image. My theory provides the resources to better understand the issues they raised.

2.   This is how Galileo characterized the common-sense position, which he rejected, as applied to the secondary qualities. See below.

3.   Descartes distinguishes qualities we "suppose to be in objects" from "that which we experience in sensation." More specifically, he states that "we do not really know what it is that we are calling a colour, and we cannot find any intelligible resemblance between the colour which we suppose to be in objects and that which we experience in our sensations." These quotations are from the *Principles*, section 70, as reprinted in Rosenthal 1991b. Locke distinguishes "Ideas . . . as they are Ideas or Perceptions in our Minds; and as they are modifications of matter in Bodies that cause Perceptions in us." (This is from *Essay Concerning Human Understanding*, Book II, Chapter VII, as reprinted in Rosenthal 1991b.) Locke calls the former "Ideas," the latter "Qualities." In these passages, we have all but an explicit claim that 'color' is ambiguous between (1) and (2).

4.   As David Hilbert does in *Color and Color Perception* (1987).

5.   The latter is suggested by Fred Dretske (1996, p. 145) as a reason why some philosophers reject phenomenal externalism. Obviously the view presented here is in opposition to phenomenal externalism, but it does not depend on an act-object analysis of sensory experience.

6.   In characterizing them as "starting points," I do not mean to subscribe to the view that they are somehow incorrigibly given, nor do I think that what I say commits me to that. I do hold that they are, at the very least, apparent facts that require an explanation and even an eliminativist regarding them has the obligation to explain why they appear to us as they do. Compare chapter 2, where I similarly talk of certain non-phenomenal data, and chapter 1, where I discuss what "explaining the appearance" comes to.

7.   The "what it is like" aspect and how it is lacking in ordinary instruments was discussed in chapter 3, the radical differences in character that I mention was also discussed there and more fully in chapter 4.

8.   There is, of course, a sense of 'real' that is independent of the perceiver. Clearly the subjective experiences are not real in this sense but, again, that point is already embedded, and granted, in the objective/subjective distinction, so *that* cannot be at issue here.

9.   See chapter 4, where I present Galileo's account. I argue that, although it is rather successful in accounting for the degree of intensity of the qualitative feature, it fails in explaining the qualitative features themselves.

10.   Recall from chapter 3 that no one would attempt to draw any negative ontological conclusions concerning the existence of voltmeter states based on the fact

that those states are similarly dependent on the voltmeter, and there is no good reason to draw such negative conclusions concerning our subjective states and their features.

11.   Galileo, as best I can tell, was never tempted to *identify* the secondary qualities with their objective external causes, as Hilbert and other contemporary writers do. He simply denied the reality of the subjective side *because* it is subjective.

12.   I am simplifying here, as the thermodynamical concept of heat preceded that of the kinetic theory. I will be more precise regarding these matters in the next section where such differences play a more consequential role.

13.   Recourse to a dictionary to determine the meaning of 'heat' is both amusing and interesting. It is amusing because the first definition of heat is "the quality of being hot" and the first definition of 'hot' is "having much heat" (and this from *Webster's Unabridged Dictionary*, second edition, 1979!). It is interesting because in the first definition of 'heat' after stating it is "the quality of being hot," it immediately continues as follows: "hotness: in physics, heat is considered a form of energy whose effect [what effect?] is produced by the accelerated vibration of molecules . . . "; this appears to conflate the subjective and objective sense of heat, unless one takes the "quality of being hot" objectively. A number of other definitions are offered, of particular note is definition 4 of heat as a sensation, which appears to conflate the objective and the subjective: "the sensation [subjective] produced by heat [objective]; the sensation experienced [subjective] when the [sentient] body is subjected to heat [objective] from any source." Some of the more metaphorical definitions of 'heat' are exclusively subjective. I take it that this is some support for my claim that the two senses are not clearly recognized as distinct.

14.   What exactly these features are is a nice question. I try to say something about this in chapters 3 and 4. We are aware of such features when our brains are in certain states, but it is the *having* of such brain states that is crucial and, importantly, this is additional to the brain states themselves.

15.   Others—for example, J. Barry Maund (1995)—also argue for the importance of the distinction between, as he puts it, "color-as-we-experience-it" and "the cause of color-as-we-experience-it." Christopher Peacocke (1983) distinguishes color qualia from colored things, holding that, say, a green quale and green grass are not "green" in the same sense. Colin McGinn (1996) wishes to develop a theory that respects the facts that color is both subjectively constituted and a feature of external objects. He holds contrary to his earlier view that a strictly dispositional theory of color does not adequately provide for the former, what he calls the "phenomenology of color perception." Though McGinn recognizes the importance of the subjective here, his account differs significantly from my own.

16.   This is granted, in a backhanded sort of way, by Michael Tye (1995, p. 170): "For the state must surely be thought of *as* a phenomenal state, *as* having a certain

phenomenal character, if it is to be *totally* understood. It follows that anyone who thought of the essence of the state solely in terms of its tracking certain external properties . . . would not fully understand it." I do not discuss his views in detail, though I think he fails to provide the required understanding; there is no improvement in this regard in his 2000 book.

17.   Larry Hardin read an earlier draft of this chapter and generously provided me with comments and criticisms. In particular, some of his remarks are what prompted me to introduce the distinction between f- reductions and t-reductions. His comments also resulted in the elimination of several pages and the correction of some errors from the earlier draft. I am most grateful to him for his constructive assistance.

18.   Though the term 'temperature' is now well entrenched in ordinary discourse, its association with a metric suggests that its entrenchment occurred well after that of 'heat' and after the scientific means were developed to measure it.

19.   I will discuss Place's and Smart's view in more detail below, and argue that recognizing the distinction does not circumvent serious objections to the identity theory, as they formulated it.

20.   I say 'modified' since at this point it is now understood that the felt heat is not an intrinsic property of an external body.

21.   Needless to say, a full defense of this requires that I deal with a number of well-known issues that are contrary to this claim, issues first raised by Hilary Putnam. To do so here would take us too far a field, however. I hope to deal with this more fully at a future time but some relevant points have already been presented in my discussion of Twin Earth in chapter 2.

22.   One thing Place and Smart thought important about the scientific identities they used as a model for sensation–brain processes identity is that they are contingent. The 'is' of composition rather than the 'is' of definition is the kind of identity at issue, and it provides the basis for the claim that the identity between sensations and brain processes is contingent. This in turn enabled them to avoid objections, which I do not rehearse here, based on the true claim that one could know sensations without knowing anything about brain processes.

23.   The same applies to the identities discussed in the previous section. For example, we do not "experience" heat and molecular motion in the same way. There are a number of complications as to just how one would characterize how we "experience" molecular motion; dealing with these complications would take us to far a field into issues in the philosophy of science (but see below regarding the observational/theoretical distinction). It is enough for the point I wish to make here that we simply notice that it clearly is different for the two cases. Compare what I say below regarding the analogous case of detecting electrical discharge.

24.   These are not normally distinguished (e.g., Question: "What is that (flash of light) in the sky?" Answer: "It is lightning.").

25.   Smart offers no candidate for what is the publicly observable lightning; he apparently expects us to just "get it." I do not, for the reasons indicated. This lacuna in Smart's discussion masks a confusion in his view and has contributed to the obscuring of the point that I am at pains to uncover.

26.   I offered such an explanation in chapter 4.

27.   It is this psychologically immediate projection that drives the false common-sense view, discussed earlier, that the experienced sensory feature is itself a feature of the external body. It is the "transparency of experience" that Gilbert Harman and Michael Tye make so much of.

28.   For Place, the "operations" for determining one's state of consciousness with regard to sensations is simply the attentive having of them, experiences. So my dropping the qualification of 'operation' in favor of just 'experiences' in statement (3) does not give reason for Place to reject (3).

29.   A similar point was made in objection to the perspectival view of subjectivity discussed in chapter 3.

30.   Louise Antony and Joe Levine made this point in conversation. Note, also, that if the identification of sensory experiences is made with states of the brain, rather than to features external to the body, then the objection presented does not apply. For the relevant brain states are certainly involved even in color dreams, though not necessarily in precisely the same way as they are when we experience color while awake. (Whether they are the same is an empirical question.) The objection is thus avoided given this identification. This is no solace to the objectivist, for the ground for the claim that external bodies (external to the perceiver) are themselves colored or hot is also lost, since the subjective feature is identical to a brain state of the per-ceiver and these are certainly not features of bodies external to the body of the per-ceiver. Indeed, objectivists who hold that our experiences represent (e.g. Lycan, Armstrong, and Tye) sometimes appear to vacillate on just what is represented, whether it is a brain state or a quality external to the body of the perceiver.

31.   David Rosenthal (1985) argues that colors of afterimages and of physical objects are not the same. (He does so by way of criticism of Jackson's argument that the identification of color with the light reflecting properties of bodies fails because after images have color but cannot reflect light.) This is another case of a dispute that is clarified once the ideas of minimal content and objective content are recog-nized. Both Jackson and Rosenthal have a point. Jackson is focusing on the minimal content, while Rosenthal is in effect identifying one sense of color with the mini-mal content and the other with the objective content. Rosenthal goes wrong, how-ever, in that he fails to see that even when spectral reflectances are the cause of the color experience, the perceiver still has a minimal content that can be exactly like

what he has when he has an after image. So, Rosenthal is right in thinking that color is ambiguous, but he has misplaced the ambiguity.

32.   But see Hardin 1988 and 2004 for powerful arguments against this claim. The 1988 book contains a probing and deep discussion of a number of central philosophical issues concerning color. Much of my thought on color has been shaped by it.

33.   I hasten to add that, although I speak of the "qualitative content" and the "subjective referent" of color, I do not endorse, nor am I in any way committed to, a sense-data theory, or to any other theory that takes the qualitative character itself to be an object. All that is meant is that qualitative character itself can be, and is, a legitimate topic of discourse. What I have in mind is along the same lines as my earlier remarks on what are legitimate topics of discussion. Ned Block makes a similar point: " . . . the phenomenist need no[t] have any commitment to phenomenal individuals" (1996, p. 35). William Lycan (in Villanueva 1996) also makes a similar point: "A quale is, not the introspectable monadic qualitative property of an actual phenomenal individual (there being no such things), but that of *what seems to be* a phenomenal individual and is referred to, individuated and counted as such."

34.   Fred Dretske, Gilbert Harman, and William Lycan defend this position in several articles; see, for example, their papers in Villanueva 1996. John McDowell defends this view in his 1994 paper, and Michael Tye does so in his 1995 and 2000 books.

35.   Michael Tye is an objectivist who finds the idea of massive error in perception unsavory. He says that "to convict such experiences of massive error . . . is just not credible" (2000, p. 46). What support does he offer for this bold claim? Astonishingly, just a common-sense intuition: "It seems totally implausible to hold that visual experience is systematically misleading in this way." (ibid.) Having favored us with his intuition, he immediately assures us that "the qualities of which you are directly aware in focusing on the scene before your eyes and how things look are not qualities of your visual experience" (ibid.) Shall I say it? This is less than compelling.

Chapter 7

1.   Burge 1979. All page references to Burge in the present chapter are to this volume.

2.   This is reflected in Burge's willingness to call embedded that-clauses "content-clauses." We will see that Burge is not as careful as he ought to be in keeping that-clauses and mental contents distinct. A further factor contributing to the blurring of these is already present when Burge says that a that-clause '*provides* the content'. For reasons that will become clear, I prefer to say that it *expresses* the content.

3.   Here I would use the word 'express'. See the preceding note.

4.   Saying this, of course, is not to deny that there is a complex interplay between a person's linguistic abilities and their beliefs. I will have more to say about this interplay in my discussion of "sophisticated notions" below.

5.   I quote at length to provide the context for parts that I will discuss in this chapter: "We suppose that in the counterfactual case we cannot correctly ascribe any content clause containing an oblique occurrence of the term 'arthritis'. It is hard to see how the patient could have picked up the notion of arthritis. The word 'arthritis' in the counterfactual community does not mean *arthritis*. . . . We suppose that no other word in the patient's repertoire means *arthritis*. 'Arthritis', in the counterfactual situation, differs both in dictionary definition and in extension from 'arthritis' as we use it. Our ascriptions of content clauses to the patient (and ascriptions within his community) would not constitute attributions of the same contents we actually attribute. For counterpart expressions in the content clauses that are actually and counterfactually ascribable are not even extensionally equivalent. However we describe the patient's attitudes in the counterfactual situation, it will not be with a term or phrase extensionally equivalent with 'arthritis'." (79)

6.   The number of other "background beliefs" required to have the target belief are extensive and varied, for example, that the subject of the experiment has a body. There is, however, no need to make these other background beliefs explicit in the discussion of the experiment, as they do not bear directly on any possible differences in content the subject might have actually and counterfactually. Although background belief (3) is not literally part of the content of the target belief, it is important in that it bears on how the agent's expresses his target belief. Apart from this, not much in this paper turns on the distinction between component and background beliefs, although I think there are important applications of it. There is some kinship between the very rough distinction as I have drawn it and the rather detailed account of a more general distinction between what Searle (1983) has called the Network and the (local) Background.

7.   I will go further than Crane by arguing below that the *having* of a sophisticated notion *requires* linguistic capabilities; moreover, I will argue that these capabilities need to be actualized to carry out the experiment, and that this requires that the agent has various beliefs, such as (3), pertaining to the use of words in his community. I take it that Crane would be sympathetic to my claim that Bert has belief (3). However, unlike me, Crane adopts a reinterpretation strategy: he ultimately argues that the subject of the experiment has a true belief involving a different notion of *tharthritis* (1991, pp. 18–22). As I have already indicated, I do not think reinterpretation is the way to go. However, I do agree with Crane's conclusion that Burge's thought experiment does not establish that intentional states are broad, though my argument for this is clearly different. I also note that In the same essay Crane argues that Putnam's famous Twin-Earth thought experiment also fails to establish that intentional states are broad. He concludes from his discussion of Putnam and Burge that we do not need a notion of narrow content, for he maintains that its intro-

duction was simply a response to the worries they raise, and he thinks he has put such worries to rest. I too have argued, though differently, for the deflation of the Twin-Earth experiment (see chapter 2), and I am here doing the same for Burge's thought experiment. I obviously disagree, however, with Crane's further conclusion, namely, that once these experiments are dispensed with no notion of narrow content is needed (23–24). In chapter 1, I argued for a new kind of narrow content, *minimal content*, independent of Burge's and Putnam's thought experiments, that is necessary for an adequate account of intentionality and phenomenality. In chapter 2 and in the present chapter, I have pressed this concept into service to deflate both experiments. (For a discussion of Putnam's thought experiment, see chapter 2 above.)

8.   The arguments of this chapter are mostly the same as those in my 1999 paper. Anthony Brueckner (2001) has challenged the sufficiency of (1)–(3) by offering a counterexample. In my 2003b paper, I argue that his challenge fails. My response to Brueckner is included in a separate section below.

9.   Rod Bertolet commented on a much shorter version of this paper at a meeting of the Central States Philosophical Association (Mt. Pleasant, Michigan, 1995). He raised some extremely useful criticisms that greatly assisted me in making important clarifications and changes in the paper. I am deeply grateful to him for the criticisms.

10.   As Burge himself has correctly argued (101), were the subject confronted with his deviation, he would not persist, insisting he meant something different, rather he would correct his word usage and, I would add, not insignificantly, his understanding of the notion associated with the word.

11.   Although I agree with Burge that the patient's deviance does not force any reinterpretation of his notion, the difference between Burge and me on the formulation of this deviance is critical. Ultimately, it comes down to whether claims pertaining to deviance should be formulated as (1) the individual has "the same notion," in *some loose sense*, but is still a bit off, which is what I will argue for, or as (2) he has the *exact* same notion, and his deviance is due to errors in his understanding. The latter formulation requires a distinct—but untenable—demarcation between one's having or understanding a notion and relevant collateral information. I argue for this below.

12.   But see the previous note and relevant text below as to the difficulty in formulating, in a neutral way, this deviance. This difficulty ensues because Burge and I locate the source of the deviance differently.

13.   This is not unusual when translating from one language to another. In fact it is curious that in one of Burge's criticisms of a metalinguistic approach, he uses the case of a foreigner sharing a notion with us but lacking the term we use as *no* reason to deny that the foreigner shares our notion (96). Perhaps Burge is assuming

here that the foreigner has some *other* term in his own language whose dictionary definition and extension is equivalent to our own, as is frequently the case. My point is broader: even if the foreign language lacks any extensionally equivalent term, a native speaker of that language may still have a notion which coincides with one of ours, though his notion would then deviate some from his fellows. And, as I have just argued, if this were not possible, Burge's thought experiment cannot even get started.

14.   As with minimal contents, the first-person perspective is essential for the concept of individual notions, though that of community notion is wide. The latter wide concept bears a direct relation to meaning. Despite the fact that meaning is a wide concept, I will argue in chapter 8 that the first-person perspective plays a crucial role in determining *which* meaning is at issue. Keeping apart the concepts of *meaning* and *which meaning* is, we shall see, very important. Finally, the discussion in chapter 8 of how the first-person perspective is related to questions about meaning contributes to an understanding of how individuals' notions and meanings are related.

15.   My position does not deny that what notions one has is partly dependent on one's understanding of them: One cannot think that arthritis has nothing to do with either aches or joints and still be said to have the community notion of arthritis. See my discussion of the difference between understanding and individuating a content in chapter 1, as it bears on a related difference between Burge and me.

16.   Compare my thesis that thoughts are systematically ambiguous between a subjective and objective reading (chapter 1) and my discussion of Twin Earth (chapter 2).

17.   In chapter 2, I examine the complicated relations between the extension of a term, the extension for an agent, and the term's application by an agent, and I argue that neither different extensions nor different applications of terms imply different mental contents. These results are grounded on my concept of minimal content, argued for in chapter 1.

18.   In this article Brueckner discusses my 1999 paper. The present chapter includes all the material presented in that paper.

19.   Of course, if Brueckner's objections to the part of my argument he does address were sustainable, *and* if he were to show that they disable the rest of my argument, then there would be no need to fully deal with the remainder of my argument. But to show the latter conjunct he would, at the very least, have to recognize those parts of my argument that I will demonstrate he ignores.

20.   Brueckner quickly raises several "doubts" about my claim that (1)–(3) is necessary (388), but he elects to pass on these. He neither explicates nor supports these doubts, but I will comment on two of them. He wonders if (1)–(3) are necessary if the subject of the experiment spoke only German, but he fails to mention that I explicitly deal with just such a case (1999, pp. 149–150). Another doubt he raises

concerns my formulation of (1), which originally read "There is an ache in my thigh" (1999, p. 148); Brueckner thinks that it suggests that arthritis always aches. That this is so is not clear to me, but in any case, I have changed (1) to "Sometimes my thigh aches." This change has no repercussions for my argument.

21.   The issues dealt with include the following: • That mental contents or notions need not be linguistic; so creatures lacking language may still have mental notions. • That having a sophisticated notion, such as *arthritis*, does require linguistic ability, but it does not require that they be English speakers and that they have the word 'arthritis' in their vocabulary. As a result, (3) needs to be indexed to the language of the agent. • Whether my analysis is unduly epistemological. (It is not.) • Although (3) is part of my analysis of the target belief, my analysis is not metalinguistic in a way that would make it subject to any of Burge's many arguments against "meta-linguistic approaches."

22.   When I argued against Burge's widely accepted view in my 1999 paper, I hoped for responses but feared neglect. I did not expect to receive both in the same paper, as I did in Brueckner's.

Chapter 8

1.   I will typically indicate intended reference and interpretation as IR and II, not so much as to save space as to remind the reader that I wish these expressions to be understood in certain specific ways; I am not simply appealing to their vernacular meanings. Though what I say of them is not unrelated to the vernacular, it is narrower in scope.

2.   Hereafter, Quine's *Ontological Relativity and Other Essays* (Columbia University Press, 1969) will be cited as *OR*.

3.   The concepts of ideal agent, individual, and community notions were discussed in some detail in chapter 7.

4.   Of course there are exceptions. See Quine on suspending the homophonic rule of translation (1969, p. 46).

5.   To speak thus of the "usual purported denotation" we must assume that in fact we know what others' IRs are and they are the same as one's own; what grounds there are for making such an assumption and the extent to which admitting II (IR) leads to a privacy of language will be considered below.

6.   I assume, as I think Quine does, that the native is a standard or typical language user.

7.   Quine allows that expressions such as 'the speaker's intended reference' have some *practical* value; this reflects his attitude toward intentional idioms generally. See *WO*, p. 221.

8.   Compare my discussion of similar problems regarding the determination of another's minimal content in chapters 1 and 3.

9.   The reasoning here is similar to that which leads one to mistakenly think that one must move to a second-order thought to talk of self-consciousness; it results from applying a strictly third-person methodology where it is inappropriate. (See chapter 2.)

10.   We will see that Quine appears to make a similar move to the one I just made when he speaks of "taking words at face value." I will argue that this move cannot do the same work for him as it does for me because he restricts himself to a third-person methodology.

11.   Long ago Chisholm argued that terms such as 'meaning' and 'reference' can only be analyzed in terms of intentional idioms such as 'takes there to be', 'believe' and 'ascribe'. I take this view, though not directed overtly against Quine's, to be compatible with mine. In fact at the end of "Sentences about Believing" (1956) he sketches a position one might take against himself, one that sounds very Quinean, though not exclusively so. It is to the effect that intentional sentences are not factual; this is reflected in Quine, when he denies there is a correct answer as to which translation to attribute to a speaker, and that the inscrutability of reference, is not an inscrutability of a fact.

12.   See, e.g., p. 92 of Quine 1960 and pp. 6–11 of *OR*.

13.   This last point is complicated for a variety of reasons. One is that in the context of radical translation one is basically assuming that one's respondents are representative of their community, that their IRs match those of the communities, match the objective references of the terms.

14.   These roughly correspond to appealing to paraphrase and ostension, respectively, discussed above.

15.   None of the preceding should be construed as saying anything about ontic reference. To talk of the "usual denotations" of a term is to talk of the inter-subjective agreement on the kinds of objects that the speakers of the language *take there to be*, and it is not to say anything about what is "really" in the world (though some may wish to take this further step). When we speak of the objects we take there to be— the usual denotations of our referring terms—we are, of course, not merely speaking of stimulations, nor of phonemic or inscriptional types (formal languages). The stimulations are the signs or evidence for the objects that are purported to be in the world. At the level of the individual agent, this is the intended reference; where there is a presumption of identity across agents' intended references it is objective reference. Both of these are independent of ontic reference.

16.   Hereafter, *Word and Object* (Quine 1960) will be cited as *WO*.

17.   The propensity to underplay the semantic part can be seen in Quine's early article "Meaning in Linguistics" (in Quine 1961). Quine consigns the semantical

part of linguistics to lexicography where the focus is on synonymy and 'having meaning' or 'significant' rather than 'meaning'. He then goes on to locate the problem of significance with the grammarian whom he describes as cataloguing short forms and working out the laws of their concatenation resulting in the class of all significant sequences. Notice though that the result is the class of all syntactically significant sequences (short forms and their permissible concatenations), not semantic significance. In fairness, he does eventually acknowledge that the grammarian needs over and above formal construction a prior notion of significant sequence for the setting of his problem and Quine admits he thereby draws on the old notion of meaning. He nevertheless does not alter the notion of a significant sequence in his article and on considering what he has said in *OR* on knowing a word it would seem that he is still leaning toward the syntactic line. Why he would do so is clear; syntax is more likely to be behaviorally ascertainable, semantics beyond use, is not.

18.   The latter conjunct does obtain if indeterminacy of translation applies to oneself, but this begs the question. For with II fully admitted, we do not have first person indeterminacy and then the second conjunct does not follow from the first.

19.   Certain distinctions must be kept clear. The sense in which the alternatives are equivalent is the sense in which the method of stimulus classes cannot distinguish them. The alternatives are not equivalent in the sense that what the sentences *assert* on different manuals is the same. At least they are different from an ordinary point of view or once intended interpretation is admitted. The properties of, say, rabbits are quite different from the properties of rabbit stages. I accept that the alternatives are equivalent in the first sense without accepting that they are equivalent in the latter sense. More on this later.

20.   If the alternatives were not genuinely different then what point would there be in intending one rather than another? The answer would seem to be that there is no point to it, and Quine would be right in rejecting the idea that some single manual is the correct one. But even this defense only works *provided* one *knows* the alternatives are equivalent. Thus, even granting the equivalence of alternatives, in some very strong sense, there would still be *some* point to maintaining a speaker intended one rather than another, provided she does not know they are equivalent. To maintain this in the situation envisioned would not lack significance. Thus, if I intend to be talking about enduring things and do *not know* that I could be equivalently, if it is equivalently, be talking about stages, then there is still some point to saying that I *intend* the one alternative and not the other. (We are here of course engaged with difficulties of substituting in opaque contexts: S intends a, and a is equivalent to b, though S does not know the latter, and hence, it is not the case that S intends b.) Independent of this, I argue that the alternatives are indeed different, but that aside, we still see that there is still some point to our talking of an individual intending one interpretation rather than another, even if the interpretations are equivalent, so long as the individual is ignorant of the equivalence. I do not put

much in this last argument, as Quine could with some plausibility respond that the ignorance supposed in the case reflects his point, made earlier, that the manuals seem different when parts are considered apart from the whole. I mention it primarily because I think the indicated connection of these issues to those surrounding opaque contexts my be of some interest.

21.   As I said, this is a view of Quine's that goes back at least to his 1961 book (pp. 40–43) and is echoed in *WO* (pp. 78–79), where he applies this idea to individual sentences in general (excepting observation sentences, which I will discuss in the next chapter).

22.   The latter locution is to be taken as a one-word observation sentence.

23.   I.e. "the grand synthetic one" that the individual ones add up to.

24.   It is interesting to compare Quine's demonstration of the inadequacy of a strictly third-person methodology to distinguish alternative translations with Dretske's demonstration of the inadequacy of that method to uncover consciousness, which I took note of in chapter 3. I accept their results but take them as a reductio of their positions.

25.   Effectively Quine is appealing to a verificationist principle. Such an appeal is explicit on p. 80 of *OR*, and comes under the guise of naturalism in *OR*—see especially pp. 29–30. His use of it to deny that there is a correct answer considered below, occurs at p. 78, *WO*, pp. 46–47, *OR* and in his discussion of the protosyntactician and arithmetician, pp. 41–43, *OR*.

26.   My argument here does not depend upon the correctness of the dynamical theory of conscious states presented earlier. The argument goes through with just the assumption that the semantic correlations are somehow realized in the bilinguals' brains, which Quine grants.

27.   Note that determining the different brain states would be objective even in the narrow sense, relying on a strictly third-person methodology.

28.   The quotation is from Dewey.

29.   In the passage just quoted, Quine seamlessly moves from the claim that meaning is primarily a property of behavior to the claim that there are no meanings beyond what is implicit in people's dispositions to behave. Clearly, the latter does not follow from the former.

30.   Compare also the discussion of objective knowledge of the subjective in chapter 3.

31.   For convenience, I quote one of the relevant passages at length: "I have urged in defense of the behavioral philosophy of language, Dewey's, that the inscrutability of reference is not the inscrutability of fact; there is no fact of the matter. But if there really is no fact of the matter, then the inscrutability of reference can be

brought even closer to home than the neighbor's case; we can apply it to ourselves. If it is to make sense to say even of oneself that one is referring to rabbits and formulas and not to rabbit stages and Gödel numbers, then it should make sense equally to say it of someone else. After all, as Dewey stressed, there is no private language." (*OR*, p. 47) Of course, having just argued that it makes no sense to say it of our neighbor and barring a private language, Quine concludes it make no sense in our own case.

32.   See Searle 1987. Searle and I agree that Quine illegitimately overlooks the first-person perspective. There are numerous other points of agreement between Searle and me regarding what is wrong with Quine's view; still, there are significant differences between us regarding the inscrutability of reference and, more generally, on the status and analysis of privileged access.

33.   Quine 1970, p. 182.

34.   Quine (1970, p. 182) takes a different tack: "When this kind of hint is available, should we say that the supposed multiplicity of choices was not in fact open after all? Or should we say that the choice is open but that we have found a practical consideration that will help us in choosing? The issue is palpably unreal. . . ." He must claim that "the issue is palpably unreal," for if he takes the first alternative—choice among the alternatives was not open—he looses the indeterminacy of translation; whereas, if he takes the second alternative, he would be allowing that there is some reason to consider one of the alternatives as "better" than others, even though not a one of them is contradicted by the method of stimulus classes. But for Quine, from a theoretical point of view, we can ask for no more than that the alternatives are not contradicted by the application of this method; so, he rejects the very significance of questions that do presume more: "The question whether . . . the foreigner *really* believes A or believes rather B is a question whose very significance I would put in doubt. This is what I am getting at in arguing the indeterminacy of translation." (1970, pp. 180–181) Indeed, as earlier quoted, he says: "we recognize that there are no meanings, nor likenesses, nor distinctions of meanings, beyond what are implicit in people's dispositions to overt behavior." (*OR*, p. 29)

Chapter 9

1.   Quine qualifies the inscrutability of reference here as *behaviorally* inscrutable; this is a qualification he normally suppresses.

2.   A similar and related point arose in my discussion of Twin Earth in chapter 2, where I argued that different extensions do not automatically imply different thought contents, for the subject of the thought content could be understood as either the minimal or objective content. See also my discussion of Burge in chapter 7.

3.   Fodor (1994) criticized Quine's claim of the inscrutability of reference for different reasons than I do. I argued in my 2000b paper that Fodor's criticism fails.

4.   Quine explicitly holds that it makes no sense to say what there is apart from doing so in some background language (see also *OR*, p. 68), but there are many other instances.

5.   Of course, there is a trivial and uninformative way that we can do this: What is there? Everything."

6.   Quine maintains that a realist view of physics is quite compatible with his position. See Davidson and Hintikka 1969, particularly p. 294 but also p. 303. Those who have read Quine over the years are familiar with this recurring claim in many of his works.

7.   I am deeply grateful to Professor Quine for his correspondence with me over several years on early versions of the material in this and the next several sections. Subsequent notes will indicate some of the points on which we came to agree and some which we did not.

8.   "I must grant the point, near the end of your paper, that taking the sophisticated observation sentences holophrastically does not free . . . their dependence on theory." (letter to me, December 13, 1993) Quine makes this explicit on p. 163 of his 1996 paper.

9.   See pp. 9, 13, and 14 of *WO*. Also the idea of an *occasion sentence* as there presented (ibid., 35–40), though broader than that of a one-word observation sentence, includes it. (See also p. 95, where he speaks of an *undifferentiated occasion sentence*.) In these cases, he is dealing with a string of marks or a sequence of sounds treated as a whole and geared to stimulation, with no attempt at parsing or the assignment of objects to terms. On the other hand, Quine also treats observation sentences, even when parsed, as occasion sentences. (See, e.g., 1960, pp. 40–46; 1993, pp. 108–109.) However, that a parsed observation sentence can be an occasion sentence is essentially dependent on its parsed history, where certain collateral information or prior theoretical considerations are the basis for the connection between current stimulation and utterance or assent to the sentence at issue. Treating parsed observation sentences as occasion sentences is of a piece with the mistakes of merging sentences of what I will call below levels 1 and 3 (because each can be treated holophrastically) and holding that they are up to doing the same epistemic work. I argue that such occasion or level-3 sentences cannot do the same epistemic work as one-word observation sentences (level 1). This is because collateral or theoretical considerations are involved in level- 3 sentences. For epistemic purposes, the levels must be kept distinct.

10.   He later remarks that a number of problems pertaining to observation and its epistemic value can be avoided by focusing on observation sentences rather than observation terms, and "Neurath and Carnap were on the right track here, in focusing on protocol sentences. But terms predominated in Carnap's further writings" (1993, p. 110). Thus, we have Quine's own emphasis on the holophrastic rather than piecemeal construal of observation sentences.

11.   Quine, in response to this particular passage, wrote: "On the contrary. I have not seen your 'objection' as an objection. It was what I had happily intended all along." (letter to me, February 23, 1997). That he intends this I certainly will not dispute. That one can embrace this point and still claim that these observation sentences are common reference points for incommensurable theories and also serve to buttress a scientific realism is precisely what I argue cannot be done. The reader must decide whether I have succeeded.

12.   This example was also discussed in on pp. 11–12 of Quine 1960.

13.   An unexpected bonus for a Kuhnian emerges. Proto-observation sentences may serve to answer those critics of Kuhn who have argued that his incommensurability thesis is incompatible with his claim that such theories are competing. How, the objection goes, can we say the theories are competing if they are incommensurable? The answer to such a worry might be: We know the theories are in competition because the same range of proto-observation sentences is at issue. This is consistent with their being incommensurable, for the latter turns on the piecemeal treatment of the sentences.

14.   Insofar as primitive observation sentences do treat of external things, present impingements are not sufficient for them—given indeterminacy of translation. Proto-observation sentences do not treat of external things—they do not treat of things at all, not even sensations. As I understand it, that is precisely why present impingements are sufficient for them. Thus, proto-observation sentences are not affected by radical translation, unlike primitive observation sentences. Primitive observation sentences, in general, do presume a "theory," albeit a widely shared one. Of course, if the competing theories are not fundamental or global, they will agree on a huge number of assumptions and so, relative to *those* theories, no questions are begged when appeal to such observation sentences is made. In that case, however, we are not looking at any fundamental epistemic or ontological issue, and there is room to question the scientist further.

15.   In another earlier letter (in response to questions concerning similar points which I put to him in the spring of 1992), Quine states: "Where then is our objectivity? Just at the checkpoints where, thanks to psychological conditioning, neural inputs are linked to our conceptual scheme; namely, the observation sentences. The objectivity of science consists in prediction of observation." But is this enough objectivity to adjudicate between theories or secure scientific realism? I think not. They do, as Quine notes, serve as *negative* checkpoints (1993, p. 111), but they cannot yield positive answers to such questions. As already observed, empirically equivalent theories must make the same predictions of proto-observation sentences; this is a necessary condition of their empirical equivalence. So this much objectivity cannot decide between them. If we move to primitive or level-3 sentences, knowledge of the world is presupposed. So using these sentences would leave one open to the

very criticism which necessitated the pristine observation sentences of level 1. Compare my discussion above.

16.   Giving (3) this "linguistic" reading fits well with what Quine has said of ontological relativity more recently (1992b, pp. 51–52): ". . . I can now say what ontological relativity is relative to, more succinctly than I did in the lectures, paper, and book of that title. It is relative to a manual of translation. To say that 'gavagai' denotes rabbits is to opt for a manual of translation in which 'gavagai' is translated as 'rabbit', instead of opting for any of the alternative manuals."

17.   Of course, Carnap allowed that various pragmatic considerations may lead us to adopt or prefer one over another.

18.   In fact, Quine rejects Carnap's internal/external distinction (see, e.g., *OR*, pp. 52–53), so one must not take the parallel I draw here too literally.

19.   Both essays appear in *Ontological Relativity and Other Essays* (1969). For interesting twists on the idea of perceptual similarity, see Quine 1996, pp. 160–162.

20.   The various moves and their shortcomings are outlined in Carl Hempel's widely anthologized classic "Empiricist Criteria of Cognitive Significance: Problems and Changes" (1950/2001).

21.   To better see this, consider one who was not trained by someone in the know and who, by most improbable chance, uttered 'There-is-copper-in-it' when appropriately stimulated. In such circumstances, the utterance would correctly be considered a one-word observation sentence, but *it would bear no linguistic relation* to the phonetically or typographically similar English sentence. Any other sounds or marks would have served as well. That this particular sequence of sounds or marks was used would be a stupendous coincidence. For such a case to have any bearing on the issues at hand, theory must have intruded somewhere, even if it did not for the ignorant subject being conditioned. I thank Ümit Yalçın for raising the possibility of someone being holophrastically conditioned to a level-3 sentence.

22.   To illustrate, consider the following sentences uttered under appropriate stimulatory conditions: "There is a cup on the desk." "There is a jet passing overhead." (as when one witnesses a stream of smoke in the sky, but not directly the jet) "There is a mass spectrometer on the desk." "There is copper in it." (as in the discussion of the chemistry example of level 3). All these are quickly decidable by anyone having the relevant knowledge and presented with the appropriate stimulatory conditions; they are all, we may allow, observation sentences. There is also some reason to maintain that as we move from the first to the last, these sentences become increasingly theory laden. The community of normal speakers of the language to which these are observational becomes ever slightly smaller as we move down the list. So the first has a higher degree of observationality to it than does the last.

23.   Just what gives rise to degrees of observationality in Quine is complicated. On p. 110 of the 1993 paper it is their theory-ladenness, their piecemeal treatment, that brings about the degrees of observationality, as it was for the positivists. But on pp. 108–109 Quine states that the degrees of observationality are attributable to two additional factors: how quickly is the quickly decidable sentence decided and whether it is corrigible. These factors, no doubt, are related to the sentences being treated in a piecemeal fashion, but they are additional. Put these complications aside. As we will presently see, these complications take a somewhat new twist in Quine's 1996 paper.

24.   These reflections were prompted by a letter from Lars Bergstrom. In addition, in a letter to me (February 20, 1996), he reports that "the degrees of observationality are rescinded in 'Progress [On Two Fronts]'."

References

Akins, K. 1996. Of Sensory Systems and the "Aboutness" of Mental States. *Journal of Philosophy* 93: 337–372.

Alexander, D. M., and G. G. Globus. 1996. Edge-of-Chaos Dynamics in Recursively Organized Neural Systems. In *Fractals of Brain, Fractals of Mind*, ed. E. MacCormac and M. Stamenov. John Benjamins.

Anderson, C. M., and A. J. Mandell. 1996. Fractal Time and the Foundations of Consciousness: Vertical Convergence of 1/f Phenomena from Ion Channels to Behavioral States. In *Fractals of Brain, Fractals of Mind*, ed. E. MacCormac and M. Stamenov. John Benjamins.

Armstrong, D. M. 1963. "Is Introspective Knowledge Incorrigible?" *Philosophical Review* 72, no. 4: 417–432. Reprinted in *The Nature of Mind*, ed. D. Rosenthal (Oxford University Press, 1991).

Armstrong, D. M. 1968. *A Materialist Theory of the Mind*. Humanities Press.

Armstrong, D. M. 1973. *Belief, Truth, and Knowledge*. Cambridge University Press.

Beckermann, A. 1988. Why Tropistic Systems Are Not Genuine Intentional Systems. *Erkenntnis* 29: 125–142.

Benacerraf, P. 1965. What Numbers Could Not Be. *Philosophical Review* 74: 47–73. Reprinted in *Philosophy of Mathematics: Selected Readings*, second edition, ed. P. Benacerraf and H. Putnam. Cambridge University Press, 1983.

Block, N. 1978. Troubles with Functionalism. In *Perception and Cognition: Issues in the Foundation of Psychology*, ed. C. Savage. University of Minnesota Press.

Block, N. 1986. Advertisement for a Semantics for Psychology. In *Midwest Studies in the Philosophy of Mind*, no. 10, ed. P. French et al. University of Minnesota Press.

Block, N. 1996. Mental Paint and Mental Latex. In *Perception*, ed. E. Villanueva. Ridgeview.

Brueckner, A. 2001. Defending Burge's Thought Experiment. *Erkenntnis* 55: 387–391.

Burge, T. 1979. Individualism and the Mental. In *Midwest Studies in Philosophy*, volume 4, ed. P. French et al. University of Minnesota Press.

Burge, T. 1988. Individualism and Self-Knowledge. *Journal of Philosophy* 85: no. 5: 258–269.

Burge, T. 1992. Philosophy of Language and Mind: 1950–1990. *Philosophical Review* 101: 3–51.

Burge, T. 1997. Two Kinds of Consciousness. In *The Nature of Consciousness*, ed. N. Block et al. MIT Press.

Carnap, R. 1956. Empiricism, Semantics, and Ontology. In *Meaning and Necessity*, enlarged edition. University of Chicago Press.

Chalmers, D. 1996. *The Conscious Mind: In Search of a Fundamental Theory*. Oxford University Press.

Chalmers, D. 2002, ed. *The Philosophy of Mind*. Oxford University Press.

Chisholm, R. 1956. Sentences about Believing. In *Minnesota Studies in the Philosophy of Science*, vol. 2, ed. H. Feigl and M. Scriven. University of Minnesota Press.

Chisholm, R. 1976. *Person and Object*. Allen and Unwin.

Churchland, P. M. 1979. *Scientific Realism and the Plasticity of Mind*. Cambridge University Press.

Churchland, P. S. 1986. *Neurophilosophy: Toward a Unified Theory of Mind/Brain*. MIT Press.

Churchland, P. S. 1996. The Hornswoggle Problem. www.merlin.com.au/brain_proj/psch_2.htm.

Churchland, P. S., and P. M. Churchland. 1983. Stalking the Wild Epistemic Engine. *Nous* 17: 5–18.

Churchland, P. S., and P. M. Churchland. 1998. *On the Contrary: Critical Essays, 1987–1997*. MIT Press.

Crane, T. 1991. All the Differences in the World. *Philosophical Quarterly* 41: 1–25.

Crane, T. 2001. *Elements of Mind*. Oxford University Press

Crane, T. 2003. The Intentional Structure of Consciousness. In *Consciousness*, ed. Q. Smith and A. Jokic. Oxford University Press.

Davidson, D., and Jaakko Hintikka, eds. 1969. *Words and Objections: Essays on the Work of W. V. Quine*. Reidel.

Davidson, D. 1984. First Person Authority. *Dialectia* 38: 101–111.

Davidson, D. 1987. Knowing One's Own Mind. *Proceedings and Addresses of the APA* 60: 441–458.

Davidson, D. 1988. Reply to Burge. *Journal of Philosophy* 85: 664–665.

Davies, M., and G. W. Humphreys, eds. 1993. *Consciousness*. Blackwell.

Dennett, D. 1978. A Cure for the Common Code? *Brainstorms*. MIT Press.

Dennett, D. 1987. True Believers. In Dennett, *The Intentional Stance*. MIT Press.

Dennett, D. 1991. Real Patterns. *Journal of Philosophy* 88, no. 1: 27–51.

Dretske, F. I. 1985. Machines and the Mental. *Proceedings and Addresses of the American Philosophical Association* 59: 23–33.

Dretske, F. I. 1996. Phenomenal Externalism. In *Perception*, ed. E. Villanueva. Ridgeview.

Dretske, F. I. 1997. *Naturalizing the Mind*. MIT Press.

Dretske, F. I. 2003. "How Do You Know You're Not a Zombie?" In *Privileged Access*, ed. B. Gertle. Ashgate.

Eckhorn, R., R. Bauer, W. Jordan, M. Brosch, W. Kruse, M. Munk, and H. Reitboeck. 1988. Coherent Oscillations: A Mechanism of Feature Linking in Visual Cortex? *Biological Cybernetics* 60: 121–130.

Fodor, J. 1986. Why Paramecia Don't Have Mental Representations. In *Midwest Studies in Philosophy*, volume 10, ed. P. French et al.. University of Minnesota Press.

Fodor, J. 1988. *Psychosemantics: The Problem of Meaning in the Philosophy of Mind*. MIT Press.

Fodor, J. 1994. *The Elm and the Expert*. MIT Press.

Freeman, W. J. 1991. The Physiology of Perception. *Scientific American* 264, no. 2: 78–85.

Freeman, W. J. 1992. Tutorial on Neurobiology: From Single Neurons to Brain Chaos. *International Journal of Bifurcation and Chaos* 2, no. 3: 451–482.

Freeman, W. J. 1995. *Societies of Brains: A Study in the Neuroscience of Love and Hate*. Erlbaum.

Freeman, W. J. 1996. Interview with Jean Burns: Societies of Brains. *Journal of Consciousness Studies* 3, no. 2: 172–180.

Freeman, W. J., and K. Maurer. 1989. Advances in Brain Theory Give New Directions to the Use of the Technologies of Brain Mapping in Behavioral Studies. In *Proceedings, Conference on Topographic Brain Mapping*, ed. K. Maurer. Springer-Verlag.

Freeman, W. J., and B. Van Dijk. 1987. Spatial Patterns of Visual Cortical Fast EEG during Conditioned Reflex in a Rhesus Monkey. *Brain Research* 422: 267–276.

Galileo Galilei. 1623. *The Assayer*. Reprinted in part as "Two Kinds of Properties" in *Philosophy of Science*, ed. A. Danto and S. Morgenbesser (Meridian, 1960).

Georgalis, N. 1974. Indeterminacy of Translation and Intended Interpretation. Ph.D. dissertation, University of Chicago.

Georgalis, N. 1986. Intentionality and Representation. *International Studies in Philosophy* 18: 45–58.

Georgalis, N. 1990 No Access for the Externalist. *Mind* 99: 101–108.

Georgalis, N. 1994. Asymmetry of Access to Intentional States. *Erkenntnis* 40: 85–11.

Georgalis, N. 1995. Review: *The Nature of True Minds*. *Philosophical Psychology* 8, no. 2: 189–193.

Georgalis, N. 1996. Awareness, Understanding, and Functionalism. *Erkenntnis* 44: 225–256.

Georgalis, N. 1999. Rethinking Burge's Thought Experiment. *Synthese* 118: 145–164.

Georgalis, N. 2000a. Minds, Brains, and Chaos. In *The Cauldron of Consciousness*, ed. R. Ellis and N. Newton. John Benjamins.

Georgalis, N. 2000b. Reference Remains Inscrutable. *Pacific Philosophical Quarterly* 81, no. 2: 123–130.

Georgalis, N. 2003a. The Fiction of Phenomenal Intentionality. *Consciousness and Emotion* 4: 243–256.

Georgalis, N. 2003b. Burge's Thought Experiment: Still in Need of a Defense. *Erkenntnis* 58: 267–273.

Georgalis, N. 2006. Representation and the First-Person Perspective. *Synthese* 149: 3.

Gray, C., P. Koenig, K. A. Engel, and W. Singer. 1989. Oscillatory Responses in Cat Visual Cortex Exhibit Intercolumnar Synchronization Which Reflects Global Stimulus Properties. *Nature* 338: 334–337.

Hardin, C. L. 1988. *Color for Philosophers: Unweaving the Rainbow*. Hackett.

Hardin, C. L. 2004. A Green Thought in a Green Shade. *Harvard Review of Philosophy* 12: 29–39.

Harman, G. 1990. The Intrinsic Quality of Experience. In *Philosophical Perspectives*, volume 4: *Action Theory and Philosophy of Mind*, ed. J. Tomberlin. Ridgeview.

Heil, J. 1980. Cognition and Representation. *Australasian Journal of Philosophy* 58, no. 2: 159–168.

Heil, J. 1988. Privileged Access. *Mind* 97: 238–251.

Heil, J. 1992. *The Nature of True Minds*. Cambridge University Press.

Heil, J. 1998. Supervenience Deconstructed. *European Journal of Philosophy* 6, no. 2: 146–155.

Hempel, C. G. 1950. Empiricist Criteria of Cognitive Significance: Problems and Changes. Reprinted in *The Philosophy of Language*, ed. A. Martinich (Oxford University Press, 2001).

Hilbert, D. 1987. *Color and Color Perception: A Study in Anthropocentric Realism*. Center for the Study of Language and Information.

Horgan, T., and Tienson, J. 2002. The Intentionality of Phenomenology and the Phenomenology of Intentionality. In *The Philosophy of Mind*, ed. D. Chalmers. Oxford University Press.

Jackson, F. 1986. What Mary Didn't Know. *Journal of Philosophy* 83: 291–295.

Kitcher, P. 1993. Function and Design. In *Midwest Studies in Philosophy*, volume 18, ed P. French et al. University of Notre Dame Press.

Kripke, S. 1982. *Wittgenstein on Rules and Private Language*. Harvard University Press.

Kelso, J. A. S. 1997. *Dynamical Patterns*. MIT Press.

King, C. 1996. Fractal Neurodynamics and Quantum Chaos: Resolving the Mind-Brain Paradox through Novel Biophysics. In *Fractals of Brain, Fractals of Mind*, ed. E. MacCormac and M. Stamenov. John Benjamins.

Levine, J. 1983. Materialism and Qualia: The Explanatory Gap. *Pacific Philosophical Quarterly* 64: 354–361.

Lewis, D. 1988. What Experience Teaches. In *Mind and Cognition*, ed. W. Lycan. Blackwell.

Loar, B. 1988. Social Content and Psychological Content. In *Thought and Content*, ed. R. Grimm and D. Merrill. University of Arizona Press. Reprinted in *The Nature of Mind*, ed. D. Rosenthal (Oxford University Press, 1991).

Lycan, W. G. 1987. Phenomenal Objects: A Backhanded Defense. In *Philosophical Perspectives*, volume 1: *Metaphysics*, ed. J. Tomberlin. Ridgeview.

Lycan, W. G. 1996. *Consciousness and Experience*. MIT Press.

Lycan, W. G. 1999. The Plurality of Consciousness. Reprinted in *Proceedings of the Sixth International Colloquium on Cognitive Science*, ed. J. Larrazabal and L. Perez Miranda (Kluwer, 2004).

Lycan, W. G. 2001. The Case for Phenomenal Externalism. *Philosophical Perspectives* 15: 17–35.

Lycan, W. G. 2003. Perspectual Representation and the Knowledge Argument. In *Consciousness*, ed. Q. Smith and A. Jokic. Oxford University Press.

MacCormac, E. 1996a. Fractal Thinking: Self-Organizing Brain Processing. In *Fractals of Brain, Fractals of Mind*, ed. E. MacCormac and M. Stamenov. John Benjamins.

MacCormac, E., and M. Stamenov, eds. 1996b. *Fractals of Brain, Fractals of Mind*. John Benjamins.

Macphail, E. M. 1987. The Comparative Psychology of Intelligence. *Behavioral and Brain Sciences* 10: 645–695.

Macphail, E. M. 1990. *Behavioral and Brain Sciences* 13: 391–398.

Martinich, A. P., ed. 1990. *The Philosophy of Language*, second edition. Oxford University Press.

Maund, J. B. 1995. *Colours: Their Nature and Representation*. Cambridge University Press.

McDowell, J. 1994. The Content of Perceptual Experience. *Philosophical Quarterly* 44, no. 175: 139–153.

McGeer, V. 1996. Is "Self-Knowledge" an Empirical Problem? Renegotiating the Space of Philosophical Explanation. *Journal of Philosophy* 93: 483–515.

McGinn, C. 1989. Can We Solve the Mind-Body Problem? *Mind* 98: 349–366.

McGinn, C. 1996. Another Look at Color. *Journal of Philosophy* 93, no. 11: 537–553.

Millikan, R. 1984. *Language, Thought, and Other Biological Categories: New Foundations for Realism*. MIT Press.

Millikan, R. 1989. Biosemantics. *Journal of Philosophy* 86, no. 6: 281–297.

Nagel, E. 1961. *The Structure of Science*. Harcourt, Brace & World.

Nagel, T. 1980. What Is It Like to Be a Bat? In *Readings in Philosophy of Psychology*, volume 1, ed. N. Block. Harvard University Press.

Nagel, T. 1986. *The View from Nowhere*. Oxford University Press.

Nemirow, L. 1990. Physicalism and the Cognitive Role of Acquaintance. In *Mind and Cognition*, ed. W. Lycan. Blackwell.

Peacocke, C. 1983. *Sense and Content*. Oxford University Press.

Pitt, D. 2004. The Phenomenology of Cognition. *Philosophy and Phenomenological Research* 69, no. 1: 1–36.

Place, U. T. 1956. Is Consciousness a Brain Process? *British Journal of Psychology* 47: 44–50. Reprinted in *The Place of Mind*, ed. B. Cooney (Wadsworth, 2000).

Putnam, H. 1975. The Meaning of 'Meaning'. In Putnam, *Mind, Language, and Reality*. Cambridge University Press.

Pylyshyn, Z. 1980. The Causal Powers of Machines. *Behavioral and Brain Sciences* 3: 443.

Pylyshyn, Z. 1986. *Computation and Cognition*. MIT Press.

Quine, W. V. 1960. *Word and Object*. MIT Press.

Quine, W. V. 1961. *From a Logical Point of View*, second edition. Harper.

Quine, W. V. 1966. On Carnap's Views on Ontology. In *The Ways of Paradox and Other Essays*. Random House.

Quine, W. V. 1969. Ontological Relativity. In *Ontological Relativity and Other Essays*. Columbia University Press.

Quine, W. V. 1970. On the Reasons for the Indeterminacy of Translation. *Journal of Philosophy* 67, no. 6: 178–183.

Quine, W. V. 1992a. Structure and Nature. *Journal of Philosophy* 89: 5–9.

Quine, W. V. 1992b. *Pursuit of Truth*, revised edition. Harvard University Press.

Quine, W. V. 1993. In Praise of Observation Sentences. *Journal of Philosophy* 90: 107–117.

Quine, W. V. 1994. Promoting Extensionality. *Synthese* 98, no. 1: 143–151.

Quine, W. V. 1996. Progress on Two Fronts. *Journal of Philosophy* 93: 159–163.

Rey, G. 1998. A Narrow Representationalist Account of Qualitative Experience. *Philosophical Perspectives* 12: 435–458.

Resnik, M. D. 1981. Mathematics as a Science of Patterns: Ontology and Reference. *Nous* 15: 529–550.

Rosenthal, D. 1985. Review of Frank Jackson, *Perception: A Representative Theory*. *Journal of Philosophy* 82, no. 1: 28–41.

Rosenthal, D. 1986. Two Concepts of Consciousness. *Philosophical Studies* 49: 3: 329–359. Reprinted in Rosenthal, *The Nature of Mind* (Oxford University Press, 1991).

Rosenthal, D. 1990. On Being Accessible to Consciousness. *Behavioral and Brain Sciences* 13, no. 4: 621–622.

Rosenthal, D. 1991a. The Independence of Consciousness and Sensory Quality. In *Consciousness: Philosophical Issues*, volume 1, ed. E. Villanueva. Ridgeview.

Rosenthal, D. 1991b. *The Nature of Mind*. Oxford University Press.

Rosenthal, D. 1997. A Theory of Consciousness. In *The Nature of Consciousness*, ed. N. Block et al. MIT Press.

Rota, G., Sharp, D., and Sokolowski, R. 1989. Syntax, Semantics, and the Problem of the Identity of Mathematical Objects. *Philosophy of Science* 55: 376–386.

Schippers, B. 1990. Spatial Patterns of High-Frequency Visual Cortical Activity during Conditioned Reflex in Man. Master's thesis, University of Amsterdam.

Searle, J. R. 1958. Proper Names. *Mind* 67: 166–173.

Searle, J. R. 1979. Intentionality and the Use of Language. In *Meaning and Use*, ed. A. Margalit. Reidel.

Searle, J. R. 1980. Minds, Brains and Programs. *Behavioral and Brain Sciences* 3: 417–424.

Searle, J. R. 1983. *Intentionality*. Cambridge University Press.

Searle, J. R. 1984. Intentionality and Its Place in Nature. *Synthese* 61: 3–16.

Searle J. R. 1987. Indeterminacy, Empiricism, and the First Person. *Journal of Philosophy* 84, no. 3: 123–147.

Searle, J. R. 1992. *The Rediscovery of the Mind*. MIT Press.

Searle, J. R. 1995. *The Construction of Social Reality*. Free Press.

Shoemaker, S. 1990a. Qualities and Qualia: What's in the Mind? *Philosophy and Phenomenological Research* Suppl. 50: 109–131.

Shoemaker, S. 1990b. First-Person Access. In *Philosophical Perspectives*, volume 4: *Action Theory and Philosophy of Mind*, ed. J. Tomberlin. Ridgeview.

Shoemaker, S. 1994. Phenomenal Character. *Nous* 28: 21–38.

Shoemaker, S. 2001. Introspection and Phenomenal Character. *Philosophical Topics*. Reprinted in *The Philosophy of Mind*, ed. D. Chalmers (Oxford University Press, 2002).

Siewert, C. P. 1998. *The Significance of Consciousness*. Princeton University Press.

Skarda, C. 1987. Explaining Behavior: Bringing the Brain Back In. *Inquiry* 29: 187–202.

Smart, J. J. C. 1959. Sensations and Brain Processes. *Philosophical Review* 68: 141–156. Reprinted in *The Place of Mind*, ed. B. Cooney. Wadsworth, 2000.

Strawson, G. 1994. *Mental Reality*, MIT Press.

Tye, M. 1995. *Ten Problems of Consciousness*. MIT Press.

Tye, M. 2000. *Consciousness, Color and Content*. MIT Press.

Van Gulick, R. 1988. A Functionalist Plea for Self-Consciousness. *Philosophical Review* 97: 149–181.

Van Gulick, R. 1989. What Difference Does Consciousness Make? *Philosophical Topics* 17: 211–230.

Van Gulick, R. 1990. Functionalism, Information and Content. In *Mind and Cognition*, ed. W. Lycan. Blackwell.

Van Gulick, R. 1993. Understanding the Phenomenal Mind: Are We All Just Armadillos? In *Consciousness: Psychological and Philosophical Essays*, ed. M. Davies and G. Humphreys. Blackwell.

Vauclair, J. 1990. Wanted: Cognition. *Behavioral and Brain Sciences* 13: 393–394.

Villanueva, E., ed. 1996. *Perception*. Ridgeview.

Yalçin, Ü. 2001. Solutions and Dissolutions of the Underdetermination Problem. *Nous* 35, no. 3: 394–418.

Index